D1706790

The Age of Garvey

AMERICA IN THE WORLD

SERIES EDITORS
SVEN BECKERT AND JEREMI SURI

A list of titles in this series appears at the back of the book.

The Age of Garvey

How a Jamaican Activist
Created a Mass Movement and
Changed Global Black Politics

Adam Ewing

PRINCETON UNIVERSITY PRESS

PRINCETON AND OXFORD

Library of Congress Cataloging-in-Publication Data

Ewing, Adam (Historian)
The age of Garvey : how a Jamaican activist created a mass movement and changed global
Black politics / Adam Ewing.
pages cm. — (America in the world)

Summary: "Jamaican activist Marcus Garvey (1887–1940) organized the Universal Negro
Improvement Association in Harlem in 1917. By the early 1920s, his program of African
liberation and racial uplift had attracted millions of supporters, both in the United States
and abroad. *The Age of Garvey* presents an expansive global history of the movement that
came to be known as Garveyism. Offering a groundbreaking new interpretation of global
black politics between the First and Second World Wars, Adam Ewing charts Garveyism's
emergence, its remarkable global transmission, and its influence in the responses among
African descendants to white supremacy and colonial rule in Africa, the Caribbean, and
the United States. Delving into the organizing work and political approach of Garvey and
his followers, Ewing shows that Garveyism emerged from a rich tradition of pan-African
politics that had established, by the First World War, lines of communication between black
intellectuals on both sides of the Atlantic. Garvey's legacy was to reengineer this tradition as
a vibrant and multifaceted mass politics. Ewing looks at the people who enabled Garveyism's
global spread, including labor activists in the Caribbean and Central America, community
organizers in the urban and rural United States, millennial religious revivalists in central and
southern Africa, welfare associations and independent church activists in Malawi and Zambia, and an emerging generation of Kikuyu leadership in central Kenya. Moving away from
the images of quixotic business schemes and repatriation efforts, *The Age of Garvey* demonstrates the consequences of Garveyism's international presence and provides a dynamic and
unified framework for understanding the movement, during the interwar years
and beyond"— Provided by publisher.

Includes bibliographical references and index.

ISBN 978-0-691-15779-5 (hardback)
1. Garvey, Marcus, 1887–1940—Influence. 2. Universal Negro Improvement
Association—History. 3. African diaspora. I. Title.
E185.97.G3E95 2014
305.896'073—dc23   2014003889

British Library Cataloging-in-Publication Data is available
This book has been composed in Sabon Next LT Pro
Printed on acid-free paper. ∞
Printed in the United States of America
1 3 5 7 9 10 8 6 4 2

To my parents,
and to Cathy

CONTENTS

ACKNOWLEDGMENTS

THIS PROJECT started nearly ten years ago when I stumbled onto the topic of Garveyism for a seminar paper. For a while I set Garveyism aside and returned to my original dissertation plans. But Garveyism crept back in. Before long it occupied my thoughts. I owe a great debt to the ingenious architects, familiar and unfamiliar, who developed a politics of such enduring importance and fascination. Writing about them has been a great privilege and a (mostly) joyful endeavor.

In the process of developing this book I have made many friends and accumulated many debts. I owe great thanks to my dissertation committee members, each of whom inspired me in different and complementary ways. Vincent Brown introduced me to the intricacies and possibilities of African diaspora scholarship. His support for my project, especially at its early stages, was a huge source of encouragement. His continued friendship and guidance has been invaluable. Caroline Elkins inspired me to extend my historical gaze to Africa, and helped me realize that I wanted to spend as much time there as possible. Her passion—in the classroom, in her work, and on behalf of Africa—has been a constant source of inspiration. Special thanks are owed to my advisor, Evelyn Brooks Higginbotham, who has remained a persistent advocate of both me and my work. I will never be able to adequately thank her for her feedback, patience, and wisdom during my years in Cambridge, and I will never forget it.

Several teachers are responsible for illuminating my path. I might not have fallen in love with history if not for Ivana Hrabek. It was in Judy Tinning's classroom that I read *The Autobiography of Malcolm X*, which introduced me to the enduring power and importance of the African American freedom struggle. At Queen's University I received early inspiration and mentoring from James Carson. At the University of South Carolina I was guided by Ronald Atkinson, Dan Carter, Bobby Donaldson, and Patricia Sullivan. During the course of completing my dissertation, I was offered key encouragement and support from Steven Hahn and James Kloppenberg.

This project has been nurtured, in ways direct and indirect, by overlapping communities of conversation and support. I have learned a lot from friends who have steered well clear of academia. Special thanks to Tiffany Barker, Galit Davies, Jon Davies, Brooks Fallis, Kaston Leung, James McDonald, Trieu Nguyen, Kirk Roth, Eric Shields, Kevin Stedmann, Lee Waxberg, and Mark Woods. At Harvard particular thanks are owed to Sana Aiyar, Daniel Barber, Chris Jones, Betsy More, Harmony O'Rourke, Courtney Podraza, Nico Slate, Tryg Throntveit, Benjamin Weber, and Ann Marie Wilson. At Johns Hopkins I am very grateful to Angus Burgin, Nathan Connolly,

Pier Larson, Tobie Meyer-Fong, Rani Neutill, Josh Walden, and to the participants of the African History seminar, the Center for Africana Studies' Critical Thought Collective, and the Mellon seminar. A special debt of gratitude is owed to the remarkable Gabrielle Spiegel, who has read much of this project, and who continues to offer encouragement, advice, and bottomless support. In my brief time at Vanderbilt I have been welcomed with open arms by several outstanding scholars and generous friends, including Dennis Dickerson, Jim Epstein, Gary Gerstle, Peter Hudson, Paul Kramer, Jane Landers, Tiffany Patterson, Dan Usner, and Juliet Wagner.

I feel very fortunate to be a member of the unofficial Garvey studies club. My work has been shaped—and improved—by conversations with Keisha Blain, Tshepo Chéry, Dan Dalrymple, Natanya Duncan, Reena Goldthree, Claudrena Harold, Asia Leeds, Rupert Lewis Erik McDuffie, Mary Rolinson, Jarod Roll, James Spady, and Robert Vinson. Steven Hahn helped bring many of these people together for a conference on Garveyism during the early stages of my project and has provided great support ever since. The Marcus Garvey Papers Project, spearheaded by Robert A. Hill, has made writing the global history of Garveyism possible. This book would not exist without Bobby's herculean efforts, and it would not be as good without his generosity, and his willingness to share with me his remarkable stores of accumulated knowledge.

This book would also not exist without the support of the Radcliffe Institute for Advanced Study and the Marcus Garvey Foundation, each of which provided key funding. Research was made possible by grants from the Charles Warren Center, the History Department, and the Graduate School of Arts and Sciences at Harvard. It was completed with the help of the brilliant and hard-working staffs of my library and archival haunts. I would particularly like to thank the librarians and archivists at the National Archives, College Park, MD; the Public Records Office, London; the National Archives of Zambia, Lusaka; the Schomburg Center, New York; and the School of Oriental and African Studies, London. Special mention is due to Barbara Burg at Harvard's Widener Library; Randall K. Burkett and the staff at Emory University's Woodruff Library; Peterson Kathuka, Richard Ambani, and Philip Omomdi and the staff at the Kenya National Archives, Nairobi; and Newton Chimala, Christopher Kwachera, and Lucciano Banda at the National Archives of Malawi, Zomba.

I am a novice in the book publishing game, but I cannot imagine a better working environment than the one fostered at Princeton University Press. Thanks to Sven Beckert and Jeremi Suri, who have generously welcomed this book into their excellent series; my editor, Brigitta van Rheinberg, who has offered me nothing but encouragement, good advice, and support; and Natalie Baan and Chris Retz, who have carried this book through the production process with important contributions and with remarkably little frustration in the face of my inexperience. Bill Nelson did a wonderful job drawing the maps that appear throughout the text.

I owe everything to my families. My parents, Guy Ewing and Miriam Hoffer, built a home for me that was safe, stable, and full of love. Dad taught me how to live in the world with compassion, enthusiasm, and wonder. Mom taught me how to love unconditionally. They also raised my sister, Megan Ewing, who over the course of this project has flowered into an amazing teacher, author, towel proprietor, shamelessly indulgent aunt, and a source of real inspiration in her own right.

I have also been welcomed with open arms by the Long family. Thanks to Barb, Peter, David, Margret, Emily, and Carter for expanding my world in wonderful and unexpected ways.

For the past fourteen years Cathy Long has given me unwavering support as a partner, friend, and critic. She has endured my bouts of periodic self-doubt and anxiety, as well as a growing number of research trips and professional relocations. The bedrock of patience, support, wisdom, and love she has given me over these years has been a gift I will never adequately repay. Our sons, Max and Jonah, were born in the midst of this project. From the beginning they have demonstrated a profound disinterest in its successful completion. But they have also taught me more, and filled me with more love, than I could have possibly imagined.

What follows is dedicated to my parents, and to Cathy.

INTRODUCTION

In 1916, Marcus Mosiah Garvey, a young Jamaican printer, entrepreneur, and aspiring race leader, sailed into New York harbor. Before the end of the First World War, from his base in Harlem he launched his great mass organization, the Universal Negro Improvement Association and African Communities League (UNIA-ACL, hereafter UNIA), ostentatiously pledging to redeem both the continent of Africa and its descendants from the thrall of white supremacy. To facilitate industrial progress and generate new mechanisms of commercial wealth, he organized the Negro Factories Corporation and founded a transatlantic shipping company, the Black Star Line, inviting the scattered members of the race to participate as clients, passengers, and stockholders. To begin the process of reclaiming occupied Africa he announced plans to transfer the central operations of the UNIA to Liberia, which was, along with Abyssinia (now Ethiopia), one of the two remaining independent nations on the continent. In August 1920, he hosted a monthlong International Convention in Harlem, the first of four such gatherings, drawing delegates to New York representing Canada, the West Indies, Central America, Africa, and nearly every American state. "We are assembled here tonight as the descendants of a suffering people and we are also assembled as a people who are determined to suffer no longer," Garvey told a capacity crowd at Madison Square Garden on August 3. "If Europe is for the white man ... then, in the name of God, Africa shall be for the black peoples of the world." Delegates crafted a charter, the Declaration of Rights of the Negro Peoples of the World, to "guide and govern the destiny of four hundred million Negroes." To great acclaim, Garvey was elected Provisional President of Africa.[1]

By the early 1920s, the UNIA had attracted tens of thousands of members, and millions of admirers. The rhetoric of "Garveyism" was carried by sailors, migrant workers, and other mobile black subjects to nearly every corner of the African diaspora. But the fall came just as quickly as the rise. Liberian colonization plans were dashed in 1921, and again in 1924, by the combined energies of the British, French, and Liberian governments. The Black Star Line was undermined by poor business management, employee graft, and government intrigue, and slid into bankruptcy in early 1922, costing its enthusiastic investors, most of whom were of limited means, an estimated $900,000.[2] Weeks earlier, Garvey had been indicted on charges of mail fraud stemming from advertisements for the Black Star Line's promised transoceanic vessel, the S.S. *Phyllis Wheatley*, which never materialized. Convicted on tenuous evidence, Garvey spent three months in the Tombs in New York City. Following a failed appeal, he then spent nearly three years in the federal penitentiary in Atlanta. Released in December 1927, Garvey was

FIGURE O.I. Marcus Garvey addresses the First International Convention of the Negro Peoples of the World, August 1920. (Library of Congress, Prints and Photographs Division, Washington, D.C.)

transported to New Orleans and put on a ship to Jamaica, never to set foot again in the United States. Unable to resurrect the fortunes of the UNIA's central infrastructure from abroad, the organization continued its decline, splitting into two factions following the contentious International Convention of 1929 in Kingston. Frustrated in a series of local political projects, Garvey and his second wife, Amy Jacques Garvey, moved their family to London in 1935, where Garvey was overshadowed by a new generation of pan-African radicals who disdained his anachronistic and "petit bourgeois" sensibilities. Garvey died in relative obscurity on June 10, 1940, after suffering a cerebral hemorrhage earlier in the year.

Garveyism is commonly recognized as one of the most important phenomena in the history of the African diaspora. "When you bear in mind the slenderness of his resources, the vast material forces and the pervading social conceptions which automatically sought to destroy him, [Garvey's] achievement remains one of the propagandistic miracles of this century," reflected C.L.R. James, no apologist of the movement, in the 1960s.[3] Nevertheless, from the beginning observers of the Garvey phenomenon have struggled to explain its success. The venerable African American journalist (and future Garveyite), John Edward Bruce, when asked his opinion of Garvey in early 1918, doubted that the young Jamaican's colorful and boorish tactics would have much traction. "We like to listen to the music of his mouth," he conceded, "[b]ut Mr. Garvey will find that the Negro race is not so easily organized as he imagines." That same year, Emmett J. Scott, secretary of the Tuskegee Institute, and special assistant to the Secretary of War, dismissed the UNIA as a "paper organization," and reported to the War Department that its activities "should not be seriously regarded." When these judgments proved wrong, when Garvey proved unexpectedly—unprecedentedly—successful at mobilizing mass support, his detractors dismissed his program of African redemption as whimsical and unrealistic, and disparaged his followers as unlettered and unsophisticated dupes. Amidst the triumph of the UNIA's International Convention of 1920, Garvey's great antagonist, W.E.B. Du Bois, observed that Garveyites "are the lowest type of [N]egroes," declared Garvey a "demagogue," and predicted that his movement would "collapse in a short time." Chandler Owen, co-editor, with A. Philip Randolph, of the black leftist journal, the *Messenger*, considered Garvey "an ignoramous," lacking "the scientific type of mind necessary to lead a big movement," and able to appeal to Negroes only through "their emotional nature." He gave the UNIA "three months of life." In a searing critique of Garveyism in the *Messenger* in 1921, Randolph dismissed the premise of racial organization as a "fallacy," argued that the UNIA's business ideas made "no practical sense," and condemned the notion of African liberation as an impossible idea, and an insidious distraction from the project of interracial worker solidarity.[4]

Garvey has traditionally fared little better with scholars. Until recently, there had been only two full-length treatments of Garvey and Garveyism published by mainstream academic presses, neither one especially complimentary. In his pioneering study, *Black Moses*, E. David Cronon argues that Garvey sold "an unrealistic escapist program of racial chauvinism" to "the ignorant black masses." In *The World of Marcus Garvey*, Judith Stein dismissively views the "methods and visions" of the UNIA as having been shaped by "the fatalism of the powerless" and "the utopias of hustlers and charlatans." Historians of the interwar period have tended to be drawn to the poetic and sophisticated dissent of Du Bois, casting Garveyism as a populist, flashy, and dangerously misguided foil. David Levering Lewis, in his magisterial, Pulitzer Prize–winning biography of Du Bois, describes Garveyism as "calamitous," and Garvey as a conservative, megalomaniacal, and naïve purveyor of "racial exclusivism." If Du Boisian Pan-Africanism offered a "prudent program for the gradual empowerment of the darker world," Garvey "threatened the continuity of these efforts with an opera bouffe act that amounted to little more, really, than pageantry and incantation—'Africa for the Africans,' a heady slogan in place of a sober program." The view expressed in all of these works—attributing the success of the UNIA to a timely convergence of mass credulity and political hucksterism—has remained remarkably durable.[5]

Thirty-seven years ago, Garvey scholar Tony Martin began his opus, *Race First*, with the observation that "no one could have organized and built up the largest black mass movement in Afro-American history, in the face of continuous onslaughts from communists on the left, black reactionaries on all sides, and the most powerful governments in the world, and yet be a buffoon or a clown, or even an overwhelmingly impractical visionary."[6] In the decades since, a growing body of literature has sought to reframe popular perceptions of Garvey, Garveyism, and the UNIA, largely, as Martin suggested, by broadening attention from the UNIA's epicenter in Harlem to the myriad communities touched by the movement, to the remarkable contours of Garveyism's reach, reception, and influence across the African diaspora. Research has made clear that the UNIA was not the mere province of the urban American north, as it was once portrayed, but a global movement that established local divisions across the United States and Canada, through the Caribbean archipelago and Central American isthmus, along the northern shores of South America, and across western and southern Africa. Garveyism, it is now understood, did not simply attract "the ignorant black masses," but an eclectic and malleable coalition of participants across diverse localities, including urban workers and farmers, aristocrats and paupers, unionists and strikebreakers, educators and the uneducated, men and women, and mobile migrant workers across Africa, the Caribbean basin, and the United States. It is hard, faced with the evidence we now possess, to deny Garveyism's persistent and broad-based appeal in the years following World War I.[7] Starting from what should by now be a firmly grounded assumption that diasporic blacks were driven by complex and generally rational motivations, this appeal is profoundly significant. Marcus Garvey built a movement that resonated with people's dreams, hopes, and expectations—a movement that encouraged them to organize against large and intractable systems of power.

Nevertheless, as historian Steven Hahn has forcefully asserted, the elision of Garveyism from mainstream academic discourse persists.[8] Much of the problem is that Garveyism continues to be remembered, for what appear to be self-evident reasons, in the terms laid out by this introduction's first two paragraphs: as a catalog of Garvey's triumphs and travails, by the most bombastic and ultimately fleeting elements of the UNIA's brief heyday, and by the years in Harlem, where Garveyism had its most visible and vocal success. This coalescence of our historical memory around the image of Garvey as, to quote one typical account, "the proverbial comet who lit up the sky before crashing down to earth," has tempered any acknowledgment of Garvey's accomplishments with the burden of their imminent collapse.[9] The problem is illustrated by Colin Grant's sympathetic and judicious new biography, *Negro with a Hat: The Rise and Fall of Marcus Garvey*, which—as the subtitle suggests—casts Garveyism in the familiar mold of Greek tragedy, its dazzling emergence obscuring for a glorious moment the fissures and contradictions that foretold its fall. Or, as historian Wilson Moses has put it, the "story of Garvey . . . contains only the possibility of defeat . . . because of his heroically irrational refusal to face an unacceptable reality."[10]

The Age of Garvey tells a story about Garvey, the UNIA, and Garveyism that seeks to align the movement along a different axis by foregrounding the latter. This orientation takes the story far beyond the peak organizational years of the UNIA, roughly 1919 to 1924, and beyond the operational reach of the UNIA entirely. Instead, the book focuses much of its attention on the influence of Garveyism on the construction of diasporic politics in the diverse contexts that the movement bridged: within urban and rural black communities stretched across the United States; among West Indian migrants and labor activists in the Caribbean; in the millennial religious revivals, local "welfare associations," and independent churches extending across central and southern Africa; and in the emerging politics of Kikuyu cultural nationalism in central Kenya. From this perspective, what was most important about Garveyism was not the bombast for which it is best remembered—the parades and shipping lines and colonization schemes— but the engagement of its proponents in a sustained and more informal project of organizing, networking, and consciousness raising. This work was perceived as a fundamentally global project, with much more of its focus directed at grassroots activism on the African subcontinent than has been previously acknowledged. It was also an orientation partly born of necessity, designed after it became clear that the radical moment of upheaval and possibility following the war was passing, that Garvey's presidency of Africa would remain provisional, and that the UNIA would not be the organizational vehicle of African liberation. Yet it was this acknowledgment of the movement's limits, and Garveyism's resulting resonance as an organizational strategy during a reactionary period of limited opportunities, that cemented its viability as a diasporic politics. Viewing Garveyism from the broader lens of the interwar diaspora both provides a clear sense of its enduring importance and demands a rethinking of the era it dominated. This was, as the book's title suggests, an Age of Garvey.

*

This study follows the spread of Garveyism throughout the United States, the greater Caribbean, and a good portion of Africa. It suggests that Garveyites stretching across the African diaspora were connected by a vast and sustained project of network building; that they pursued a common set of aims, structured around broad appeals to pan-Negro unity, political education, and racial pride; and that they shared a common understanding about the opportunities presented by global events, and a faith in the liberatory implications of racial preparation and organization. The political movements that grew from this network owed as much to local conditions as to diasporic currents; they responded to the particular opportunities available in particular places and at particular times, and flowed from homegrown traditions as well as global organizing. Some Garveyites sustained an official relationship with the UNIA; others, confronting harsh political realities, could not. In Africa, some black subjects borrowed the rhythms of Garveyism, others the attendant mythologies that it carried abroad, and transformed them in ways that Garveyites in the Americas could hardly have imagined. Amidst this diversity, Garveyism provided a powerful organizing principle, a political approach that combined caution and ambition, that proposed both a practical and an inspiring means to confront a postwar world dictated by the logics of colonial domination and white supremacy. For subaltern black subjects living in the decade-and-a-half after the First World War, Garveyism provided usable materials for political engagement.

"Garveyism" has been traditionally viewed as a product of the "philosophy and opinions" of Marcus Garvey, as an ideological foundation for the political activism of the UNIA. The characterization of Garveyism as an ideology has never really fit. As Wilson Moses derisively noted several decades ago, Garvey's intellectual program was a pastiche, a derivative compilation of greatest hits from nineteenth-century black intellectuals, updated to reflect the new currents of world anticolonial activism and racialism.[11] More than this, attempts to characterize Garveyism at a point along an ideological or political spectrum do not hold up to scrutiny: Garveyism was radical in some moments and reactionary in others, strident in some places and cautious in others. As we have learned more about the local and regional manifestations of the movement, we have been confronted time and again by its fundamental diversity. Scholars have attempted to resolve the divide between the "tenets" of Garveyism and its execution in practice by noting the movement's flexibility, its multidimensionality, its transformation on the ground.[12] But to acknowledge that these were the essential properties of Garveyism is to say that Garveyism was not essentially an ideology.

The Age of Garvey views Garveyism not as an ideology but as a method of organic mass politics. Garvey variously presented himself as an ideologue, as a liberator, as a prophet, but he was first of all an organizer and a propagandist. The movement he founded relentlessly spread a series of broad and relatively fixed assumptions: a belief that African redemption and Negro redemption were coterminous and biblically ordained; a view of the "Negro race" as a unified and ancient category of belonging; and an understanding of history that suggested a declining white civilization and an ascendant Negro one. These beliefs were sufficiently dramatic enough to demand action, while remaining capacious enough to ensure that the work done on their behalf would be malleable, adaptable to changing circumstances and fortunes, and amenable to local and regional innovations. The effect of Garveyist organizing was to empower black communities to direct attention to their own needs, to build upon their own traditions, to confront systems of power within the purview of their own discretion. Framing this work was the understanding by local Garveyites that their often mundane and limited political efforts were joined to a vast, expanding, and dazzling project of diasporic connectivity and international organization. Garveyism not only generated local political activism but connected otherwise isolated efforts within a sophisticated network of communication; it encouraged black men and women to believe that their modest work of racial organization, education, and preparation was not in vain, that it was inexorably undermining the status quo, and that it was hastening the end of global white supremacy and colonial rule.

Broadly speaking, the success of Garveyism as a mass movement suggests the need to think carefully about the relationship between ideology and political action. Garveyism privileged "process" over "stance."[13] It was fashioned not as an ideology—structured to reside outside of and remain critically detached from systems of power—but as a politics, shaped to operate within existing relations, to engage in the unequal negotiations out of which those systems were tested, contested, and ultimately recreated. Confronted with powerful white gatekeepers, Garveyites' sensitivity to the spectrum of the possible allowed their movement to flourish beyond the unsettled years of the postwar period, providing an organizational framework for diasporic black politics during a period of limited political opportunities. Dedicated to the mobilization of black subalterns, Garveyites likewise began with process, with the act of organization itself, building on the premise, either explicitly or intuitively, that politics is not enacted on inert populations, that political action must be nurtured by—and grow out of—communal practices and beliefs, modes of association, and relations of power. The history of Garveyism demonstrates that to organize communities is to stir deep wells of political knowledge and wisdom, and to encourage the development of new, hybrid, and organic forms of belief and possibility.

✳

If Garveyism was an organic mass politics, it was also a sustained project of diasporic identity building. The term "diaspora" (from the Greek, διασπορά, meaning "scattering," or "dispersion"), most closely associated with the forced exile of Jews from modern-day Israel and Palestine that began in the sixth century BCE, was introduced to global black studies nearly fifty years ago by the legendary historian George Shepperson. Central to Shepperson's project, as diaspora scholar Brent Hayes Edwards argues, was the desire to deploy a concept that was neither beholden to a specific political history, like Pan-Africanism, nor limited in the scope of its analysis by a unitary focus on the "idea and practice of African unity." As an alternative to such frameworks, Shepperson projected the idea of African diaspora studies widely, as "the study of a series of reactions to coercion, to the imposition of the economic and political rule of alien people in Africa, to slavery and imperialism." Such an approach proffered a field of analysis—structured first by the global system inaugurated by the Atlantic slave trade, then by imperialism—without precluding the fundamental heterogeneity of black experience. It offered the possibility of solidarities and affinities across national and natural boundaries without assuming their emergence, or ignoring the complexities of difference, or of competing affinities. Importantly, Shepperson eschewed the binaries of exile and return, diaspora and homeland, instead observing the ways in which continental Africans were themselves constituted by diasporic dispersals: by the internal slave trade, by the migrations of refugees and former slaves, and by the movements of African soldiers, clerks, laborers, and missionaries facilitated by the economic and political geographies of colonial rule. Considering the lack of attention given to Africa in many subsequent articulations of an African diaspora, it is notable that Shepperson's paper was first delivered in Dar-es-Salaam, Tanzania, and published three years later in a volume dedicated to enumerating new themes in African history.[14]

Over the past half century, the best theoretical work on diaspora has reinforced the foundational principles established by Shepperson. Defining diaspora as a "framework of analysis" constituted by "a shared, ongoing history of displacement, suffering, adaptation, or resistance," scholars have noted the persistence of the African diaspora as an "identity option," a site for the construction of "alternate public spheres" in order to dwell within systems of white economic, political, and cultural privilege.[15] Echoing Shepperson, cultural theorist James Clifford observes that "transnational connections linking diasporas need not be articulated primarily through a real or symbolic homeland," but can be mediated by "[d]ecentered, lateral connections," such as those forged by the "imperial formations" of what historian Frank Guridy has recently called the "US-Caribbean world."[16] This decentering of the "homeland" does not preclude its importance, but rather draws attention, as J. Lorand Matory notes, to the ways in which Africa is not a subject of past desire or future reward but "coeval," involved in the ongoing, transatlantic "dialogue" that invents black identity again and again. The promise of diasporic solidarities, warns Brent Edwards, offers not the "comfort of abstraction," an easy appeal to cross-border racial and cultural affinities, but rather insight into the ways communities residing within different national borders, speaking different languages, and bearing different local traditions might—under the right circumstances—forge cultural and political linkages "through and across difference." This awareness of the "practice of diaspora" focuses attention not only on the "routes" of transnational identity making, but also on its "roots"—those local communities that must filter the raw material of hybrid transnational culture through "overlapping diasporas" (ethnic, vernacular, gendered, etc.) and extant power relations.[17] For all of its mobility and flexibility, diaspora does not transcend the messiness of place and localness. It must, as anthropologist Jacqueline Nassy Brown insists, be articulated "through place and localness."[18]

Marcus Garvey—like his intellectual forebears in the pan-African tradition[19]—imagined Negro identity in far different terms. The "race," he argued, was a fixed signifier, connecting peoples of African descent to a single, ancient history, and guiding them to a common destiny. The ruptures of slavery and imperialism, rather than inventing an African diaspora (or Africa, or the Atlantic world), submerged from view a fundamental Negro unity. The primary aim of his organization was to reawaken the scattered peoples of Africa to their natural solidarity, refocus their gaze on racial cooperation and progress, and by doing so hasten the day when the African continent would be returned to its proper Negro owners.

Yet Garvey, to his great fortune, was rarely forced to face the pretensions of racial unity. The realities of global politics in the 1920s and 1930s ensured that Garveyites would never have to organize a Negro empire, or a United States of Africa, or transform their "portable eschatology" into concrete policy.[20] Instead, Garveyism flourished during the interwar years as a diasporic politics, its claims of solidarity facilitating and inspiring the organization of local initiative, its global vision of Negro ascendance and anticolonial resistance cutting through and across difference in creative and generative ways. Garveyites, as Frank Guridy has brilliantly shown, participated in a "relentless effort to use performance to enact an African diaspora." By engaging in embodied practices big and small—the inauguration of two shipping lines, but also the execution of parades, elocution contests, newspaper distribution, poor relief, uniform wearing and local institution building— Garveyites broadcast a global sense of race dynamic enough to seem real, and seem useful, for black subjects across the world.[21]

*

The Age of Garvey pursues a selection, rather than the sum, of stories that can be written about the consequences and uses of Garveyism between the two world wars. A comprehensive history of the movement would follow its influence from Canada to Australia, would devote considerably more attention to Caribbean hotspots of Garveyite activity such as Cuba, would ask searching questions about the unwritten influence of the movement in places like Brazil. Regrettably, to acknowledge Garveyism's primary importance as an organizational and inspirational device for interwar black politics making—rather than as a metonym for the Universal Negro Improvement Association—is to acknowledge the logistical difficulty of writing a truly inclusive history of the movement. For the global spread and impact of Garveyism becomes truly apparent only by digging into local or regional sites of struggle and following its translations on the ground, often far removed from the centers of bureaucratic Garveyism. By design, *The Age of Garvey* traces the rhythms of Garveyism more vigorously than its reach. It narrates not a linear history of an organization's rise and fall but rather a method of understanding the legacy of a man and a movement that came, in ways both direct and indirect, to dominate an era.

Part 1, "The Rise and Fall of Marcus Garvey," follows the emergence of the UNIA and its institutional decline, paying particular attention to the global contours of racial discourse, empire building, and pan-African politics that helped dictate Garveyism's growth and evolution. The movement was in many respects a product of the extended, and profoundly uneven, negotiations surrounding the parameters of citizenship, economic agency, and racial identity following the abolition of Atlantic slavery—and the rich traditions of diasporic politics that emerged as a result. It was galvanized by the Great War, which violently tore the world apart, and cast established verities and assumptions briefly into doubt. The UNIA that emerged from the war was radicalized, eager to spread its message abroad as a means of participating in the anticolonial uprisings that were erupting across Asia, the Middle East, Africa, and the Caribbean. As the tectonics of racial domination were reestablished, and as the UNIA entered a period of institutional crisis, Garveyites began to formulate new, and decidedly more cautious, strategies for hastening the moment of African, and Negro, liberation.

Part 2, "The Age of Garvey," explores some of the myriad ways in which Garveyism's influence was fruitfully sustained in the decade following Garvey's incarceration and the disintegration of the central edifice of the UNIA. In the United States, Garveyites embraced a rhetoric of global, anticolonial agitation that projected its radical implications abroad, to Africa, and forward, to a moment better suited to strident politics. Such a stance helped shield Garveyites from the repressive consequences of white supremacy, and allowed them to sustain vibrant local communities of organizational work that offered adherents a new and shifting platform upon which to participate in politics, challenge hierarchies, and negotiate racial, religious, class, and gender identities. In southern and central Africa, the wide transmission of Garveyism—and its popular translation as a series of rumors predicting the imminent arrival of black American liberators—provided the vocabulary for a series of millennial religious revivals spreading from the Eastern Cape to Northern Rhodesia (Zambia). At the same time, Garveyite organizing in the region facilitated the proliferation of local "welfare associations" and independent churches, modest and creative efforts by a cadre of clerks, ministers, traders, and workers to nurture the movement—which was anathema across colonial Africa—under the guise of cautious reformism. In Kenya, young activists translated the lessons and tactics of African Garveyism to meet the needs of a nascent Kikuyu cultural nationalism.

In late 1924, months before his imprisonment in Atlanta, Garvey declared the inauguration of the UNIA's "second period." Much of what we remember about Garveyism was a product of its earlier iteration: the militancy, the pomp and circumstance, the ambitious refusal to accept the constraints of global white supremacy. And yet much of Garveyism's legacy was forged after 1924 in more cautious and mundane circumstances, a product of the second period commitment to what Garvey described as the work of "quiet and peaceful penetration."[22] This work would be directed less by the provisional president of Africa than by millions of men and women inspired and energized by his message, who saw in the call to Negro unity and organization an opportunity to enact local political projects, to confront the indignities of disempowerment in their own lives. *The Age of Garvey* seeks to tell this story.

PART ONE

The Rise and Fall of Marcus Garvey

Chapter One

THE EDUCATION OF MARCUS MOSIAH GARVEY

ON THE morning of October 11, 1865, men and women streamed out of the small black settlement of Stony Gut, Jamaica and trooped in military formation toward the town of Morant Bay, in the parish of St. Thomas in the East. They were armed with sticks and cutlasses; some carried guns. At their head was a Native Baptist preacher and peasant farmer named Paul Bogle. The columns marched first to the police station, which was ransacked for weapons, then headed to the courthouse, where they confronted the volunteer militia. As the Queen's representative in the parish, Custos Baron von Ketelhodt, read the Riot Act, stones were lobbed at the volunteers by a group of women in the crowd, and the volunteers returned a volley of fire. In the ensuing chaos twenty-nine people were slain, including von Ketelhodt and seven volunteers. The rebellion quickly spread through neighboring sugar plantations and among freeholders. Bogle returned to Stony Gut and declared Jamaica liberated. "The iron bar is now broken in this parish," he proclaimed. "War is at us, my black skin. War is at hand."[1]

If the bloody Christmas revolt of 1831–32 hastened emancipation in the British Empire, the Morant Bay rebellion unleashed the forces of reaction. Governor Edward John Eyre declared martial law and inaugurated a ruthless "reign of terror" that included indiscriminate and "barbarous" floggings, the burning of a thousand homes, and the deaths of more than four hundred—guilty and innocent alike—most by execution. Among the innocent was George William Gordon, the mulatto assemblyman, ally of Bogle and defender of Jamaica's poor, shepherded from his home in Kingston to Morant Bay to face the military tribunal. Bogle was captured on October 23, and hanged the next day. By the end of the year, warning that Jamaica was on the verge of becoming "a second Haiti," a haven for black licentiousness and creeping savagery, the governor had convinced the Legislative Assembly to suspend self-government and embrace the "strong government" of the Queen.[2]

The Morant Bay rebellion was one of the remarkable events of a remarkable year best remembered for the close of the Civil War—and with it, the

FIGURE 1.1. Paul Bogle.

institution of slavery—in the United States. For British subjects of African descent, already released from bondage, the rebellion marked a "symbolic turning point" in the contest to define the parameters of citizenship and freedom in the postemancipation era, its destruction foreshadowing the coalescence of new and assertive imperial regimes by the end of the century.[3] Since the revolutionary decades of the late eighteenth century, peoples of African descent had forged a rich intellectual tradition premised on an uncompromising commitment to abolitionism and natural rights, an investment in black "nation" making, and an unswerving faith in racial destiny, guided by the understanding that human perfectibility depended on the fulfillment of providential design—that "Princes shall come out of Egypt"; that "Ethiopia shall soon stretch forth her hands unto God" (Psalms 68:31). At times, as at Morant Bay, the advocacy and activism of transatlantic black spokesmen converged explosively with the radical democratic cultures of the black peasantry, often mediated by the contested public sphere of black Christianity. At other times, black intellectuals sustained their faith in a partnership with white allies, wagering that the European and American commitments to free labor, "civilization" building, and global proselytization would hasten the day when they and their race would be respected as equal partners—"co-worker[s]," as W.E.B. Du Bois put it, "in the kingdom of culture."[4]

By 1900, when delegates from Africa, the West Indies, Europe, and the United States assembled at the historic Pan-African Conference in London, the idealism and possibility of the postemancipation period had been undercut by a reinvigorated racial order that deemed Africans and their descendants perpetual hewers of wood and drawers of water, consigned for the distant future to tutelage under the administration and care of "civilized" European administrators. For members of the black intellectual diaspora, bearers and proponents of the pan-African tradition, the two decades before the First World War were a period of experimentation and halting steps. At the Tuskegee Institute in Alabama, Booker T. Washington established a détente with white supremacy that had unexpected reverberations across the world. From the Gold Coast (now Ghana), barrister, author, and activist J. E. Casely Hayford struggled toward a philosophy of political Ethiopianism that paid homage to the legacy of his mentor, Edward Wilmot Blyden, while articulating a more defiant, anticolonial posture.[5] In London, at the offices of the *African Times and Orient Review*, Dusé Mohamed Ali, aided by his network of journalists, correspondents, and agents in Asia, Africa, Europe, and the Americas, chronicled the first gestures toward the New Negro radicalism that would erupt during and after the war.

The education of Marcus Garvey, who was born in 1887, was both grounded in the decades-old discourse of global pan-Africanism and shaped by the ferment of his era. His youthful experiences and experiments in Jamaica, Central America, and Europe—many of which seem to fly in the face of popular understandings of Garvey and Garveyism—suggest much about the diversity of the pan-African tradition out of which he emerged, and hint at the model of politics Garvey ultimately embraced. Pan-Africanism provided less of a blueprint than a set of assumptions about the common origins of the "race," its shared destiny, and its inevitable, providentially assured ascent. For political activists, it offered what Eddie Glaude has called "vocabularies of agency," a critical arena in which to construct and negotiate identities, build alliances, and invoke shared traditions of experience and fictive meaning.[6] Thinking of pan-Africanism less as an ideology than as an historically conditioned social, cultural, and political field of meaning explains why a tradition dominated by elitism, infused with an abiding scorn for black folk cultures, and partial to Western theories of "civilization" has been able to mobilize peoples of African descent again and again. Proscribing neither radicalism nor conservatism, neither boldness nor caution, neither separatism nor interracial cooperation, the pan-African tradition offered clever and ambitious activists like Marcus Garvey a "potter's clay" that, under the right conditions, might unite a scattered race.[7]

1865

Morant Bay, St. Thomas in the East, Jamaica

The Morant Bay rebellion was not entirely unexpected. Early in January 1865, Edward B. Underhill of the Baptist Missionary Society penned a letter to the British Parliament warning of the rapidly deteriorating conditions on the island. The drought of the past two years had exacerbated an employment crisis created by the decline of the sugar industry. The American Civil War had curtailed the importation of food and cotton products from the North, driving food prices to levels that threatened starvation, and clothing prices to levels that reduced vast numbers of people to a "ragged and even naked condition." The political hegemony of the small white planter class was further cemented in the Franchise Act of 1859, which dramatically reduced the number of Jamaica's eligible voters, and which ensured that the Legislative Assembly—like the planter-dominated courts—would remain unresponsive to the needs and entreaties of the island's majority. The Underhill letter sparked a series of public meetings across the island, many facilitated by George William Gordon, representative to the Legislative Assembly for St. Thomas in the East, and expressing the emerging political voice of what Mimi Sheller describes as an "alternative public—an African, poor, black, urban working class and rural peasant public." Rather than accepting the grievances expressed at the meetings in good faith, or pursuing measures to alleviate the peasantry's misery and discontent, Governor Eyre responded with furious contempt, introducing harsher methods of discipline, including punishments for petty larceny and other minor crimes that bore no small resemblance to those enacted during the days of slavery. Efforts by peasant workers to squat on unused Crown lands and abandoned plantations—to rely on their own productive capacities rather than the island's faltering plantation economy—were rebuffed. When rumors of rebellion and the impending "deliverance of the sons and daughters of Africa," as one placard foretold, emerged in the western parishes over the summer, Eyre responded by sending two men-of-war as a precautionary measure, but demonstrated no inclination to reconsider his government's increasingly perilous course.[8]

Contributing to this lackluster response was the widely shared view that Jamaica's economic misery could be laid at the feet of the island's black population. The architects of the Colonial Office's emancipation policy had expected the formerly enslaved, released from the enervating shackles of their bondage, to exercise their freedom according to the "rational" principles of classical liberalism. They would serve a period of tutelage on their old plantations, imbibe the values of hard work and self-reliance in the school of wage labor, and progress carefully and inexorably toward the attainment of political responsibility. Before the apprenticeship system ended on August 1, 1838, Lord Glenelg, the Colonial Secretary, ordered a sweeping review of colonial law to ensure the unlimited exercise of personal freedom and equality for the newly freed peoples of the British West Indies. But when freedom came, the freed refused to play their assigned part. Jamaica's black peasantry struggled to defend their own understandings of freedom, pursuing an amalgam of strategies that combined independent proprietorship, market production, supplemental wage labor, and the reproduction and expansion of social relations crafted during the long era of slavery, and in Africa itself. Rather than engendering a review of liberal democratic theory, the behavior of the formerly enslaved lent purchase to the possibility that the rules of rational economic behavior may not apply to the "Negro." And if the "Negro" could not be entrusted with the maintenance of the plantation system, it was doubtful that he was suited for the exercise of the franchise, even those who qualified to vote and hold office under Jamaica's restrictive formula. By the 1850s, British policymakers had begun to view their West Indian colonies in a different light than their dominions in places like Canada and Australia, where white settlers were being groomed for self-government. As Thomas C. Holt has demonstrated, the outlines of the "white man's burden" were traced not during the Scramble for Africa at the close of the nineteenth century, but in the struggle between policymakers, planters, and peasants in the postemancipation West Indies.[9]

In a broader sense, then, the Morant Bay rebellion gave credence to an emerging narrative about the lessons of the West Indies. For James Hunt of the newly formed Anthropological Society of London, the rebellion illustrated the folly of a "philanthropic sentimentality" that posited an inherent equality between the Negro and the European, confirmed the consequences of luring the Negro from his "natural subordination to the European," and demonstrated that "English institutions are not suited to the negro race." *The Times* of London viewed the rebellion as a greater "disappointment" than the Indian Mutiny of 1857. "It seemed to be proved in Jamaica that the negro could become fit for self-government," lamented the paper. "Then they show themselves so wonderfully unchanged. . . . We have been trying now [for] the best part of a century to wash the blackamoor white, with all kinds of patent soaps, infallible dyes, sweet oils, soothing liniments, rough towels, and soft brushes. But he remains as black as ever, as thick-skinned as ever, his hair as wooly, and his cranium as hard."[10]

By the time James Anthony Froude visited Jamaica in 1887, the year Marcus Garvey was born, the official story about the rebellion was settling into place. Froude argued that the fault lay neither with Governor Eyre and his excesses and neglects, nor with Gordon and his machinations, but with those who, by insisting on "applying a constitutional form of government" to a country with a large majority of black subjects, had ignored the tragic calculus of the "negro problem." The power of Froude's formula, as with subsequent such renderings, was that it subsumed individual and group agency—white and black alike—within a series of abstract and timeless "truths." In Jamaica, Froude argued, an "intelligent white minority" would never submit to an "unintelligent black majority," but neither could Jamaican whites be trusted to resist the exploitative instincts that had been so horribly manifested in the slave trade. The black man had a right to "his prosperity, his freedom, his opportunities of advancing himself," but he must accept his lowly position as a "child race," marked by "thousands of years" of inequality, capable of civilization only under the guidance of the white man. The end of slavery did not mean the end of naturally delegated authority: as wives and children must submit to patriarchal power, blacks must submit to their wiser brothers. Master and servant must conduct themselves well. Essential in maintaining this equilibrium was the steady hand of England, exercising impartial rule, acquitting itself of its "self-chosen responsibilities." The West Indies were to remain "a small limb in the great body corporate of the British Empire," the islands themselves naturalized in a hierarchical relationship that preserved their health and forestalled their decay.[11]

To this fate, Froude assured, the "docile, good-tempered . . . and faithful" Negro would happily submit, provided he was "kindly treated," and provided he was denied the poison pill of self-government. But failure to heed the former threatened a war of "extinction." Giving ground on the latter augured a descent into "absolute barbarism." Froude toured nearby Haiti, where he reported sickening smells, overwhelming dirt and disease, shameless sexual immorality, and a "horrible revival of the West African superstitions; the serpent worship, and the child sacrifice, and the cannibalism."[12] Since 1791, when slaves in Haiti (then the French colony of Saint-Domingue) had inaugurated their successful revolution, the New World's second independent republic had been a beacon of inspiration for transatlantic blacks, a place of refuge, a powerful representation of black nationality, of violent resistance in pursuit of freedom. With slavery abolished from the New World and with the reevaluation of black capacities for "improvement" in the postemancipation era, Haiti was transformed from a specter of slave militancy into a cautionary tale, a teaching tool, an early test—as Lothrop Stoddard would later declare—"between the ideals of white supremacy and race equality." If the solution to the vexing "negro problem" remained unresolved, by the turn of the century European policymakers and intellectuals were agreed on the lesson of Morant Bay, on the lesson of Haiti, and on the lesson of "philanthropic sentimentality." As J. A. Hobson, the great British critic of imperialism, wrote in his 1902 masterwork, "the old Liberal notion of our educating lower races in the art of popular government is discredited."[13]

House of Commons, London, England

On February 21, 1865, a Select Committee was formed in London to consider the prospects for, and future of, Britain's colonial presence in West Africa. Since its transition toward a policy of "legitimate commerce," accelerating with Parliament's abolition of the slave trade in 1807 and the adoption of Sierra Leone as a Crown colony, Britain had sustained a modest presence on the coast. When Lagos Colony was established in 1862, it joined Sierra Leone, the Gambia, and the Gold Coast as the fourth British enclave, coexisting alongside equally modest French, Portuguese, and Spanish territories, the independent republic of Liberia, and large and small African polities and kingdoms stretching into the interior. The British settlements were populated by a cosmopolitan collection of European missionaries, traders, and officials; African American, West Indian, Brazilian, and Cuban emigrants; and tens of thousands of "recaptives," formerly enslaved men and women from all over Africa who had been liberated by the British naval blockade of the west coast. A creole culture had developed that—while certainly not free of racial prejudice—had convinced many coastal Africans that they were involved in a shared project of establishing centers of commerce, Christianity, and civilization at the edges of the Dark Continent. An emergent, European-educated black elite had risen to prominent roles in the colonies as doctors, lawyers, educators, and traders, and several held senior positions in the missions and in the colonial administrations. In 1861, the Church Missionary Society of the Anglican Church (CMS) established the Native Pastorate, intended to lay the groundwork for the establishment of African-governed episcopates. Three years later, Samuel Ajayi Crowther—former recaptive, the first African student of the CMS-run Fourah Bay College in Sierra Leone, pioneering evangelist in Yorubaland—was ordained the continent's first black bishop.[14]

For residents on the coast, the gradual assumption of leadership by Western-educated black men was regarded as part of the natural course of events. Tropical Africa was widely viewed as the "white man's grave," its climate and disease-rich environment inhospitable to permanent European settlement. The colonies themselves were the product of an interracial antislavery tradition with roots dating back to the evangelical awakenings of the mid-eighteenth century and the revolutionary decades that followed. The turmoil of the Age of Revolution produced what Michael O. West and William Martin have described as a "diaspora within a diaspora," the flowering of a black international tradition that joined missionaries, sailors, teachers, traders, and writers in a transatlantic conversation about racial destiny. This vibrant exercise in pan-African nation building, as West and Martin point out, veered in both reformist and revolutionary directions. Educated black men and women scattered throughout Canada, the United States, the Caribbean basin, and West and South Africa ascribed not to a fixed ideology but rather a dynamic public discourse rent by disagreements over tactics, the advisability of emigration to Africa, and the relative value (or lack thereof) of African indigenous and Afro-diasporic folk cultures. Nevertheless, members of this vanguard diaspora within a diaspora accepted a broad set of common beliefs that remained compatible, in principle, with the rhetorical commitments of European social activism in the nineteenth century: a Christian, postmillennialist faith in the perfectibility of human relations, concomitant on an equitable readjustment of race relations; confidence in the capacity of properly administered European modes of education, civilization, and free market capitalism to revive the fortunes of Africa and its scattered and fallen peoples; and an unwavering belief that members of the race were joined to a single garment of destiny. As David Walker put it in his famous jeremiad, God's plan for their redemption would not be fully consummated "but with the entire emancipation of your enslaved brethren all over the world." For black activists, the fact of Africa's regeneration was decided. The question was how, and by whom, and whether Europe was to be met with divine retribution for its procrastination.[15]

Thus, when the Select Committee presented its findings to the House of Commons on June 26, recommending the gradual withdrawal of British administration from West Africa and the transfer of authority to creole self-government, the conclusions were both welcomed and not unexpected by West Africa's black intelligentsia.[16] For James Africanus Beale Horton, the Sierra Leonean physician, the committee's report served as both a rebuke to the pseudoscientific theories of the Anthropological Society, and an acknowledgment that the British "civilizing mission" could only go so far, that "tropical Africa must be left eventually for the Africans." In his dynamic volume, *West African Countries and Peoples*, Horton traced the contours of an emerging West African nationalism. The current "barbarism" of the Negro race, he argued, was reflected not in the past, when ancient Africa had been "the nursery of science and literature" for Europe, nor did it predict the future, when Africans would again "take a prominent part in the history of the civilized world." As "harbingers of civilization," as the bearers of Christianity, and as models of industrious achievement, European pioneers and missionaries had set Africa back upon a proper course. Now it was incumbent on Africans, with the help of their civilized brethren, to shed their superstitions and splintered allegiances in the interests of racial unity and national spirit. Horton proposed the foundation of a "University of West Africa," and a comprehensive investment in education, particularly for African women who—removed from "debasing" field labor—might from their proper sphere "become the best expounders of civilization to the subsequent generation." With "undaunted courage and industry, by real hard work and application . . . by an uncompromising, disinterested adhesion to the truth," Africans would settle the question of racial advancement. And in so doing they would regenerate the continent.[17]

For Horton, as George Shepperson has noted, civilization was "the application to West Africa of European learning, technology, and religion."[18] For Reverend James Johnson, CMS clergyman, politician, and champion of the Native Pastorate, African civilization must take account of the continent's unique history, its racial distinctiveness, and its cultural traditions. Like Horton, Johnson shared the European view of tropical Africa as a fallen land. Like Horton, he viewed Christianity as the primary motor of civilization: The continent's ancient glories, he argued, dated from the establishment of the Christian Church in North Africa; its decline was assured by the failure of the Church to expand below the Sahara Desert. But for Johnson, the revival of Christian civilization in Africa was predicated on the latent genius of Africa itself. And because Africa's reconstruction relied on the expression of a "native character and power," the work must be performed by Africans themselves, first in the training ground of the Native Pastorate, then in a continental Church, and finally in a self-governing nation. "In the work of elevating Africans, foreign teachers have always proceeded with their work on the assumption that the Negro or African is in every one of his normal susceptibilities an inferior race, and that it is needful in everything to give him a foreign model to copy," declared Johnson. "[N]o account has been made of our peculiarities; our languages enriched with traditions of centuries; our parables, many of them the quintessence of family and national histories; our modes of thought, influenced more or less by local circumstances, our poetry and manufactures, which though rude, have their own tales to tell." God, argued Johnson, "does not intend to have the races confounded, but that the Negro or African should be raised upon his own idiosyncracies." The failure to heed this call had resulted in the loss of "our self-respect and our love for our own race." Like Horton, Johnson supported the establishment of a West African university, one that would keep exceptional students at home, trained under an African curriculum and by African teachers. And more forcefully than Horton, Johnson subscribed to the transatlantic doctrine of Ethiopianism, viewing Africans and their "brothers in exile" in the Americas as members of a shared civilization, divided only by accident and tragedy, destined to rule Africa by "divine right" and biblical prophecy.[19]

The centrality of religious faith in nineteenth-century West African nationalism helps account for the enduring optimism of its most famous proponent, Edward Wilmot Blyden. Indeed, one of the persistent themes of

Blyden's masterpiece, *Christianity, Islam, and the Negro Race*, is the author's unshakable confidence in Africa's ultimate destiny. Blyden, who was born in St. Thomas, Dutch West Indies and emigrated to Liberia in 1851, accepted the view that humankind was divided into discrete races, but rejected the European assumption "that the Negro is on the same line of progress, in the same groove, with the European, but infinitely to the rear." Rather than being a question of superiority or inferiority, the question revolved around "difference of endowment and difference of destiny." The two races were moving "on parallel lines," distinct but equal. The goal of African nation building was not to "attempt to Europeanize the Negro"—a fruitless task—but to groom the African to perform "his specific part in the world's work, as a distinct portion of the human race." As the Scramble for Africa gained momentum, Blyden remained serene, convinced that the climate of equatorial Africa made European occupation untenable. So confident was Blyden that he openly solicited the expansion of white philanthropy in the interior, first to Britain, then the United States. If Blyden remained a cultural—rather than a political—nationalist, it was only because of his expectation that the politics would sort itself out in due time.[20]

Blyden, of course, was wrong. The year 1865 was a chimera. By 1884–85, European leaders were meeting in Berlin to discuss the ground rules for the expansion of imperial power in Africa. The doctrine of formal intervention acquired momentum from several overlapping directions: from international rivalries for markets of standardized raw materials to feed industrial growth; from concerns about the global stability of trading and banking interests, reflecting the rise of finance capital in the metropole and resistance to its prerogatives on the periphery; from the political machinations of "gentlemanly" elites in the City of London, and of politicians eager to sate industrial unrest at home; and from the maneuvering of "men on the spot"—representatives of charter companies, merchants, industrialists, and mining interests.[21] Meanwhile, scientific and technological progress offered a means—for the first time—to subdue the interior of the continent. Medical breakthroughs, including the use of quinine to combat malaria, dramatically reduced the dread of sub-Saharan Africa's tropical disease environment. Advances in transportation and communications made empire more affordable. And the invention of new and more terrible weaponry, particularly the Maxim gun in 1884, handed European powers the means of domination. At the 1898 Battle of Omdurman, Sudan, British forces massacred nearly 30,000 Mahdists, while suffering a mere forty-eight casualties. Despite the persistence of resistance and the periodic eruption of rebellion throughout the pre–World War I period, by the turn of the century the colonial map had been established.[22]

An emerging racial consensus given scientific imprimatur by the rise of social Darwinism offered compelling ideological support to the new

FIGURE 1.2. Edward Wilmot Blyden. (Library of Congress, Prints and Photographs Division, Washington, D.C.)

imperialism. In his *The Descent of Man*, Charles Darwin left no doubt that his theory of evolution applied to the "races" of men, and their relative successes and failures.[23] By the early twentieth century, with the aide of theorists like Herbert Spencer, the idea of nations and races locked in a geopolitical struggle for survival, demonstrating variegated levels of fitness for the rigors of civilization, had attained a powerful popular and academic hegemony.[24] "The negro, more than any other human type, has been marked out by his mental and physical characteristics as the servant of the other races," wrote Harry Johnston in his sweeping history of the colonization of Africa. For all of the horrors of the slave trade, it had contained within it "an underlying sense of justice," its European and Arab facilitators "the unconscious agents of the Power behind Nature in punishing the negro for his lazy backwardness." With the colonial occupation of the continent, Africans had been given a second chance. But if blacks did not apply themselves "zealously under European tuition to the development of the vast resources of Tropical Africa," if they continued to lead "the wasteful, unproductive life of . . . baboon[s]," then "the force of circumstances, the pressure of eager, hungry, impatient outside humanity" would "once more relegate the Negro to the servitude which will be the alternative—in the coming struggle for existence—to extinction."[25]

Seemingly incontrovertible evidence of black inferiority thus cast colonial domination as a noble project of humanitarianism, an effort to save inferior peoples from themselves. Led by the swashbuckling explorer and crusading missionary David Livingstone, European travelers to Africa relayed to readers back home the stark brutality of life under the tyranny of Negro misrule. Particularly galling was the persistence of slavery and the internal slave trade. If free labor societies in the Caribbean had demonstrated the incapacity of African descendants to become rational economic actors, the inability of African rulers to end the trade suggested the failure of black self-government to protect free labor principles entirely. Joined with the metalanguage of scientific racism, the question of outside governance of African affairs devolved to a question of outside governance by whom. As J. A. Hobson scolded advocates of a "hands off" policy in Africa, "If organised Governments of civilised Powers refused the task, they would let loose a horde of private adventurers, slavers, piratical traders, treasure hunters, concession mongers, who, animated by more greed of gold or power, would set about the work of exploitation under no public control and with no regard to the future."[26]

In 1865, Western-educated Africans had imagined themselves an emergent coastal elite, collaborators and essential agents in an interracial civilizing mission that would in due time be left to their care. It was a vision that relied on a romantic rendering of "African" unity, one that depended on a chauvinism that tended to reduce sophisticated African polities, cultural practices, and religious observances to abstract props in a cosmic drama of redemption. But it also insisted on an underlying equality between European and African peoples, posited surface environmental, rather than ancient biological, explanations for the supposedly benighted condition of the African interior, and—in its most hopeful manifestations—implied an African exceptionalism destined to one day surpass the global achievements of European civilization. By the 1890s, such beliefs were not only discordant with a sweeping new iteration of white supremacy and white rule, but were viewed as an inconvenient hurdle to the administration of an expanding colonial order. In the reconstituted version of the civilizing mission, Africans must undergo an indefinite period of patient tutelage, nurtured within the timeless order of "traditional" African custom that was best suited to their stage of racial development. Those smartly dressed subjects on the coast who spoke the Queen's English, had trained for advanced degrees in Britain,

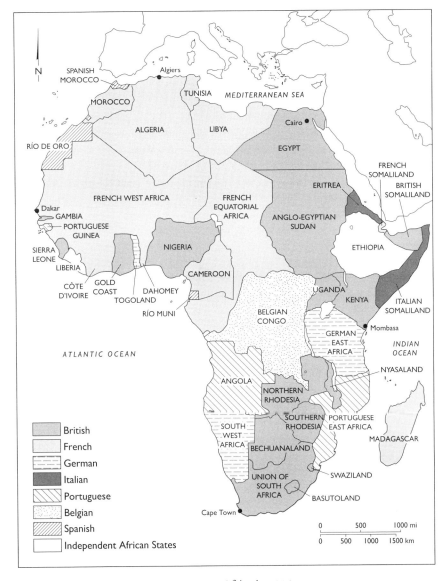

FIGURE 1.3. Africa in 1914.

and held senior positions in the civil service would have no place in the new order. Instead, they were cast as impostors—able, as one official put it, to exhibit the "parrot-like knowledge" of a child but incapable of performing the "higher intellectual functions" necessary to succeed in European civilization. When James Johnson complained about the shrinking opportunities for educated West Africans, his dilemma was exquisitely captured in a remark by the Colonial Office's Reginald L. Antrobus. "Generally speaking, the highest education fails to impart to the African something which the European possesses, and which makes him competent to administer and to occupy positions of trust," Antrobus explained. He added: "It would be impossible to explain this to Mr. Johnson but I don't think his appeal on this score need cause us much searching of heart."[27]

Savannah, Georgia

United States General William Tecumseh Sherman issued his "Special Field Order No. 15" on January 16, 1865 in the aftermath of his triumphant march to the sea from Atlanta, and before heading north to Columbia, South Carolina, toward General Robert E. Lee's Confederate armies in Virginia. The order reserved the rice lands along the Carolina and Georgia coastline for liberated African Americans, subdivided into parcels of forty acres. In March 1865 when Congress established the Freedmen's Bureau, it empowered its head, General Oliver Otis Howard, to issue titles to black families on the lands confiscated within the insurrectionary states of the South. For the 40,000 men, women, and children who claimed homesteads on "Sherman's Land," or the black residents who claimed land on the Carolina Sea Islands in 1861, or the emancipated slaves working their own fields at Davis Bend, Mississippi, the promise of land affirmed the expectations and legitimized the sacrifices inspired by the outbreak of the Civil War. African Americans had not merely been given their freedom. By participating in what W.E.B. Du Bois described as a "general strike" on Southern plantations, by running away to Union lines, and by demanding participation in the Union war effort, former slaves ensured that the war would not end with slavery intact. They waged what historian Steven Hahn has called the greatest slave rebellion in modern history. For a few tantalizing months in 1865, their victory appeared complete. Before Howard was sent to South Carolina in October by president Andrew Johnson to return Sherman's Land to its former white ownership; before the nearly 900,000 acres of confiscated land owned by the federal government was returned to Southern planters; before Thaddeus Stevens thundered impotently that land redistribution offered the last, best chance for the United States to become a true republic—it looked as though freed people might have their forty acres and a mule.[28]

Instead, the demise of the world's most powerful slave society inaugurated a fierce contest between competing visions of freedom. The dogged efforts by freedpeople to carve for themselves a foothold during Reconstruction— the struggles to unite families, to pursue educational opportunities, to achieve labor autonomy and wage fairness, to participate in an interracial political order—have received thoughtful and voluminous attention. The gains were not insubstantial, and were reflected in rising literacy rates, modest land acquisitions, political office holding, and the proliferation of churches, schools, universities, mutual aid societies, fraternal orders, and Union League councils. Kinship-based political networks established during slavery were strengthened and enriched during the postbellum period. After the withdrawal of the Federal army from the former Confederate states in 1877, Southern blacks continued to find creative means, both big and small, to deploy their increasingly fragile economic and political power in pursuit of communal and individual goals. Rayford Logan's oft-repeated observation that the end of Reconstruction precipitated a "nadir" in American race relations should not imply that the black freedom struggle was forced into submission.[29]

But the nadir did come. By the turn of the century, the American South had emerged from decades of turmoil as the world's most advanced racial regime, supported by pillars of economic, legal, and political domination, undergirded by institutionalized racial terrorism, naturalized by transatlantic discourses of white supremacy. The abandonment of land redistribution robbed freedpeople of a measure of leverage at a crucial moment of vulnerability and thrust the vast majority back into a reconstituted and capricious cotton economy. Resisting planter efforts to resume old relations of labor control, prioritizing independent production free of white oversight, rural blacks swallowed the poison pill of sharecropping. The arrangement was simple enough: families rented plots on plantation lands under an agreement to share a portion of the yields with the owner. But with the Southern banking system in ruins, and in order to acquire provisions and supplies to sustain the production of those yields, farmers were compelled to enter into credit relationships with country merchants, borrowing against their expected profits, and purchasing food and equipment at monopolistic prices. The crop lien system steered farmers toward cotton, which enjoyed high market value in the late 1860s and early 1870s. But with the collapse of prices following the depression of 1873, sharecroppers were thrust into a cycle of perpetual indebtedness, unable to square their accounts, their autonomy increasingly undermined by the demands of their creditors. The plantation Negro is "the victim of a cunningly devised swindle," seethed Frederick Douglass, "one which paralyzes his energies, suppresses his ambition, and blasts his hopes." Slavery was resumed without a sense of responsibility for the well-being of the workers, Douglass complained. Emancipation was revealed as "a stupendous fraud."[30]

The reestablishment of rural labor control was facilitated and accelerated by the restoration of white political and juridical hegemony. The economic collapse of 1873 illuminated the limits of Northern patience for Reconstruction, and returned Democratic majorities to the House of Representatives and Senate for the first time since the war. With federal interest in the protection of blacks waning, Redeemer governments swept through the former Confederate states, sometimes legitimately, often with the aid of fraud, intimidation, and violence. Creative efforts to break the power of planter rule in the upper South were isolated and overwhelmed. The final blow came in Wilmington, North Carolina in 1898, where the specter of "negro rule"—a tenuous interracial fusion government of Populists and Republicans—was decisively crushed in a race riot that killed dozens of blacks and drove hundreds of black residents out of town. Once entrenched, white power became self-sustaining. Black labor's negotiating power was further undermined by a catalogue of laws designed to depress wages, restrict worker mobility, and offer sweeping powers to employers. Disenfranchisement laws in the 1890s erased millions of black and white voters from the rolls, and established decades of one-party Democratic rule. Segregation laws in the 1880s and 1890s dictated separate schools for black and white children, separate accommodations on trains, separate sections on buses, and restricted black access to public and private space, including parks and libraries that were partially funded by black taxpayers. The new order was codified by the Supreme Court, which dramatically undercut the equal protection clause of the Fourteenth Amendment, affirmed the legality of "separate but equal" facilities for whites and blacks, and upheld the right of states to pass voter laws designed to circumvent the Fifteenth Amendment so long as they did not explicitly discriminate on the basis of race—although that was both the intention of the laws and their result.[31]

Violence was never far below the surface. In *U.S. v. Cruikshank* (1876), the Supreme Court repudiated the Enforcement Acts of 1871, enacted to empower the federal government to suppress the paramilitary counterrevolution of the Ku Klux Klan. With the absolute power to criminally prosecute individuals returned to the states, white supremacists were given free rein to renew their campaign of extralegal punishment and terrorism. By the mid-1880s, lynching had emerged as a visceral demonstration of white power. As a practical tool of domination, lynch mobs served their purposes well. Lynchings surged during a period of labor agitation in the late 1880s, reached their peak in the 1890s during the final push for disenfranchisement and segregation, and declined to a more modest equilibrium after the formalized system of Jim Crow was firmly established. Extralegal violence was used to suppress union activities, to enforce labor contracts, to dissuade political organizing, to punish conspicuous demonstrations of black success, and to generally prevent blacks from getting "bigotty," as one southerner put it.[32] But mob murder was more than a functional weapon serving the cause of economic and political interests. Lynchings were elevated to the level of spectacle, occasions for family gatherings, a reason for children to miss school. Photographs of hangmen and charred corpses were turned into postcards and mailed by mob participants to their friends. Methods of torture became more inventive and more sadistic, as mobs competed with each other to exact a maximum degree of punishment on their victims. For blacks, the menace of extralegal death was ever present, unpredictable, capricious. For whites, the power to bring death upon a hapless victim for "disrespectful" language, for a sideways glance or sardonic grin, for "being troublesome generally," dramatically reinforced the fundamental fact of social custom and belief: white supremacy.[33]

Racial violence, like racial domination in general, was powerfully gendered. It was fueled by a mythology that cast black men as sexually unrestrained savages—unmanly by Victorian standards—and white men as chivalrous defenders of white female purity. The canard of the black man as rapist was a fairly transparent invention, emerging only in the late 1880s, easily disproven. But as Jacquelyn Dowd Hall has argued, "the emotional circuit between interracial rape and lynching lay beyond the reach of factual refutation." It simply explained too much: the Negro's condition; his lack of civilization; the necessity of his disenfranchisement and his segregation; his marginalization. No matter, as Ida B. Wells bitterly remarked, that the so-called chivalry of white men was "written in the faces of the million mulattoes in the South." The "southern rape complex" recast white barbarity as a linchpin of social order. As James Vardaman suggested during his successful 1900 gubernatorial campaign in Mississippi, "We would be justified in slaughtering every Ethiop on the earth to preserve unsullied the honor of our Caucasian home."[34]

During Reconstruction, Northern reformers had been enlivened by the same free labor assumptions that had guided early postemancipation policy in the British Caribbean. If freed people were released from their bondage, they believed, allowed to compete in a fair labor market, their rise from slavery would be commensurate with their work ethic.[35] By the dawn of the twentieth century, any confidence in the assimilative power of American institutions had been replaced by the powerful new transatlantic paradigm of racial competition and difference. The assumptions of social Darwinism swept triumphantly across the sciences, social and natural, and embedded themselves deeply into popular culture.[36] America's foray into empire building in the South Pacific and the Caribbean following its triumph in the Spanish-American War in 1898 reoriented the "negro problem" in the South within the broader global framework of the white man's burden. For supporters of the new imperialism, the identification of an Anglo-Saxon (or Caucasian, or Nordic) race as the purveyor and protector of a superior civilization crystallized America's mission to bestow its wisdom, tutelage, and protection on its hapless wards. In his "Corollary" to the Monroe Doctrine, President Theodore Roosevelt described American expansionism not as "land hunger" but as "welfare," protection against "a general loosening of the ties of civilized society," assistance—in the case of the Philippines—for peoples "utterly incapable of existing in independence at all or of building up a civilization of their own." For advocates of eugenics and Mendelian genetics—both of which suggested that biology, rather than environmental factors, shaped individual and racial destiny—the lessons of racial hierarchy were more dire. Foreign peoples, both abroad and at home, were not to be tutored but contained. The goal of Anglo-Saxon civilization was to preserve the purity of the bloodlines from which that civilization had emerged. Regardless the brand of white supremacy, the nationalization and internationalization of the race problem had the effect of further entrenching and naturalizing the political, economic, and social predicament black people faced at the turn of the century. As in the Caribbean and in Africa, efforts to include black people in the social compact were viewed in retrospect as hopelessly naïve.[37]

The Problem of the Twentieth Century

The twentieth century opened early in the African diaspora, on September 18, 1895, when Booker T. Washington stepped to the podium to deliver his address at the Cotton States and International Exposition in Atlanta. The Negro, Washington argued, must accept that Reconstruction was a mistake. He must accept that "agitation of questions of social equality is the extremest folly," and that political "privileges" must be earned by "severe and constant struggle," by self-improvement and demonstration of worth rather than by "artificial forcing." He must begin at the "bottom of life," in the fields, working with his hands, in the commercial and industrial world where the southern states offered him a real opportunity. In return, the Negro must be afforded the freedom by whites to acquire an education, to prove his worth, to contribute to the "business and industrial prosperity of the South" rather than be reduced, by self-defeating prejudice, to a source of its social decay and stagnation. "It is important and right that all privileges of the law be ours," Washington reminded whites. But not yet. It was "vastly more important" that Negroes be first "prepared for the exercise of these privileges."[38]

Washington was born on a plantation in Franklin County, Virginia, a slave. He remembered the day an officer of the United States army arrived at the plantation to declare its black residents free, remembered the tears of joy streaming down his mother's cheeks. After the family reunited with his stepfather in West Virginia, Washington worked in a salt furnace, and then a coal mine, and traveled several miles to attend night school. Eventually, he secured employment in the home of Viola Ruffner, the mine owner's wife, a strict taskmaster whom he won over with his soon-to-be-legendary work ethic and discipline. In 1872, long harboring a desire to acquire a proper education, Washington set out for the newly established Hampton Normal and Agricultural Institute, trekking nearly five hundred miles, mostly by foot, or by begging rides. Along the way, he worked for his food, and spent several days sleeping under an elevated sidewalk in Richmond. When he finally arrived at Hampton, starving, filthy, and nearly penniless, he won admittance to the school by impressing the head teacher with his thorough sweeping and dusting of the reception room. As a student, Washington was such a success that when money was raised for a new normal school in Tuskegee, Alabama, he was recommended to head it by his mentor, Hampton's principal and founder, General Samuel C. Armstrong.[39]

For General Armstrong, Washington was an ideal disciple, a testament to his view that if the "weak tropical races" are to "work out . . . [their] own salvation," they must "learn how to work." When Hampton opened in 1868, Armstrong envisioned it as a more practical alternative to the crop of academically rigorous Negro universities emerging across the South—Atlanta University in 1865, Fisk in 1866, Howard in 1867. Raised by his missionary parents among the "grown-up children" of Hawaii, commander of black soldiers during the Civil War and superintendent for the Virginia Freedmen's Bureau, Armstrong considered himself an expert in the character and needs of "inferior" peoples. A Western-style liberal arts education would "exhaust the best powers of nineteen-twentieths of those who would, for years to come enter the institute." Instead of deferring to the ghosts of an abstract tradition, an educator must soberly consider the "real needs and weaknesses" of his students. The Negro's weakness was a "deficient character." His need was the sober discipline of manual labor. The thing to be done was clear," reflected Armstrong in 1890.

> [T]o train selected Negro youth who should go out and teach and lead their people, first by example by getting land and homes; to give them not a dollar that they could earn for themselves; to teach respect for labor; to replace stupid drudgery with skilled hands; and, to these ends, to build up an industrial system, for the sake not only of self-support and intelligent labor, but also for the sake of character.

The twentieth student, Armstrong explained, could go to Howard.[40]

When Booker T. Washington arrived in Tuskegee in 1881 he established his school in a "broken-down shanty" with a leaky roof. His first

FIGURE 1.4. Booker T. Washington speaking in Mount Bayou, Mississippi, 1912. (Library of Congress, Prints and Photographs Division, Washington, D.C.)

class contained thirty students. By the end of the century, marshaling his trademark determination and exercising the full capacities of his wit, Washington had built an industrial institution that matched the prestige of its forebear, Hampton. The school boasted fourteen hundred students from twenty-seven states, and from across Africa and the Caribbean; nearly one hundred teachers, including agriculturalist and scientist George Washington Carver; and a 2,300-acre campus with sixty-six smart red brick buildings erected by student labor. A healthy endowment was fueled by an impressive network of philanthropic support that also sustained Washington's national political, media and business machine. President William McKinley visited Tuskegee in 1898. The next year, during a trip to Europe, Washington sat for tea with Queen Victoria. In October 1901, at the invitation of Theodore Roosevelt, Washington became the first African American to dine in the White House.[41]

Washington's Atlanta Exposition address—the "Atlanta Compromise" as Du Bois later dubbed it—was an oratorical masterpiece, an extrapolation of the insights of the Hampton-Tuskegee education model as social policy, as a grand bargain. Southern moderates responded with ecstatic approval. "I do not exaggerate when I say that Professor Booker T. Washington's address yesterday was one of the most notable speeches . . . ever delivered to a Southern audience," raved Clark Howell, editor of the *Atlanta Constitution*. "The address was a revelation. The whole speech is a platform upon which blacks and whites can stand with full justice to each other."[42] As Jim Crow settled over the South, the Hampton-Tuskegee philosophy established dominance over every aspect of black educational pedagogy, dictating the flow of philanthropic support, teacher training, and school curriculums at all levels. White power brokers eagerly sought to replicate Washington's success abroad: in Cuba, where the United States military helped distribute Spanish-language translations of Washington's memoir, *Up from Slavery*; in Togo, where German agents invited Tuskegee students to reproduce Southern techniques of cotton production and labor discipline; in the Anglo-Egyptian Sudan, South Africa, Southern Rhodesia (Zimbabwe), and the Gold Coast, where officials sought Washington's aid and council.[43]

Both at home and internationally, the Hampton-Tuskegee model and its famous black spokesman added powerful rhetorical support to the coalescing discourse of "liberal imperialism" that demanded "fair" treatment for the world's peoples of color while consigning them to positions of economic, cultural, and political tutelage. For a growing collection of white progressives, missionaries, educators, and reformers—horrified by the abuses of white rule but convinced of its necessity—industrial education offered an exciting medium of civilization, one that facilitated the moral and mental growth of inferior peoples, protected them from self-defeating ambitions to rise above their current state of development, and offered them a productive role as junior partners in the production of raw materials, providing an economic incentive for "equitable, understanding government" from white superiors. Like the liberal imperialists, the Hampton-Tuskegee model accepted as its starting point a hierarchy of racial abilities that placed peoples of color below whites. It posited as the foundation of racial development a devotion to industrial labor that would, if patiently pursued, provide lower races with the wealth and moral integrity to achieve respect and political recognition from their rulers. But practically speaking, the removal of peoples of color from the political sphere ensured the safe continuation of their economic subordination. And in turn, their economic subordination remained powerful proof of their immaturity and unpreparedness for civil equality. In the hands of the liberal architects of colonial rule, the Hampton-Tuskegee model was, as historian James Campbell puts it, "a reactionary doctrine, a pedagogical prop for white supremacy."[44]

Washington's apparent betrayal of the black freedom struggle has become an indelible part of his legend. Yet to dismiss him as a capitulator or a collaborator is to obscure the breadth and the complexity of his legacy. Washington's apolitical public persona was deeply political, a wager that it was more prudent to maneuver within, rather than directly against, relations of

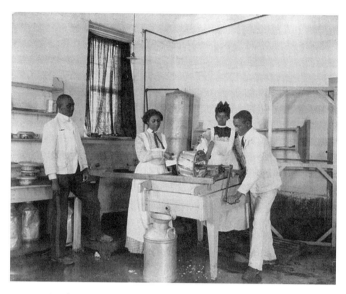

FIGURE 1.5. Students operating small cotton gin at Tuskegee Institute, c. 1905.
(Library of Congress, Prints and Photographs Division, Washington, D.C.)

power that were gathering strength during his lifetime—a calculation, as he put it, that it was better "to encourage those you come in contact with in the direction in which they are right than it is to oppose them in the direction in which they seem to be wrong." Washington used his influence as "king of a captive people" to quietly lobby for black voting rights, to launch legal challenges to Jim Crow, and—with stunning success—to marshal American diplomatic support to sustain Liberia, at least nominally, as a free black republic.[45] If the Tuskegee Institute was used as a prop of liberal imperialism, it subverted the Hampton model by rendering it in blackface, Tuskegee's gleaming campus and African American leadership standing as a physical refutation of racial theories, its famous principal affirming the capacity of a man with black skin to rise from slavery to a position of command, prestige, and influence in half a lifetime.[46]

Indeed, the flip side of white regard for Tuskegee was the tremendous enthusiasm it evoked from peoples of African descent. Like Garveyism after the war, the Tuskegee idea established a broad pan-African site of meaning that resonated with local traditions throughout the diaspora, and that proved amenable to transformation and rearticulation at its various sites of enactment. For many African Americans, Tuskegee embodied the promise of postbellum education established during Reconstruction, a secular manifestation of racial destiny that cast Washington as the Moses of his people, and a program of mutual self-help and Victorian respectability that matched the dominant strain of black institutional and ecclesiastical activism between the dawn of Jim Crow and the First World War.[47] In both Cuba and Puerto Rico, Washington's narrative of personal triumph and his school's promise of upward mobility attracted an "aspiring class" of skilled workers.[48] In West Africa, where support for both African-controlled institutions of higher learning and schemes of industrial education dated back to James Africanus Horton's writing in the 1860s, Tuskegee was an institution of racial uplift to be emulated. So too for the group of mission-educated South Africans who founded the South African Native National Congress, later renamed the African National Congress, many of whom, like John Dube, viewed Washington as their "guiding star," and industrial education as their "salvation."[49] In 1912, when Washington hosted his International Conference on the Negro, it served as a forum for the views of liberal internationalists like E. D. Morel, Maurice Evans, and Robert Park, but also elicited support from leading pan-Africanists like J. E. Casely Hayford, Gold Coast barrister and activist, who praised Tuskegee as a "mighty uplifting force for the race," and expressed hope that the efforts of West Africans might be joined with their "brethren in America" to arrive at a "national aim." From Johannesburg, Ethiopian Church members expressed hope that Washington's scheme might be adopted in South Africa, and suggested that God's plan for the redemption of the continent may be routed through the Tuskegee Institute. In seeking to work through the challenges of a resurgent white supremacy, Washington had managed to simultaneously provide cover for doctrines of racial exclusion and transform Tuskegee, as Frank Guridy has suggested, into "the prime epicenter of Afro-diasporic activity in the world."[50]

*

From the perspective of turn-of-the-century pan-African politics, Washington's "Atlanta Compromise" was one of a series of attempts to refocus global black activism in the aftermath of imperial Thermidor. The final years of the nineteenth century witnessed not only the national and international ascent of Booker T. Washington and the Tuskegee Institute but the emergence of a number of new organizations and alliances that deepened existing connections among educated members of the diaspora. In 1896, the year after Washington's Atlanta address, the Ethiopian Church in South Africa merged with the American-based African Methodist Episcopal (AME) Church, strengthening a transnational relationship that already saw many of South Africa's brightest black students educated in the United States at African American colleges.[51] The National Association of Colored Women (NACW) was founded the same year, evincing a "global commitment to women of color" that was given more formal structure when members of the NACW, including Washington's widow, Margaret Murray Washington, established the International Council of Women of the Darker Races in 1920.[52] In 1897, Henry Sylvester Williams organized the African Association in London, the vehicle for the historic Pan-African Conference in 1900, while Alexander Crummell brought together the elite American Negro Academy in Washington, DC. This "articulate chorus," as David L. Lewis puts it, was joined in a shared dialogue by organizational affiliation, correspondence, missionary bulletins, and journals like the *Lagos Standard*, *Gold Coast Chronicle*, and J. Robert Love's *Jamaica Advocate*.[53]

If Washington's Tuskegee network established the agenda for a conservative pan-Africanism, the Pan-African Conference in 1900 suggested the possibilities of a more assertive Afro-diasporic politics. In many respects, the conference was backwards looking, sustaining the nineteenth-century optimism about the destiny of the race, eager to work with sympathetic white philanthropists and government officials, confident that the advantages of British rule in theory would ultimately prevail over the "capricious greed" of empire builders in practice. Among the all-star roster of transatlantic black activists brought together by Williams was the omnipresent Washington, who participated in a preparatory session for the conference and offered advance praise in the press, predicting that the conference would comprise "the most effective and far reaching gathering that has ever been held in connection with the development of the race."[54] Yet several of the addresses at the conference also gestured forward, adopting the note of warning that would swell by the First World War: that the progress of the race was inevitable, that its onward march would either shower European civilization in glory or engineer its destruction. "The problem of the twentieth century is the problem of the colour line, the question as to how far differences of race . . . are going to be made, hereafter, the basis of denying to over half the world the right of sharing to their utmost ability the opportunities and privileges of modern civilization," announced W.E.B. Du Bois in the conference manifesto, "To the Nations of the World." The future belonged to the "darker races"—black, brown, yellow—because of their gathering political consciousness and numerical strength. The question remained whether "the world of culture" would "hasten human progress" by providing "the broadest opportunity for education and self-development," or whether peoples of color were to remain "exploited and ravished and degraded"—a path that threatened Christian civilization itself.[55]

Cast in the light of an ascendant, rather than receding, European imperialism in Africa, the millennial underpinnings of Blyden's cultural nationalism projected their own foreboding shadows at the dawn of the twentieth century. The development of an "African personality," Blyden's disciples had come to believe, required the articulation of an independent and indigenous African Christianity, unencumbered, as Reverend Mojola Agbebi declared, of "the white man's style, the white man's name, the white man's dress," and other "props and crutches affecting the religious manhood of the Christian African."⁵⁶ It required the preservation of native institutions, land rights, and social customs amidst the introduction of European innovations. This difficult task required, as always, the enlightened leadership of Western-educated Africans, those able to navigate through, and appreciate the complexity of, both European and African worlds. In his influential collection of essays, *Ethiopia Unbound*, published in 1911, Casely Hayford argued that what Africa required was not "redemption," but rather "emancipation from the thralldom of foreign ideas inimical to racial development." West Africans must learn from Japan, now an international power, which had acquired authority and respect not by replacing its own national character with a European one but by imbibing the best of Western culture within a framework of its own national genius and custom. If Hayford continued to declare himself an "ardent imperialist," it was increasingly hard to avoid the conclusion that his proscriptions for West Africa's development were incompatible with the prerogatives of European administration. "West Africa shall not for ever remain a hewer of wood and drawer of water," warned Hayford in 1913. "West Africa cannot continue for ever watering the feet of the Empire without her own feet being watered."⁵⁷

No prewar organ did more to sow the seeds of anticolonial consciousness in the African diaspora than Dusé Mohamed Ali's London-based journal, the *African Times and Orient Review* (ATOR). The journal emerged out of the Universal Races Congress of 1911, an interracial effort to promote "a heartier cooperation" among "the peoples of the West and those of the East," and to combat the ascendancy of biological racism with scientific research. According to Ali, a shadowy figure who claimed Sudanese-Egyptian provenance, the Congress had "clearly demonstrated that there was ample need for a Pan-Oriental, Pan-African journal at the seat of the British Empire which would lay the aims, desires, and intentions of the Black, Brown, and Yellow races—within and without the Empire—at the throne of Caesar." Providing a mouthpiece for peoples of color, argued Ali in the ATOR's inaugural edition, would both direct agitation through a reasonable channel and force British policymakers to confront the underlying causes of colonial resentments. "We, as natives and loyal subjects of the British Empire," he wrote, "hold too high an opinion of Anglo-Saxon chivalry to believe other than that African and Oriental wrongs have but to be made manifest in order that they may be righted."⁵⁸

From the beginning, however, it was clear that the ATOR would do more than simply parrot the Congress's humanitarian commitment to a more "cordial" and scientific imperialism. Instead, Ali's journal more precisely mirrored the aims of *Ethiopia Unbound*'s fictional "Gold Coast Nation and

FIGURE 1.6. Dusé Mohamed Ali as a young man. (Courtesy of Robert A. Hill)

Ethiopian Review," which Hayford imagined embracing the needs of the "Ethiopian" race, circulating through the African diaspora, "moulding the spiritual atmosphere of the world," providing a conduit of communication and debate for "leading thinkers of the race."[59] What was perhaps most impressive about the ATOR was its remarkable network of agents and correspondents, linking readers across Asia, the Middle East, Africa, and the Americas, from Canada to Argentina. Reflecting this reach, the journal sustained a sincere commitment to the presentation of a myriad of viewpoints and vantage points from which to assess the progress and predicaments of peoples of color. Travel diaries appeared alongside political tracts by Hayford and Sundara Raja, an Indian nationalist; articles on West African marriage customs alongside advertisements for the Uganda Railway and the British shipping line, Elder Dempster and Company; tributes to notable colonial agents alongside reports on the advance of Pan-Islamism and racial violence in the American South. At the same time, the ATOR constructed out of this cacophony an unmistakable synthesis reflecting the editorial and political prerogatives of its editor: a persistent invocation of racial destiny, a proclivity for commercial and economic schemes to hasten the arrival of peoples of color, and a tone of conciliation toward the honest brokers of empire joined by an increasingly strident denunciation of the practices and long-term future of white rule. "Your place in the Sun has been and will come again," Ali assured his readers. "As darkness overtook you for a space, it must also overtake Europe. The future of Africa, the future of India, will not be decided in the Chanceries of Europe, but upon the hills of India and the plains of Africa. See that your loins are well girded and that you have your staff firmly in your hand when you once more take your place in the Sun."[60]

Like Hayford, Ali articulated a framework of pan-African and pan-Asian ascendance that offered a more militant set of conclusions than those proffered by Washington's Tuskegee thesis. For Washington, race work must take honest stock of the Negro's loss of political control in the United States and abroad. For Ali, the monumental victory of Japan over Russia in 1905, the nationalist awakenings of China and India, the spread of Pan-Islamism across the colonial world, and the quickening collaborations of peoples of African descent suggested for peoples of color a gathering, rather than receding, strength on the global stage. The ATOR would serve in these struggles as "a rallying point for the scattered forces of the non-European peoples," a "bond of brotherhood" that would join common struggles against "the European aggressor" and thus give colonial governments pause. "Neither South Africa, North Africa, West Africa, nor East Africa can ever be a white man's country," wrote Ali, "and the sooner that illusion is cast overboard the better it will be for all parties concerned." During the white man's "temporary sojourn" in Africa and Asia, he might as well turn his honest attention to the needs and aspirations of peoples of color, to foster cooperation, understanding, and common good. The alternative, Ali warned, was violence, upheaval, world revolution.[61]

The Education of Marcus Mosiah Garvey

When Marcus Garvey established his first newspaper in Kingston in 1910, he named it *Garvey's Watchman*, a tribute to George William Gordon and his legendary broadsheet, the *Jamaican Watchman and People's Free Press*. As a young man, Garvey's father, Malchus, had attended one of the Underhill Meetings at Saint Ann's Bay, chaired by Gordon. Later, Garvey would pay tribute to the martyrs of Morant Bay, those who "sounded the call of unmolested liberty" and whose success would have made Jamaica "as free to-day as Haiti."[62]

Marcus Garvey's early life was shaped by a series of dynamic apprenticeships that drew him—along with his persistent enthusiasm and ambition—into the shifting currents of turn-of-the-century pan-African politics. In the shop of his godfather, Alfred "Cap" Burrowes, Garvey learned the printing trade while listening to Burrowes and his friends reminisce about the slave rebellions of yore, about Paul Bogle and George William Gordon. In 1908, after being promoted to manager of a large printing firm in Kingston, he lost his job after helping to lead a printers' strike for higher wages and better working conditions. In 1910, Garvey was elected secretary of the National Club, Jamaica's first nationalist organization, whose founder, S.A.G. Cox, called for the political alliance of Jamaica's colored and black people "with all Negroes in all parts of the world."[63]

According to Garvey, the primary source of his "early education in race consciousness" was his elocution tutor, J. Robert Love, publisher of Jamaica's essential vehicle of pan-African discourse, the *Advocate*, which ran from 1894 to 1905. Love's commitment to elevating "the destiny of the Negro Race" was manifest in his journal's reporting on the activities and writings of Washington, Du Bois, Crummell, and John Edward Bruce in the United States; and Williams, Blyden, and Hayford on the other side of the Atlantic. The *Advocate* publicized the Pan-African Conference of 1900, and published its "Address to the Nations of the World." When Williams arrived in Jamaica in 1901 to help organize a branch of his Pan-African Association, which was launched at the close of the conference to continue its work, Love participated in the meetings and offered his support. In that same year Love expressed his allegiance to a policy of "Africa for the Africans," which he acknowledged as "the new shape of an old cry," one that would "waken the so-called civilized world to a consciousness of the fact that others who are not accounted as civilized, think with regard to natural rights, just as civilized people think." Love, according to his eulogist, lacked the "organizing powers" needed to transform his vision into "constructive" action.[64] It would remain for his onetime pupil, Garvey, to transform "Africa for the Africans" from a slogan into a call for mass organization after the First World War.

In the fall of 1910, Garvey sailed to Costa Rica, joining thousands of his fellow West Indians in their attempt to navigate the economic decline and restructuring of the British colonies and the emergence of new opportunities in Central America, Cuba, the Dominican Republic, and the United States.[65] Garvey spent a tumultuous year abroad, most notably in Costa Rica and Panama, where he established two newspapers—the *Nation* in Limón and *La Prensa* in Colón—and clashed with both local authorities and West Indian leadership in the labor enclaves. After a few months home in Jamaica, Garvey sailed to London in the spring of 1912, where he read Blyden's *Christianity, Islam, and the Negro Race*, Washington's *Up from Slavery*, and other classic works of the black literary canon at the British Library. He also took a menial job at the offices of the *African Times and Orient Review*. In October 1913, Garvey published an essay in the journal, in which he prophesied that "the people of [the West Indies] will be the instruments of uniting a scattered race who, before the close of many centuries, will found an Empire on which the sun shall shine as ceaselessly as it shines on the Empire of the North today."[66]

Garvey returned to Jamaica in 1914 prepared to make a name for himself. Writing nearly a decade later, Garvey cast his return in the most heroic and fateful of terms. "I was determined that the black man would not continue to be kicked about by all the other races and nations of the world, as I saw it in the West Indies, South and Central America and Europe, and as I read of it in America," Garvey recalled.

> I saw before me then, even as I do now, a new world of black men, not peons, serfs, dogs and slaves, but a nation of sturdy men making their impress upon civilization and causing a new light to dawn upon the human race. I could not remain in London any more. My brain was afire. There was a world of thought to conquer. I had to start ere it become too late and the work be not done. Immediately I boarded a ship . . . for Jamaica. . . . The Universal Negro Improvement [and Conservation] Association and African Communities (Imperial) League was founded and organized five days after my arrival, with the program of uniting all the negro peoples of the world into one great body to establish a country and Government absolutely their own.[67]

In a pamphlet published soon after his arrival in Kingston, Garvey confidently invited his fellow "Afro-West Indians" to participate in a "world-wide movement of doing something to promote the intellectual, social, commercial, industrial, and national interest" of the "downtrodden Negro race." The intellectual architecture of Garvey's scheme rested comfortably within the spectrum of pan-African discourse, appealing to the "[s]ons and daughters of Africa" to "take on the toga of race pride," to celebrate the glorious Negro civilization of antiquity, to inaugurate an era of racial renewal by joining hands in a struggle to replace the "lethargic and serfish" qualities of the "ignorant and backward" black masses with discipline, education, industriousness, and piety. For good measure, Garvey included an extensive passage from Blyden.[68]

Fundamental to Garvey's vision was his critique of the island's colored and black aspiring class, the members of whom Garvey accused of adopting the false and destructive airs of an "aristocracy." No such thing could exist, he argued, until the "race as a whole brings itself into respect" among the "cultured and progressive races." The UNIA would accomplish this work of racial development on a global scale by raising the fallen and civilizing the backward, establishing an infrastructure of Negro leadership, conducting "world-wide commercial and industrial intercourse," and promoting Christian worship and educational opportunities. Locally, the organization would promote a variety of uplift measures, most ambitiously the establishment of an industrial farm and institute "on the same plan as . . . Tuskegee." Garvey declared the organization "non-political," and aggressively courted the favor of white elites in both Jamaica and England, demonstrating a Washington-like faith in the advantages of white philanthropy and friendship. Privately, he hinted to Washington's successor at Tuskegee, Robert R. Moton, of "many large schemes . . . for the advancement of my people" that must remain hidden for the moment from the public and his many enemies.[69]

The organization Garvey founded in Kingston in 1914 bore the scars, and projected the ambitions, of eight decades of racial struggle and reorganization inaugurated by the dawn of freedom in the British Empire. As the optimism of the postemancipation era gave way to new regimes of political, economic, social, and intellectual control, members of the educated diaspora in Europe, Africa, and the Americas experimented with new vehicles for projecting a roughly shared vision of racial redemption and freedom. In so doing they brought a pan-African tradition with roots in the eighteenth century into the twentieth, a tradition defined not by uniformity of opinion but by a shared belief that Providence had not condemned them and their race to perpetual servility, that a new age was on the horizon, that Ethiopia would soon stretch forth her hands.

And then war came, and the world fell apart.

Chapter Two

THE CENTER CANNOT HOLD

Turning and turning in the widening gyre
The falcon cannot hear the falconer;
Things fall apart; the centre cannot hold;
Mere anarchy is loosed upon the world . . .

—*William Butler Yeats, "The Second Coming" (1919)*

JOSEPH BOOTH arrived in the Shire Highlands in 1892, and established his Zambesi Industrial Mission at Michiru, north of Blantyre. Invasions by Yao-speaking people, the expanding slave trade, and a devastating famine in 1862 had left the once-populous region nearly uninhabited. After a protectorate was declared over the area that became Nyasaland (today Malawi) by the British Foreign Office in 1891, colonists faced the problem not of engineering land alienation—large tracts had been purchased in 1880s by speculators hoping to draw British interest in the highlands—but of establishing a reliable labor force. The year Booth arrived, the first tax was imposed on the peoples living south of Lake Nyasa (now Lake Malawi), later revised as a hut tax in 1894. When taxation proved an insufficient mechanism to compel Nyasalanders to the farms, migrant workers were recruited from neighboring Portuguese East Africa (Mozambique), drawn by promises of cultivable land on the large European estates. In return, workers agreed to contribute one month's labor for the estate owner, a system known as *thangata*. An additional month of labor could be contributed in lieu of paying the yearly hut tax.[1]

As was customary, missionary contact predated political rule. The famed Livingstonia mission of the Free Church of Scotland was established at Cape Maclear in 1875, to the north, and later moved to its permanent location further north at Bandawe. Legend has it that the mission's namesake, David Livingstone, drew his pistol against African belligerents for the first time while traveling through Magomero, in the highlands.[2] Within this grand tradition of African proselytization, it was clear that Booth was peculiar. He was deeply troubled by the widespread abuses of the *thangata* system, by African poverty, by European ownership of vast and often unused tracts of arable land. Booth offered his converts unusually high wages to work on mission-owned property. To demonstrate his fundamental equality with his flock, he sat with Africans for meals. He insisted that the end of missionary work was African independence, that Europeans were not honest brokers in this pursuit, and that Africans must "rise up" and save their country. One day Booth met M. M. Chisuse, an African convert of the Church of Scotland mission, gazing out at the Indian Ocean from a beach at Chinde in Portuguese East Africa. "I love the sea, because the sea do[es] not tell any lies," Chisuse remembered Booth reflecting. "[Y]ears ago we Europeans use to sail in this Ocean on to the coast and got you Africans as slaves and sold you in America; but now Europeans have got another plan of just coming to take away the land from you and make you slaves together with the land."[3]

Upon his arrival in the highlands, Booth launched an industrial mission scheme designed to establish self-sufficient, industrious, and multiplying communities of African Christians through the production of coffee and other cash crops. The industrial mission, he argued, provided an ideal mechanism for spreading the Gospel, offering a "ladder" and a helping hand "while the man himself climbs to the higher life by his own labor." The foundation of Africa's future strength depended simultaneously on the spread of Christianity across the continent, and in the continent's "undeveloped power" to furnish the world with cotton, coffee, and other "tropical and subtropical articles of commerce." It did not take Booth long to realize that his European compatriots were unlikely partners in Africa's regeneration. The partition of Africa, he wrote in 1897, "is a proposal to deprive 200 million . . . people of their birthright, seize upon their property and permanently drain the wealth of Africa and the African's labor into European channels." Missionaries, he argued, served merely as "the forerunner of another set of men, sent to appropriate, to kill, to tax and subjugate," bringing words of peace in order to facilitate acts of war. Instead, Booth proposed the establishment of an African Christian Union that would align Africans—in need of agricultural, commercial, and spiritual education—with "Afro-Americans" from the West Indies and the United States in need of a country to call their own. The Union would encourage unity among members of the "African race," and pursue proposals to develop the continent's industrial infrastructure. It would stand in protest against anyone who would "ruthlessly assert their purpose, power, or right to take from the African race the African's land." To express this protest Booth adopted a motto that he acknowledged was hardly new: "Africa for the African."[4]

Booth's first convert was a young man named John Chilembwe, who was taken on as a domestic servant in the Booth household and became, especially after the death of the Booths' son, John Edward, more of a surrogate

FIGURE 2.1. John Chilembwe (L). (Library of Congress, Prints and Photographs Division, Washington, D.C.)

son to the family.[5] In 1897, when Booth traveled to the United States to lecture on "Africa for the Africans" and raise money for his African Christian Union scheme, he brought Chilembwe with him. At first, Chilembwe participated with Booth on his speaking tour. But over time Chilembwe gravitated, with Booth's encouragement, toward the orbit of African American independent Christianity and the National Baptist Convention (NBC). With the help of Lewis Garnett Jordan, secretary of the NBC's Foreign Mission Board, Chilembwe secured a place at the Virginia Theological Seminary and College, in Lynchburg. While there, he developed plans for an American Development Society that adopted the basic premises of the African Christian Union. A large fortune in cash crop production was to be earned in the fertile soils of East Central Africa, Chilembwe wrote in his prospectus. Christian natives were awaiting the arrival of Afro-Americans prepared to direct them "in the development of the rich resources of their country," and to bring them the benefits of "Christian civilization."[6]

FIGURE 2.2. Providence Industrial Mission. (Library of Congress, Prints and Photographs Division, Washington, D.C.)

By the time Chilembwe returned to the Shire Highlands in 1900 he had retreated from Booth's brand of uncompromising dissent. Booth had returned a year earlier, and had been forced to flee to Portuguese East Africa after printing a petition to Queen Victoria demanding, among other things, the expenditure of hut tax revenues on native education and the transfer of the protectorate to native government by 1920. Chilembwe's Providence Industrial Mission (PIM), by contrast, seemed organized to demonstrate the viability and respectability of African independent Christianity. The mission boasted "tidy gardens," a "handsome" brick church, and a growing community of industrious, well-dressed members—Chilembwe himself wore a three-piece suit, his wife Ida silk stockings and Empire gowns. PIM's curriculum focused on agricultural instruction for men and domestic education for women, whom Chilembwe lauded as the "mothers of the race."[7] If PIM's pedagogy would not have been out of place at Tuskegee, Chilembwe's African Industrial Society (AIS), composed of members of the highlands' mission-educated, property-owning, petty-capitalist elite, pursued an agenda not unlike Booker T. Washington's National Negro Business League. Rather than directly criticize the practices of colonial rule,

Chilembwe courted approval. In 1910, he invited local Europeans to PIM to observe the mission's progress, to view its neat facilities and smartly attired community—to observe, in short, living proof of African self-government along the lines of meticulous European behavioral patterns.[8]

At some point between 1910 and 1914, Chilembwe came to believe that he had made a mistake. Perhaps it was the reports carried by PIM's migrant worker followers of widespread labor abuses on the neighboring A. L. Bruce Estates: *thangata* requirements extended to four months, and to women and children; "months" extended to five or six weeks; beatings, hut burnings, and evictions for noncompliance. Perhaps it was the raising of the hut tax to eight shillings in 1912, or the rush to expand cotton production on the Bruce estate amidst the food shortages of 1911–13, or the ban on Christian mission schools on the estates, or the burning of the informal grass-hut churches erected by Chilembwe's followers in defiance of the ban. Or it may have been the District Administration (Native) Ordinance of 1912 which, rather than praising the work of Chilembwe's ambitious flock, criticized "the rising generation of natives who, finding themselves without the restraining influences to which their parents were accustomed, have of recent years evinced an inclination to emancipate themselves from the disciplinary responsibilities of village life and obedience to authority." As Landeg White has observed, white settler society seemed less worried by the defiant radicalism of Booth "than by Chilembwe's notions of African advancement—by his activities as a planter and employer, by his relations with African businessmen and his industrial training schemes, in short by his assault on the paternalism of planter, administrator and missionary which left no scope for African initiative." Translated to British Central Africa, Washingtonianism embodied a subversive challenge to the colonial project.[9]

The outbreak of the world war was the last straw for Chilembwe. News of the intention to mobilize forces in Nyasaland was confirmed on August 5, 1914, and had spread throughout the highlands by August 8. In November Chilembwe sent an angry letter to the editors of the *Nyasaland Times*—his first recorded expression of dissent since his involvement in Booth's African Christian Union in 1897. The letter revealed that Chilembwe's embrace of nonconfrontational respectability had been less a rejection of Booth than a carefully calibrated strategy.[10] "We understand that we have been invited to shed our innocent blood in this world's war," Chilembwe began angrily. Even though Africans had little stake in the outcome, they had already "unreservedly stepped to the firing line" as they had in previous conflicts, understanding not what they would face. "Shall we be recognized as anybody in the best interest of civilisation and Christianity after the great struggle is ended?" wondered Chilembwe sardonically. Because "in the time of peace the Government [has] failed to help the underdog. In times of peace everything for Europeans only. And instead of honour we suffer humiliation with names contemptible."[11]

Shortly after the beginning of the war, reports began to surface that Chilembwe was organizing secretly, collecting weapons in preparation for a war against the Europeans.[12] By November he was baptizing hundreds of workers on the Bruce Estates.[13] If Chilembwe did not himself ascribe to the popular view—spread widely through Central Africa by the Watch Tower Bible and Tract Society—that the millennium would arrive in October 1914, he certainly seems to have embraced an eschatological interpretation of his own plans. Rumors swirled that PIM was a new Noah's ark, that John Chilembwe's Christians alone would be saved in the coming deluge.[14] In January Chilembwe held a meeting and told his followers the story of John Brown, whose frustrated assault on the slave power in America had helped unleash the country's bloody emancipation. Let us follow John Brown and "strike a blow and die," he told his flock. "Let us . . . strike a blow and die."[15]

*

The Great War tore the world asunder; things fell apart. Across Asia, Africa, Europe, and the Americas, men and women mobilized to defend the spoils of decades of empire building—"to decide," sneered Vladimir Lenin, "whether the British or German group of financial marauders is to receive the most booty."[16] Millions died. The German, Austro-Hungarian, Ottoman, and Russian empires were shattered. Protests erupted in Ireland, Egypt, India, China, and Korea. Europe was reduced to rubble.[17] Africa's participation in the war, observed John Harris of the Anti-Slavery and Aborigines Protection Society, "may easily mean the greatest revolution in negro and white relationships since the commencement of the Christian era."[18] But no one knew exactly what that meant. Peoples of color from every corner of the world shed their "innocent blood": More than 200,000 laborers and fighters from Nyasaland were joined in the conflict by millions of Africans serving Britain, France, Belgium, Portugal, and Germany, nearly a million Indians, hundreds of thousands of Chinese, 370,000 African Americans and 16,000 West Indians.[19] By enabling new interactions and migrations, by unraveling old structures of custom and control, by unleashing waves of hunger and disease, and by facilitating new dialogues—in particular, surrounding the explosive principle of "self-determination"—the war both offered dramatic opportunities to challenge global white supremacy and provided mechanisms to protect and strengthen its flank. From every corner of the globe, observers wondered if the "problem of the color line" had forever escaped its bounds, if new and more terrible wars for racial domination inevitably lay ahead.

The war did not by itself generate the black militancy that erupted during the conflict and that continued in its wake. As the story of Joseph Booth and John Chilembwe suggests, the war acted as a catalyst in which old and richly drawn contests of authority and power were shifted on their axis, disrupted, transformed. Concerns that African soldiers had slain whites in battle, that the veneer of European invincibility had been torn away, that the moral authority and leadership of Western civilization had been undermined, were suggestive less for their insight than for what they revealed about the vulnerability of the moment. The colored nations and races, warned W.E.B. Du Bois in 1915, "composing as they do a vast majority of humanity, are going to endure . . . [their] treatment just as long as they must and not a moment longer." From the perspective of Du Bois and like-minded compatriots in the colored world, many linked in conversation by the global reach of the *African Times and Orient Review*, the time of opportunity had arrived. But the hopes of these reformist-minded internationalists for a rational settlement of their grievances were soon outpaced by the horrors invited upon peoples of color during the war. From the ascendant black capital of Harlem, a militant "New Negro" movement burst forward, its proponents hoping to more dramatically leverage the "new theater" created by the war to reshape global relations of race and class inequality, to celebrate militant and respectable black masculinity, and to replace an old cadre of elitist and ineffectual black leadership with a new brand of uncompromising mass politics. Joining the stream of West Indians heading for New York, Marcus Garvey was a fortunate witness to the birth of the New Negro movement. By the end of the war, thoughts of returning to Jamaica forgotten, he had begun to pull the movement's center of gravity toward himself and his organization.[20]

Falling Neither as Whites Nor as Blacks

Britain declared war on Germany on August 4, 1914. The first shots discharged on its behalf were fired by West Africans, at West Africans, in the brief and successful invasion of German Togo. The symbolism was fitting. The Great War was a war of empires, a truly global affair, and it engulfed peoples of African descent. Nearly two hundred thousand troops, the *tirailleurs Sénégalais*, were recruited from West Africa to fight for the French on the Western front, in Turkey, and in Togo and Cameroon. Recruits drawn from across the British Caribbean were sent to Egypt, Palestine, Mesopotamia, East and West Africa. More than 20,000 blacks were enlisted in the South African Native Labour Contingent (SANLC) and shipped to France, joined—after United States entered the war in April 1917—by the roughly 200,000 African American members of the American Expeditionary Forces (AEF). Except for the nearly one thousand Nigerians who worked with the Inland Water Transport Service in Mesopotamia, British African troops and

FIGURE 2.3. Black Soldiers in South Africa (above) and Jamaica. (Originally printed in *The Crisis*, January 1918)

laborers remained stationed in Africa for the duration of the war. But the hostilities nevertheless brought the world to them. The bloody stalemate of the East African Campaign (1914–18), the most important front in the African theater, drew manpower from a dizzying number of countries and colonies: England, South Africa, Belgium, Germany, Portugal, the United States, India, the West Indies, the Seychelles, Somalia, Kenya, Uganda, German East Africa (Tanzania), Nyasaland, Northern Rhodesia (Zambia), Southern Rhodesia (Zimbabwe), Portuguese East Africa, the Belgian Congo, Nigeria, the Gambia, Sierra Leone, and the Gold Coast.[21] For many colonial subjects, the war provided an opportunity for material and personal reward. Kande Kamara, from an aristocratic Susu family in Guinea, enlisted with the *tirailleurs Sénégalais* to honor his warrior heritage, one that had been disrupted by the advent of French rule. Chiefs and headmen willing to impress colonial officials with their rigorous recruitment practices hoped to be rewarded with the backing of the state after the war. Peasants in search of wages to fulfill the expectations of colonial taxation enlisted to secure the promise of a steady income and the opportunity for upward mobility.[22] Senegal's Blaise Diagne, the first African elected representative in France's Chamber of Deputies, turned wartime leverage into an art form. In laws of 1915 and 1916, he used the occasion of the war to win French citizenship status for residents of Senegal's four communes, the *originaires,* and their descendants.[23] During the final year of the war, with the French desperate for fresh troops, Diagne was appointed to the prestigious post of Commissioner of General Recruitment, and was empowered to offer new *tirailleurs* an exemption from the hated *indigénat.*[24] Eschewing the clumsy and brutal methods that had attended earlier conscription efforts in West Africa, Diagne sold recruits on the benefits of service. "Those who fall under [German] fire," he noted, "fall neither as whites nor as blacks; they fall as Frenchmen and for the same flag." The drive was a triumph, winning more than 60,000 new recruits.[25]

Across the British Empire, black and brown subjects argued that colonial peoples' loyal and brave participation in the Allied cause constituted a "war loan" that would produce dividends after the fighting was over. "It is the duty of everyone within the British Empire to loyally support the Empire to the last drop of blood and the last penny remaining within their coffers," proclaimed Dusé Mohamed Ali from the pages of the *African Times and Orient Review.* "If you do this loyally and willingly, when the day of settlement arrives you cannot be left out of the reckoning." Following Ali's admonition to Indians and Africans to exercise patience in the redress of their grievances while the war continued, the South African Native National Congress declared its loyalty to the King and vowed to temporarily suspend its agitation against the insidious Land Act of 1913. From West Africa, Casely Hayford's *Gold Coast Leader* likewise urged solidarity with the war effort,

FIGURE 2.4. French propaganda poster from World War I. (Library of Congress, Prints and Photographs Division, Washington, D.C.)

arguing that the shared defense of the Empire by white and colored troops would have portentous consequences. "We are, above all British citizens of the Great British Empire," remarked Mahatma Gandhi, who during the war participated in the effort to recruit Indian soldiers for the Allied cause. "Fighting as the British are at present in the righteous cause for the good and glory of human dignity and civilization ... our duty is clear: to do our best to support the British, to fight with our life and property."[26]

After the United States entered the war, the vast majority of African American leaders and intellectuals adopted a similar approach.[27] The new principal of the Tuskegee Institute, Robert Russa Moton, penned an open letter to President Woodrow Wilson, assuring him that the he could "count absolutely on the loyalty of the mass of the Negroes to our country and its people, North and South." Colonel Charles Young, the nation's highest-ranking black officer, urged that "negroes must have a part ... in the destiny of this country—Our Country." "Let us do nothing to divide our people in this hour of our country's trials," he counseled. "When the storm is past we can take up the idealism of the cause." Veteran African American jour-nalist John Edward Bruce argued that blacks must demonstrate the same "unswerving loyalty and fidelity to the flag" as they had in previous wars, noting that "although the Negro has not been treated fairly nor justly by this Government as a soldier and sailor, either as regards pay for his services and position in the ranks, he has been just as courageous as a fighter on half the pay and in a subordinate position as white men on full pay." At a conference of black leaders in Washington, DC, organized by the National Association for the Advancement of Colored People (NAACP) and spear-headed by W.E.B. Du Bois, the participants registered their "deep sympathy with the reasonable and deep-seated feeling of revolt among Negroes at the persistent insult and discrimination to which they are subject," but never-theless deemed the Allies' side "the greatest hope for ultimate democracy," and "earnestly" urged their "colored fellow citizens to join heartily in this fight for eventual world liberty."[28]

As the war progressed, illustrations of the jarring discordance between persistent discrimination against African Americans at home and the brave service of black soldiers abroad emerged as a pervasive rhetorical strategy deployed by race leaders, citizens, and soldiers petitioning federal authori-ties for a redress of their grievances. The participants of the Washington conference of 1917 made this connection explicit from the beginning, link-ing their "unfaltering loyalty" to an insistence "that neither the world nor America can be happy and democratic so long as twelve million Americans are lynched, disfranchised, and insulted." Although the loyalty of the Negro could not be questioned, declared a collection of petitioners from Norfolk, Virginia, it was difficult to "assume sponsorship for democracy" abroad "while we foster the most poisonous, unholy, unreasonable and degrading

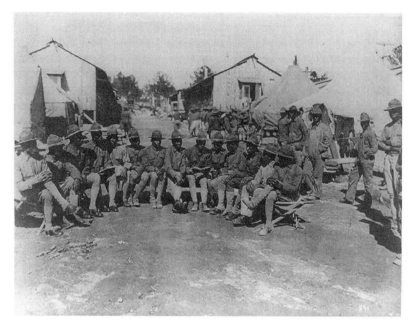

FIGURE 2.5. African American Soldiers at Camp Gordon, Georgia, 1917–18.
(Library of Congress, Prints and Photographs Division, Washington, D.C.)

form of caste known in modern times." For a group of petitioners from
Atlanta, it was hard to square black service on the battlefield with the persistent threat of lawless violence invited upon blacks throughout the nation.
"We . . . regard lynching as worse than Prussianism, which we are at war to
destroy," they declared. "The nations of the world have a right to demand
of us the workings of the institutions at home before they are promulgated
abroad," wrote Kelly Miller, the influential dean of the College of Arts and
Sciences at Howard University, in an open letter to Woodrow Wilson. "The
German press will doubtless gloat with ghoulish glee over American atrocities against the Negro. The outrages complained of against the Belgians
become merciful performances by gruesome comparison. Our frantic wail
against the barbarity of the Turk against Armenian, German upon Belgian,
Russian upon Jew, are made of no effect."[29]

In developing this argument, African Americans were aided, along with
their colored brethren abroad, by the lofty objectives attached to the war
by Woodrow Wilson. In his war address to Congress on April 2, 1917 Wilson famously declared that "[t]he world must be made safe for democracy."
Over the next several months, aided by the massive wartime propaganda
campaign of the Committee on Public Information (CPI), Wilson's defense of weaker nations against the strong, his advocacy of international

justice, and, most explosively, his support for the rights of people to "self-determination," were widely broadcast and became widely associated with the wartime aims of the Allies. Wilson's idealism, and his calculations for postwar peace, were elucidated with Western, "civilized" peoples in mind. Along with his contemporary white liberal internationalists, Wilson viewed "self-determination" as a right that applied to nonwhite peoples, but one that must be bestowed upon them only after a period of tutelage and preparation for the rigors of independent governance. Nevertheless, as historian Erez Manela has so brilliantly demonstrated, Wilsonian idealism was gleefully coopted by colonial peoples around the world. The phrase "self-determination" was "simply loaded with dynamite," remarked Secretary of State Robert Lansing in December 1918. "It will raise hopes which can never be realized.... What a calamity that the phrase was ever uttered! What misery it will cause."[30]

For a savvy critic familiar with Wilson's foreign and domestic policy before the war, well aware of the near-universal assumption among whites that peoples of African descent were unfit for self-government, the expectation that Wilsonianism was intended to apply to African peoples on the continent and in the diaspora required an act of imagination.[31] But the widespread embrace of Wilson's wartime rhetoric was hardly a group exercise in delusion. Just as Haitian free blacks and slaves had used the occasion of the French Revolution to expand the parameters of its meaning, and just as American slaves had ensured that Abraham Lincoln's war to preserve the Union became a war of emancipation, so advocates of color hoped to transform the cataclysm of world war into a mandate for colonial and racial liberation.[32] Reformers studied the pronouncements of Allied leaders like legal scholars, building a case that wartime declarations in defense of the rights of nationalities and individuals, weak as well as strong, must definitively apply to the nonwhite peoples of Africa, Asia, and the Americas. To deny Africa and the African races "the benefits which this war will offer the weaker States and nations of Europe" would reveal the Allied powers "as hideous and immoral monsters devoid of all sense of honour, and the very allies of Germany, whose estimation of declared and written agreements is nothing but a 'scrap of paper,'" argued the *Lagos Standard*. After British Prime Minister David Lloyd George declared that the inhabitants of Germany's African colonies "should be placed under the control of an administration acceptable to themselves," and affirmed that "[t]he general principle of national self-determination is . . . as applicable in their cases as in those of occupied European territories," Dusé Mohamed Ali cheered: "there is not the slightest attempt at equivocation. The Allies are REALLY fighting for a lasting peace and the RIGHTS OF ALL small nationalities." Likewise Du Bois argued that "if English is English and Justice is Justice," Woodrow Wilson's "flaming arrows" elucidating postwar rights must be "aimed at the Vardamans in Mississippi as well as the Huns in Europe," Cameroon as well as Serbia.[33]

For these commentators, the principle of "self-determination" was predicated not merely on the good faith of American and European policymakers, but on the acknowledgment of an inexorable shift in global politics. The rise of Japan as a world power, the drama of the Easter Rising in Ireland in 1916, the "awakening" of "Ethiopianism" in Africa and nationalist sentiment in Egypt and India, and the participation of black, brown, and yellow subjects in the defense of democratic freedom, had quickened the rise of people of color that Du Bois had prophesied at the beginning of the century.[34] "The war is an End and, also, a Beginning," Du Bois now wrote.

> Never again will darker people of the world occupy just the place they have before. Out of this war will rise, soon or late, an independent China; a self-governing India, and Egypt with representative institutions; an Africa for the Africans, and not merely for business exploitation. Out of this war will rise, too, an American Negro, with the right to vote and live without insult. These things may not and will not come at once; but they are written in the stars.

From this perspective, Wilsonian self-determination was less the trumpet of a new age than a final, desperate opportunity for European peoples to atone for centuries of plunder, exploitation, and brutality. If the catastrophe of the present war had emerged from the "jealousies and greed" of imperial rule, warned Du Bois, "how much wider and wider will be the conflict when black and brown and yellow people stand up together shoulder to shoulder and demand recognition as men!" The Allies' struggle to "save the world for democracy" was more than empty sloganeering. It was a chance "to postpone if not to make unnecessary a world war of races."[35]

RACE FIRST

The approach adopted by Du Bois and his allies at home and abroad was premised on the power of the war to compel white recognition of African American and colonial grievances. Support for the war, they insisted, was a necessary precondition: "*first* your Country," exhorted Du Bois, "*then* your Rights."[36] It was a strategy born partly of necessity. The passage of the Espionage Act of 1917 and the Sedition Act of 1918 afforded the federal government sweeping powers to criminalize dissent. The war gave birth to the modern surveillance state, dramatically expanding the censorship powers of the Post Office, the intelligence operations of the new Bureau of Investigations (BOI, later the Federal Bureau of Investigations), and the domestic reach of the War Department, which in the fall of 1917 recruited retired

FIGURE 2.6. W.E.B. Du Bois in the office of *The Crisis*. (Photographs and Prints Division, Schomburg Center for Research in Black Culture, The New York Public Library, Astor, Lenox and Tilden Foundations)

black army major Walter Loving to head its effort to monitor "Negro Subversion." By mid-1918, both the BOI and Loving's Military Intelligence Branch (MIB) were exerting pressure on the NAACP to moderate the tone of the *Crisis*. Across the nation, reactionary patriotism ran high, manifest in the mobilization of the volunteer American Protective League (APL) and the widespread anti-German, anti-foreign, anti-union, and anti-radical excesses of "100% Americanism." In this climate, observed NAACP organizer James Weldon Johnson, "the bald truth is that the Negro cannot afford to be rated as a disloyal element of this nation. Imagine the result if he should for an instant arouse against himself the sentiment which is now directed against the pro-German element."[37] The choice, argued Du Bois on the eve of the war, was not between "volunteering and not volunteering," but "between conscription and rebellion." He scolded shortsighted critics who advised the Negro "to add treason and rebellion to the other grounds on which the South urges discrimination against them."[38]

As the war carried on, admonitions of patience and pragmatism became increasingly jarring amidst the widespread instances of abuse, discrimination, and suffering inflicted upon peoples of African descent in the United

States and abroad. The refusal by Du Bois and other black leaders to push further in their wartime demands created space for the emergence of a radical young vanguard in Harlem, eager to build out of the war a "New Negro Manhood Movement." On June 12, 1917 Hubert Henry Harrison called to order the first meeting of the Liberty League, at Bethel AME Church in New York, an organization he hoped would represent "the new demands and aspirations of the new Negro." It was time, declared Harrison, for the Negro masses to break away from "the grip of old-time leaders." The New Negro would demand, rather than request, equal treatment. He would meet white racial violence with arms rather than with sorrowful editorials and appeals for justice. He would respond to global white supremacy by declaring his primary allegiance to his own race, and to the clamoring millions across Africa, Asia, and the Americas—allegiance to race, not country, first.[39]

*

For white defenders of Southern racial mores, America's declaration of war created an interesting thought puzzle that elicited starkly divergent conclusions. For many prominent members of the business, intellectual, and political elite, comfortable that the subordination of the Negro was securely entrenched, the war provided an opportunity to demonstrate the loyalty of their black citizens, and by extension the successful reconstruction of the New South and its management of the "negro problem." For officials of local draft boards, control over the machinery of recruitment provided an occasion to ensure that white registrants were "take[n] care of" and black Southerners were drafted in disproportionately high numbers. For Tom Heflin, a congressman from Alabama, large enough numbers of black men must be enlisted to protect the homeland from the menace of "negro boys" in the absence of white men. On the other hand, for Congressman Thaddeus Caraway of Arkansas black enlistment must be barred entirely, lest the Negro, "the blood of his forefathers forg[ing] to the front," become "a menace to the lives and liberties of those he is sworn to defend." James Vardaman, senator from Mississippi, was most persistent and agitated on this front. "[C]ompulsory military training will leave a problem in this country more difficult of solution, more disastrous . . . in its consequences than the sudden emancipation of the slave a half century ago," he warned. "Impress the negro with the fact that he is defending the flag, inflate his untutored soul with military airs, teach him that it is his duty to keep the emblem of the Nation flying triumphantly in the air—it is but a short step to the conclusion that his political rights must be respected."[40]

Black conscripts hoping service in the army would afford them an opportunity to transcend the restrictions and indignities thrust upon them in everyday life were treated to a rude awakening. Army officials had no interest in adjudicating civil rights; instead, they sought to reproduce relations of Southern life in the barracks. In a deeply racist and segregated society, this meant a deeply racist and segregated army. As always, it was incumbent upon blacks to "know their place." In March 1918, Major General Charles C. Ballou issued Bulletin No. 35 to black soldiers of the Ninety-Second Division stationed at Camp Funston, Kansas. It advised them to place "the general interest of the Division above personal pride and gratification" by avoiding "every situation that can give rise to racial ill-will" and "refrain[ing] from going where their presence will be resented." After southern white recruits engineered a race riot at Camp Merritt, New Jersey, leaving one black man dead and three injured, G. B. Perkins, chief of the Military Morale Section, placed the blame on black YMCA secretary William Lloyd Imes, who, by seeking to protect black soldiers' right to equal facilities, had failed "to contribute to a better mutual understanding and more harmonious relations."[41]

The symbolic power, and subversive potential, of the black soldier was well understood by army officials, who did their best to minimize opportunities for blacks to test their bravery on the battlefield. Of the roughly 370,000 African American draftees, an estimated 3,700 saw duty as combatants in the all-black Ninety-Second and Ninety-Third Divisions—the latter on loan to the French Army, and fighting under the French flag. The vast majority of the African American soldiers in the American Expeditionary Force—nearly 200,000 strong—served in France in labor battalions, working on the docks, laying railroad track, digging trenches, building roads, barracks, and warehouses.[42] In the camps at home, officers often saw no point in training or drilling black soldiers whatsoever. Instead, draftees were given a pick and shovel, and commanded to perform painstaking manual labor from sunrise to sunset. At Camp Lee, Virginia, the two best-drilled companies of black troops were sent to the officers' school to serve as bellhops and waiters. Another soldier at Camp Lee complained that blacks were assigned to perform ditch-digging work and to set up targets on the rifle range on Sundays while the white draftees lounged in the YMCA facilities or attended church. At some camps, when work was scarce, soldiers were simply contracted out for civilian projects. Across the country, in ways big and small, direct and indirect, white officers confirmed the view of a captain at Camp Jackson, South Carolina, who informed his black troops that they "were not soldiers, that all niggers are made to work." Disgruntled black letter writers described their experiences in the camps using the same metaphors: Slavery; the penitentiary; the chain gang.[43]

Like their counterparts in the United States, British officials endeavored to strike a careful balance between their need to involve colonial subjects in the war and their desire to protect their carefully delineated imperial hierarchies of racial status. Until the end of October 1915, the War Office resisted pressure from subjects of Britain's Caribbean colonies to participate in the defense of the Empire. When the British West Indies Regiment (BWIR) was finally established, Caribbean volunteers were classified as "aboriginal troops": held away from the European theater where they would confront white soldiers on the battlefield; denied promotion above the rank of sergeant; provided second-class facilities and medical attention; and expected to perform the most degrading and humiliating tasks. British officers and soldiers greeted members of the BWIR with a remarkable torrent of name calling, discrimination, and unbridled contempt. "On our arrival in Egypt in 1916, our men, hungry and tired, entered the YMCA at Gabbary Camp to the strains of 'Rule Britannia,'" remembered Corporal Samuel Haynes. "Imagine our surprise when we were confronted by a number of British soldiers and the question asked: 'Who gave you n——s authority to sing that! Clear out of this building—only British soldiers admitted here."[44]

In Africa, the geopolitical demands of the war easily eclipsed concerns for the welfare of colonial subjects. The dynamics of African warfare, particularly during the extended East African Campaign, hinged on the establishment and maintenance of massive lines of transport and communication across undeveloped and inaccessible terrain. The vast majority of the participants in the African theater served as laborers and porters, performing with sheer numbers the punishing work that would otherwise be done by modern vehicles or draft animals. The unpopularity of this work, and the endless need for it, encouraged the use of forcible conscription. In Nyasaland, recruitment tactics—the kidnapping of wives to leverage their husbands, nighttime raids on villages, the binding of captured recruits with rope—evoked uncomfortable memories of the slave trade. Once enlisted in the Carrier Corps, recruits were required to perform backbreaking work over long distances, and with unreliable access to food, water, and medical treatment. Those who remained at home suffered from food shortages and famine occasioned by wartime crop requisitions by the army, a problem exacerbated by the manpower shortages created by recruitment which left fields untended. Most of the men and women who died during the war in Africa were killed not on the battlefield but by the devastating logistical requirements created by the conflict. The result, lamented the *Beira* (Mozambique) *News and East Coast Chronicle*, was "an almost inconceivable wastage of human lives."[45]

Living conditions on the home front were truly dreadful for African American soldiers as well. Draftees complained about rancid food and unfit drinking water, inadequate shelter and bathing facilities, lice-infested cots and widespread sickness.[46] Breaking from the tradition of assigning black non-commissioned officers (NCOs) to command black soldiers, white NCOs were assigned to black labor battalions based on their previous experience "handling negro labor"—on plantations, or on public works projects, or on turpentine farms. Officers relied on those experiences when they referred to soldiers as "niggers" and "black sons of bitches," when they beat them with sticks and revolvers, when they denied them furloughs to visit family members, and when they tolerated widespread intimidation of black soldiers by white soldiers and military police. Harassment of black soldiers stationed at Camp Sevier on the streets of nearby Greenville, South Carolina by military police became so provocative that Major Loving urged immediate action before mass violence erupted.[47]

Elsewhere, violence did erupt. The dramatic race riot at Camp Merritt was joined by lesser clashes at Camp Mills, New York, Camp Hill, Virginia, and Camp Meade, Pennsylvania. Outside of the barracks, racial terrorism continued apace throughout the war: the *Crisis* recorded forty-four lynchings of black men and women in 1917, sixty-four in 1918.[48] In southern Georgia, near Valdosta, Walter White, assistant secretary for the NAACP, collected the gruesome details of the death of Mary Turner, one of the most horrifying episodes of lynching ever recorded. Hampton Smith, owner of a large plantation and notorious for his poor treatment and manipulation of black employees, had been murdered by a disgruntled worker, Sidney Johnson, over a wage dispute. Johnson fled. Suspecting a conspiracy, a white posse lynched three men believed to be in cahoots with Johnson, and another man, seemingly for sport. One of the slain was Hayes Turner, husband of Mary Turner, who at the time was eight months pregnant. Grieving and furious, Turner publicly determined to have warrants issued for the men, and to see them punished in court. Deciding to "teach her a lesson," the posse seized Turner and dragged her to a small oak tree near the Little River. "Her ankles were tied together and she was hung to the tree, head downward," reported White.

> Gasoline and oil from the automobiles were thrown on her clothing and while she writhed in agony and the mob howled in glee, a match was applied and her clothes burned from her person. When this had been done and while she was yet alive, a knife . . . was taken and the woman's abdomen was cut open, the unborn babe falling from her womb to the ground. The infant, prematurely born, gave two feeble cries and then its head was crushed by a member of the mob with his heel. Hundreds of bullets were then fired into the body of the woman, now mercifully dead, and the work was over.

Before the orgy of violence was over, two more men were killed, including the finally cornered Sidney Johnson. In the months following the lynchings, ignoring threats by whites commanding them to remain at work in Valdosta, more than five hundred African Americans fled.[49]

Nothing, however, could match the scale or the horrors of East St. Louis. Tensions had been building in the blue-collar Illinois city since America's entry into the war, as thousands of southern blacks streamed north to take advantage of new opportunities in industrial production. Migrants were viewed by the labor unions as strikebreakers, by Democratic politicians as Republican plants, and by the press as a criminal menace. Near the end of May, Edward F. Mason, secretary of the Central Trades and Labor Union, promised to call on the mayor and city council to "take some action to retard this growing menace and also devise a way to get rid of a certain portion of those who are already here." In the early hours of July 2, 1917 white rioters decided to do just that. What followed, as one writer put it, was "a veritable pogrom." Black residents of the city were "shot down like rabbits," hung from telegraph poles, left for dead in the gutters. Two white girls dragged a black girl from a streetcar and beat her unconscious with her own shoe as a crowd cheered them on. Another man was beheaded with a butcher's knife, his head thrown over the side of the Free Bridge. The Negro section of town was set ablaze, while members of the mob waited outside of residences and fired upon anyone trying to escape the flames. A baby was snatched from its mother and thrown into the fire, while white women held the mother back. Members of the police and the militia took sides with the mob. Militia members told an NAACP investigator that they were instructed to disarm blacks of their weapons, and boasted of killing "niggers." "The only trouble with the mob," reflected an East St. Louis postman after the four-day massacre had ended, "was that it didn't get niggers enough."[50]

There were few outside of East St. Louis willing to so brazenly condone the savagery of the rioters. As many as 125 African Americans were killed, hundreds injured, and thousands forced to flee their homes.[51] It was a telling reflection of the times, however, that when Theodore Roosevelt condemned the "unspeakable brutalities" of the race riot he was celebrated for his "courage" in the *Crisis*. Woodrow Wilson remained steadfastly silent. For advocates of the white South, long condemned for their toleration of mob violence, East St. Louis provided a satisfying silver lining. "Never again can one section of the country select and set apart any other section as barbarians to a greater extent than other places," wrote Reverend Dr. J. W. Lee, a Methodist minister from Atlanta. "All parts are guilty under the stress of mob hate of giving way to the vilest passions of which human nature is capable. . . . The best people of East St. Louis are not to blame, as the best people in the South were never to blame for the lynchings in that section." Senator Benjamin Tillman of South Carolina was heartened that the North was finally "beginning to understand the South and to understand the race problem," observing that the "more the northern people know of the negro the less they like him." James Vardaman declared the riots "very regrettable," but also "fortunate in the fact that it is the outward expression, cruel and brutal though it may be, of that inward, dominant, and dauntless spirit of the white man, which would prefer death rather than surrender its superiority or yield in any way any of its rights or privileges, industrial or political, to the less favored and congenitally inferior race." Despicable as their gloating was, southern boosters hit on a fundamental truth. "There is no escape for the Negro in flying from the South to North, or from East to West, or in any direction whatever," reflected the New York *Call* somberly. "He can, en masse, no more get away from his 'problem' than a man can abandon his shadow." Once again, in vivid terms, East St. Louis revealed white supremacy as a national, not a sectional, project.[52]

*

If the suffering inflicted upon peoples of African descent during the war inspired faint interest in itself, the extent to which that suffering might translate into insurrectionary behavior was a source of great interest and concern. In the United States, the military illustrated this mind-set in the naming and execution of its "Negro Subversion" subagency, an Orwellian framing for what often amounted to the compilation of reports on lynchings, race riots, assaults on black soldiers, and complaints about the horrible and inequitable conditions endured by blacks in their segregated army barracks.[53] White letter writers from across the country, worried that disgruntled and supposedly credulous blacks were likely targets of German propaganda and other radical agents, gave somber attention to every hint of rumor and read evidence of sedition into every untoward glance. In Illinois, it was rumored that colored people were collecting arms and ammunition and drilling at night. In West Point, Georgia, Negroes were reportedly giving lectures "tending to promote undue race ambitions." A concerned citizen from Lexington, Kentucky worried that Negroes were showing "rather a coolness" toward the flag. Bolton Smith, a wealthy businessman from Memphis, viewed recent episodes of defiance against the city's segregation laws on its streetcars as evidence "of a changed attitude on the part of the negro," who "is not as jolly, care-free, and good-natured as he once was." Smith recommended an end to lynching to undercut the "extremis[m]" of the NAACP, and a repeal of the Fifteenth Amendment to restore "normal political life" to the South.[54]

In Africa, colonial officials worried that the hardships of the war were dangerously weakening the prestige of the government. In 1917, concerned that France's relentless recruitment campaigns of 1915 and 1916 had brought French West Africa to the brink of revolt, Governor-General Joost van Vollenhoven recommended an end to conscription, and resigned his position when his apprehensions were ignored. Across the continent, observers worried about the danger of military mobilization—as Jan

Christiaan Smuts, then commander of the South African Defence Force, put it—"to civilization itself." In a detailed report for the British War Office, Captain J. E. Phillips warned of the deleterious effects of the "unprecedented meeting of the tribes of Africa" during the East Africa Campaign. "Round the camp fires," reported Phillips, Africans from every corner of the continent were sharing stories of common suffering, "touching on the killing of white by black as illustrated before their eyes," and wondering why the powerful empires of Europe were forced to rely for their defense on black soldiers. Just as damaging, "Black privileges in the Cape and Sierra Leone" were being discussed and "distorted into concessions wrung from white by black." The politics of "Africa for the African" were spreading with "no conception" of the "intermediate process" of white tutelage bridging savagery and civilization. The war, wrote Phillips, is engendering in East Africa for the first time "a conscious feeling of the possibilities of a black Africa."[55]

Fears of this nature were mischaracterized, but not ungrounded. Expressions of defiance exploded on both sides of the Atlantic. Africans responded to forced recruitment tactics by escaping military agents in large numbers, often crossing colonial borders in an effort to elude capture. The combination of wartime opportunity—occasioned by the weakened bonds of imperial power—and wartime deprivations proved a potent formula for rebellion. Along with John Chilembwe's uprising in Nyasaland, violent resistance erupted in Portuguese East Africa, in the Transkei region of South Africa, and in northern and southern Nigeria. In West Africa, the French were forced to extinguish multiple rebellions of varying intensity. In the western Volta region of what is today Burkina Faso, the Volta-Bani uprising escalated into an anticolonial war that lasted well over a year, extended over 100,000 square kilometers of territory, and for a time threatened French control of the entire Niger Bend region.[56]

For members of the British West Indies Regiment, the war was a radicalizing experience. On December 6, 1918, after years of facing abuse as second-class representatives of the British army, frustrations erupted in Taranto, Italy, where members of the Ninth Battalion mutinied against their commanding officers. The final indignity was their exclusion from Army Order No. 1 of 1918—awarding an across-the-board pay raise—because of their official classification as "Natives." As if to emphasize the point, BWIR soldiers at Taranto were commanded to clean the latrines used by the Italian Labour Corps and to wash their laundry. After several days of unrest, order was finally restored, dozens arrested, and one man executed. Eight battalions of the BWIR were disarmed by British military authorities, and promptly escorted back to the Caribbean.[57]

When they arrived home, members of the BWIR were confronted with equally tense conditions. Wartime inflation more than doubled the prices of basic foodstuffs, antagonizing workers who accused white merchants of profiteering, and who blamed white employers for failing to raise wages to meet the rising cost of living.[58] Labor disturbances and strikes flared in British Guiana (Guyana), Trinidad, St. Lucia, and Jamaica. In St. Kitts-Nevis and Antigua, agitation was led by men who would emerge as leading Garveyites after the war. J. A. Nathan, a leader of the St. Kitts Universal Benevolent Association and founder of the first UNIA division in St. Kitts in 1920, penned a letter to the secretary of state for the colonies, indicating the intention of the island's laboring class to do "our bit to make the world safe for DEMOCRACY" by protesting their condition as "SLAVES to the land-monopolists." In the Panama Canal Zone and Canada, West Indians organized the National Association of Loyal Negroes, demanding self-determination for Africans to match the wartime promises made to the small nationalities of Europe, a recognition of "our inalienable rights to a domain in Africa," and the establishment of "a large African State"—a reward "for our loyalty and service of our race in the past and in the war."[59]

In the United States, the war shifted the center of political gravity away from the cautious guardians of Tuskegee and toward the explosive ferment of Harlem. For a time it appeared as though the wartime dynamics of opportunity, dislocation, and disillusionment would transfer the influence of the Tuskegee Machine to the National Association for the Advancement of Colored People. Founded in 1909, the New York-based interracial organization sought to use political lobbying, legal activism, and publicity of racial discrimination and violence to spark "the renewal," as founding member Oswald Garrison Villard wrote, "of the struggle for civil and political liberty" rhetorically conceded by Booker T. Washington. By 1917, fueled by the southern organizing work of Field Secretary James Weldon Johnson, and the brilliant and militant editorship by W.E.B. Du Bois of the NAACP's monthly journal, the *Crisis,* the organization had been established as a legitimate force in national and African American politics. During the war membership exploded, from 9,500 in March 1916, to approximately 40,000 by 1918. The number of NAACP branches more than doubled, no longer clustered in the Northeast and Midwest but spread across the country and through the South. Circulation of the *Crisis* expanded from 41,000 in 1917 to 75,000 in 1918, and reached monthly figures topping 100,000 in 1919.[60]

But even as support for the NAACP continued to rise—membership approached 75,000 in 1919—events had begun to outrun Du Bois and his colleagues.[61] Part of the transformation was sparked by demographic upheaval. The year Booker T. Washington died, 1915, was also the first year of the massive exodus of African Americans to the North that came to be known as the Great Migration. Southern blacks were pushed north by a series of natural disasters that struck the cotton belt—floods in middle Alabama and Mississippi, boll weevil infestations that destroyed cotton yields across much of the South—and by a desire to escape the violence, discrimination, and poverty of rural southern life. More importantly, the war created a massive demand for domestic industrial production at a moment when European immigration—also because of the war—was dramatically reduced. Suddenly, lily-white industries in the big urban centers and industrial towns of the Northeast and Midwest began offering employment to black workers. The migration was cheered by northern black activists as a promising, grassroots manifestation of protest against Jim Crow, a means to both build black political power in the North and to acquire leverage over suddenly nervous employers in the South, who depended on a reliable base of cheap, exploitable labor. By the end of the war, half a million men and women had trekked north, to be followed by a million more over the next decade. The migration transformed small pockets of black settlement in the urban north into dynamic, volatile ghettoes. Harlem was reborn as the Negro Mecca, the black capital of the world. Working-class migrants streaming into New York, Pennsylvania, Illinois, and elsewhere would soon help comprise the northern base of the UNIA.[62]

Migrants from the southern United States were joined in northern metropolises, particularly in Harlem, by emigrants from the Caribbean. Since the first years of the century, black workers from the West Indies had included New York, often via the American-controlled Panama Canal Zone, as a stop in their increasingly complex and overlapping migratory patterns. The completion of the canal in 1914, the wartime decline of banana exports, and the opening of industrial jobs in the United States increased the importance of New York as a destination, a trend that continued through the first half of the 1920s, when yearly arrivals from the Caribbean spiked to 7,300. In all, nearly 150,000 black people arrived in the United States between the end of the Spanish-American War and World War II—the vast majority before immigration restriction in 1924. Like migrants from the southern states, they established thick and mobile networks of contact and association that contributed to what Frank Guridy has called the "US-Caribbean world," and which established an infrastructure for the rapid spread of Garveyism after the war.[63]

The leaders of what became known as the New Negro movement were migrants themselves. A. Philip Randolph, from Florida, and Chandler Owen, from North Carolina, met while studying at Columbia University and launched the class-conscious journal, the *Messenger,* in November 1917. Cyril Briggs, born in Nevis and a resident of New York since 1905, founded the radical *Crusader* in September 1918, and the militant African Blood Brotherhood after the war. The most important voice of black wartime radicalism in the United States was Hubert Henry Harrison. Born in St. Croix, Harrison arrived in New York in 1900 at the age of 17. A brilliant lecturer and voracious reader, by 1912 Harrison had emerged as the Socialist Party's most influential black advocate. Over time, however, Harrison grew dissatisfied with the Party's class-based orthodoxy, disillusioned by its indifference toward the dynamics of racial injustice, and increasingly convinced, as he put it in 1919, that the "international Fact to which Negroes in America are now reacting is not the exploitation of laborers by capitalists," but "the social, political and economic subjection of colored peoples by white"—not the "Class Line" envisioned by the Socialists but a global "Color Line." By the end of 1916, Harrison had established the framework for what he coined the New Negro Manhood Movement: a tactical embrace of "Race First" politics designed to confront the "race first" realities of white supremacy; the development of autonomous and uncompromising black leadership at home and internationally; and the mobilization of a mass-based movement informed by the theories of class-based exploitation but grounded in the vivid and practical realities of global race prejudice.[64]

Harlem's young radicals adopted much of the same rhetoric that intellectuals like Du Bois, Casely Hayford, and Dusé Mohamed Ali had championed before them. The explicit confluence of New Negro and manhood rights in Harrison's formulation of the movement was of a piece with the long-enduring effort by male intellectuals to hinge racial emancipation on the redemption of black masculinity—a discourse, as recent work has made clear, that was "both revivified and revised" by the spectacle and service of black soldiers during the war.[65] Although Harrison viewed the internationalist perspective of the New Negro as a point of departure from the supposedly parochial "old Negro," the effort by Randolph, Owen, Briggs, and Harrison to find common ground with the liberation struggles of peoples in Ireland, India, China, and throughout Africa mirrored both Du Bois's interest in the solidarity of the colored world and the mission statement of the *African Times and Orient Review*. Like the "old guard" before them, the young radicals wrote eloquently about the consequences of whites' failure to heed the warnings of the world's brown, yellow, and black peoples. "Truly it has been said that 'the problem of the Twentieth Century is the problem of the Color Line,'" declared Harrison, invoking Du Bois. "And wars are not likely to end; in fact, they are likely to be wider and more terrible—so long as [the] theory of white domination seeks to hold down the majority of the world's people under the iron heel of racial repression."[66]

FIGURE 2.7. Hubert Henry Harrison. (Photographs and Prints Division, Schomburg Center for Research in Black Culture, The New York Public Library, Astor, Lenox and Tilden Foundations)

What was new about the New Negro movement was the conclusion of its members that the time for compromise was over. From the beginning of the war, black leaders had measured the costs of disloyalty and the benefits of cooperation, and had wagered their hopes on the capacity of wartime service to compel legislative reform in peacetime. For Harrison, the time for the Negro masses to rely on "old-time leaders," on the counsel of "good white people," and on the power of reasoned appeal to compel the favor of white power brokers, had reached an end. Harrison's Liberty League proposed a different set of propositions. The global push toward democracy, declared League members—"the right of every people to rule their own ancestral lands, free from the domination of tyrants, domestic and foreign"— had acquired a momentum that no longer relied on the will of white rulers and spokesmen. As the Russian, Irish, and Indian peoples had seized their moment, so too must Negroes. To fail to act courageously in an "era of revolutionary ferment," to set aside racial grievances in support of the war effort, was an act not of pragmatism but of cowardice, and "would be to brand ourselves as the only people in the world who are quite fit for serfdom." The League declared loyalty "to our race first in everything," and called on Negroes to organize their own political power, and in their own self-defense—to meet murderous white mobs "with the weapons of murder." It proclaimed a readiness to affiliate "with similar organizations of the darker races in other lands," and a determination to win liberation for Africans and Asians. For its flag, the League adopted the colors black, brown, and yellow, reflecting the "dual relationship to our own and other people" in the struggle against white supremacy.[67]

At the outset of the war, Marcus Garvey would have seemed an implausible candidate to rise to the pinnacle of the New Negro insurgency. Operating out of Jamaica, heading a fledgling and unknown organization, frustrated in his ambitions by the island's colored elite, Garvey appeared to be going nowhere fast. Moreover, he appeared comfortable embracing the pragmatic patriotism of his old mentor, Dusé Mohamed Ali. In September 1914, members of the UNIA met in Kingston, where they composed a message to the governor declaring their prayers "for the success of British arms on the battlefield" and expressing their "loyalty and devotion" to the King and the Empire, mindful as they were of "the great protecting and civilising influence of the English nation and people." Over the next year, Garvey preached patriotism, lecturing on the virtues of the British Empire and the tyranny of German rule in Africa, and bragging that the UNIA had been the only society in the West Indies to send a message of support to England at the beginning of the war. In November 1915, the UNIA hosted a farewell meeting for the Jamaican volunteers of the British West Indies Regiment, Garvey "impress[ing] on the men the good wishes of the meeting, and the duty of every true son of the Empire to rally to the cause of the Motherland."[68]

Garvey's journey to the United States, ostensibly to raise money for his proposed Industrial Farm and Institute back home, began innocently enough. Embarking in New York on March 24, 1916, Garvey toured thirty-eight states, making a pilgrimage to Tuskegee to "pa[y] respects to the dead hero, Booker Washington," visiting local churches, examining black business ventures and prospects in major urban centers across the Northeast and Midwest.[69] But back in Harlem, toiling in poverty as an obscure step-ladder orator, contemplating a return home, Garvey's life took major turn. Through his old colleague in the National Club, W. A. Domingo, Garvey was introduced to Hubert Harrison, and invited to speak at the founding meeting of the Liberty League. The next month, Garvey cemented his embrace of New Negro militancy when he delivered a blistering address on the East St. Louis "massacre," declaring it "one of the bloodiest outrages against mankind" in history, and scolding the United States for lauding its experiment in democracy before the world despite the nation's history of slavery, lynching, burning, and butchering.[70]

Four days earlier, Harrison had published his own assault on American hypocrisy in East St. Louis. Indeed, by the end of the war Garvey had adopted much of Harrison's and the Liberty League's platform as his own. Harrison had founded the League in the hopes of building a radical, mass-based alternative to the NAACP. After the war it would be Garvey, and the UNIA, that would carry Harrison's vision to fruition. "Everything that I did he copied," Harrison later complained in his diary. "[M]y work which had failed had laid the foundation for his success."[71] On November 10, 1918, the day before Armistice, members of the UNIA met at Palace Casino in New York to draft postwar resolutions "representing the interests of new spirited Negroes of America, Africa and the West Indies." The gathering represented Garvey's emergence as a major figure in the New Negro movement, attracting to him for the first time the attention of federal authorities. Among the meeting's demands were self-determination for Africans at home and abroad; the right to equal educational facilities and representation in world governments; and that the colonies captured from Germany be turned over to the control of "educated Western and Eastern Negroes." "We have been slaves for four hundred years and we now come not to compromise but to demand that we be recognized as a nation and a people," declared Garvey. "We are backed by four hundred million who we will mobilize if necessary and fight for what is our just rights."[72]

*

On the night of Saturday, January 23, 1915, on the orders of John Chilembwe, a group of two hundred rebels stormed the homes of white residents on the estates of the Shire Highlands in Nyasaland. Three men were slaughtered, including the manager of the Bruce Estates, W. J. Livingstone, who was decapitated with an axe. Three women and their children were taken hostage and sent into the bush for their transport to the government center in Chiradzulu. A second party raided the stores of the African Lakes Corporation in Blantyre, hoping to acquire guns and ammunition. A third group waited near Ncheu for the signal to launch their attack. The telegraph line between Blantyre and the capital, Zomba, was cut.

Almost from the beginning, the plan began to unravel. Mrs. MacDonald, a guest of the Livingstones, escaped the house undetected with the help of a servant and fled to a neighboring plantation, from where word of the uprising was sent to Zomba. At Ncheu, the district resident was warned by a friendly chief of the planned attack, and was able to mobilize adequate defenses. The combined forces of the Nyasaland Volunteer Reserve and roughly one hundred untrained recruits of the King's African Rifles (KAR), freshly mobilized to replace casualties in the war, were able to overpower the rebels and sack Chilembwe's village, razing the mission and its gleaming new church. On February 3, Chilembwe was cornered while fleeing to Portuguese East Africa and shot dead when he resisted capture. Thirty-six of his conspirators were hung, and three hundred more received prison sentences.[73]

The extent to which John Chilembwe expected his rebellion to succeed has been disputed, but at the very least he prepared for the possibility of success.[74] The East African Campaign had drawn local troops of the KAR to Karonga, hundreds of miles to the north, leaving the protectorate's tiny population of 831 white settlers, nearly all clustered in the highlands, more exposed than usual. The presence of new recruits in Zomba at the time of the rebellion was an unfortunate coincidence for the conspirators. As an additional plank of his plan, Chilembwe dispatched a secret letter to authorities in German East Africa, requesting assistance in a war against their common enemy. Testimony collected in the aftermath of the rebellion suggested its broad ambitions. On January 24, the women hostages were handed a note instructing them to "tell all the white men that the Chiefs of all the tribes have agreed to kill all the white men as they have robbed us of our motherland." An official commission assembled by Governor George Smith to investigate the rebellion submitted a fair reading of the evidence when they concluded that the participants sought "the extermination or expulsion of the European population, and the setting up of a native state or theocracy of which John Chilembwe was to be the head."[75]

For the governor the rebellion "open[ed] up a new phase in the existence of Nyasaland." Before the war, he observed, resistance had been localized, and attributable to "the conquest and settlement of a savage country." Chilembwe's rising grew out of Christian mission work, spread over many years, attracting followers across multiple ethnic groups. The commission cited the influence of "Ethiopianism," which "has as its watchword 'Africa for the Africans,' and aims at securing for the native soil political control." It noted the pernicious influence of Chilembwe's correspondence with African Americans, and his subscriptions to their publications. It questioned the wisdom of permitting the existence of religious sects in the protectorate without the proper leadership and oversight of trusted Europeans. And it noted the danger of Watchtower proselytization and prophecy to excite untutored native minds. It was a prescient report. After the war, Garveyism would work through each of these channels, rebuilding—with more caution and patience—the ministry of John Chilembwe.[76]

After parting with Chilembwe in the United States, Joseph Booth continued his remarkable and dogged campaign against what he described as "the colour lie and the race supremacy lie" in Africa. After his expulsion from Nyasaland in 1899, Booth was allowed to return in 1900, only to be expelled again, in part for his involvement in a repatriation scheme that included the cooperation of Bishops Henry McNeal Turner and Levi Jenkins Coppin of the AME Church in the United States and South Africa.[77] In 1906, while in Scotland, Booth was introduced to the teachings of the Watch Tower Bible and Tract Society (WTBTS). The next year, he relocated to Cape Town, from where he channeled Watch Tower materials into central Africa, and won a convert, Elliott Kenan Kamwana, who returned to Nyasaland and sparked a mass revival that established the African Watchtower movement as a permanent feature of the colonial landscape.[78] By the eve of the war, Booth had drifted away from the WTBTS and back toward politics. In May 1914 he organized an appeal to the King on behalf of the "million natives" of Nyasaland and the Rhodesias, declaring British rule a fraud, and demanding that authorities take "immediate and decisive steps" to preserve African land and liberties, "as well as the speedy uplifting and education" of the native "on an equal basis with the British settler," and immediate political rights and representation for those already educated. The next year, he organized the British African Congress from Basutoland (now Lesotho), repeating his demands and noting that there would be no "deserved or lasting victory" for the Allies until they were willing to extend to Africa "the same degree of liberty, protection and enlightenment for which they themselves so justly and resolutely contend." If "peaceful appeals" failed to work, he warned, "a forceful and extensive effort to obtain either equality or independence on African soil" would likely be the result.[79]

Booth once wrote that of all the people he had known, no one had had a greater influence on him than John Chilembwe. In October 1911 Booth sent a letter to his former student, noting his own estrangement from most of his former white friends because of his efforts "to follow God's Bible Truth," and wondering why "we do not find a way to still work together." In December, Booth wrote to Chilembwe again, enclosing lengthy instructions for a "true path for Africa," and expressing a desire for Chilembwe to "speak out, and speak boldly . . . for your people and country," as he once had with Booth in 1897. Soon after the outbreak of the war, Booth sent Chilembwe a copy of his petition of May 1914. When the rebellion erupted, Booth was in Basutoland, likely unaware of what had happened. Viewed as an instigator, although not a participant, in the rising, he was ushered by authorities back to Cape Town, then placed on a ship to England, never to return to Africa. A lifelong pacifist, Booth could not reconcile himself to

Chilembwe's final, dramatic act of defiance. "Poor kindhearted Chilembwe, who . . . wept, laboured with and soothed the dying hours of my sweet son John Edward," he wrote in 1919. "[G]ladly would I have died by my coun-trymen shot, to have kept thee from the false path of slaying: far better to die a slave than die stained with others' life blood."[80]

Chapter Three

AFRICA FOR THE AFRICANS!

SEVERAL MONTHS after the war, serving as a colonial agent in a remote out-post in northern Nigeria, the aspiring Anglo-Irish novelist Joyce Cary was summoned to adjudicate a peculiar case. A young man had been arrested by the local emir after he had been overheard "talking sedition" about a black king, armed with a great iron ship and an army of black soldiers, preparing to set out for Africa to drive the whites from the continent. To his great surprise, Cary was informed by his trusted political agent, an elderly Hausa man named Musa, that the story of a "white man's ship" operated by black sailors had been spreading widely through the local markets, where it was being discussed with breathless enthusiasm. Musa, a cosmopolitan, shrewd, and pragmatic operative, was himself swept up by the idea. "[T]he notion of a ship with black officers and crew, coming across the ocean, moved him to some deep and private excitement," wrote Cary. "He was unwilling to believe that such a ship did not exist."

It was only later, when Cary learned of Marcus Garvey, his Black Star Line, and his designs for Africa, that the rumors made sense. In his antico-lonial tract, *The Case for African Freedom*, Cary retold the story to emphasize his own dawning realization of the futility of British rule. The prevailing narrative of the Black Star Line's rise and fall, he noted, cast Garvey as a comical figure. And yet "Garvey's Manifesto went all through Africa." It had reached Cary's tiny station, several days' journey from the nearest telegraph office and even further from the railway. "Seeing primitive people in their isolated villages, I assumed their ideas of the world were primitive, that they were isolated also in mind," wrote Cary. "But they were not. In a continent still illiterate, where all news goes by mouth and every man is a gatherer, news of any incident affecting the relations of black and white, a strike in South Africa, war with Abyssinia, spreads through the whole country in a few weeks. It is the most exciting of news, above all, if it tells of a black victory."[1]

In the years following the First World War, Marcus Garvey and adher-ents of his Universal Negro Improvement Association captured scores of followers by broadcasting this very narrative of victory. They did so on a scale, and with a dramatic flourish, previously unimagined by peoples of African descent. The end of the war unleashed a massive wave of labor agitation, anticolonial mobilization, and civil violence—an "ecumenical radicalism" that posed a hydra-headed challenge to capitalists, empire builders, white supremacists, and other purveyors of the status quo.[2] Garveyites argued that this "reconstruction period" offered a crucial opportunity for the members of their race to renegotiate the terms of their relations with the white masters of the world. Peoples in Ireland, in Egypt, in India, in China were demanding their right to nationhood and self-determination. Negroes must likewise organize, pool their capital and resources, and construct the foundation of their own statehood-in-exile. Just as Europe was for the Europeans and Asia for the Asians, Africa was for the Africans. On this premise rested the fate of the Negro race, at home and abroad. The consequence of European intransigence was revolution, race war.

Garveyism was carried with impressive thoroughness to every corner of the "Negro world" by an engaged collection of sailors, migrant workers, activists, and community leaders. Recent work has correctly emphasized the extent to which members of the British West Indian diaspora acted as what Robert A. Hill calls a "transmission belt" for the establishment of a global UNIA infrastructure.[3] But the spread of radical Garveyism transcended this West Indian skeleton, enlivening the dreams of black men and women throughout the Americas and Africa, projecting a dazzling interpretation of world events and scriptural destiny that built on and paid respect to rich histories of struggle while plotting a new future and a new identity—a New Negro. Radical Garveyism urgently articulated a moment in which the outlines of the postwar world were uncertain, and in which peoples of African descent sensed an opportunity to redraw them. Its dramatic reception both explained a moment of global mass politics and catalyzed new and often explosive expressions of dissent.

THE RISING TIDE OF COLOR

"Whether the Caucasian reads the news despatches from Egypt or from West Africa, from the Capital of the United States or from the West Indies, from Chicago or from Panama, it must be now dawning upon his junker mind that his self-constituted lordship of the world is at an end," crowed Cyril Briggs in the *Crusader* in September 1919.[4] When Briggs and his allies in the New Negro movement surveyed the global landscape from Harlem in the months following the war, they saw everywhere social orders upended, radicalism ascendant, disempowered people on the march. The editors of the *Messenger* cheered the "strike influenza" that spread across Europe, Asia, the

Americas, and to Africa, where dockworkers struck in Cape Town, railway employees walked out in Thiès, and migrant workers, the urban poor, and the unemployed launched a series of strikes and riots in Freetown.[5] With great satisfaction, W. A. Domingo observed a "new spirit . . . abroad in the world," and celebrated the coalescing unity of subject races, small nationalities, and oppressed workers from Korea to Africa to the West Indies.[6] Protest and rebellion erupted in Germany, India, Syria, Palestine, Iraq, China, Indonesia, Turkey, and Egypt. Leaders of the Russian Revolution raced to capitalize on the shattered expectations of Wilsonianism by launching the Third International and announcing global communism's solidarity with the anticolonial struggles of colored peoples in Asia and Africa.[7] White observers like the American author T. Lothrop Stoddard broadcast with blaring headlines the theory that the Nordic races had suffered their Peloponnesian War, that a "rising tide of color," aided by Bolshevism, "the arch-enemy of civilization and race," threatened to sweep away the social order of the last hope for humankind: the white man. Hubert Harrison, delighted by the clarity with which Stoddard had presented the crisis of Nordic supremacy, sent him a congratulatory letter.[8]

The United States was roiled by its own wave of massive unrest. In 1919, nearly fifteen percent of all American workers went on strike, including tens of thousands during the general strike in Seattle in February. During what Chad Williams has called the "long Red Summer," stretching from the end of the war to the bloody Tulsa riots of 1921, whites struggled desperately to restore the prewar balance of racial privilege they feared was slipping away. Lynchings and white vigilantism surged, with returning black soldiers too often finding themselves singled out as victims. Twenty-five race riots rippled across the country in 1919, including explosive confrontations in Washington, DC and Chicago. In Philips County, Arkansas, efforts by black farmers to seek a measure of economic justice by organizing a sharecroppers' union were met by accusations of "Negro insurrection." Sufficiently agitated, whites launched a pogrom that drew support from nearby counties in Arkansas, Tennessee, and Mississippi—along with federal troops armed with machine guns from Camp Pike—and resulted in the murder, execution, imprisonment, torture, and displacement of over one thousand African Americans. In Florida, a massive voter registration drive following the passage of the Nineteenth Amendment, spearheaded by African American women, was overwhelmed on election day 1920 by a systematic campaign of terror launched by the newly resurgent Ku Klux Klan.[9]

During the long Red Summer, black men and women were in no mood to turn the other cheek. Amidst steady urban migration, within growing and increasingly fortified northern ghettoes, facing rising levels of unemployment, and nursing wartime frustrations and daily racial grievances, black soldiers and civilians met white violence with coordinated and often

Figure 3.1. Return of the Fifteenth Regiment, New York. (Originally printed in *The Crisis*, May 1918)

cathartic acts of self-defense. "In all the bloody trail of riots in the 'Land of the Free' . . . there never was another wherein the Negro took so much pride and jubilation," wrote W. E. Hawkins in his colorful account of the Washington riots.

> When the long pent up floods of race hate broke their bounds, trans-forming men into demons, and bands of armed mobs hunted each other like the wild cla[n]smen in the South during Reconstruction, groups of Negroes roamed the streets shouting jubilant war songs as if it were a carnival and gala day. And to them it was a carnival indeed, in which the sleeping Demon of Race Consciousness aroused to fury by the constant pricking of his pride, sensed the flavor of the glory of hate and dropped the sting of death into the white man's cup of arrogance.

During the Chicago riots, black residents, led by returning soldiers, formed a "Hindenburg line" along State Street, three-and-a-half miles long, and or-ganized into squads to defend their neighborhoods. Canvassing the north-west section of Washington during the riots, James Weldon Johnson was surprised to discover a similar mood of calm and fearlessness, a resolve not to flee but to fight. "If the white mob had gone unchecked—and it was only the determined effort of black men that checked it—Washington would have been another and worse East St. Louis," he wrote. "As regrettable as are the Washington and Chicago riots, I feel that they mark the turning point in the psychology of the whole nation regarding the Negro problem."[10]

Black activists in Harlem across a wide spectrum of belief, from ministers to "race first" activists to socialists, were united in agreement about the value and valor of armed self-defense in the immediate postwar period. Indeed, to the radical side of the crude fault line that young insurgents like A. Philip Randolph relentlessly drew between the "Old Crowd" and the "New Negro," there existed for a moment a broad solidarity of aims.[11] In January 1919 an eclectic collection of black notables—including Randolph, Reverend Adam Clayton Powell, businesswoman Madam C. J. Walker, secretary of the Foreign Mission Board (and former John Chilembwe associate) Lewis Garnett Jordan, Niagara movement founder and Socialist Party candidate Reverend George Frazier Miller, and UNIA president general Marcus Garvey—organized the short-lived International League of Darker Peoples (ILDP), an effort to coordinate a united front ahead of the peace conference, and to establish a permanent international council of Asians, Africans, African Americans, and Afro-Caribbeans "with a view of preventing the expropriation of the darker peoples of their natural resources and labor." Through the spring of 1919, Randolph and Chandler Owen, the socialist editors of the *Messenger*, participated in UNIA meetings, and Randolph was one of three delegates nominated by the UNIA to represent the organization in Paris. Until September, the *Negro World* was edited by another socialist, Garvey's boyhood friend W. A. Domingo.[12]

This moment of "ecumenical radicalism" is important for understanding the emergence of radical Garveyism. Because radical Garveyism was something different than the politics Marcus Garvey brought to the United States in 1916, and different than the politics he returned to in 1921. Viewing the vast "reconstruction" of the world following the war as a remarkable opportunity, Garvey accelerated the scope, the pace, and the menace of his program. If, before the war, Garvey had been content to let vast historical trajectories and social forces run their course, wartime ferment convinced him, as it had the Bolsheviks, to seize history by the throat. It was a role well-suited to a master propagandist. By the middle of 1919, Garvey had emerged in the eyes of the federal intelligence community as the most important "Negro radical agitator" in New York, the most likely to sow the seeds of racial violence. Liberty Hall, the newly inaugurated headquarters of the UNIA, at 135th Street and Lenox Avenue was "sort of a clearing house for all international radical agitators," reported an agent. "[B]lacks and yellows from all parts of the world . . . radiate around Garvey, leave for their destinations, agitate for a time, and eventually return to Garvey's headquarters." In the spring of 1919, Randolph and Owen had issued a call for a "great mass movement among Negroes" behind the banner of socialism and interracial class solidarity. But by the end of the year, it was clear that the plurality of the black masses—and the reins of the New Negro movement—had been seized by the UNIA. "Where Negro 'radicals' of the type known to white radicals can scarce get a handful of people," wrote Hubert Harrison, "Garvey fills the largest halls and the Negro people rain money on him. . . . [He] holds up to the Negro masses those things which bloom in their hearts— racialism, race-consciousness, racial solidarity."[13]

Garvey spent the first months after the war awaiting the results of the Peace Conference in Paris. "If the delegates of the Peace Conference would like to see no more wars we would advise them to satisfy the yellow man's claims, the black man's claims and the white man's claims, and let all three be satisfied so that there can indeed be a brotherhood of man," he declared weeks after the armistice. The choice in Paris was between "abolishing racial discrimination" or "many more wars," fought to liberate lands occupied by Europeans and belonging to peoples of color. In Africa, the UNIA demanded that the colonies ceded by Germany, won in battles fought mainly by African troops, be handed over to the administration of Western-educated blacks. Along with Randolph, the UNIA selected Ida B. Wells-Barnett and a translator, the Haitian-born Eliezer Cadet, to travel to Paris. After Randolph and Wells-Barnett were denied visas, Cadet represented the organization alone. He wrote home brimming with enthusiasm about his position, boasting that after the conference he would travel to Africa to contribute to the administration of the new black government.[14]

It is hard to imagine that Garvey expected much to come of this exercise in high diplomatic theater. Regardless, the failure of the Covenant of the League of Nations to extend the principles of democracy and self-determination to peoples of African descent was a teachable moment. The mandates clause, wrote Garvey, which placed control of the former German colonies under the "tutelage" of white governments, revealed once and for all "the intention of the European powers to shackle the millions of black people on the continent of Africa and to further exploit them for the development of their respective nations." The time for petitions and begging was past, the "farce of brotherhood" proven a lie. If whites were to continue their policy of "race first," so too must Negroes view their politics through the prism of race. "The next twenty-five years will be a period of keen competition among people," Garvey argued. "It will be an age of survival of the fittest. The weaker elements will totter and fall. They will be destroyed by the upbuilding of the greater powers." In their preparation for "this titanic industrial and commercial struggle that is in the making," Negroes must seek their salvation in the unity and collective strength of their brethren scattered across national borders. Only through organization on a global scale might the race wrest power from their oppressors and establish a more healthy racial equilibrium.[15]

FIGURE 3.2. Black Star Line stock certificate. (Photographs and Prints Division, Schomburg Center for Research in Black Culture, The New York Public Library, Astor, Lenox and Tilden Foundations)

In January 1919 John Edward Bruce observed that Garvey had "reorganized his society into a 'great world movement' for the redemption and regeneration of Africa." Indeed, the UNIA's emerging agenda was breathtaking in the sweep of its ambition. In April, Garvey announced the inauguration of his Black Star Line Steamship Company, the cornerstone of his plan to establish a thriving commercial network between West Africa, the Caribbean basin, and the United States. The Black Star Line, Garvey explained, was not a private company but "the property of the Negro race." By purchasing shares at $5 apiece, black men and women in Africa and the Americas were buying ownership in a collective project that would ultimately comprise a fleet of black-owned ships, carrying raw materials and goods manufactured in black-owned factories, sold in black-owned stores, underwritten by black-owned banks. The idea of the Black Star Line, a shining symbol of emerging New Negro industrial potential, captured the imagination of peoples of African descent like few projects before or since. By 1920, seemingly "unlimited amount[s] of money" arrived daily at Liberty Hall. At points stretching across Africa and the Americas—as at Joyce Cary's remote outpost—it elicited vivid expectations of gathering Negro strength and imminent liberation.[16]

Figure 3.3. International Convention of the Negro Peoples of the World, 1920. (Photographs and Prints Division, Schomburg Center for Research in Black Culture, The New York Public Library, Astor, Lenox and Tilden Foundations)

The Black Star Line was the flashiest manifestation of the broader UNIA effort to project itself as a government-in-exile, the germinal manifestation of a black republic in Africa, or, more ambitiously, a "vast Negro empire."[17] Garveyites composed a national anthem, established business, military, and nursing auxiliaries, and crafted a red, black, and green tricolor flag. The First International Convention of the Negro Peoples of the World, held over the month of August 1920, gathered delegates from around the world to unite in common congress, elect the leaders of the race, and write a constitution, the Declaration of Rights of the Negro Peoples of the World, that Garvey envisioned governing future generations of the race. The convention itself was designed to announce the beginning of a "new age" for the Negro, reflecting the spirit "born of the bloody war" and propelling peoples of color across the world to demand their liberty. The convention, declared Garvey, was "an epoch-making event" from which there was "no turning back." "Destiny leads us to liberty, to freedom," he wrote. "that freedom that Victoria of England never gave; that liberty that Lincoln never meant; that freedom, that liberty, that will see us men among men; that will see us a nation among nations; that will make of us a great and powerful people."[18]

In December 1919 Garvey announced that the headquarters of the UNIA would be relocated to Monrovia after the convention, and that Liberia would be the staging ground for the rebuilding of the African continent. So long as Negroes remained without a powerful country of their own, he argued, any gains in the Americas would be fleeting, insecure, subject to the whims of white governments. "Back to Africa" did not mean relocating all

Western blacks to the continent, but rather organizing a cadre of scientists, mechanics, and artisans to build railroads, establish schools, and broadly perform the "pioneering work" necessary to resurrect the struggling black republic as a flourishing Negro homeland. Once UNIA "missionaries in the cause of freedom" had been established in West Africa, the spirit would inexorably expand outwards and across the continent. "Liberia is the hope of Africa," Lewis G. Jordan assured a rapt audience at Liberty Hall in April 1920, after his return from the country. "If you make Liberia what she ought to be it would be like the ef[fervesc]ing of soda in a glass of water. Whatever goes out from there would spread all over Africa, and all Africa would be blessed if you strike Liberia."[19]

As in the earlier emigration schemes of Edward Blyden or Henry McNeal Turner, the UNIA's secular vision of a powerful African state was inseparable from the spiritual expectation of providential destiny. "Do you think that my forebears were brought into this Western Hemisphere to suffer and bleed and die for nearly 250 years that I might get the civilization that I have now and the Christianity that I have now—for naught?" demanded Garvey.

> The God that we worship and fear has never been asleep, and because He has never been asleep, He has ever been watching over the Negro, and He has brought him out of his trials and tribulations to see the light of a new day—the light of liberty for all people—the light of liberty when Ireland cries out for freedom—when Egypt cries out for freedom—when India cries out for freedom—when the Jew cries out to get back and to be restored to Palestine. We have lived to see the day when Ethiopia is stretching forth her hands unto God. . . . No power on earth can stop the great onward rush of the UNIA.[20]

What was so potent about Garvey's invocation of nineteenth-century Ethiopianism in the long Red Summer was that he embraced biblical prophecy in the present tense, and cast himself as divine vessel of its realization. Amidst the great postwar rumblings for liberty and justice, he argued, Ethiopia's "hour [had] come." "During this twentieth century there came a man upon the scene to teach his people race loyalty, to teach them to fear God and know him, to teach them to unite the world over," declared leading Garveyite, Reverend James W. H. Eason, in Chicago in the aftermath of the riots. "Black but honorable, a Negro but with motives pure, . . . a man who traces his ancestry back for thousands of years until it goes back to the mighty black kings who founded the pyramids of Egypt; he is now upon the scene as the president general of the Universal Negro Improvement Association." After he was shot and nearly killed by a disgruntled UNIA member a month later, Garvey generously cast the movement itself as the work of provenance, greater than any one man. "The Universal Negro Improvement Association is too strong to be destroyed by any human agency," he wrote. "We have our part to play on the stage of life." If Garvey were to fall, one hundred more would spring up to carry on the cause. Africa would be redeemed just as God had dictated it.[21]

To this language of religious conviction Garvey added the martial language of war and revolution. "The time for the peaceful penetration of the black man's right by the white man is past, and the time for determined resistance has come," he declared. "We are determined to fight and die free men." The war had both demonstrated Negro manhood and courage and convinced Negroes that the time for fighting for the cause of white civilization had reached an end. Now that the "old-time Negro" had been "buried with Uncle Tom," it was time for the New Negro to fight so that "future generations of the Negro race shall be declared free." In the gathering storm that would pit civilizations against one another—white, yellow, brown, black—Negroes must mobilize their resources, their determination, and their courage to liberate their God-given homeland. "[T]here is no turning back for us now," thundered Garvey. "The war must go on . . . in the African plains, there to decide once and for all in the very near future whether black men are to be serfs and slaves or black men are to be free men."[22]

The "radicalism" of the UNIA, like much else about the movement, has traditionally been viewed from the prism of American politics. Yet Garvey, from the beginning, viewed his activism as a global project. Why storm the ramparts of white supremacy in the United States, where Negroes were "hopelessly outnumbered," when the white man could be made to "eat his salt" in the black-majority colonies of Africa and the West Indies? In November 1920 Garvey confided to an undercover agent in New York that the *Negro World* "was used for propaganda purposes . . . to spread discontent among the races, not only in America, but in Africa, and the West Indian islands." This would not have been news to British governors in the Caribbean, who for two years had been waging an unsuccessful effort to stem the flow and the influence of the paper.[23] As labor agitation rippled across the region, the *Negro World* emerged as the paper of record for West Indian workers, contextualizing local struggles with dramatic reports of riots in the United States and Great Britain, and revolution throughout much of the colonial world.[24] The rise of the UNIA in the region, as in the United States, benefited from the accumulation of wartime and postwar grievances, but it also galvanized them by drawing an exhilarating conclusion—that a New Negro had arrived on the scene, mobilizing, gathering strength, preparing to overturn the bulwarks of the racial status quo.

AN ETHIOPIAN TENT: RADICAL GARVEYISM IN THE CARIBBEAN

It was fitting that the UNIA would exert its most explosive immediate impact on the British colonies of the greater Caribbean. As a number of scholars have recently noted, Garveyism's emergence as a global movement owed much to the expansive "migratory sphere" fashioned by members of the British West Indian diaspora. For decades, and accelerating with the extension of United States hegemony in Latin America following the Spanish-American War, West Indian migrants forged a vast, mobile labor force that connected the eastern seaboard to the Gulf of Mexico, the Caribbean islands to Central and South America, the British Caribbean to the Hispanic and French Caribbean. Within this transnational community, West Indians established thick networks of associational life, religious and cultural practices, family and social ties. They were connected by the multidirectional traffic of workers and newspapers, and by the significant presence of West Indian sailors aboard British and American ships, who acted as important vectors for the spread of information and rumor throughout the Atlantic world. When the UNIA emerged as a hemispheric force following the war, it was dominated by West Indians and West Indian leadership in American cities like New York, Philadelphia, Newport News, Detroit, and Miami; in the migrant enclaves abutting banana and sugar plantations in Central America, the Dominican Republic, Puerto Rico, and Cuba; and at home, in the islands of the British Caribbean, where Garveyites became embroiled in a series of contentious labor disputes and nascent rebellions. The UNIA's rapid expansion owed much to its capacity to catalyze the West Indian diaspora within a single frame of reference, to infuse an emerging West Indian identity with a broader sense of global racial solidarity.[25]

Garveyism was carried widely to the greater Caribbean from the beginning of the UNIA's reestablishment in New York. By late 1918 and early 1919, local UNIA divisions had emerged in the region; according to the British War Office, Garvey was also in correspondence with soldiers in the British West Indies Regiment (BWIR) stationed abroad.[26] From island to island, officials noted with concern the contributions of Garveyist propaganda to a new and pervading climate of hostility toward whites. Henry Baker, American Consul at Port-of-Spain, Trinidad, warned that the British West Indies were "on a social volcano . . . which is liable to burst into eruption at almost any time," and blamed the *Negro World* for a "growing bad temper against white people," and for a "spirit of lawlessness" that seemed "likely to prove a very serious menace in the future."[27] Across the region, government agents worked furiously—and ineffectively—to suppress the flow of Garveyist materials.[28] In British Honduras (now Belize), authorities banned the *Negro World*, only to watch in dismay as copies continued to arrive in the colony through Guatemala and Mexico in greater numbers than before.[29] In Costa Rica, the American consul reported that "hundreds of thousands of copies" of the paper were shipping each month to "foreign countries having large negro populations," and estimated that at least five thousand copies were circulating in Limón despite the best efforts of Costa Rican authorities.[30] By May 1920 the governor of British Honduras,

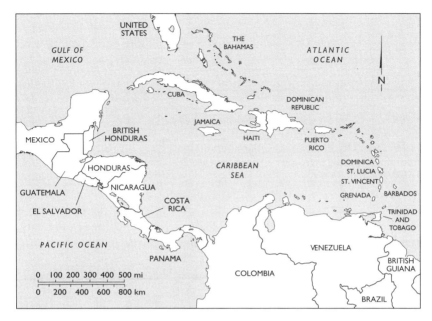

FIGURE 3.4. The Greater Caribbean, 1919.

Sir Eyre Hutson, had given up. Observing the widespread failure of official suppression, he conceded the futility of searching every person arriving in the colony. As an alternative, he proposed informing members of the local UNIA that government officials were themselves subscribing to the *Negro World;* that they, like thousands of readers stretching throughout the greater Caribbean, were receiving copies of the paper and studying its directives carefully.[31]

The message that Garveyites crafted for the Caribbean in 1919 and 1920 was unabashedly provocative. "If political freedom is good enough to be forced upon Germans [by Great Britain], then it is certainly good enough for Jamaica, Trinidad, Barbados, St. Kitts, and the other islands of the Antilles," wrote W. A. Domingo in a *Negro World* article that was republished in the *West Indian* (Grenada). "In the West Indies after the war there should remain not a single vestige of economic serfdom or political slavery." West Indians must demand self-government, and usher in a "West Indian renaissance." Dominican Garveyite J. R. Ralph Casimir was more direct. "The Negro is tired of being ruled by the pale-faced oppressors," he wrote to the *Negro World*. "The Negro must and will rule." In January 1920 Garvey cheered that the British islands had become "powder houses," ready to explode if whites were "to start anything." George Tobias, treasurer of the Black Star Line, advised British administrators to suppress the *Negro World* while they could, because the time would soon come "when they will have to run for their very lives with shoes in their hands to find refuge in the Caribbean sea."[32]

Garveyist propaganda encouraged Afro-Caribbeans to view their discontent as a reflection of the geopolitical racial status quo. It was a lesson that the returning soldiers of the British West Indies Regiment were prepared to accept. In Trinidad, "strong feeling[s]" were rekindled in July 1919 when the S.S. *Oriana* brought forty military prisoners from the BWIR ashore en route to Jamaica. The day earlier, during a parade of local forces, several soldiers refused to participate, and instead hurled insults at their marching comrades. Similar discontent was reported in the city of Belize, British Honduras, where soldiers reportedly refused to come to attention when "God Save the King" was played, and hissed at the Union Jack.[33] Local anger at rising food prices, low wages, and disenfranchisement was quickened by dramatic stories of the race riots exploding across the United States and Great Britain. In Belize, massive riots erupted days after the Garveyite-friendly local newspaper, the *Independent*, published an article documenting the violence in Liverpool, England, and Cardiff, Wales, during which "infuriated crowds hunted every negro from pillar to post, wrecked and fired their lodging houses," and stalked the streets armed with revolvers, razors, and knives. According to Governor Hutson, during the Belize disturbance "the cry arose that the whites generally should be treated as the negroes had been treated in Liverpool." In Trinidad, massive labor resistance was likewise preceded by reports of gangs of white soldiers and sailors "savagely attacking, beating and stabbing every negro they could find" in the streets of Liverpool, including a Trinidadian, Charles Wooten.[34] Garvey, for his part, cast black resistance against white mobs across the United States as an expression of revolt, "a rising of the blacks and the turning of the oppressed worm upon the oppressor." Across the front page of a copy of the *Negro World* seized by authorities in the Bahamas blazed the title, "Negroes Should Match Fire with Hell Fire."[35]

At the same time, Garveyites successfully conveyed the idea that the emergence of the UNIA represented a profound break for members of the race, the inauguration of a new era of prosperity. The arrival of the S.S. *Yarmouth*, the first ship purchased by the Black Star Line, in the Caribbean in December 1919 had a profound effect on the men and women who flocked to the docks of Cuba, Jamaica, and Panama to shower the crew with flowers and fruit and lay eyes on the ship's jet-black captain, Joshua Cockburn.[36] "The star that shone on Bethlehem had hardly a greater significance to the wise men than the success of this venture will have on the minds and attitudes of the people of the Negro race," gushed an editorial in the *Dispatch* (Panama). "It will serve to show them that beyond a doubt ... the Negro is here; he has arrived and is arriving. ... The day is at hand." The arrival of the *Yarmouth* in Cristóbal, Panama, offered proof "that the 'Black Star Line' is a real organization with vim and vigor behind the capital of thousands of dollars subscribed solely and entirely by Negroes in the United States, Central America and the West Indies," reported the *Workman*. "Never before in the history of the Negro has any proposition originating among our race received such world-wide recognition and discussion as this new scheme proposed and executed by the New Negro in this new age of racial independence." The emergence of Cockburn on deck suggested that "Ethiopia shall stretch forth her hand" was no longer prophecy, but an accomplished fact.[37]

This view, which conflated the remarkable rise of the UNIA with the rejuvenation of the Negro race, partly explains the galvanizing effect of bans on the *Negro World* across the region. In St. Vincent, R.E.M. Jack, the local agent for the newspaper, complained that "the Government everywhere is determined to stop the progress of us, poor and innocent Negroes." In Grenada, efforts to ban the *Negro World* were resisted by an impassioned campaign led by T. Albert Marryshow, managing editor of the *West Indian*, who organized meetings that drew thousands and were described as the largest in living memory. In Belize, the suppression of the *Negro World* was cited as one of the causes of the riots that erupted in July 1919. "The intended suppression of the *Negro World* is causing much uneasiness among the inhabitants," reported J. R. Ralph Casimir in Dominica. "Is it not necessary for the Negro to know of his capabilities, the history of his race in the past and the future? . . . What harm is in a paper which teaches the Negro to unite, teaches him about his race, and to better his conditions? Must the Negro stay in darkness in this age of civilization, Christianism and freedom? By jove, not as long as there is life in the Negro!"[38]

The labor agitation and anticolonial sentiment that erupted across the Caribbean region after the war was framed by this discourse of racial solidarity. Labor was mobilized, as the Trinidadian activist Tubal Uriah "Buzz" Butler observed in the 1930s, under an "Ethiopian tent."[39] In Castries, St. Lucia, a "wave of strike fever" and "racial antipathy" was traced by authorities to secret meetings held by local Garveyites, who were holding laborers' collections for Black Star Line stock in reserve as a strike fund.[40] During the massive canal workers' strike in Panama, in 1920, Garveyite leaders refashioned the struggle as one between whites and blacks (rather than capital and labor), sold union activity as a demonstration of loyalty to the race, and emphasized the broader project of Negro organization and unity. When William Stoute, de facto leader of the union movement in Panama, ordered his workers back to the job, leading local Garveyite Eduardo V. Morales begged the workers to "stay out and die" if they had to. "We are not fighting any government nor for any government, we are fighting for the uplift and the betterment of ourselves," Morales argued. "I say . . . it is a racial cause and if we divide ourselves we are going to fall." Much of the local Garveyites' confidence was inspired by the presence of UNIA organizers Henrietta Vinton Davis and Cyril Henry, who had arrived in Panama on the *Yarmouth* and spent the weeks leading up to the strike addressing huge crowds, touring the country, and organizing local divisions. When the strike commenced, Garvey cabled $500 from New York, and Davis assured the strikers that the UNIA would "help them to the limit financially."[41]

In Belize, a major rebellion may have been narrowly avoided. On the evening of July 22, 1919 a band of men, members of the BWIR, spread out strategically on street corners, communicating with verbal instructions and whistle blasts. At 8:30, the electricity was cut across the northern half of the city under suspicious circumstances, and a dense crowd of onlookers, perhaps four thousand, began to gather in the streets. Rioters attacked storefronts, directing their anger toward the merchants they blamed for wartime profiteering while workers suffered stagnant wages. Protesters set upon white men they encountered in the streets, and were heard singing, "We are going to kill the white sons of bitches tonight. . . . This is the black man's night." Ominously, a group of five hundred soon crowded in front of the Drill Hall which—thanks to the quick thinking of officials—had been locked up in time, the weapons removed and hidden. The situation remained tense throughout the night. Major Henry Schnarr of the British Honduras Territory Force later testified that he refrained from using force because he believed the "infuriated mob" would have turned the streets of Belize into "rivers of blood." Only the arrival of the warship H.M.S. *Constance* on the morning of July 24 returned the colony to order.[42]

In Trinidad, a strike initiated by black dock workers in Port-of-Spain escalated into a wave of uprisings that spread across the island and into Tobago, what W. F. Elkins describes as "[o]ne of the earliest effusions of [mass-based] black nationalism."[43] Preceded by "wild and persistent rumors about the blacks rising in a body against the whites," the strike was organized by the Trinidad Workingmen's Association (TWA), whose leadership was mainly sympathetic to Garveyism. During the strike, organizers circulated "verselets" that cited Garvey and the Black Star Line; at TWA meetings, passages from the *Negro World* were read, and Garveyist ideas were encouraged. "You are a powerful race and our power was proved in the gigantic struggle for British liberty," declared James Braithwaite, TWA secretary, at one meeting. "You don't think it is a shame for the intelligent negro to remain sleeping and waiting for amelioration? No, we must fight. If we can die for the white man against his German brother we can die better for ourselves." After the unrest was quelled, a solicitor-general's report detailed the numerous ties between strike leaders and the UNIA.[44] Indeed, James Braithwaite and his brother Aaron Fitz Braithwaite served as local officers of the UNIA in the 1920s. William Bishop, who edited the *Labour Leader*, the TWA's newspaper in the 1920s, was a committed Garveyite. John Sidney de Bourg, who was deported for his involvement in the strike, traveled to New York, where he attended the UNIA's First International Convention, became an official signatory of the Declaration of Negro Rights, and was elected Leader of the Negroes of the Western Provinces of the West Indies and South and Central America.[45]

MORE DANGEROUS THAN RIFLES: GARVEYISM IN AFRICA

Garveyism's transmission to Africa was not as explosive as in the Caribbean, but—considering the level of difficulty—perhaps more impressive. The movement spread like brushfire through southern Africa after the war, becoming an essential part of the region's political "ecology."[46] Carried on the lips of black sailors, relayed through the post, splashed across the pages of the *Negro World*, news of the UNIA and its magnificent Black Star Line reached the docks of Cape Town by 1919, then dispersed widely to rural hamlets, bustling labor compounds, and urban centers throughout South Africa.[47] Local agents fanned out across the country; in 1924, a worried postmaster general reported that "thousands of copies" of the *Negro World* were being received each week at a Kimberley address, and then sent throughout the diamond and mining region and into other territories.[48] Garveyite organizers, working clandestinely, planted their seeds from Cape Province to Natal and then throughout the region, up the western coast to South West Africa (now Namibia) and Angola, north to Bechuanaland (Botswana), and in the east through Basutoland (Lesotho), Portuguese East Africa (Mozambique), and as far as Tanganyika (Tanzania).[49] Garveyist literature was concealed inside food shipments, distributed along bicycle paths, and dispersed along the vast "human chain" of information and migration that connected the region and fed the escalating and coercive demand for cheap, rootless, and exploitable labor.[50]

Garveyism was carried with equal rigor through the British, French, and Belgian colonies on the west coast. News of the movement started to flow through well-connected channels in 1919, and organizational work had begun in Freetown, Monrovia, and Lagos by early 1920.[51] By the end of 1920, reported A. W. Wilkie, a missionary stationed in the Gold Coast (Ghana), Garveyism had "gripped the coast and many of the towns are seething with it."[52] Organizing work was conducted in nearly every colony from Senegal to Cameroon.[53] Aided by worker mobility and the expansion of the railway, word of the movement spread far into the hinterland, especially in Nigeria, where Garveyist activity stretched north through Ibadan, Illorin, Minna, Zaria, and Kano.[54] Nnamdi Azikiwe, the future president of independent Nigeria, learned of the UNIA from a fellow student while he was studying

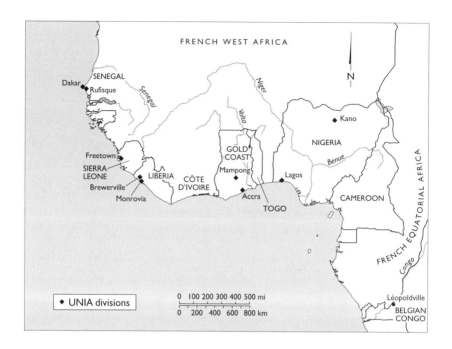

FIGURE 3.5. West Africa.

at the Hope Waddell Institute in Calabar. French authorities worried that their students in Dakar were being exposed to Garveyist propaganda, which they viewed as "more dangerous than rifles," but conceded that there were "no walls thick enough" to stop the spread of informal rumor and gossip. In 1923 a writer for the *Cape Argus* complained that "[a]t almost every West African port the inquisitive voyager has only to get into the 'black quarter' and to scratch a little below the surface to find signs of the organization." Trekking through the Belgian Congo, from the east coast to the west, the American adventurer Hermann Norden was astonished to find at post after post Belgian officials eager for information about "Marcus Garvey, his Black Star line, and other details of that mad dreamer's plan to win the continent back for its scattered people."[55]

Outside of the Americas, the UNIA had its greatest organizational success in South Africa and the closely linked colonies of Basutoland and South West Africa. In South Africa, Robert Vinson counts eight official divisions, and numerous informal ones, emerging in rural, urban, and industrial regions stretching from Cape Town to Durban.[56] In South West Africa, thanks in large part to the tireless organizing work of West Indian emigrant Fitz

Herbert Headly, lively divisions were established in Luderitz, Windhoek, and Swakopmund, and activism reached Usakos, Karibib, and Okahanja.[57] In West Africa, the UNIA also had a notable, if mostly fleeting, presence. Garveyites managed to establish six divisions in the British colonies, two in Liberia, and two—briefly and secretly—in Senegal.[58] As in the United States and the Hispanic Caribbean, the formal spread of the UNIA owed much to the energies of West Indian migrants like Headly. Scholars have stressed the importance of West Indian sailors and port workers in the growth of Garveyism in South Africa, particularly in Cape Town, but West Indians also played a crucial role in the establishment of the UNIA in Nigeria, and there is every reason to believe that West Indian influence extended beyond the degree to which is currently known.[59]

Emphasizing the organizational accomplishments of the UNIA in Africa rather dramatically understates the influence of Garveyism on the continent, however. Everywhere, as Helen Bradford has suggested of South Africa, "'common sense' was Garveyized and Garveyism was domesticated."[60] Garveyism had a profound influence on the early development of the African National Congress (ANC) and the Industrial and Commercial Workers' Union (ICU), South Africa's two most important black political organizations in the 1920s, and was fiercely debated among members of the path-breaking National Congress of British West Africa (NCBWA), whose vice president and Gold Coast delegate J. E. Casely Hayford continued to receive smuggled copies of the *Negro World* from friends in the United States and the West Indies long after the paper was officially banned throughout much of the region.[61] In West Africa, news of Garveyite activities were sympathetically reported in African-run newspapers like the *Sierra Leone Weekly News*, the *Times of Nigeria*, and Hayford's *Gold Coast Leader*.[62] In South Africa, where the *Negro World* was not officially suppressed, its propaganda was complimented by several African newspapers that featured *Negro World* articles, advertised for Garvey, and, to varying degrees, supported the aims of the UNIA editorially. So clear was the influence of Garveyism on *The Black Man*, the newspaper published by ICU founder Clements Kadalie, that Garvey referred to it as "the *Negro World* of South Africa."[63]

Over time, Garveyites in Africa established an organizational framework that carefully measured the long-term goal of African liberation against the constraints of overwhelming European power on the continent. But in the reconstruction period after the war, as was the case in the greater Caribbean, the spread of Garveyist information had explosive consequences that fulfilled—and perhaps at times exceeded, Garvey's wildest expectations. In the Eastern Cape, the millennial Israelite movement of the prophet Enoch Mgijima was radicalized by Mgijima's correspondence with his nephew, Gilbert Matshoba, a clerk in Queenstown, who relayed to Mgijima's camp in the Bulhoek sub-location news of postwar droughts and food riots, civil disobedience by workers on the Rand and students in Lovedale, and reports about the growing Garvey movement and its plans to liberate Africa. Reporting on the UNIA's International Convention in 1920, Matshoba told Mgijima that Garvey had declared,

> We will not ask England, France, Italy or Belgium . . . why are you . . . in this place [Africa]. We will only direct them to get out. . . . The blood of all wars is about to arrive (its compensation is due). Then Europe puts her might against Asia. Then it will be time for the negroes to lift up their sword of the liberty of the Africans. Father that is the news of our black countrymen.[64]

When Mgijima and his followers entered into a lengthy standoff with South African authorities, refusing to acknowledge the secular power of the state, several prominent African moderates condemned the Israelites for plotting the overthrow of the white government, and for believing that their cause would be aided by black Americans and by American airplanes commanded by Marcus Garvey.[65] On May 24, 1921 the confrontation came to a bloody end. Israelites carrying swords and assegais were met by hundreds of policemen and army troops, who opened fire with machine guns. Nearly two hundred members of the sect were slaughtered.[66]

Similar rumors of Garveyist mobilization contributed to the radicalization of the Kimbanguist revival in the Congo. In the spring of 1921, a young Bakongo Christian named Simon Kimbangu announced that he had been called to heal and preach in the name of the Lord, broke from his European mission, and inaugurated an independent African ministry. Thousands flocked to Kimbangu's village, which became known as Jerusalem.[67] European observers, at first delighted by Kimbangu's assault on traditional beliefs and his strict condemnation of alcohol and "lascivious dance," soon became alarmed by reports of Kimbanguist prophets urging people not to work for whites, nor to pay taxes to the state. The Léopoldville-based newspaper, *L'Avenir Colonial Belge*, reported in hushed tones that Kimbangu had declared the true God to be black, and that he had called for whites to be expelled from the colony, perhaps thrown into the sea. The paper noted the peculiar similarity between these extreme utterances and the propaganda of the "American agitator," Marcus Garvey, at his great convention in New York the past August.[68]

By the inauguration of Kimbangu's ministry, the *Negro World* had been filtering into the colony for several months, carried by West African migrants who joined the "invasion" of skilled workers hired to fill positions in European firms as mechanics, carpenters, ironworkers, and clerks.[69] In October 1920 authorities had captured and expelled from the colony an organizer for the UNIA and the Black Star Line who was carrying a document announcing the formation of a great organization in the United States that was committed to redeeming the Negro race and to mobilizing Africans throughout the continent.[70] Garveyism received an enthusiastic reception from a dynamic group of intellectuals based in Kinshasa, including a successful trader and bricklayer named André Yengo. Yengo and other members of this group would become the primary financial backers of the nascent Kimbanguist church.[71]

Kimbangu's personal allegiance to Garveyism remains a matter of speculation. Belgian officials, the European press, and several observers were nevertheless convinced that the spark for the movement had been lit, as Territorial Administrator Léon-Georges Morel put it, by "the pan-African movement which prevails in America." As the movement gained momentum, rumors circulated among adherents that the Belgians would be expelled from the colony by an arriving black American army. One popular version imagined the arrival of a great ship sailing up the Congo River—surely a garbled reference to the Black Star Line.[72] Along the rail line, the colony's only artery connecting Kinshasa and its west coast, rumors of a mass walkout of African workers on the occasion of Kimbangu's arrest threatened to halt the transportation of people and goods and bring production to a standstill. Thomas Moody, of the American Baptist Foreign Missionary Society, suggested that the workers were "thrilled at the chance to join the movement initiated by Marcus Garvey." As Father J. C. Van Cleemput of the Redemptorist Mission observed, "the battle cry of the [Kimbanguist] movement . . . [is] to found a prophet religion, a Negro religion, to destroy the whites and expel them, to gain independence: in a word, 'Africa for the Africans.'"[73]

Harry Thuku and the Radical Moment in Central Kenya

In November 1920 the *East African Chronicle* published a short report on the "Conference of Negroes" in New York, noting that a group of American, West Indian, and African delegates had assembled to tell Europeans to "clear away from the soil of Africa."[74] The *Chronicle* was a Nairobi-based paper, edited by the secretary of the East African Indian National Congress (EAINC), M. A. Desai. It was one of the mouthpieces of a cosmopolitan group of young activists—African, Indian, Arab, Swahili—who had been brought together in Nairobi, radicalized by the war, and inspired by the wave of anticolonial agitation and colored solidarity rippling across the world in its wake. Out of that milieu would emerge a dramatic challenge to colonial authority, what the leading missionary in Kikuyuland, John W. Arthur of the Presbyterian Church of Scotland Mission (CSM), described as "the first native rising in Kenya."[75] As elsewhere in the unsettled postwar years, it was a challenge explicable only in the convergence of global discourses and local particularities and frustrations. In central Kenya, the provocative narratives of Indian self-determination and Garveyist mobilization together generated the subversive idea that amidst the gathering clash of peoples of color, global and local experiences spoke to a shared history, and gestured to a common, liberated future.

The trouble in central Kenya can be traced back to the violent birth of the colony. The British "pacification" of the region began in earnest after the Imperial British East African Company transferred control of the protectorate to the Foreign Office in 1895.[76] Heavily armed expeditions of British commanders, regulars of the King's African Rifles, Swahili from the coast, Masai warriors, and Kikuyu collaborators stalked through Kikuyuland, burning villages, seizing livestock and supplies, and engaging in a series of local battles against pockets of Kikuyu resistance that left thousands dead.[77] By cruel chance, British aggression was accompanied by a series of plagues that devastated the land one after the other. The arrival of rinderpest and an outbreak of bovine pleuropneumonia devastated cattle stock; locusts and drought decimated crops. The severe famine that followed produced mass dislocations, which in turn sparked a smallpox epidemic. For some local populations, mortality rates reached as high as seventy percent.[78]

With administrative control established over much of what became the Kikuyu districts of Fort Hall (Murang'a), Kiambu, Nyeri, Embu, and Meru by the next year, attention shifted to the solemn burden of the imperial "civilizing mission." The CSM reached central Kenya by 1898, followed by the Anglican Church Mission Society (CMS) in 1899, the American-based and interdenominational Africa Inland Mission (AIM) in 1901, and the Methodist Missionary Society in 1909. Rather than compete for converts, the missions divided the spoils of Kikuyuland into distinct spheres of influence. When this informal arrangement became unwieldy, representatives of the four missions established a central governing structure, the Alliance of Protestant Missions, to facilitate cooperation, resolve disputes, and coordinate strategy.[79]

British officials, for their part, set to work on the second plank of the "civilizing mission," establishing the infrastructure for a commercial export economy that would allow the Protectorate to become self-supporting— thereby sustaining the exercise of white tutelage without burdening taxpayers at home—while disciplining Africans in the virtues of Protestant work ethic and labor capitalism. Beginning in 1902, a year after the completion of the Uganda Railway, which snaked through the fertile agricultural lands of central Kenya on its way from the coast to Lake Victoria, the government opened up large tracts of land to white settlement in the highlands of southern Kiambu and in the Rift Valley Province. The logistics of land alienation fell particularly hard on the Kikuyu; by the outbreak of the First World War, 60,000 acres had been transferred from Kikuyu *mbari* (sub-clans) in

Kiambu to white ownership. Confined to reserves with insufficient land, compelled to pay hut and poll taxes, debarred from growing cash crops of their own, Kikuyu men entered into squatters' contracts with the new white aristocracy, or entered into seasonal labor arrangements. Women were left home to shoulder the burden of domestic production, or they were driven to nearby Nairobi, where many carved careers for themselves as brewers, traders, landlords, and prostitutes.[80] "Thus the chain is complete," wrote Jomo Kenyatta grimly.

> The Kenya Africans are robbed of their land, and driven by taxation which they cannot escape to enter into a forced contract, oral or written, as tax earners; if, in spite of everything, they refuse to enter into any such contract they can be arrested and thrown into prison and thereby forced to labor at less than the current rate of wages with which to pay their taxes, which means that they will have to work harder and longer.[81]

Norman Leys, the former Kenyan official and an increasingly vocal critic of the British colonial administration, lamented the irony that in abolishing formal slavery in East Africa—the supposed capstone of imperial morality—officials and settlers had in short time established a new coercive mechanism of perpetual servility.[82]

The war and its aftermath brought new and more horrible deprivations. Abandoning all pretense of support for free labor principles, the government pursued an aggressive policy of forcible labor recruitment, conscripting tens of thousands of men, often by press-gang and raiding, to serve in the Carrier Corps as porters. At home, the governor officially endorsed the use of compulsory labor for infrastructure work and cash crop production. Those not among the estimated 23,000 Kenyan Africans who died during the war, mainly from disease, returned home to find villages in disrepair and decay, and domestic food production in crisis. The resulting famine claimed the lives of 14,000 people. The next year, the great influenza epidemic claimed the lives of 155,000 more. Out of nearly a million Kikuyu, roughly 120,000 perished.[83]

Several observers voiced alarm at the extent of African suffering. Norman Leys, who had been transferred from Kenya to Nyasaland (Malawi) in 1913, was convinced that an insurrection on the order of the Chilembwe rising was inevitable unless the government acted immediately to secure adequate tribal lands and to end forced labor in all forms.[84] Fueling this concern was the common belief that the East African Campaign had irreversibly shattered one of the foundational mythologies of the colonial project: the prestige and respect bestowed on men with white skins by awed and deferential tribesmen. The supposed boon of the imperial project—the vaunted protection against the fierce intertribal warfare of colony mythology—was now

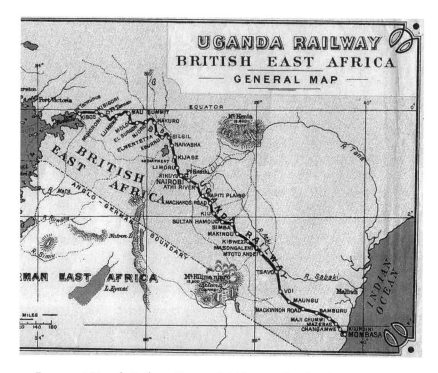

FIGURE 3.6. Uganda Railway. (Source: *British East Africa* [brochure], Newland, Tarlton & Co., Ltd, 1909–10)

revealed as a hypocritical construct. Observers worried about the psychological consequences of black troops witnessing the shooting and bayoneting of Europeans by enemy black soldiers.[85] Perhaps most disturbing was that in drawing together black peoples from across the continent and across the sea in common cause, the East African Campaign had scattered the seditious seeds of race consciousness among heretofore loyal subjects.[86] Suggesting that reconciling the claims of white settlement with "the acknowledged rights of a 'Protectorate' people" in Kenya was a "stupendous task," Handley D. Hooper of the CMS mission at Kahuhia, Fort Hall warned that the rising tide of color consciousness could only be stemmed by compassionate and liberal reform.[87]

Rather than heed these warnings, the Kenyan administration, bowing unambiguously to the aspirations of an increasingly powerful settler community, chose to double down. To enforce labor discipline on the farms, the government introduced the *kipande* system, which required African males over the age of sixteen to carry registration papers at all times, placed in metal containers and worn around the neck. Failure to produce one's papers meant fines or imprisonment; by February 1922, approximately two years after the introduction of the system, over 8,000 men had been convicted, and tens of thousands detained. The papers themselves placed workers at the mercy of their employers. "There was one space where the employer had to sign when he engaged you and also when you left," remembered Harry Thuku.

> You could not leave employment without permission, and if you did, you could be taken to the DC's [District Commissioner's] court. Also, no other employer would take you if the space for discharge was not filled up. Another thing in the early kind of *kipande* was a space for remarks; and here, if an employer did not like you, he could spoil your name completely by putting "lazy," "disobedient," or "cheeky."[88]

To meet the mounting labor demands, created by demographic catastrophe and exacerbated by booming coffee production, the new governor, Sir Edward Northey, doubled the hut and poll taxes. When this intervention did not satisfy needs, he issued the infamous Northey Circular in October 1919, encouraging "Government officials in charge of native areas"—African chiefs and headmen—to "exercise every possible lawful influence to induce able-bodied natives to go into the labour field," including women and children. Chiefs and headmen—a collection of men with no claim to legitimacy among the formerly stateless Kikuyu other than their loyal execution of administrative directives—would be monitored by district commissioners, who would "keep a record of the names of those Chiefs and Headmen who are helpful and those who are unhelpful." Opposition came from the Alliance of Missionary Societies, which supported the idea that young African men were better off at work rather than "loafing about the Native Reserves, dressing themselves in paint and feathers and dancing their immoral dances," but worried about the "evil effects" resulting from the legislation—perhaps a reference to the paramilitary press-gangs assembled by chiefs to round up labor conscripts, or perhaps a nod to widespread instances of bribery, corruption, and exploitation of female workers, including physical and sexual abuse. One unexplored solution to the labor crisis was the raising of wages. Instead, settlers took the opportunity of vigorous state repression to reduce farm wages by a third.[89]

*

In April 1921, the Kikuyu Association (KA) was organized in the Kiambu Reserve by four headmen led by Koinange wa Mbiyu, with the intention of establishing a legitimate channel for Kikuyu subjects to express their mounting disaffection with the operation of the colony. On June 24, at a large *baraza* attended by senior chiefs, government officials, missionaries, and members of the KA, the organization was afforded "virtual recognition," and, with the help of A. R. Barlow of the CSM, drafted a "Memorandum of

Grievances," to be submitted "constitutionally" through the proper hierarchy of command. The meeting was historic: The KA was the first political organization formed by Kenyan Africans in the colonial era. Yet its emergence was almost immediately overshadowed. With the KA's official secretary unable to attend the *baraza* with an illness, the role of transcribing the memorandum was given to Harry Thuku, a young, mission-educated man from a prominent lineage in Kiambu. At the close of the meeting, Thuku found himself still in possession of a copy of the document. Rather than submit it to the elders, he tucked it away and returned to Nairobi.[90]

Thuku had moved to Nairobi in 1911, at the age of sixteen, and was by 1921 employed as a telephone operator in the government Treasury. He inhabited a cosmopolitan space a world removed from the Kiambu district, which abutted Nairobi to the north. Living in the neighborhood of Pangani village, Thuku rubbed shoulders with young African clerks from Luo, Kamba, Kikuyu, and the coast; with Baganda migrants, Indians, Arabs, and Swahili; with Christians, Muslims, and animists. Together this multiethnic community was beginning to remake Kenya's colonial capital as a hub of East African political activity. The East African Indian National Congress, launched in 1914 as a cautious reformist vehicle, had by 1920 been radicalized in step with the rising tide of anticolonial activism in India. The EAINC was joined by the Arab Association in 1921, and the National Union of Baganda Workers, which represented the interests of Baganda clerks, teachers, and workers living in Nairobi, and published the journal *Sekanyolya*.[91] European observers like Handley Hooper attributed "the growth of modernism" in Nairobi to the machinations of Indian agitators, but the truth was far more complex.[92] The "Indian question," as elsewhere in the colony, was indeed a source of bitter dispute, and opened up a gulf between the advocates of Indian rights in the *East African Chronicle* and advocates of African rights in *Sekanyolya*.[93] Non-European denizens of Nairobi inhabited a dynamic public sphere in the making, with multiple points of connection and division, solidarity and contestation.

Thuku's politicization began just before the war, when he was hired by the settler-friendly weekly, the *Leader of British East Africa*, as a compositor and machine man, and exposed to the unrelenting hostility of settler opinion toward African aspirations. Near the end of the war, he met M. A. Desai, and the two men established a close friendship, meeting often to have long discussions about politics. Thuku was introduced to another future collaborator, Abdulla Tairara bin Assuman, a distant relative and head of the small Kikuyu-Muslim community residing in Pangani. And he made numerous contacts with politicized Bagandans, including S. K. Sentongo, editor of *Sekanyolya*, and Joswa Kamulegeya, secretary of the Young Baganda Association (YBA), a Kampala-based clique of educated young Africans committed to nonconfrontational political advocacy.[94] By the time Thuku learned that a *baraza* had been called in Kiambu to form a new organization for the Kikuyu, his immersion in Nairobi's activist networks had convinced him both of the need for such an organization and of the importance that it reflect the sensibilities of his colleagues in the capital rather than those of the established authority figures in the reserves.

Before attending the meeting in Kiambu, Thuku had hastily assembled his own group, the Young Kikuyu Association (YKA), which he modeled on the YBA. Back in Nairobi, however, in possession of the Barlow Memo, he began to formulate broader ambitions. On July 1, the members of the YKA met and renamed their organization the East African Association (EAA)—"so that anyone in the whole area could join," explained Thuku. At a mass meeting, fiery speeches were delivered by Kikuyu, Kamba, and Luo representatives, new resolutions were drawn up, and, with the help of Desai, a cable was composed and sent to the prime minister in England. Three days later, Thuku sent the full text of the EAA's resolutions, along with the Barlow Memo, to the chief native commissioner in Nairobi. Adding to the list of KA grievances—against the forced labor of women, land alienation, the *kipande* system, high taxes, the paucity of resources for African education—the EAA declared African solidarity with Indians, demanded the franchise for all educated subjects, and empowered a delegation led by Jeevanjee, headed to London to argue the Indian case before Winston Churchill, then Secretary of State for the Colonies, to represent the African cause as well. The entire exercise was provocative. In bypassing acceptable protocol and appealing directly to the highest officials of British administration, Thuku was implicitly challenging the legitimacy of local administrators to resolve African grievances. And by acting unilaterally without the consent or the knowledge of the KA, he was forcefully claiming his own organization as the legitimate voice of his people.[95]

To solidify this claim to leadership, Thuku launched an extensive organizing and propaganda tour of the African reserves. Enjoying limited success in the KA stronghold of southern Kiambu, the EAA won large numbers of followers, primarily among young Christians, in the Kikuyu reserves of Fort Hall and Nyeri, and among squatters on the European farms.[96] Traveling west of Kikuyu Province to Machakos District, Thuku convened a meeting with local leaders to explain the aims of the organization and to win an alliance with the Kamba, but without success.[97] In Luo country, however, several "enthusiastic" meetings were held at Maseno Mission Station, and money was raised for the cause.[98] By the end of 1921, Thuku had amassed a collection of supporters that remained largely Kikuyu, but which included Christians and Muslims, Nandi and Luo, Kamba and Masai. The beginnings of an organizational edifice had been established, comprised of district branches, delegates, and secret meetings.[99] Followers were asked to take an oath pledging loyalty to the country and promising allegiance to the

EAA—rather than the white man—on pain of death.[100] Handley Hooper, who believed as late as January 1922 that the EAA was restricted to "a few clever educated native boys," was invited to a secret session with anti-Thuku Christians and was shocked to learn of the reach of the organization in his own district, Fort Hall. From Kiambu, J. W. Arthur observed that "[t]he [political] development of the native peoples in Kenya . . . is simply past thinking," and suggested that Thuku "has now got ahold of . . . the majority of young Kikuyu Christians."[101]

Thuku's political message during this period of mobilization combined a broad attack against the legitimacy of European, missionary, and chiefly authority with a dynamic appeal to pan-African unity as the foundation of a new political order. At the end of November, the EAA organized a mass meeting in Fort Hall and drafted a new series of resolutions that demanded authorization, upon the failure of local government agents to redress grievances, for the chairman of the organization to appeal directly to Churchill in London. But by this time Thuku was no longer satisfied with official memoranda. "[T]he District Commissioner is nothing to us, nor is any European anything to us," he declared near the end of December. "Now if anyone wants a friendship with us we also want to be friendly with him, but with him who does not want to be friends with us we do not want friendship, even if he is a European, may he perish at a distance." In a series of mass meetings, culminating in a large gathering at Weithaga in Fort Hall at the end of February, Thuku instructed his followers to embark on a campaign of non-cooperation, to throw away their *kipande* papers, to refuse to perform unpaid work on roads and in the camps, to refuse to provide porters with firewood or food, and to prevent others from doing so. In meetings and in his broadsheet *Tangazo* he accused European missionaries of conspiring to "cover the land with darkness," and to keep their flocks "unenlightened." Salvation depended on the willingness of Kenya's "black people" to set aside their quarrels with each other, to unite behind a new idea of leadership that replaced tribal boundaries with the idea that Africans "were all one family and that there was no difference between all the tribes of Kenya."[102]

Thuku's argument creatively built on and synthesized the two dominant anticolonial discourses swirling through east Africa in the years following the war: Indian nationalism and Garveyist radicalism. Thuku's immersion in the politics of the EAINC went far beyond his friendship with Desai. The EAA office was located in the same building as the *East African Chronicle*, and Thuku used the *Chronicle* press to publish *Tangazo*, which first appeared in December 1921. While EAA leaders were not the "political pawns" of Indian interests that Hooper assumed them to be, they benefited from the experience, connections, and advice of activists in the pan-Indian *Swaraj* movement. When Gandhi's close friend and advisor, Reverend C. F.

Andrews, visited Nairobi in the second half of 1921, he was introduced to Thuku by Desai, and met with him "nearly every day." While canvassing the reserves, Thuku likened himself to Gandhi, whom he noted had been ignored at first, but now had grown "very powerful with many followers."[103]

It is clear that Thuku was influenced by the editorial perspective of the *East African Chronicle*. Like the *Negro World*, the *Chronicle* assiduously chronicled and celebrated the "spirit of combination and unity" emerging from all the "subject races" within Kenya and abroad. Praising the emergence of the Arab Association and the "awakening" of the "natives of this country ... from their long sleep" under the influence of the EAA, Desai envisioned a future alliance of colored peoples "in one common propaganda for a common cause—the political and racial rights of those concerned." In a long article published on August 27, 1921, Desai argued that the British Empire was at a crossroads: along one path, a "wonderful conglomeration of races and creeds and nations" enjoying equal rights; along the other a perpetuation of an "aggressive and autocratic policy" that rested on a temporary "suppression of the coloured races," and assured the destruction of the imperial project by those same darker peoples.[104]

In the same issue, the *Chronicle* published a report on the UNIA's Second International Convention, noting with enthusiasm that Garvey had sent a cable to Gandhi on behalf of the Negro peoples of the world expressing support for "the speedy emancipation of India from the thralldom of foreign oppression." For Desai, the cable was further proof of a "Great World Movement" that was coalescing around the demand for the subject peoples of the world to manage their own affairs. "The Negro Congress has outlined its ideas and aspirations of 'Africa for the African,' and the day may not be so far distant as some people imagine when this continent will not be ruled solely by those of European origin," he wrote. "It would seem to be impossible to stem this ever-growing flood of national desires and aspirations."[105]

The suggestive content of the report, and the timing of its publication—just prior to the EAA's organizing push in the reserves—lends credibility to the view that it had a formative effect on Thuku's developing activism. During the war, many East Africans had come into contact with African Americans for the first time while serving with the Carrier Corps. In Dar es Salaam, Max Yergan and other secretaries of the Colored YMCA of America established night schools for stationed African carriers, and frequently advertised the advantages of pursuing further education in the United States. After the war, Joswa Kamulegeya established contacts with administrators at the Tuskegee Institute, and successfully petitioned to send his younger brother to the school in 1920. Through his correspondence with Kamulegeya and the mission-educated network of Africans centered in Kampala and Nairobi, Thuku had access to the stream of African American literature, including the *Negro World*, which entered the colony via black sailors and through private correspondence. Like Kamulegeya, Thuku interpreted African American politics through a prism that narrowed intra-racial rivalries and competing political visions into a singular visage of black sophistication, independence, and solidarity. From his perspective, Marcus Garvey, W.E.B. Du Bois, and Tuskegee's president Robert Moton were engaged in a shared project that mirrored the struggle of the Indian diaspora. One can imagine that he read the report from New York with a quickening sense of excitement.[106]

Less than two weeks later, Thuku penned a pair of letters, one to the secretary of the UNIA, the other to the secretary of the Tuskegee Institute. Unfortunately, only the second letter has survived. Thuku attacked the hypocrisy of the British civilizing mission, declaring the project of colonial uplift "a hollow boast" and a "horrid myth" that threatened to "annihilate and wipe out native races from the land of their fore-fathers at no distant date." The remedy, in Thuku's view, was "unification" and education; his reading of "books and newspapers . . . dealing with the condition of Negro races in America," he wrote, had convinced him of the "necessity . . . of having our own man—a kinsman brother, and a leader, who has devoted his life and renounced everything for the elevation and uplifting of . . . [our] primitive race." But Kenya was hampered with an insufficient number of "educated natives" to complete the task on their own. Thuku wondered if "a Booker T. Washington or a Du Bois can be spared for founding a 'Tuskegee' in the African wilds and for the holy Mission of up-lifting and emancipating the hopeless, hapless struggling 3,000,000 nude Native souls from deep ignorance, object porvity [sic], and grinding oppression of the white settlers" of the colony.[107]

If Thuku had any doubts about the reach and influence of the UNIA, they were dispelled over the next few months. First, Thuku began receiving Garveyite missives and materials from New York. At around the same time, Ugandan activist Daudi Basudde returned to Kenya from England with a breathless account of Garveyism's gathering strength. "The progress of the Blacks, especially in America and West Africa, astonishes the people and causes those in Europe and other countries everywhere to fear," Basudde explained in an interview published in *Sekanyolya*. The UNIA had acquired "their own ships on the sea" and a membership of "close to five million." The organization now had "under consideration the question of Africa for the Blacks," and was "convinced that . . . Blacks in the world [will] undoubtedly acquire a kingdom in their land of Africa."[108]

By the first months of 1922, Thuku had cast himself as an East African Moses, Kenya as Pharaoh's Egypt. "He is seen as a deliverer of the prophetic type, and religious fervour is contributing to his popularity," observed Handley Hooper with concern in early March. In a prayer published in the *East African Chronicle*, "Christians of all districts of Africa and Uganda" were asked to "pray from Bwana Harry Thuku our leader and the elders," who had been "set apart by our God to be our guides in our present condition of slavery which we knew not before the Europeans came into this our country of East Africa." Africans were encouraged to remember the story of David and Goliath, and "to pray for our Guide and his supporters" in the same manner that Europeans prayed for King George. At a meeting in Fort Hall on March 11, standing astride a motor car, Thuku declared witness to his own power:

> If anyone takes a Government officer milk it is the duty of any one of my followers to spill it; if anyone takes wood it is to be thrown away. The chiefs are nobody. If I send a letter to the Governor a chief would be dismissed at once. If any man is called for road work, he is not to go unless he gets paid.

According to a witness, Thuku said, "I want to drive the Europeans from this country because God has appointed me to be your leader."[109]

Thuku was seized by authorities three days later. A hasty investigation and a raid of the offices of the *Chronicle*, ordered after the publication of Thuku's prayer, demonstrated to shocked officials the extent to which the EAA had galvanized and emboldened its rank and file. Learning of Thuku's arrest on the morning of March 15, EAA leaders called for a general strike in Nairobi, which they supported with pickets, patrols of the town to ensure compliance, rallies, and a march to the police station, where Thuku was being held, to demand his release. By midday on March 16 the crowd had swelled to seven or eight thousand men and women, facing off against a wall of *askari* armed with bayonets. After a long meeting between six representatives of the protesters and Colonial Secretary Sir Charles Bowring the representatives returned to the crowd and attempted to disperse it. But as some moved to leave, a group of between 200 and 250 women began to taunt the men for their cowardice. According to EAA organizer Job Muchuchu, another participant in the EAA, Mary Muthoni Nyanjiru, "leapt to her feet, pulled her dress right up over her shoulders and shouted to the men: 'You take my dress and give me your trousers. You men are cowards. What are you waiting for? Our leader is in there. Let's get him.'"[110] As the crowd surged forward, pushing a wave of bodies toward the *askaris*' bayonets, a shot was fired, followed by several more. According to Muchuchu, white settlers watching the unfolding events from the nearby Norfolk Hotel also opened fire on the crowd. After an investigation, the government reported the death toll at twenty-one, among them Mary Nyanjiru. A mortuary worker sympathetic to the EAA counted fifty-six bodies in the morgue.[111]

On March 19, at Liberty Hall in New York, Marcus Garvey started his weekly address by reading a press dispatch from London relaying news of the "disturbance" in Kenya. "In all civilized communities men are allowed, even subjects are allowed the right, to protest," thundered Garvey. "The shooting was done because these 6,000 white 'aristocrats' were afraid of their own skin; because they knew from the Christian sense of righteousness that they had no right in those people's country, and because they saw the people in an attitude wherein they were indignant to what had been done to them, and they were not prepared to take any chances." In the "spirit of disgust," Garvey sent a cablegram to David Lloyd George:

> Four hundred million Negroes through the Universal Negro Improvement Association hereby register their protest against the brutal manner in which your government has treated the natives of Kenya, East Africa. You have shot down a defenseless people in their own native land for exercising their rights as men. Such a policy will only tend to aggr[a]vate the many historic injustices heaped upon a race that will one day be placed in a position to truly defend itself, not with mere sticks, clubs and stones, but with modern implements of science. Again we ask you and your government to be just to our race, for surely, we shall not forget you. The evolutionary scale that weighs nations and races, balances alike for all peoples; hence we feel sure that some day the balance will register a change.

White observers in Kenya, for their part, breathed a partial sigh of relief. H. D. Hooper remarked that the bloodshed in Nairobi "very probably prevented a much bigger loss of life in a more general commotion." J. W. Arthur, who on the day of Thuku's arrest had addressed an urgent letter to London predicting a "native rising," observed that the "ghastly tragedy" would have been "infi[ni]tely more serious if it had started in the country . . . with the massacre of isolated Europeans." "We are thankful today," he wrote, "because we believe that the trouble is well in hand and with Thuku's arrest things should quieten down all over."[112]

Chapter Four

"THE SILENT WORK THAT MUST BE DONE"

THE OPENING parade of the Second International Convention of Negroes of the World stretched two miles, up and down the wide avenues of Seventh and Lenox. Large crowds assembled along the parade route, and residents hung streamers bearing the UNIA tricolor, the red, black, and green. Harlem, the *Negro World* boasted, had declared an unofficial public holiday. Leading the estimated ten thousand parade participants was Captain E. L. Gaines, the head of the Universal African Legions, astride a horse. The Black Star Line band and Liberty Hall choir played behind him. Then came the officials of the High Executive Council, each riding in their own automobile: Honorable Gabriel M. Johnson, High Potentate and Mayor of Monrovia; the Chaplain General, Reverend Dr. George Alexander McGuire; Leader of American Negroes Reverend James W. H. Eason; International Organizer Miss Henrietta Vinton Davis; and President General of the UNIA and Provisional President of Africa Marcus Garvey. After the executive council came crew members of the S.S. *Yarmouth*, followed by uniformed members of the New York African Legion, Motor Corps, Black Cross Nurses, and Juvenile Corps. Representatives of divisions, foreign and domestic, stretched into the distance. The infantry band of the 369th regiment—the famed Harlem Hellfighters—delighted the crowd with jazz music. Banners were unfurled block after block broadcasting fragments of collective Garveyite wisdom: "Scattered Africa united"; "The Negro gave civilization to the world"; "Negroes, hitch your wagon to the Black Star"; "Africa shall be redeemed."[1]

The parade offered persuasive visual evidence of the UNIA's spectacular growth in the year since the convention of 1920. By the Second International Convention, which opened on August 1, 1921, the organization had expanded to over four hundred chartered divisions, with another four hundred awaiting official approval from the parent body. Circulation of the *Negro World* tripled in 1921, rising to 75,000 and providing the UNIA with a reliable source of weekly income. Garvey's tour of the Caribbean and Central America from February to July attracted throngs of enthusiastic supporters and left observers marveling at the president general's fundraising prowess. The sale of Black Star Line stock certificates continued apace; according to one estimate, from February 1919 to August 1921, the shipping venture raised more than $750,000.[2]

By late 1921, however, outward displays of UNIA strength were belied by an accelerating and multipronged institutional crisis. In the United States, the return to "normalcy" following the war and its unsettled aftermath was one manifestation of a global wave of conservative readjustment that sharply circumscribed the landscape of black politics for the remainder of the decade. Federal authorities were in the midst of manufacturing a legal case against Garvey that would cast a shadow over his activities from his arrest in January 1922, through his trial, imprisonment, and ultimate deportation in December 1927. Despite repeated assurances to the contrary, the finances of the Black Star Line were in ruin, the impressive fundraising tallies overwhelmed by mismanagement, inexperience, and graft. By December, the *Yarmouth* had been sold for a fraction of its purchase price, and in February, shortly after Garvey's arrest, the operations of the Black Star Line were shut down entirely. As the infrastructure of his government-in-exile began to rot, Garvey's leadership became increasingly authoritarian, paranoiac, and reckless. Acrimonious feuds with his enemies in the black intelligentsia—both real and perceived, both inside and outside his organization—were exacerbated by Garvey's retreat from radical politics, and his increasingly bold embrace of racial purity and separatism. Mounting pressures revealed the UNIA's ugly, violent subculture, culminating in the assassination of Eason months after his split with the organization.

The day after Garvey's arrest, the *New York World* declared an end to his "bizarre career." In February 1923 W.E.B. Du Bois published a smug article in *Century Magazine*, comprehensively detailing Garvey's financial and organizational failures, ridiculing his "childish ignorance of the stern facts of the world," and congratulating members of his generation for surviving the "two grand temptations" of Washingtonianism and Garveyism.[3] Such eulogies were premature. Somewhat paradoxically, the Age of Garvey would rise, phoenix-like, from the ashes of the UNIA's imperial dream. The decline of Garvey's institutional empire provided space for the emergence of a "second period" of modest organization building and consciousness raising, generated as much by the needs and expectations of the Garveyite rank and file as by Garvey himself, as much by the limits and constraints of a reactionary age as by the "freedom dreams" of energetic black activists.[4] As the chapters of part two seek to demonstrate, the lasting legacy of Marcus Garvey would be forged not in the radical moment of 1919–20, nor in the grand theatrics and ostentatious scheming that made Garvey famous, but in the sustained commitment to movement making—locally rendered, globally framed.

MANDATES, MONGRELS, AND THE SACRED TRUST OF CIVILIZATION

On February 3, 1924, hours after the death of Woodrow Wilson, Marcus Garvey took the opportunity in his weekly address at Liberty Hall to offer his thoughts on the oversized legacy left by the former president. Wilson, suggested Garvey, did not fully understand what he was doing when he pledged to make "the world safe for democracy" and to affirm "the freedom of the weaker peoples of the world." He had nevertheless "started the world aflame." To his horror, he "found the people of Asia had taken up the cry; he found that the scattered Negroes of the world and Africa had taken up the cry." He found that he had "stirred up one billion men" who were held in bondage by the world's white minority. The League of Nations, argued Garvey, amounted to an effort to put the genie of global self-determination back in the bottle, an attempt by the assembled delegates to draw together the "scattered forces of . . . [the] race" in a united effort to reestablish the racial infrastructure of the prewar world. It is "the special duty of the white people to mourn for a great white leader," Garvey declared, for "as a white man Woodrow Wilson's loftiest purpose and idea was to see the perpetuation of the white man's rule of the world."[5]

Garvey's history lesson lacked a certain amount of nuance, but in 1924 it was certainly easy enough to understand his point. By then the radical demands for racial justice that characterized the postwar period had been overwhelmed by a powerful counterrevolution of policy, ideas, and often stark repression. Conservative governments were ascendant across the Western world, most spectacularly in Italy, where Benito Mussolini's fascists swept into power. Colonial regimes across Africa, briefly staggered by the war, waged successful battles to reestablish control. In French West Africa, the canny political negotiations of Blaise Diagne gave way to a new emphasis on racial separation, new anxieties about interracial sexual contact, and a governing philosophy that expressed new doubts about the prospect of Africans acquiring a fitness for full French citizenship. Custodians of the British Empire, now conceding that the status quo in South Asia could not hold, renewed their energies in Africa with what P. J. Cain and A. G. Hopkins describe as a "crusading zeal."[6] In the United States, the hyperpatriotism of "100 percent Americanism" was redirected after the war into populist campaigns against Bolshevists, labor organizers, blacks, Jews, feminists, and foreigners of all stripes. By 1924, a reconstituted Ku Klux Klan claimed five million members across the country—ordinary, middle-class (white, Protestant) citizens—and wielded decisive political power in several states. The same year, Congress passed the Johnson-Reed Act, a landmark nativist bill designed to virtually eliminate immigration from Asia, reduce immigration from southern and eastern Europe to a trickle, and generally

FIGURE 4.1. Ku Klux Klan parade in Washington, D.C., 1926. (Library of Congress, Prints and Photographs Division, Washington, D.C.)

ensure, as President Calvin Coolidge remarked as he signed the bill into law, that "America . . . be kept American."[7]

By 1924, the League of Nations was indeed viewed by many as the institutional bulwark of a renewed, and more refined, white supremacy. The war and its aftermath had unleashed the twin—and, in the minds of many administrators, conjoined—dangers of Bolshevism and anticolonial radicalism, both of which aspired to overturn the imperial world order. For liberal internationalists like Woodrow Wilson, such a reckless application of the slogan "self-determination" posed a threat to global governance by unnaturally elevating "backward" peoples untutored in the arts of civilization. "Commonsense," wrote John Harris of the Anti-Slavery and Aborigines Protection Society, "forces us to admit the impracticability of summoning to a European Peace Congress illiterate Mandingos, Fiots, Herroros, Fans, the senile Polynesian, or the wild Bedouin." The Covenant of the League of Nations, in extending this principle, demarcated a clear line of separation between national citizens with rights and stateless subjects deemed unprepared for the exercise of those rights. Article 22 established a system of "mandates" in the colonies and territories ceded by Germany in the war, places inhabited by "peoples not yet able to stand by themselves under the strenuous conditions of the modern world," and delegated to the "advanced nations" of Britain, France, Belgium, and South Africa so that they make undertake the responsibility of administration and "tutelage."[8]

During the postwar reconstruction period, liberal internationalists in Britain, thoroughly convinced that the benefits of empire far outweighed any concerns, set themselves to the task of polishing the rhetorical armor of the civilizing mission. Article 22, argued Leonard S. Woolf of the Labour Party and Fabian Society, was "the antithesis of imperialism," its emphasis on the well-being of those peoples of color "not able at once to adapt themselves to the world's changed conditions" an antidote to the excesses of stark "economic exploitation" in the colonies. The task of the "new era" in Africa, agreed E. D. Morel, was to "convey a clear notion of the atrocious wrongs which the white peoples have inflicted upon the black," take stock of old failures, and soberly "lay down the fundamental principles of a humane and practical policy in the government of Africa by white men." Divided in the precise application of imperial rule, policymakers and members of the intelligentsia were nevertheless united in the conviction that the governance of peoples of color after the war must be handled with more intelligence and foresight than in the past. "There must be no reversion to the Congo regime, however much it may recommend itself to British captains of industry," declared Sir Harry H. Johnston. "The White man must realize straightaway that the time for exploiting the Black men and the Yellow man is over," that "the days of forced labour are gone," that, for example, the "magnificent results of the White man's engineering in Egypt are overcast by the bad manners of the English officer … and British tourist towards the Egyptian."[9]

As Frederick Cooper has wonderfully illustrated, the model of imperial governance that became entrenched after the war—"indirect rule" in the British colonies, "association" in the French ones—was a case of administrators declaring victory in the face of defeat. Attempts to transform tropical African colonies into rational export economies in the preceding decades were resisted by African peasants, forcing officials to relinquish their project of steady proletarianization in favor of hybrid forms of tenancy and smallholder production. For Frederick Lugard, the primary architect of indirect rule, these unexpected contingencies on the ground offered proof of the existence of inescapable cultural differences that precluded the development of African colonies along European lines, and suggested a need to revisit "traditional" forms of African governance and social organization that might more effectively stabilize British rule. "We are perhaps somewhat too apt to take it for granted that the introduction of civilization must add to the happiness of the natives in Africa," wrote Lugard in his masterwork, *The Dual Mandate in British Tropical Africa*. "The ascent of man to a higher plane of intelligence, self-control, and responsibility is a process not unattended by pain." Rather than force a "revolution" in African social life and custom, administrators should embrace "representative institutions" and the local government of "hereditary dynasties" and "native chiefs" more in accord with "racial instincts and inherited traditions." The "dual mandate" of "civilized administration" following the war need not amount to "pure philanthropy," because it offered attractive and reciprocal benefits: for "backward races," the opportunity to develop their "national genius" at their own pace, and shielded from the pressures of the modern world; for war-torn Europe, a steady and reliable supply of tropical foodstuffs and raw materials, and a promise that white entrepreneurs might continue to "employ their technical skill, their energy, and their capital . . . in fulfillment of the Mandate of civilization."[10]

The revised civilizing mission of mandates, indirect rule, and association had roots in the articulation of segregationist regimes in South Africa and the American New South; as Andrew Zimmerman has argued, postwar administrators codified Jim Crow as a worthy model for the global governance of nonwhite peoples.[11] Across tropical Africa, statesmen, missionaries, and philanthropists collaborated on the most effective means of preserving the integrity of newly "invented" modes of traditional "tribal" custom, while maintaining generous pools of cheap, mobile labor to service the continent's extractive and export economy.[12] By the 1920s, thanks in large part to the oversized influence of Thomas Jesse Jones of the American Phelps-Stokes Commission and J. H. Oldham of the British International Missionary Council, the insights of the Hampton-Tuskegee model of Negro education—fundamentally, as Lugard noted, that education must be adapted to the racial particularities of its pupils—had been widely applied in colonial pedagogy. "Here then is the true conception of the interrelation of colour," wrote Lugard in 1921, invoking Booker Washington's Atlanta Compromise. "[I]n matters social and racial a separate path, each pursuing his own inherited traditions, preserving his own race-purity and race-pride; equality in things spiritual; agreed divergence in the physical and material."[13]

The stiffening, "crustaceous borders" of the global color line in the 1920s were given added priority by the era's ascendant, and pervasive, understandings of racial difference.[14] Intelligence tests, developed in the decade before the war, were read as conclusive proof of white intellectual superiority, and seemed to confirm the theories of eugenics and Mendelian genetics, which presupposed biological, unchanging differences across generation and race type.[15] Citing the work of some of the world's most eminent scientists, popular writers devised sweeping new theories of history, sociology, and politics through the lens of the "new biological revelation," what bestselling American author Lothrop Stoddard described as "the mightiest transformation of ideas that the world has ever seen." For Stoddard, the scientific breakthroughs of Darwinism and eugenics had conclusively lifted the veil of environmentalism, revealing the natural rights tradition of Locke, Hume, Jefferson, and Mill a "pernicious delusion." All civilization, argued Harry Johnston, expressing a common opinion, flowed through white blood, the contributions to human history of places like Egypt, India, China, and Latin America explained by white travelers and intermarriage, tropical kingdoms springing from "the diluted form of the half-breed." The old idea that the Negro, with a generation of proper training, might ascend the hierarchy of civilization, was absurd; "the Backward peoples have mostly stopped in some rut, some siding of human culture," wrote Johnston, "whereas the White man during the last thousand years has gone speeding ahead until he has attained the powers and outlook of a demi-god." Synthesizing the current research in heredity, genetics, eugenics, "race culture," and Mendelian principles of inheritance, Seth K. Humphrey observed that "it is a common mistake to regard non-Aryans as races in their infancy, delayed in maturing, and destined for later emergence." In truth, the races were "contemporary," their "different courses" the result of divergent physical and mental developments thousands of years in the past.[16]

The conclusion that, as Earnest Sevier Cox put it, "[c]ivilization's every pulse-beat is Caucasian," generated profound anxieties about internal and external threats to the purity and integrity of the white race. Stoddard called the Great War the "White Civil War," and warned that the two doctrines of white world politics emerging from the conflict—"national-imperialism" and "internationalism"—disregarded "the essential solidarity of the white world." Unity, argued Stoddard, was essential to stave off the menace of Bolshevism—which aspired to unravel the integrity of civilization in a "dysgenic" spree of "enforce[d] leveling, proletarian equality," and anti-racism—and the "rising tide of color" against white supremacy in the colonial world. At home, evidence that the "melting pot" was nothing but "mongrelism," and that the dilution of white racial purity through miscegenation explained the decline of ancient civilizations and threatened future ones, necessitated strict immigration laws and strictly enforced codes of social behavior. Western nations, counseled Lugard in a glowing review of Stoddard's book, "would be better engaged in legislating in the matter of eugenics than in competing with each other in armaments." After all: the "future of Western civilization" was at stake.[17]

Considered together, innovations in international politics, colonial administration, and scientific inquiry supported the conclusion, as President

Warren G. Harding declared in his famous "Birmingham Address," that "the race problem" was no longer merely a Southern concern, but a problem with global consequences and requiring a global solution. Praising the insights of both Stoddard and Lugard, Harding suggested that a grand bargain of interracial peace hinged on the recognition of "fundamental, eternal, and inescapable difference" in "things social and racial," on the hope that the "colored race" would acquire the "self-respect . . . to improve itself as a distinct race, with a heredity, a set of traditions, an array of aspirations all its own." The achievement of "natural segregations" and the abandonment of questions of "social equality" would foster "racial ambitions and pride," and set a course away from "old prejudices and old antagonism" in favor of sectional, racial, and international cooperation. Harding's speech, like much of the racial thinking in the 1920s, inverted W.E.B. Du Bois's prediction that the problem of the twentieth century would be the problem of the color line. Differences of race were not the barrier to peace and harmony, but their necessary precondition. Only by guarding the color line in perpetuity might the fevered nightmares of Bolshevism, mongrelization, and barbarity remain at bay.[18]

Retreat from Radicalism

While racial regimes were establishing new mechanisms of control in the early 1920s, the Universal Negro Improvement Association began its descent into institutional crisis. The two circumstances, of course, bore some relationship to each other. As Theodore Kornweibel has demonstrated, "[n]o black militant drew more investigation and surveillance by the Military Intelligence Division, State Department, and Bureau of Investigations . . . than Marcus Garvey." American authorities assigned a dizzying number of agents across the country, some undercover, to carefully chart the growth of the UNIA, to document the rhetoric of its leaders, and to engage in acts of economic and interpersonal sabotage. By the fall of 1919, frustrated by their failure to establish "concrete evidence" of sedition, agents at the Bureau of Investigations began to cast around for other means to establish Garvey as an "undesirable alien" and to effect his deportation. In October, J. Edgar Hoover, the new head of the Bureau's anti-radical division, noted that "there might be some proceeding against him for fraud in connection with his Black Star Line propaganda." The suggestion bore fruit nearly two-and-a-half years later, when Garvey was arrested for mail fraud related to the selling of Black Star Line stock.[19]

American and British authorities also played their part in the collapse of the Black Star Line. Most consequentially, efforts by local and federal authorities to block the purchase of the shipping company's first vessel, the S.S. *Yarmouth*, drove up the sale price far beyond the ship's value. Negotiations to purchase a transoceanic vessel from the U.S. Shipping Board in order to carry passengers and supplies to West Africa were first drawn out, and ultimately undermined, by the Bureau of Investigations. UNIA efforts to advertise passage on this ship, to be named the S.S. *Phyllis Wheatley*, and the subsequent failure of the Black Star Line to complete the sale, formed the core of the Department of Justice's prosecution against Garvey.[20]

Nevertheless, it would grossly exaggerate their influence to blame the fall of the Black Star Line on nervous white authorities. From its inauguration, the shipping company was beset by a lethal combination of inexperience, poor business management, bad luck, and widespread graft among Garvey's subordinates. The *Yarmouth* was purchased after foregoing the customary pre-sale mechanical inspections, and on the recommendation of Joshua Cockburn, the man hired by Garvey to captain the ship, who received a healthy portion of the broker's commission. The *Yarmouth* was an old vessel, in need of expensive retrofitting and constant repairs. By its third—and final—voyage to the Caribbean, the enthusiasm of the triumphant maiden voyage months earlier had completely faded. Pulling into port in Charleston, South Carolina, in August 1920, the British consul observed the vessel in "a miserable plight." "She was short of coal and provisions; there was a small pox on board; the Master complained of difficulties with his crew," he reported. If the *Yarmouth* was a fair representation of the Black Star Line, "the operations of such a concern are unlikely to accomplish any large commercial or political objects, but are better calculated to weaken the professed cause in view and to confirm prevailing conceptions as to the limitations of the negro race in the conduct of affairs."[21]

Poor management of the Black Star Line was exacerbated by the line's importance as a propaganda vehicle for the UNIA. From the beginning, as Garvey confided to an undercover agent, the ships had been purchased not only as a business proposition but "in order to better stir up the Negroes in all parts of the world" in the hopes of quickening racial and African redemption. To admit defeat, or even a temporary setback, cut across the narrative that Garvey and his organization had been carefully crafting for nearly two years. On this point there was some agreement: From the perspective of undercover agent Herbert S. Boulin (Agent P-138), "the foundation and strength of Garvey's anti-white movement rests solely on his retaining ownership of these ships"; for Garvey, the thought of revealing to his supporters the true state of affairs for the Black Star Line drove him to consider suicide.[22] Instead of acting with transparency, Garvey deepened the growing financial and organizational crisis by pushing ahead with new fundraising schemes, like the Liberian Construction Loan, that could funnel money into the repayment of unacknowledged debts, and continued to publicly celebrate the triumphs of the Black Star Line as if nothing was wrong. In early January 1921, Garvey announced that plans to transfer operations to Liberia were on track, that the *Phyllis Wheatley* would set sail for West Africa by the end of the month, and that by midyear between 50,000 and 75,000 supporters would follow the first group. When the Black Star Line's board of directors, in a hastily called meeting, asked Garvey how he intended to secure the purchase of the new transatlantic ship with no funds and mounting bills, Garvey stormed out without responding.[23]

Desperate to raise money for his sinking shipping line, in early 1921 Garvey announced plans to embark on a speaking tour of the West Indies and Central America. The calculations surrounding the trip exquisitely captured the gathering political dilemma facing both Garvey and the UNIA. On the one hand, a fundraising blitz through comparatively untapped black communities promised a financial windfall that might rescue the Black Star Line from ruin. On the other, as worried advisors warned Garvey, to leave the United States was to risk permanent exile. Indeed, after Garvey sailed out of Florida to Cuba in late February, State Department officials did everything in their power to deny him a means of return. The planned five- or six-week tour stretched into nearly five frustrating months, as Garvey's lawyer worked desperately to secure his client a visa. In the end, Garvey may have been allowed to reenter the United States only because American law enforcement officials were confident they could build a legal case against him. As William L. Hurley of the State Department observed days before Garvey's visa was finally issued, it was better to discredit Garvey in the court of law than to "martyrize him" by "insisting upon exclusion."[24]

Facing mounting legal, political, and economic crises, Garvey embarked on what Robert A. Hill has described as a tactical "retreat from radicalism." From the beginning convinced that the future of the Negro race depended on a free and liberated Africa, disdaining the engagement of organizations like the NAACP in the "white man's politics" as a "waste [of] time," Garvey now began to couch his program of African redemption in carefully crafted declarations of noninterference with constituted authority outside of the Motherland. "We are not organizing to fight against or disrespect the government of America . . . we are organizing to drive every pale-face out of Africa," Garvey told an audience in Chicago on February 1, three weeks before departing for the Caribbean. "I have been talking over the country for five years, and I know I have said nothing against the government of the United States. In fact, I think Uncle Sam is very pleased with the fact that the Negro is getting ready to protect himself and not bother Uncle Sam so much."[25]

Garvey's tour through the Caribbean and Central America—with stops in Cuba, Jamaica, Panama, Costa Rica, British Honduras, and Guatemala— was framed in similarly nonconfrontational terms. In Kingston, Garvey assured his audience—and by extension, concerned authorities—that he had "not come to Jamaica to stir up any revolution or race strife," and instructed his followers to pursue constitutional means to demand their rights. In Colón, Garvey observed that he was not there "to criticize Panama nor any Government whatsoever." In Costa Rica, Garvey met amicably with President Julio Acosta, and told West Indian migrant workers that "they should not fight" the United Fruit Company (UFC), the region's dominant employer, because the work the UFC gave them was "their bread and butter." An ecstatic G. P. Chittendon, manager of the UFC's Costa Rica division, reported after one meeting that "Garvey was the most conservative man" in attendance.[26]

Upon his return to the United States in late July, mere days before the opening of the Second International Convention, Garvey launched a multipronged propaganda campaign to reposition the UNIA on more stable political ground.[27] Crucial to this project was a new emphasis on the points of agreement between Garveyites and proponents of the racial status quo. Echoing the architects of postwar white supremacy, Garvey argued that the world had reached an age when "each race will travel in its own direction, when each national group will travel in its own avenue." Because both Negroes and whites had a distinct social, cultural and political destiny, he wrote, "the fullest opportunity should be given to both Races to develop independently a civilization of their own."[28] Furious with W.E.B. Du Bois, whom he suspected of colluding with authorities to bring about his downfall, and eager to distance his politics from the integrationist and increasingly besieged NAACP, Garvey launched a reckless and dishonest assault on Du Bois's support of the principle of social equality.[29] For decades, white supremacists had conflated the defense of social equality—by which African Americans meant, as James Weldon Johnson put it, "the right of the Negro to participate fully in all of the common rights of American citizenship and to arrange his own personal associations"—with the specter of miscegenation and unrestrained black sexuality. Now Garvey made the same gesture, accusing Du Bois, Du Bois's Pan-African Congress, and the NAACP of seeking "to produce a new race type by an amalgamation of black and white, which, to our belief, is destructive to the designs of nature." Rather than endorsing "a wholesale bastardy in the Race," Garvey lavished praise on President Harding's Birmingham Address, particularly his "uncompromising" stand "against the idea of social equality."[30]

From Garvey's perspective, these concessions to white supremacy reflected merely the reality of geopolitics in the 1920s. The Negro had squandered the opportunity of the Great War by being caught unprepared and disorganized.[31] Now that world powers had reestablished themselves, it was "a waste of time" to think that the Negro problem could be solved by "working for a better understanding between black and white people," or by making appeals to philosophy, or constitutional rights, or man's better nature—in other words, the domestic agenda of the NAACP.[32] The only answer to white power in America was black power in Africa. The fight of the "Western Negro" was not with the Ku Klux Klan, or with other white Americans, but with "the Negro himself," with those who had "accomplished nothing" and needed to "build up a nation" in order to win true respect.[33] From this perspective, argued Garvey, the Klan had done Negroes a real favor by having the nerve to speak openly to "the spirit, the feeling, the attitude of every white man in the United States of America." Once Negroes stopped believing the empty platitudes and promises of white "friends" and recognized that "the spirit of the Ku Klux Klan is in 80 or 90 percent of white Americans," they would abandon the hope that the United States promised anything for the Negro other than perpetual servitude, if not outright extermination, and turn to the real work of redeeming Africa. In June 1922, declaring the Klan "the invisible government of the United States," Garvey arranged a meeting in Atlanta with Acting Imperial Wizard Edward Young Clarke, later touting his courage in "speaking to a man who was brutally a white man" while "speaking to him as a man who was brutally a Negro."[34]

Garvey's increasingly vocal embrace of racial separatism and racial purity infuriated his rivals in the black intelligentsia. In *The Crusader*, Cyril Briggs excoriated Garvey as a "traitor" for "his shameless compromises and servile surrender of Negro rights," and condemned him for "catering to the worst passions of the Negro-hating white South." Du Bois declared Garvey "an open ally of the Ku Klux Klan," either "a lunatic or a traitor," and advised that Garvey be "locked up or sent home." The editors of the *Messenger*, Chandler Owen and A. Philip Randolph, vowed to expose his schemes, which were "calculated not to redeem but to enslave Africa and the Negro everywhere," and launched a campaign to "drive Garvey and Garveyism in all its sinister viciousness from the American soil." During the UNIA's International Convention of August 1922, Owen, Randolph, and the NAACP's Robert Bagnall and William Pickens held a series of "Garvey Must Go!" meetings in Harlem. In January 1923, the same men penned a letter to Attorney General Harry M. Daugherty, declaring the UNIA a "menace to harmonious race relationships," and requesting that the Justice Department do something to halt "the imminent menace of this insidious movement which, cancer-like, is gnawing at the very vitals of peace and safety."[35]

Garveyites responded to these attacks with threats, intimidation, and violence. Anti-Garvey meetings were besieged in New York, Philadelphia, and Los Angeles. In Cincinnati, an anti-Garvey lecturer was stabbed and hit with a chair. During an attempt to break up an anti-Garvey meeting in Chicago, a Garveyite shot a police officer. Pickens, Owen, and Du Bois were all threatened. Randolph was mailed a severed human hand, signed "KKK," and with instructions for him to join the "nigger improvement association."[36] In the months leading up to Garvey's trial for mail fraud, which

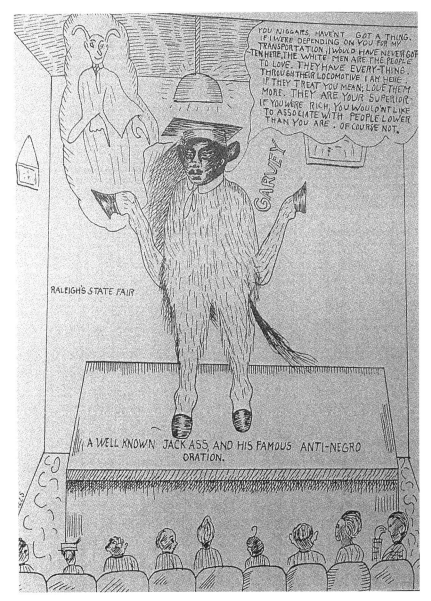

FIGURE 4.2. *Messenger* Cartoon during "Garvey Must Go" campaign, 1922.
(*The Messenger*)

commenced in May 1923, several government witnesses received death threats. Dorothy Lawson, a dressmaker who had invested her life savings in the Black Star Line, was walking with her husband one night when she was approached by a man who drew a revolver and threatened both Lawsons with death unless Dorothy stopped her attacks on Garvey. Hugh Mulzac, former officer of the Black Star Line, and John Sidney de Bourg, signee of the UNIA's Declaration of Rights and former Leader of the Negroes of the Western Provinces of the West Indies and South and Central America, were threatened by Linous Charles, a member of the UNIA's paramilitary auxiliary, the African Legion, who told Mulzac that he would "get them" if took the rest of his life.[37]

By this time, Garvey's authoritarian instincts and increasingly paranoiac leadership had driven many of his former supporters, like Mulzac and de Bourg, from the UNIA. During the International Convention of 1922, Garvey responded to a challenge from the Leader of American Negroes, Reverend James Eason, by staging an elaborate impeachment trial and expelling Eason from the UNIA, a move that further inflamed simmering tensions between West Indian and African American members.[38] Eason, uncowed and defiant, launched the Universal Negro Alliance and set out across the country, hoping to bring Garveyites over to his side, claim control of the UNIA from Garvey, and return the organization to its original principles. He also agreed to testify against Garvey in court. On January 1, 1923, leaving a meeting in New Orleans, Eason was ambushed by three men and fatally shot. Before he died, Eason identified two of the assailants—Frederick Dyer and William Shakespeare, members of the local UNIA's "secret service"— and told police he was "positive" that his assailants "were acting on instructions to put me out of the way and prevent my appearing as a witness against Garvey at the trial." Agents later identified the third assailant as John Jeffries (alias Esau Ramus), who had been sent to New Orleans by Garvey to organize the secret police outfit. According to Garvey's longtime supporter William Ferris, who was deeply shaken by Eason's murder, Garvey sent Jeffries to New Orleans to kill Eason, received a telegram from Jeffries informing him of Eason's death, and provided Jeffries with money to flee to Detroit. Federal agents, for unknown reasons—perhaps because by this time Garvey had been convicted of mail fraud and was facing five years in prison and certain deportation thereafter, perhaps because of the difficulty extracting actionable testimony out of Jeffries, Dyer, or Shakespeare—ultimately abandoned efforts to connect Garvey directly to the murder.[39]

By the middle of 1923, Garvey found himself imprisoned in the Tombs, his organization rent with internecine feuding, his Black Star Line defunct, and colonization plans in West Africa on hold. For his opponents it seemed that all that was left to do was to take account of the tornado that had blown briefly, unexpectedly, and violently through their lives. Garvey was a "half zealot and half faker, who, able to play upon the prejudice and imagination of the black masses of the Western world and parts of Africa, had seduced from them hundreds of thousands of dollars and squandered it upon self-glorification and visionary projects," eulogized a satisfied George W. Harris, editor of the *New York News* and leading participant in the "Garvey Must Go" campaign. "His case should be an example to all those agitating black demagogues who seek to serve themselves first and their race afterwards. His removal should enable all those whom he divided to get together to fight the common enemies of the black race. Marcus Garvey was a menace. His race will now be the better off for his removal."[40]

The Birth of Second-Period Garveyism

In mid-November 1924, Garvey delivered a seldom-remembered speech at Liberty Hall in Harlem, entitled "The Silent Work That Must Be Done." "We have practically reached the [end of the] first period in our organization history, and we are now about to launch out into the activities of the second period," Garvey announced. Whereas the war and its aftermath had occasioned the need for a "radical program" and "a policy of aggression," the reconstitution of white regimes in the 1920s now called for a more pragmatic focus on "quiet and peaceful penetration." Whereas the UNIA of the first period had been known as a "great institution," heretofore the organization would pursue its agenda in the shadows, with secrecy, caution, and patience. "We will no longer shout from the platform of Liberty Hall our plans," explained Garvey's chief officer William Sherrill. "[T]he real work will be largely carried on through secret missions, embassies, agents and representatives." The focus would not be on shipping lines and grand provocations but on education, modest institution building, propaganda work, and the shaping of "world sentiment" among Negroes and "other colored races."[41]

The UNIA's second period was inaugurated at a moment of reckoning, its aims articulated after it became clear that Garveyites would have to re-imagine their contribution to the project of Negro and African redemption. It was certainly not Garvey's first instinct. Following his release from prison on bail, pending appeal, in September 1923, Garvey sought to revive the fortunes of his organization with a renewed commitment to grand, ostentatious scheming. In December, a UNIA delegation embarked for Liberia to resuscitate the organization's colonization plans. With much fanfare, in early 1924 the organization announced the launching of a second steamship line, the Black Cross Navigation and Trading Company. By the convention in

August, however, negotiations with the Liberians had unraveled, and in a manner that seemed designed to inflict maximum embarrassment upon the UNIA.[42] The Black Cross Company was in crisis, and by early 1925 defunct. On February 5, two days after his appeal was denied, Garvey was seized by authorities at the 125th Street train station in New York, and shepherded to the Atlanta Federal Penitentiary, where he would spend most of the next three years. Awash in debt, Liberia a dead end, the central edifice of his organization pulling apart at the seams, Garvey looked for a new way to understand the UNIA's mission. He found it in the work that Garveyites had been performing on behalf of the movement across the United States, the greater Caribbean, and Africa from the beginning—work wedded less to the fortunes of the UNIA's central infrastructure, or to the top-down, bureaucratic, imperial vision of its founder, than to the dynamic impact of Garveyist organizing on local politics making. Like Frederick Lugard, Garvey had the good sense to recognize what he had wrought, to rearticulate his priorities accordingly, and to declare victory amidst certain, bracing failure.

The origins of the second period can be traced to 1921, as Garvey began to explore the implications of his retreat from radicalism. Crucial to the conceptualization of both was a new rendering of the UNIA's programmatic timeline. As late as January 1921, Garvey had described the UNIA's project of African liberation in the present tense, and in unequivocal terms. "In two years I predict we will have ten to fifteen million [N]egroes ready for action in Africa," he boasted in Pittsburgh. "I am positive that the interpretation in the Bible—'Eth[i]opia shall stretch forth her hand'—the time is nigh . . . When the bugle sounds for the final conflict I expect to be there and not be ninety years old either." By August, Garvey was warning that "Rome was not built in a day," that a free Africa may not be seen in their lifetimes, and that it may be their children and grandchildren who would benefit from the spadework of the organization. Garvey now pointed to the example of Ireland, which had struggled for freedom for hundreds of years, and whose painful and bloody history suggested that African redemption was still decades away. In a lecture on "Liberty and Patience" in late 1924, he stressed that the "titanic" struggle of the race required "a continuous grind," an acceptance of partial success mixed with partial failure, and "a repetition of the same thing, until ultimately you reach the objective." This blend of spadework, patience, and deferred victory was perfectly captured in the aspirational language surrounding the founding of the UNIA's Liberty University in Claremont, Virginia in 1926. "As it is not possible to change our present environment," explained Garveyite official Ethel Collins, "it is highly necessary that schools and universities be established to educate and inculcate in the minds of our sons and daughters love and respect, race purity and race pride."[43]

As Garveyites shifted the expected influence of their work into the future, they embraced the idea of Garveyism as an organic form of decentralized, mass organization. The UNIA "has not been as successful in its commercial ventures as the promoters had hoped," admitted Sherrill in 1926, but "[f]or seven years scores of speakers have gone to and from in different parts of the world," preaching Garvey's message of unity, and now "Negroes everywhere have begun to look upon one another as brothers." The form of the organization—the awarding of long titles, the particulars of business schemes, the wording of the constitution—mattered less than its function to "organize the Negro, to bring about a better relationship between Negroes everywhere; to arouse Negroes to a sense of loyalty to themselves and to their race." Amy Jacques Garvey celebrated the "men and women who will take a *Negro World* into certain districts of Africa, where to be caught with one is a death sentence," and praised "those who translate the philosophy and opinions of Marcus Garvey by sections into different dialects and carry their parchment from village to village spreading the gospel of Garveyism."[44] The suggested similarity between the spread of Garveyism and missionary work was hardly accidental. As the momentum of the UNIA stalled, Garvey began to be described by his followers less as a "Negro Moses" who would lead them to the promised land than as a Christ figure, the vessel of a divine cause. With or without their "prophet," declared Bishop George McGuire, "the soul of the movement, which [Garvey] has fanned into flame . . . will not perish," nor will "the spiritual yearnings of his legions of converts." The primary task of the second period was less to "put over" the program of the UNIA than to grow the number of believers and to encourage them in their endeavors. "All that Mr. Garvey has said during the past ten years was merely in an effort to get the Negro peoples of the world to do one important thing," wrote Garveyite J. Milton Batson in 1928. "Organize."[45]

As the next chapter will demonstrate, Garveyism flourished in the United States for the remainder of the decade by projecting its global vision as a dynamic framework for local black politics and community building, particularly in the Jim Crow South. In the greater Caribbean, Garveyites demonstrated a similar versatility. As the wave of radicalism that swept the region in 1919 and 1920 gave way to a decade-and-a-half of relative calm, Garveyism flourished under a variety of guises as a cautious, reformist, and primarily nonconfrontational politics. In the migrant labor enclaves of Central America, Liberty Halls functioned as important meeting places, the UNIA as a secular vehicle of community building. In Cuba, which boasted more UNIA divisions than any other country outside of the United States, but where race-based political organizations were banned, Garveyites foregrounded the mutual aid and recreational aspects of their work. In the West Indies, Garveyites worked closely with labor activists to establish the foundation of a labor politics that emphasized organization and constitutional reform rather than direct action and worker resistance, a politics that flourished in the Trinidad Workingmen's Association, in the British Guiana Labour Union, in the Barbados Workingman's Association, and ultimately in the organizations associated with Garvey upon his return to Jamaica in 1927, including Garvey's People's Political Party and the Jamaica Workers and Labourers Association, for which Garvey served as chairman. Garveyism spread primarily among English-speaking peoples, but also to some extent among Spanish and French speakers. The UNIA, fueled by West Indian migration, remained robust in the Hispanic Caribbean, boasting more than fifty divisions in Cuba by the mid-1920s, joined by nearly the same number of divisions and chapters in Panama and the Canal Zone, twenty-three divisions in Costa Rica, and three dozen more stretched across Colombia (6), Brazil (1), Guatemala (5), the Dominican Republic (6), Mexico (4), Nicaragua (5), Honduras (7), Puerto Rico (1), Ecuador (1), and Venezuela (1).[46]

The UNIA's second period also consummated the organization's shifting perspective on the parameters of African Garveyism. In 1919, when Garvey announced his plans to transfer UNIA headquarters to Monrovia, the UNIA had promoted Liberia as its future staging ground for the raising of a modern black state, a point of embarkation through which to facilitate the mobilization of the scattered peoples of African descent around a common project of racial emancipation. Enacting the well-worn tropes of emigration movements dating back to the eighteenth century, Garveyites envisioned a cadre of Westernized and Christianized Negroes returning "home" to rebuild the fallen continent, armed with the skills acquired during their trials abroad and guided by the hand of providence. These plans, and the UNIA's subsequent dalliances with Liberia, established the widely held view that Garveyism was a "Back to Africa" movement. It was here, also, that Garvey's rather facile expectations of race solidarity were exposed; as Ibrahim Sundiata puts it, the "poesy of trans-Atlantic longing ran headlong into African sociopolitical reality," dashed on the rocks of colonial machinations, Liberian high politics, and the complexities of African ethnic diversity.[47]

By 1921, as negotiations with the Liberian government broke down for the first time, Garvey began to consider a broader, more dynamic model of African Garveyism. Spurned by the Liberians, Garvey now challenged the idea that the UNIA had settled on Liberia, or any part of the continent, as a point of emphasis in its African campaign. "[W]e recognize not only Liberia as belonging to the Negro, but all Africa," Garvey observed at the Second International Convention. "Whether we land in the South or the West or the North or in Central Africa there shall be the battleground for African freedom." State building remained the final goal, but the task of "resurrect[ing] the civilization of the Nile" required "patience, sacrifice and determination." For the moment, explained Sherrill, Garveyites must adopt a policy of "silent and peaceful penetration into Africa," carrying news of the movement to the continent, "awakening Negroes to their duty and responsibility." The nature of this work meant that wide publicity would not be given to their every move. "But the truth is that the Universal Negro Improvement Association today is more active in its African program than ever in its history," assured Sherrill in 1925. "We have today more representation, more agents in Africa working in the interest of the propaganda of Africa for the Africans than we had in 1918, 1920 and 1921 when we did most of our platform talk."[48]

The success of UNIA organizing, consciousness raising, and networking in the preceding years meant that agency and authority could be transferred from the parent body in Harlem to local agents on the ground. Garvey now suggested that Africans, rather than Africans in America, would be the primary agents of the continent's rebirth. Western Negroes must "further link hands and hearts" with their brothers and sisters in Africa, and offer mechanical, organizational, and rhetorical assistance. But now that the "information [had] . . . gone abroad," the burden shifted to Africans themselves to absorb its implications, apply its directives to the exigencies of the continent, and "do their own redeeming." "Tonight Africa stands one great organized continent, one great organized section for the Universal Negro Improvement Association," boasted Garvey in 1923. "Our work is half done. If half has been completed in five years, give us ten years more and we will sweep Africa—we will sweep the world." Opponents of the UNIA failed to realize that the great work of raising Negro consciousness was not a human force, but "a spiritual force that cannot be stopped." Halting the progress of the UNIA, or of Garvey, did not reverse the inexorable momentum of Africa's redemption. "As they tried to oppose the religion of Christ by nailing Christ to the cross," declared Garvey, "so in the death of one leader of the Universal Negro Improvement Association, the work . . . will be carried forward with stronger force and power."[49]

Left for dead in 1923, the UNIA was reborn in its second period. As was the case with the "New Negro" following the war, the rebranding of the organization was rhetorical, an attempt to capture a Zeitgeist that had emerged not from top-down decision making but from acts big and small, by blacks and whites, by citizens and subjects in Africa, Europe, and the Americas. Marcus Garvey's genius was not in his ability to imagine new futures or craft new ideas, but to give expression to—and provide an organizational vessel for—the unruly stream of black internationalism as it flowed down from the ages and crashed against the dikes of interwar white supremacy. Garvey's success at building a workable mass politics out of the ferment of the Great War is well known. But his true contribution to global politics came later, during the frustrating decades of the 1920s and 1930s, and through the agency of men and women who adopted the infrastructure of Garveyism to pursue their own ends, and not always in ways that Garvey himself would have approved. For Garvey, a man with autocratic impulses and imperial ambitions, this must have been a perplexing irony indeed. The organizational insights that sustained his movement, that broadcast his name and his program across the world, precluded much of Garvey's participation. He shone too brightly to work in the shadows. Yet it was here, amidst ostensible retreat, and in a variety of guises, that the Age of Garvey was forged.

PART TWO

The Age of Garvey

Chapter Five

THE TIDE OF PREPARATION

> I can now see the tide rising to bring us into what truly belongs
> to us. . . . I am going to follow because the living program [of
> Garveyism] is the tide of preparation and the seed is the power-
> ful nation that will ultimately evolve . . . to establish with dignity
> the seat of government in Africa.
>
> —*Ruth E. Jerome, Garveyite from Atlantic City, NJ, 1926*

ON THE evening of March 12, 1927 Arthur S. Gray found himself sharing
the stage with a compelling cast of characters. Edgar Owens of the Communist Party sat to his side, accompanied by a representative from the Socialist
party; a young Chinese student and an older Chinese man were joined by
a representative of the People's Party in India. The occasion was the second
anniversary of the passing of Sun Yat-Sen. A celebration was being held at
the headquarters of the Chinese Nationalist Party (Kuomingtang) in San
Francisco. A nationalist icon in China, Sun was also revered as a symbol
of anti-imperialism and self-determination for nonwhite peoples. Months
before his death Sun had delivered an impassioned speech in Kobe, Japan,
appealing for a "Pan-Asianism" that would combine the resources of nations stretching from Egypt and Turkey to China and Japan, thereby ending
European aggression and interference, relieving the sufferings of Asian peoples, and restoring the continent to its former glory. Sun challenged Japan,
which he warned had assimilated the Western "rule of Might," to lead the
Orient in a civilizational clash: to seek "a civilization of peace and equality
and the emancipation of all races" rather than one guided by power, prejudice, and chauvinism.[1]

Befitting the occasion, the speakers, one after the other, echoed Sun's refrain. Edgar Owens advocated a direct and unflinching assault on the ramparts of Western imperialism, noting that China had received the recognition and consideration of the foreign powers only after she had ceased
to be peaceful. The representative from India declared Asian civilization

superior to the "utilitarian and militaristic civilization of the Occident," expressed outrage at the crimes of English empire builders and caretakers, and launched into an appeal for the cooperation of the "darker races" of the world against white supremacy and "overlordship." Enumerating the hundreds of millions of Indians, Asiatics, and Africans, he declared, "if we will all unite against this common imperialism, we can obtain our freedom in the next fifteen years!"[2]

Arthur Gray was the leading light of the Oakland division of the Universal Negro Improvement Association, longtime Garveyite, *Negro World* contributor, and soon to be named High Commissioner for the States of Arizona, Utah, Nevada, and California. He was enthralled and energized by the meeting. Asked to deliver a short speech, he outlined the "striking similarity" between the programs of Sun and Marcus Garvey. Negroes, he noted, were a little further behind in their program of political emancipation, in "the educational and organization stage" and "hoping to advance to the development and national stage soon." But they were "very much encouraged by the progress made by the Chinese in their rapid awakening and adjustment of their own affairs." In his breathless report to Amy Jacques Garvey, Gray boasted that he had been invited to attend regular mass meetings of the San Francisco Koumintang, and that he had arranged for a Chinese representative to speak at an upcoming meeting of the Oakland UNIA. Having already established contacts with Asian activists, both in formal meetings like this one and more informally at local restaurants and cafés, Gray hoped that the enthusiasm demonstrated for the UNIA's program of African redemption by his Chinese friends and by Japanese "men of affairs" might translate into concrete political alliances in the pursuit of common goals.[3]

Garveyism was built, disseminated, and sustained in the United States on the foundation of an intoxicating narrative of revolution. Viewing the recently completed war as a portentous turning point in world history, and anticolonial struggles across Africa, Asia, Europe, and the Americas as evidence of an inexorable rise of peoples of color against a decadent and declining white civilization, Garveyites projected their efforts to awaken, organize, and educate African Americans onto a global canvas of reorganization, mobilization and—in the event of white intransigence—international race war. As the heady days of the immediate postwar period gave way to the reaction and intolerance of the 1920s, and as the primary vessel and purveyor of Garveyism, the Universal Negro Improvement Association, began to crumble under the combined weight of economic insolvency, state-sanctioned repression, and internecine feuding, Garveyites continued to nurture alliances across the African diaspora and throughout the "colored" world, and they continued to imagine their often mundane local politics against the backdrop of world anticolonialism. By framing their political aims internationally, and by projecting their radical demands for African liberation forward into an undefined future, Garveyites sustained vibrant local communities of political activism amidst the decline of the national UNIA and the constraints of Jim Crow America.

The best scholarship on American Garveyism in recent decades has focused on grounding the movement in the mundane and the practical, and on entangling its genealogy in the vibrant web of African American and Afro-Caribbean social, religious, and political traditions it so effectively cultivated. The results have been startling. From its humble incorporation in New York City in September 1918 news of the UNIA swept across the United States in the years following the war, carried by Pullman porters, rural ministers, *Negro World* subscribers, Garveyite organizers, and Garvey himself, who toured the country relentlessly until his incarceration in 1925. In the urban centers of the Northeast and Midwest, Garveyism offered an appealing political vessel for recent arrivals from the South and from the West Indies, men and women who found themselves alienated from class-based organizations dominated by whites and race-based organizations dominated by established black elites.[4] In the port towns of Hampton Roads, Virginia, the UNIA pulled together a diverse collection of labor activists, skilled and unskilled laborers, domestics and laundresses, theologians, and members of the black middle class, including entrepreneur and activist Maggie Lena Walker, who hung a large photograph of Marcus Garvey in her study, alongside a framed copy of Garvey's essay, "African Fundamentalism."[5] So too in the coastal hubs of Brunswick, Georgia, Charleston, Mobile, and New Orleans, where the UNIA attracted a solid working-class constituency that included recent migrants from the rural hinterland, port workers, washerwomen, and common laborers.[6] Garveyism flourished among tobacco workers in and around Winston-Salem, lumber workers, cane cutters, and cotton pickers in Louisiana, coal workers in West Virginia, Bahamian communities in Miami and Key West, and entrepreneurs, doctors, preachers, and unskilled workers in California.[7] In isolated rural communities, especially in the cotton-growing regions of Worth County, Georgia, the Arkansas and Yazoo-Mississippi Deltas, and the Missouri Bootheel, Garveyism enjoyed perhaps its greatest and most sustained success, attracting both local elites and sharecroppers, older farmers with deep regional ties and recent migrants searching for land and opportunity.[8] By the end of 1922, the UNIA had blanketed the country, and Garvey stood abreast of the largest and most inclusive mass movement in African American history.[9]

Research into the local praxis of UNIA activism in the United States remains incomplete, and numerous exciting discoveries promise to reward diligent investigation. There should be little enthusiasm for a return to readings of Garveyism unmoored from the pragmatic manifestations of its appeal. But it is also important that we do not lose sight of the expansive

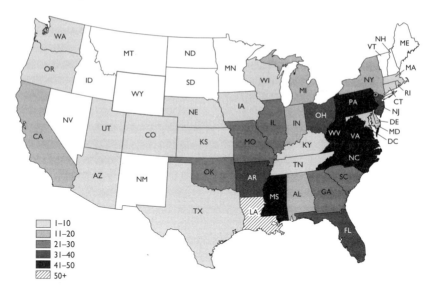

FIGURE 5.1. UNIA Divisions, 1925.

and oversized ambition—the diasporic orientation and global vision—
that provided a subtext for the modest work of day-to-day organizing. Recently, Steven Hahn has challenged scholars to develop better answers to
explain the tremendous and sustained appeal of Garveyism among African
Americans in the interwar period.[10] Part of the solution involves shifting
the conceptual geography of UNIA politics from the United States to the
global arena in which Garveyites themselves measured their success and
articulated their hopes and dreams. By joining peoples of African descent
in common purpose, in both an imagined and a real sense, and by connecting the struggle for African redemption to what was viewed as a relentless
and worldwide assault on white supremacy, Garveyites constructed a global
metalanguage within which local political identities—along with racial,
religious, class, and gender ones—were conceptualized and negotiated.[11]
Scattered UNIA divisions, as Emory Tolbert and others have so wonderfully
demonstrated, were grounded in, and shaped by, the complexity and diversity of local challenges.[12] But Garveyism offered a "vocabulary of agency," an
organizational and discursive forum for debate, that allowed participants to
understand the impact of their work, in the words of one Garveyite, "on a
larger scale."[13] During a period of limited political opportunities, in which
African American activism was fraught with danger, Garveyites built a massive political movement committed to modest aims at home, but premised
on the notion that members were involved, in the words of a Garveyite
from Tennessee, in a "world movement . . . which is now felt throbbing in
every corner of the globe."[14]

An Army of Millions

By the end of 1919 Marcus Garvey had settled upon a grand vision for his work, a broad political strategy of race unity and color consciousness that would remain remarkably consistent throughout the 1920s. Amidst wild shifts in tactics, and wild shifts in fortunes, the UNIA projected a relentlessly hopeful narrative that allowed Garveyites to view themselves as "unbreakable link[s]" in a "world-wide Negro movement," and to contextualize the struggle to redeem Africa as part of a global effort stretching across Asia, Africa, Europe, and throughout the Americas.[15] By imbuing the mundane work of organizing and consciousness raising with world-historical significance, Garvey was able to project the radical implications of his program into a nebulous future. And by projecting the aims of the UNIA globally, both Garvey and Garveyites were offered the latitude to make strategic short-term accommodations to white supremacy that, especially in the South, were less accommodations than preconditions of political life.

At every opportunity, UNIA officials worked to affiliate their organization with fellow travelers from the colonial world. With great fanfare, Garvey exchanged cables with Éamon de Valera and Mahatma Gandhi, expressing solidarity with the Irish and the Indian peoples. Garveyites welcomed guest speakers at Liberty Hall in Harlem, and at divisions throughout the country, from West and South Africa, Japan, China, and especially India.[16] In October 1919, UNIA officials worked with Japanese representatives to purchase a vessel for the organization's Black Star Line, and the *Negro World* encouraged members to attend a talk by a Japanese speaker on the prospects of the fledgling shipping line. Garvey sent a letter to the Japanese press begging "[f]ollowers of the world" to prepare for the day when "Asia will lead out to [defeat] Europe." "The New Negro has fought the last battle for the white man, and he is not getting ready for the redemption of Africa," he declared. "With mob laws and lynching . . . fresh in our memories, we shall turn a deaf ear to the white man when Asia administers to him his final 'licking.'"[17]

Some UNIA divisions forged dynamic relationships with peoples of color. In San Francisco, the Pacific Street chapter made contacts with local Japanese businessmen, and was linked with the Emanuel Gospel Mission, a congregation that, according to a government informant, brought together "Mexicans, Hindus . . . and a number of negroes" to preach the necessity of unity among all colored races, and to celebrate the successes of the Gandhi movement, Bolshevik success in Russia, the rise of the Japanese empire, and the establishment of a free state in Africa. Local UNIA organizer George Farr claimed that Garvey and Gandhi had been classmates in England and India, and that they had remained close friends. Farr, branch president J. J. Adams, and several other speakers spoke on numerous occasions at UNIA meetings about learning lessons from the Japanese, about struggles in Ireland, Egypt, and India, and about a broad vision of world liberation that included all oppressed peoples.[18]

Arthur Gray's Oakland division also made a sustained commitment to pursuing alliances with local activists of Chinese, Japanese, and Indian descent. After a scheduled joint meeting with representatives of the Chinese Nationalist Party fell through because of difficulties acquiring a suitable translator, Oakland Garveyites were treated to a lecture by B. V. Ghayanee of the Hindustan Gadar Party. The next year, the division was visited by Kaoru Nakashima, executive-secretary to the Japanese consul general, who called Garvey a "prophet," and celebrated the nationalist struggles of the "colored race" across Asia and Africa. In a 1930 letter to the editor of the *Negro World*, Gray suggested the establishment of a "Brotherhood of Colored Peoples" that would join Negroes with China, the Philippines, and India under the leadership of Japan. The suggestion was enthusiastically adopted by the paper in the next issue, the editorialist noting, "We want every member of our race to be ever on the alert and willing to cooperate with all those brave peoples who are now successfully fighting the white man's yoke so that the liberation of our own dear Africa may soon come."[19]

As dynamic as these alliances could be, especially at the local level, cooperation among the so-called yellow, brown, and black peoples of the world served a far more important symbolic and discursive function for UNIA organizers. For Garvey and his lieutenants, the "rising tide of color" was an abstraction that could be put to useful effect as an organizational vehicle. Precision mattered far less than effect. In speeches, and in columns and news items emblazoned across the pages of the *Negro World*, Garveyite officials constructed a totalizing narrative of creeping world revolution, and of the central place of the UNIA in that struggle.

The *Negro World* boasted an impressive collection of national and international news, selected, organized, and headlined to create the greatest possible effect. Not only did the paper print more world news than any other newspaper in the country, enthused a reader from Louisiana, but, unlike the white newspapers, it presented the news in a manner that allowed readers "to grasp its racial significance."[20] By far the most common narrative cultivated by news items was one of a world awash in anticolonial revolt. The *Negro World* carried news of mounting opposition to US stewardship in Haiti, the Dominican Republic, Puerto Rico, the Virgin Islands, Nicaragua, and especially the Philippines. Even more attention was given to clashes of colonial subjects with British authorities across the Middle East, Africa, and especially in India, where Gandhi's exploits were celebrated with great fanfare. Japan's rise on the world stage, Chinese nationalist struggles, and Abd el-Krim's daring revolt against the Spanish and the French in Morocco, were afforded sustained and detailed attention. To ensure the message was not missed, the paper reprinted essays by statesmen like David Lloyd George and the former Kaiser Wilhelm, warning of the sinister confluence of these episodes throughout the colored world. Garvey provided his own guided analysis in his popular front-page editorials, as did UNIA intellectual leaders in reprinted speeches, editorials, and recurring columns.

Together, Garveyite writers both popularized and sustained a dialogue of colored internationalism given momentum by the First World War, a confidence, as leading Garveyite John E. Bruce put it, that "[t]he future of the white race is imperiled by the spectre of the yellow, black and brown perils, which, like a 'mighty army,' is moving on the works of their oppressors."[21] Negroes were urged to awaken to the import and the opportunity afforded by world anticolonialism, to prepare for the likelihood of a terrible clash between white empire builders and the darker races. "If you keep organized, as the Hindus are organizing, as the Indians are organizing, as the Egyptians are organizing, as the Irish are organizing, I tell you these heretofore oppressed groups will shake the foundations of the world," declared Garvey at Liberty Hall. Noting the intention of radical movements in Turkey, Egypt, India, and China to "take their destinies out of the hands of the white lords of misrule," *Negro World* contributor Hubert Harrison argued that only by "join[ing] hands across the sea" and "link[ing] up with the other colored races of the world" would the black man have the capacity to overcome the superior economic, political, and military power of the white man. "The conflict of color is the call to the black race, the brown race, the yellow race today," he wrote. "It is a bid for their self-emancipation." Not content merely to attach the organizing efforts of the UNIA to struggles in the colonial world, Samuel Haynes argued that it was Garvey himself who had stirred the darker peoples of the world to action. "The universal influence of his philosophy among black and yellow peoples and the steady growth of his organization constituted a dark cloud on the universal horizon," wrote Haynes. "Europeans who are ambitious to make Africa and Asia subservient to their will now realize the possibility of a cultural and spiritual cohesion between the two, out of which may be born a common brotherhood looking towards a unification of efforts in checking the ambitions of white men."[22]

There is ample evidence to suggest that local Garveyites internalized this discourse of colored internationalism, and that they viewed their work in this global context. In Philadelphia, remembered Thomas Harvey, the biggest draw at Sunday meetings was a reading of world news "and how it affected Negroes and other people." The Philadelphia division reported that Garveyites were "learning from the Turks and the Irish," and emboldened by the news of "races everywhere getting together, working together, planning together, preparing together for the next great conflict." Likewise, a Garveyite from Oklahoma argued that the "Moors" in Morocco, struggling against the Spanish and French, were "kith and kin of 400,000,000 black people all over the world," and expressed confidence that "[u]niversal peace cannot be obtain[ed] in this world until all nations and races are willing to show respect one to the other regardless of creed or color."[23]

For Garveyites, one marker of their divergence from "old" Negroes is that they had awoken to a less provincial view of their condition. A woman from Arizona reported that enthusiasm was high in Mesa despite the modest size of their division, and implored Negroes to "wake up and use just a little common judgment . . . and see our condition the world over." The vision of a new future precipitated by the unity of peoples of color filled local Garveyites with purpose and hope. One Garveyite from Coffeyville, Kansas celebrated the "rapid approach of the climax in the human affairs of the universe." Another, from Kansas City, shared Garvey's vision of a new race war, envisioning "an army of many millions coming out of Asia, yellow and brown men, linking with the continent of Africa." The unity of the colored races throughout the world, across Africa and stretching to China, represented the only hope of the "dark world," argued a Garveyite from Chicago. "The New Year belongs to the darker races and to the new generations of the colored races throughout the world."[24]

*

If providing Garveyites with a global backdrop against which to situate their activism was an essential plank in the UNIA's propagandistic work, demonstrating the organizational reach of the UNIA and its role in facilitating the steady work of African redemption was another. The UNIA survived its "fall," at least until the Great Depression, by nurturing a domestic vision that was conservative enough to allow its work to continue, especially in the South, amidst violent racial intolerance. It matched this modest American agenda by projecting its subversive vision of African redemption into the future, by exporting its activism abroad, and by convincing its adherents that the very work of organizing—"the tide of preparation," as one Garveyite put it—was sowing the seeds of a better day.[25]

Those who criticized the UNIA for its so-called failures, argued Garvey, misunderstood the "international character" of the movement, and misjudged the capacity of the organization to spread "the growing and persistent sentiment for African freedom and redemption" that comprised its most meaningful work.[26] The UNIA was mobilizing a global community of Negroes, weakened by their dispersal, but growing stronger in their dawning realization of a common purpose, and a common destiny. "Through the entire world, in the most remote parts of the globe, Negroes of all shades and hues are meeting together under the banner of the Universal Negro Improvement Association," claimed Amy Jacques Garvey. "Even in those parts termed darkest Africa where the white man dares not go and stay very long—even in those parts we have branches of the Universal Negro Improvement Association singing the same songs we are singing here, making the same speeches." With the help of the UNIA, Africa was biding her time, "uniting her tribes, linking hands with her scattered children in all parts of the world," and organizing carefully and purposively for the moment of liberation.[27] "Thousands who have caught the spirit of the new philosophy have and are matriculating in the leading universities of the world," boasted Samuel Haynes in 1928. "We have inspired Negrodom to a new sense of racial security and are responsible for the new leadership now being developed." Patiently, Garveyites were sowing the seeds for a new and more hopeful generation.[28]

Focusing on long-term and diasporic consciousness building afforded American Garveyites the space to pursue a more pragmatic politics, especially in the South, where the UNIA enjoyed remarkable success throughout the 1920s.[29] During a decade in which the integrationist National Association for the Advancement of Colored People (NAACP) faced oppressive scrutiny, violent reprisal and—despite the heroic efforts to preserve the organization by local members—a period of marked decline and retrenchment,[30] Garveyites were able to sustain hundreds of Southern divisions by eschewing a direct engagement with Jim Crow, embracing separatist traditions of self-government, self-defense, and communal politics dating back to slavery, and by framing their strategic, temporary acquiescence to the racial status quo as a necessary precondition to the liberation of the race on an international scale.[31] Garveyism, explained Reverend James N. Bridgman, was not a theory but "a workable, practicable plan to save men and unite them." It resonated because it "call[ed] men from absorption in local and limited views of the valley, to climb up the mountain steeps for universal glances at African communities."[32] It was this convergence of local praxis and global vision that allowed the UNIA to recruit southerners to Garveyism in racial cauldrons like southern Georgia, the Mississippi Delta, and the Missouri Bootheel. It allowed Garveyites not merely to sustain the storm of the reactionary twenties, but to offer southern blacks a vibrant and, for most of the decade, a growing base upon which to organize, network, and shape their political aspirations.[33]

In an effort to sustain a reliable base of support in the United States, UNIA officials and recruiters consciously adapted their organizational style to the rhythms and complexities of southern life, a strategy born of recruiting efforts in the South during the frenetic years of 1919–21. Such a strategy involved a careful appraisal of the forces arrayed against black political activism, and required a privileging of locally grounded, situational tactics, over abstract appeals for shibboleths like "social equality," which both local Garveyites and national officials deemed dangerous and impractical.[34] In some places, such as the West Virginia coalfields, UNIA divisions formed in defensive response to intense working-class conflict and Ku Klux Klan activity; more commonly, in places such as the Missouri Bootheel, or in Phillips County, Arkansas, site of the notorious Elaine race riots, Garveyites were able to translate their overlapping goals with white supremacists— race purity, social separatism, African emigration—into uneasy accords.[35] This ostensible outreach to white racists, as the previous chapter notes, had the effect of deeply alienating much of Marcus Garvey's remaining support in the black intelligentsia, and stoked the fires of the "Garvey Must Go" campaign. Yet in response to charges from African American opponents, even the most fair-minded, that the UNIA was "conced[ing] America" to the Klan, Garveyites argued that they were merely being realistic about the totalizing power of white supremacy, a strength that had real consequences.[36] As Garvey noted with only minor exaggeration, "[t]he farmer is a Klansman, the policeman is a Klansman, the police captain is a Klansman, the Mayor of the city is a Klansman; the Governor is a Klansman."[37] Garveyites vigorously and creatively debated the best methods for approaching this threat. After a lively conversation about the Klan at the UNIA Convention in 1924, William Sherrill, then the titular "Leader of the American Negroes," suggested a policy of "neutral opportunism," one that condemned the Klan's cowardly acts, but also took stock of its power and strength. Garveyites would remain "watchful," careful not to antagonize the Klan, prepared to take advantage of elements of its program, clear that the UNIA did not endorse its fanaticism. It was an approach that was unsatisfying to some Garveyites, but it was also a policy that allowed the vital work of the organization to continue. "We have thousands of little divisions dotted all over Alabama, Texas, Tennessee and Mississippi, many of them who have just simply formed themselves into little African bands to carry on the propaganda of the Universal Negro Improvement Association, if not so publicly, silently," boasted Sherrill a month before the convention. "[I]t takes a whole lot more courage to be a member . . . in Texas than it takes here in Harlem."[38]

Because of the global metalanguage within which UNIA officials sold their program, local Garveyites viewed the challenging dynamics of their work with a startling degree of optimism and hope.[39] For African Americans who had, for good reason, trouble envisioning a constructive means of confronting white supremacy, Garveyism offered "sunshine," a "measure of hope and encouragement," an opportunity to dream anew, and what Garveyites viewed as a sophisticated and constructive means to ensure racial redemption. "We cannot talk much down here about the things that we have in heart concerning the work, but we read everything that we can get and it helps us," wrote an Arkansas farmer to the editor of the *Negro World*. "Negroes who have been oppressed so long are glad to look forward to a time when things will be different. The Negro World keeps us encouraged as we work." Several Garveyites echoed J. H. Blackwell, manager of the UNIA's Liberty University, when he exulted that Garvey had "lifted the veil that obstructed our view and has given us a race consciousness that has created us anew, and we see as we have never seen before, feel as we have never felt before, know as we have never known before, desire as we have never desired before, hope as we have never hoped before." For a Chicago Garveyite, becoming a member of "our gigantic movement" made him feel "as if I have done something that is right and that I am released from some burden."[40]

Crucial to the UNIA's appeal was the notion that no matter how dire one's circumstances, no matter how isolated the community, no matter how modest one's effort, he or she—by the very nature of his or her participation in a global awakening—was a crucial link in the chain. If the Negro was poor and politically weak in the United States, the UNIA was everywhere, demanding respect all over the world. "As I stand before you this afternoon and look at the dial of the clock," marveled S. A. Owens, vice president of Newport News Division No. 6, "I can truly state that at this present moment there are thousands of Negroes standing on platforms somewhere throughout the various countries of the world, expounding the doctrines of the Universal Negro Improvement Association." Attending the UNIA's International Convention in 1924, a Garveyite from Fort Wayne, Indiana was deeply moved by the display of racial unity among the delegates. "It is so stupendous that the minds of the uninitiated could not grasp its amazing wonders," he gushed. "Little did I know that thousands of black folk were able to meet in a great conclave, acting in unison, although of diversified nationalities." By successfully expanding Garveyites' field of vision, UNIA officials created a space for consciousness raising, and a local politics fired by radical imagery of redemption. The nurturing of a grassroots politics helped prepare African Americans to take advantage of a better day. "In this age of racial unrest, when the darker peoples of the world are struggling for political independence and social equality, when oppressed millions of Chinese, Indians, Negroes, and Philippinos [*sic*] are determined that there shall be liberty or death, our noble leader has come on the scene," wrote a Garveyite from Chattanooga. Like a "whirlwind," Garvey "swept into a mighty organization millions of black men and women throughout the world." This "prophet sent from God" may not live to see his dream realized, but he had set it inexorably in motion. For the time being, explained a UNIA member from Pittsburgh, Garveyites would robe themselves in "the garment of preparedness." For they had been "swept . . . up above the poverty and the prejudice" by which their lives had been limited. They had glimpsed the horizon.[41]

A Working Idealism: Negotiating Identities in American Garveyism

If the UNIA transmitted a global metalanguage, the terms were played out locally, and in diverse ways. Scholars who have judged Garveyism as a theoretical or abstract discourse have failed to appreciate the extent to which, as Amy Jacques Garvey suggested, it flourished as a "working idealism," or as Emory Tolbert puts it, "a growing, experimenting, debating movement."[42] Garveyites constructed an organic political community, one that drew on existing traditions and projected them onto a world stage; they created a discursive field that included ordinary blacks in the project of diasporic identity building. Within this idiom, racial, religious, class, and gender identities were consciously recalibrated to reflect the New Negro's global outlook. This reorganization did not follow an even pattern. In some places, it bolstered existing relations of power within the black community. In other places, it unsettled them. Everywhere, it offered Garveyites a new, unfinished, and malleable platform upon which to participate in politics, challenge hierarchies, and negotiate extant identities. The success of Garveyism in the United States is inseparable not only from its global vision, but from the dynamism with which that vision was projected on the ground.

Garvey's political communion was founded on the principles of racial unity, interconnectedness, and organization. As Michele Mitchell has demonstrated, debates about racial destiny had dominated African American thought since the end of Reconstruction. Garvey adapted this language to the narrative of rising colored consciousness emerging from the war, giving his movement a fresh sense of urgency, and allowing him to enrobe what amounted to a derivative discourse in the language of rebirth and regeneration.[43] "Race first," Garveyites argued, was a pragmatic and strategic program of cooperation among Negroes that found "its highest justification in the practices and methods of their oppressors." It was only by uniting behind a common purpose and recognizing a common condition that Negroes might weather the racial reorganization of the postwar world; it was only by acknowledging "One God! One Aim! One Destiny!" that Negroes might hope to establish a great "Racial Empire" in Africa that might foster, sustain, and protect the interests of the race the world over.[44]

Garvey's message of international racial cooperation struck a responsive chord with African Americans who had endured the disappointment and horrors of the wartime years, and found in Garveyism a path through the

morass and darkness. "Your brother and mine was lynched on demobiliza-
tion from overseas before he could get the uniform off his back," seethed
Lois Pittman, lady president of the Oakland division, to the *Negro World*.
"When my heart was in despair after reading how your sister and mine
hung by the heels and the limb of a tree, her belly ripped open, her babe
yet unborn falling to the ground . . . crushed by the heel of him for whom
we fought . . . there cometh Marcus Garvey saying 'Never mind, Negroes,
Africa is over there—ours by right of birth and of God, let us prepare a
home where we can have peace of mind and complete freedom of body.'"[45]

With avenues to interracial, class-based activism overwhelmed by a combination of postwar repression and white intolerance, African Americans
embraced a unionism premised on diaspora and the breaking down of
intra-racial boundaries.[46] Garveyites hailed the efforts of the UNIA to answer the cry of the masses for unity, to bring "into close touch the American
Negro, the West Indian Negro, the African Negro, and the Negroes from
all other parts of the wide world," to bring scattered members of the race
under one roof in conversation and cooperation. In this reading, the war
was cast as Providence, a divine and terrible act that had, in the words of one
Garveyite, "cultivat[ed] for America an international mind and quicken[ed]
the imagination of black men and women." The war, according to William
Sherrill, had opened "new avenues for the race," given birth to a new ambition, given the Negro a greater sense of his own destiny. The war had facilitated the rise of a powerful organization that aimed to awaken the Negro, to
break down arbitrary national boundaries, to join a race strewn throughout
the world.[47]

Membership in the UNIA was framed in a language of religious revival
and prophecy that was inseparable from notions of racial destiny, and was
perhaps even more steeped in African American cultural traditions.[48] Garvey's crucial insight was not ideological but conceptual. He not only held
the twin goals of African redemption—political and eschatological—in
fruitful dialogue, as Randall Burkett has argued, but he constructed a mass-
based, diasporic vessel—the UNIA—within which to reorient and subli-
mate the power of the black church.[49] Rejecting an old and corrupted black
theology obsessed with the hereafter, Garvey and his disciples proposed a
new ministry founded in biblical prophecy—"Princes shall come out of
Egypt; Ethiopia shall soon stretch out her hands unto God"—but dedicated
to an "applied Christianity" that demanded sacrifice and toil in the here and
now, and which viewed the gathering of a scattered flock in the apocalyptic
language of racial Armageddon.[50] In this new era of religious awakening
and rebirth, the UNIA would serve not only to spread the good news, but to
exist as a physical manifestation of God's will on Earth, with Garvey cast in
the role, as circumstances dictated, of Noah, or Moses, or John the Baptist,
or Christ himself. The UNIA would not supplant organized Christianity;

rather, it would provide a global umbrella under which to unite Negroes of diverse religious beliefs and sects in a single, African ministry.

Garveyite attacks on the duplicity and poverty of the African American clergy were vociferous and numerous enough that scholars once assumed the UNIA to be unreservedly hostile toward the black church.[51] In truth, the UNIA attracted a large number of clergymen, who held numerous positions of importance within the organization, both in national office and local leadership.[52] Garveyites sought not to cast religious traditions aside, but to weed out "old Negro" preachers who had failed to cater to the needs of the race, and to reorient the goals of the church around active and vigorous service. Self-serving ministers of the faith, Garvey charged, had long conspired to redirect their congregations' gaze from their miserable condition toward the promise of redemption in the afterlife. As Amy Jacques Garvey put it, "Preachers had told them about the sweet 'bye-bye,' but he [Garvey] was telling them about the 'now-and-now.' The good books says that 'your just reward shall be in Heaven on that great Day'; but Garvey said, 'Work for it right here, and get it here, or take it; then the spiritual reward shall surely come.'" Or, as Garveyite preacher William Henry Moses argued, "the problem in the past has been that Negroes have not been asking for anything worthwhile; but Garvey has taught us to pray for stores, mills, factories, railroads, and ships. He has taught us to seek our salvation here and now, rather than in the far off tomorrow." At best, "old" ministers were accused of complacently keeping their followers in the "darkness."[53] More often, they were charged with collaborating with the white power structure by promoting an irrational liturgy of meekness, accommodation, and servitude.[54]

Attacks on the leadership of the black church reflected a broader organizational assault against established black leadership, and cleverly exploited class tensions within black religious communities that had been exacerbated by the Great Migration that brought thousands of rural and West Indian migrants to urban centers across the country.[55] Members of the more affluent clergy themselves stoked these fires, dismissing Garveyites as "the poorest and most ignorant class of our race."[56] Rank-and-file Garveyites responded in kind. "It does seem strange that ministers who, themselves Negroes and depending on the poor Negroes for their living would be so willing to lend the white man a hand to hold the race in slavery," noted one Garveyite in Hartford, Connecticut. "No Negro minister in Hartford will speak from his pulpit in favor of the UNIA. . . . Yet these same fellows are sucking blood from our necks to live on." A Chicago man who had recently arrived from Camden, Arkansas told the *Negro World*, "I heard a minister remark in his sermon not long ago in speaking of the atrocities of our people: 'Let them lynch you; they mobbed Christ.' This kind of advice and teaching from the church of God and from the 'big' Negroes of this country is what largely brings upon us such hellish treatment as we are receiving." Negroes were tired of "false-hearted leaders," who told their followers to abdicate the material world for the afterlife while expecting them to fund their "$100,000 churches," explained a Garveyite from New Bern, North Carolina. Negroes needed "more ships and fewer high-priced churches." They needed "to worship God and not the house." And they needed leadership more in the visage of the New Negro than in an old elite that had proven self-serving, corrupted, and anachronistic.[57]

Because, as Samuel Haynes argued, the masses were to be found in the churches, because the churches wielded enormous influence, and because spiritual leaders were failing to cater to the "needs of a struggling race," a new religious leadership was needed, versed in a program of "human uplift" aligned to achieve the redemption of Africa.[58] Garveyites self-consciously framed the passing of the "old slave" Negroes and the "awakening" of the New Negro in the language of baptism and revivalism.[59] "Before Marcus Garvey came upon the scene three or four years ago we Negroes were dead," explained George Alexander McGuire, chaplain general of the UNIA. Like Lazarus, Garveyites had been raised from their former condition; they were now "resurrected Negroes." New Negroes had been "regenerated and baptized in the lake of purity," noted William Ferris. For another Garveyite, to be a New Negro was to be "born again."[60] William Sherrill, who became a lifelong Garveyite after hearing Garvey speak for the first time in Baltimore, remembered his conversion to the movement as a religious experience:

> Mr. Garvey spoke for about an hour and a half and I stood all that time and it looked like just ten minutes to me. . . . I don't know how people feel when they get that old-time religion that makes you want to jump and scream and shout; but I want to say that when I heard Mr. Garvey that night I had a fair example. . . . His speech was so different—the program he brought was so much in the opposite of those speeches and those programs I had heard before, that, for an hour and a half I stood motionless—transfixed—completely astounded and amazed. For that hour and a half I did not know whether I was standing on the floor or in the air, or whether I was sitting down; and from that night on I realized that the Universal Negro Improvement Association brought the hope for which I had longed ever since I had been old enough to think independently on the race question.[61]

Garvey, who considered himself a "born again" citizen of Africa, framed this ritual of organizational "baptism" in secular terms.[62] As Jesus had been resurrected "to save a fallen humanity" and to change the spiritual attitude of man, the UNIA sought "a resurrection from the lethargy of the past," from the false notion that "God intended that we should occupy an inferior place . . . in the world." As Jesus had risen from the dead, Negroes under the banner of the UNIA would be "risen from the slumber of the ages; risen in thought to higher ideals, to a loftier purpose, to a truer conception of life."[63] Garveyites were not content to stop at metaphor; children of UNIA members were both baptized as Christians and as soldiers dedicated to the principles of the organization.[64]

Once awoken to the doctrine of the New Negro, Garveyites sought to fashion, as Randall Burkett has argued, a "Black civil religion," one that combined aspects of the spiritual and the secular, old and new, in a powerful mythology that posited a common purpose and a common destiny for members of the Negro race.[65] For Garveyites, the secular goal of racial organization and unity was a predicate for the psalmic prophecy of African redemption. "I have dreamed dreams and seen visions, and have come to the conclusion that the Almighty Spirit has made of one blood all nations to dwell upon the face of the earth, and that they themselves are to teach the world the grand and glorious lesson of the fatherland of God and the brotherhood of man," preached the Reverend James W. H. Eason in Chicago. "[W]e feel that if we can get this same spirit imbued in the hearts and minds of the four hundred millions of our people of African descent throughout the world, that we can be able to help make the world safe for every human being that trods this mundane sphere."[66] Garveyites considered themselves members of a "new religion," on a "spiritual crusade" to shed light upon the "gigantic confraternity of African brotherhood."[67] Complaining that the field of missionary work had for too long been dominated by ineffectual blacks and duplicitous whites, Garveyites called for an emphasis on practical religious and educative efforts, and viewed the *Negro World* as their foremost "missionary" in this effort.[68] The gospel of Garvey may embody a spiritual force, but it was also, as Garvey reminded his followers, a "religion of hard work," a "religion of toil," and it was driven by a worldly prize. As one Garveyite put it, "We don't want to go to heaven, unless heaven is in Africa."[69]

If Africa was Heaven, and the UNIA God's vessel, Garvey cast himself in the role of the prophet. Garvey has been remembered as a "Negro Moses," and it is unsurprising, considering its importance in the historical praxis of black Christianity, that Garveyites viewed their movement as a symbolic recreation of Exodus.[70] But Garvey also had something more ambitious in mind. By infusing his mission in the language of resurrection, martyrdom, and divine appointment, Garvey fashioned himself as a secular Christ, an earthly parallel to the Son of God. Garveyites were careful to compare Garvey to Jesus in simile, and not in literal terms. "Not styling Marcus Garvey as a Jesus, I do style him as a Savior for the Negro people of the world," wrote William Ware. "He has trodden in the footsteps of our Savior, Jesus Christ. . . . The gospel of Marcus Garvey shall be preached in all the world to every nation, and then the end shall come to barbarism."[71] In a similar

working poor. It was an organization that not merely served the masses, but came from them; that was premised, as Garvey declared, on the notion that "[t]he masses of our people must rule."[83]

In providing an inclusive forum for the working poor, the UNIA forged, as George Fredrickson has suggested, an "interclass coalition" that divided the community along a unique axis that did not comport neatly with income or occupation: the "masses," who were awakening to their condition, and with whom rested the ultimate hopes of the race; and the "classes," who since emancipation had pursued their own selfish interests and had betrayed the trust of their people.[84] Arguing that a race without leaders was doomed, Garvey dismissed the "big Negroes," the so-called "aristocracy of the Negro race," as unfit for the task. "We have to take them out of the pulpits, off the platforms and from the public places, and relegate them to the scrap heap of racial treachery," he declared. "They have conspired for decades and are still conspiring to rob and exploit the masses." Driven by a hate toward, and a fear of, the common people, the old Negro leader used his advantages of education and privilege to stultify the growth of the less fortunate.[85]

Encouraged by Garvey's common condemnations of the "classes," but also drawing on personal and communal frustrations, Garveyites complained consistently and often about the self-serving machinations of the established elite.[86] A UNIA member from Philadelphia compared black leaders to famous traitors such as Benedict Arnold and Judas Iscariot, complaining that "these Negro leaders keep [their wealth] to buy houses, lands, and automobiles and would sell more Negroes to get more [wealth] to buy more plunder." Garveyites also remembered the "betrayal" of the war. Told by their "so-called leaders" that their service and bloodshed in Europe would be repaid with rights and respect at home, the Negro was repaid instead with "hemp rope, fire, flames, rifle balls, bombs from airplanes, together with the renewed decree that we shall not live," complained a Garveyite from Chicago. "Shall we render up all hope, pride, self-respect and our manhood because these imposters indirectly advise us to do so?" he asked. "Shall we be simple enough to further take and accept such teachings from a class of men that have, for lo these many years, made us their prey?"[87]

Garveyites resented the black elites for what they perceived to be their willingness to make sacrifices for the United States and its white leadership, while refusing to represent and support the aspirations of poor and working-class blacks. A member from Norfolk, Virginia pointed out that "our doctors, lawyers, preachers, bankers, real estate and insurance corporations" are "consumers, waiting for our laboring people's dollars in order that they may operate," and yet unlike the leaders of other races, were unwilling "to call the Negro people of the world together for the purpose of uniting our entire group and directing them to seek to become producers, commercially, industrially, politically, and financially." The UNIA offered a means for black women and men who were frustrated with the leadership of their "social betters"—businessmen, politicians, ministers—to embrace a more community-driven, egalitarian vision of black unity. "It does not matter how highly a man is educated," argued a female Garveyite from Cleveland. "It does not matter how much money he has, how he stands in with the powers that be, he can never be a true leader to this people until his heart beats even and fair and true with his people. Unless he is willing to go up or down with them he is incapable of understanding them." Another Cleveland Garveyite argued that while both the "classes" and the "masses" would be needed to redeem Africa, the masses, with their ingenuity, their diverse skills, and their willingness to sacrifice for the race, were essential for the rebuilding and development of the continent. "We need the classes too," he noted, "but the redeeming faction will be the masses."[88]

Garvey and his officers situated the UNIA as a populist alternative to the old guard of leadership. Speaking at Liberty Hall after returning from an organizing trip to Boston, Garvey boasted that he had seized the city from the "400 people . . . who call themselves the aristocracy of the Negro race," undermining their authority by raising consciousness and buffeting the Boston UNIA with another six hundred members. Captain E. L. Gaines, titular head of the African Legions, related a story from an organizing trip in Asheville, North Carolina, where "big Negroes" tried to buy him off with a fancy car rather than allow him to speak candidly to the African American residents of the city. Gaines refused, explaining that he had not joined the UNIA to better his financial condition, did not fancy aligning with "these 'dictie' big Negroes, who have been putting their hands down into the pockets of my people the last fifty years," and most importantly he did not need to submit to their overtures. "I have found in my travels over the country that the UNIA is not particularly catering to big Negroes anywhere, but is catering to the masses of the people," he explained. Instead of taking guidance from the "selfish Negro," Garvey implored blacks "to evolve from among themselves as a common people, as a common mass, their own leadership, that will feel with them, that will think with them, and will not be afraid to suffer for the ideal of a higher and a nobler life for all the people." The UNIA would provide a staging ground for the emergence of a Negro leadership dedicated to the needs of the community rather than the interests of a few.[89]

Garveyites backed up this populism by providing a tangible visage of UNIA leadership. Divisions mirrored the work of more "respectable" fraternal and benevolent associations, emphasizing a similar mixture of mutual benefits, entrepreneurship, and charitable service to the community.[90] The UNIA guaranteed each of its members funeral insurance, an aspect of the organization that proved especially appealing to poor, rural supporters.[91]

Local Garveyites in urban divisions established laundries, restaurants, groceries, meat markets, shoe-shine parlors, tailor shops, drugstores, and theaters. In East Berlin, Connecticut, Garveyites ran a brickyard; in Louisiana they established two packing houses.[92] Liberty Halls became multifaceted social centers which catered to the needs of the working poor. As Amy Jacques Garvey remembered,

> Liberty Halls, wherever located, served the needs of the people—Sunday morning worship, afternoon Sunday Schools, public meetings at night, concerts, dances were held, especially on holidays and Saturday nights. Notice boards were put up where one could look for a room, a job, or a lost article. In localities where there were many members out of work during the winter the Black Cross Nurses would organize soup kitchens, and give them a warm meal daily. The Legions would make portable screens for a corner of the hall, where men who could not be temporarily housed with fellow members, could sleep on benches at night. In the freezing winter days stoves had to be kept going to accommodate the cold and homeless, until they "got on their feet" again.[93]

Despite Judith Stein's confusing assertion that "UNIA divisions could not provide services for impoverished blacks," local branches performed an impressive number of charitable functions and communal services for both members and nonmembers alike, including medical clinics, adult and Sunday schools, and a variety of relief programs, including aid to flood victims in New Orleans, grocery baskets for the poor in Pittsburgh, legal defense in Philadelphia, and clothes for the needy in Africa.[94] "The Universal Negro Improvement Association is our church, our clubhouse, our theatre, our fraternal order and our school," explained leading female members of New Orleans Division No. 149. It provided an alternative staging ground to the one proffered by "the Negro 400 of New Orleans," who spent their time "imitating the rich whites," and trying vainly "to be able to pass for anything but a Negro."[95]

In all, the UNIA offered an organizational apparatus within which to reconceptualize notions of respectability, pursue new positions of leadership, and provide meaningful service to the race. "Aristocracy" was recast not as a reflection of education, or profession, or wealth, or ancestry, but as something conferred by one's investment in the principles of the organization, and by one's sacrifice and toil for the race. "Outside of Booker Washington and Frederick Douglass, there is not another aristocratic Negro in America," argued Garvey. "It was not a matter of money that made these two men big Negroes. It was nobility of soul, of spirit, to do service to suffering humanity, and that made them different from the rest of the people. That made them aristocrats among their own." The UNIA offered "a chance and opportunity for every man who wants to distinguish himself just at this time," an opportunity "for every man who really wants to be an aristocrat to be an aristocrat." Garveyites could become "honorably distinctive" through service. It was a dazzlingly democratic vision that offered tangible opportunities; it proved a powerful and successful appeal.[96]

*

Garveyites embraced a proudly masculinized language that fetishized Victorian gender norms, celebrated the reclamation of a fallen manhood, and relegated women to the roles of nurturer, mother, helpmate, and guardians of racial purity and nationhood.[97] Women were idealized as inert vessels of tradition, bodies of comfort for the weary male warriors of the organization, addendums to assertive manhood.[98] They were denied all but a small number of leadership positions within the UNIA's organizational structure, and were segregated in ladies' auxiliaries that, as Barbara Bair writes, were "not separate and equal but separate and hierarchical." The UNIA's emphasis on race purity, argues Michele Mitchell, facilitated a sexual politics that resulted in proscriptive gender roles, and made women "targets of protection, coercion, and control." Women who transgressed "the accepted rules of female self-actualization," as Bair puts it, risked censure, banishment, and—in the case of dissident UNIA organizer Laura Adorker Kofey—assassins' bullets.[99]

Scholars who have stopped their exploration of gender politics within the UNIA there, after a cursory examination of some of the dominant discursive tropes embraced by members of the organization's male leadership, have missed a far more compelling story about gendered constructions within the movement.[100] Discourses that project particular relations of power and authority are not hegemonic, totalizing, or fixed, but in a constant process of negotiation and recreation. They are also, as Barbara Bair, puts it, "lively and multidimensional," composed of overlapping dialogues rather than projected along a single, unbending track.[101] As a number of scholars have suggested, Garveyites, especially women within the movement, found in the UNIA a felicitous vehicle within which to both embrace idealized male fantasies of pure womanhood and champion feminist causes, to pursue traditionally proscribed roles as organizers and informal leaders and to ascend to real positions of authority and power.[102] If at times and in places the UNIA sustained existing gender inequalities among African Americans, at other times and in other places it offered a promising vehicle within which women might negotiate better terms. By embracing a movement that considered their role in the redemption of the race indispensable, women did not submit to a masculinist discourse, but afforded themselves an opportunity to shape the conversation. Following the efforts of Garveyite women to navigate a constructive course within the UNIA is not to ignore the serious limitations the organization posed for women, but to emphasize that in a

FIGURE 5.2. Marcus Garvey in uniform. (Library of Congress, Prints and
Photographs Division, Washington, D.C.)

society dominated by male authority and power, the UNIA offered a rather
remarkable space for the transgression and testing of those limitations.

The gendered structure of the UNIA mirrored the structure of the black
church, in which men dominated the pulpit and women the pews, and
anticipated the structure of the mass-based civil rights organizations that
emerged in the 1950s and 1960s, in which men monopolized positions of
visible leadership while women organized, filled out membership roles, and
provided the unglamorous, unrecognized leadership work that sustained
the movement.[103] Garveyite women served in important posts as community, regional, and national organizers, often dominated the membership
lists of local divisions, and exercised considerable influence behind the
scenes as informal power brokers, but only infrequently ascended to positions of real authority as local presidents and national leaders.[104] These

FIGURE 5.3. Three Universal African Legion officers. (Photographs and Prints Division, Schomburg Center for Research in Black Culture, The New York Public Library, Astor, Lenox and Tilden Foundations)

were the "Poets in the Kitchen" of Paule Marshall's memory, women burdened with "invisibility" as black, female, and, for Marshall's mother and her friends, foreign subjects, who contributed their meager earnings to the UNIA, bought shares in the Black Star Line, and marched in Garvey Day parades as members of the Universal African Black Cross Nurses.[105]

Whereas Garveyite men were encouraged to reclaim their manhood by immersing themselves in the UNIA's ubiquitous martial spirit, most clearly embodied by the organization's flagship male auxiliary, the Universal African Legions, Garveyite women were celebrated as the conservators of racial virtue and purity, and were expected to heal and nurture a fallen race, embodied in the organization's flagship female auxiliary, the Black Cross Nurses.[106] In this equation, men were cast as the protectors of honorable and unsullied black womanhood. By restoring the balance of masculine authority that had been lost in slavery, and defending a female sexuality that had been desecrated and unmoored by the twin legacies of rape and lynching, male Garveyites sought to both establish a chivalric New Negro manhood and to place women upon a pedestal from which they could safely perform their work for the race as mothers and educators of the young.[107]

Some Garveyite women blithely followed this script.[108] Others, however, viewed the discourse of Garveyism as a jumping-off point from which to expand definitions of women's roles within the movement, as a relation of power that might be manipulated, negotiated with, and challenged. One felicitous strategy deployed by Garveyite women was to cast women's rights in the language of awakening used to characterize the rise of the New Negro. "From the brow-beaten, dominated cave woman, cowering in fear at the mercy of her brutal mate; from the petted toy reared for the sensual indulgence of the Roman and Greek nobility, from the safely cloistered woman reared like a clinging vine, destitute of all initiative and independence . . . we find her at last rising to a pinnacle of power and glory so great, so potential that she has actually become the central figure of all modern civilization," wrote Saydee E. Parham in the *Negro World*. The "new woman" had mastered clerical work in the business world, production in the factories, reformism in politics. Now she was at the front of all movements for "the redemption of the oppressed masses," the "great civilizer of all future civilization." Eunice Lewis, a Garveyite from Chicago, argued that the "New Negro Woman['s]" place was not only in the home, but beside men in the office and on the platform. In Lewis's rendering, male chauvinists were cast as "old" Negroes, and women pioneers at the vanguard of racial politics. In this sense, it was important not only for Garveyite women to assume positions of leadership, but to "revolutioniz[e] the old type of male leadership." Lewis suggested a five-point "Plank for the New Negro Woman, at home and abroad," that joined a traditional definition of women's role in the movement—the importance of teaching their children to love their race—with a demand for absolute respect from men and an equal influence in the organization.[109]

Perhaps no Garveyite was as adept at traversing masculinist gender conventions than Amy Jacques Garvey, who self-consciously embraced the limitations implied by her membership in a proudly patriarchal political vehicle as a means to pursue undeniably feminist aims, not to mention real power and influence.[110] Working behind the scenes in her early years with the UNIA, Jacques Garvey began to emerge as a more visible voice in the organization in 1923, during Marcus Garvey's incarceration in the Tombs. After Garvey was released on bail, pending appeal, Jacques Garvey accompanied him on a national speaking tour, cataloguing the trip in a series of popular articles that ran in the *Negro World*, and delivering well-received speeches from the stump.[111] From February 1924 to April 1927 Jacques Garvey became an associate editor of the *Negro World*, editing the full-page feature section, "Our Women and What They Think." During Garvey's longer incarceration in Atlanta, which began in early 1925, Jacques Garvey served as a de facto leader of the organization, delivering regular addresses at Liberty Hall, emerging as the most visible presence in the *Negro World*, and acting as Garvey's most trusted ally and filter.

Jacques Garvey's genius as a polemicist was to frame her argument for women's participation in the organization, and their expanded role in society at large, within the paternalist paradigms projected by the larger movement. Recognizing that her authority emanated—even more meaningfully in her case—from her role as a wife and mother, she sought not to overturn socially constructed views of women's "natural" virtues, but to expand Garveyites' understanding of the means by which those virtues might be expressed and actualized. Celebrating the work that women had done as the "backbone" of the home and as the educators of Negro children, Jacques Garvey argued that a "larger life . . . is being carved for womanhood," and that "modern" women must be prepared to extend their "holy influence outside the realms of the home" in both the workplace and in politics. Noting the active role of women in liberation movements in India, Egypt, and Turkey, Jacques Garvey argued that "[the] exigencies of this present age require that women take their places beside their men," to infuse the ranks of Negro leadership with the "softening, conscientious effect of woman's entry." Excoriating Negro men for holding their women back with their "old-fashioned tyrannical feelings," Jacques Garvey served notice that as Sarojini Naidu could be president of the Indian National Congress, and as the United States Congress could open its doors to white women, "Negro women will demand equal opportunity to fill any position in the Universal Negro Improvement Association or anywhere else without discrimination because of sex." Women were becoming so "impatient" that they were "getting in the front ranks . . . [to] serve notice to the world that we will brush aside the halting, cowardly Negro leaders, and with prayer on our lips and arms prepared for any fray, we will press on until victory is ours."[112]

Jacques Garvey's editorship of the *Negro World*'s woman's page, "Our Women and What They Think," was by any measure a dazzling and groundbreaking accomplishment. At a time when other journals devoted their woman's pages to fashion, home hints, and love advice, Jacques Garvey created an eclectic forum for Garveyite women to expound on a wide range of topics, engage in debates about the proper place for women in the movement and outside of it, and generally nurture a more complex and fluid conception of themselves than some of the organization's male rhetoricians and writers would consider.[113] The page carried columns that offered recipes and child-rearing advice, and also printed stories about the activities of women from around the world pursuing careers as lawyers, doctors, and politicians; essays that extolled woman as "the great homemaker of the world," and others that celebrated their achievements at the

FIGURE 5.4. Amy Jacques Garvey. (Courtesy of the Marcus Garvey and UNIA Papers Project)

vanguard of African American politics, and in independence struggles in places like India and the Philippines.[114] In one edition, men and women contributors debated the question, "Will the Entrance of Woman in Politics Affect Home Life?" with most writers agreeing that women's expanded participation in civic life would only enrich their work at home. This sentiment was reinforced in subsequent issues, in articles about the value of female education for the health of marriage, and the importance of women maintaining a "vast and varied" field of activity.[115] Jacques Garvey's column focused predominantly on international anticolonialism, women's issues, and the relationship between the two, and was the clearest projection of the page's effort to project the "woman's viewpoint" far beyond the confines of traditionally rendered female interests.

Garveyite women did not save their critiques for print. They expounded their positions at speakers' podiums, participated in lively conversations with men at meetings, and at times directly challenged their male colleagues to respect and reward their contributions to the organization.[116] At the 1922 convention, the majority of women delegates, represented by Victoria W. Turner of St. Louis, drafted, signed, and submitted a list of resolutions to the floor that included calls for greater autonomy and control of women's auxiliaries, and greater representation as committee members, officeholders, and field workers. After the chair of the session opened the floor, a Mrs. Morgan from Chicago declared that women "were not willing to sit silently by and let the men take all the glory while they gave the advice." Women had earned the right to hold executive positions, and could be effective advocates in the field as commissioners and organizers. Mrs. Hogue, also from Chicago, stated that "it was not the intention of the women to get in the way of the men or to take the men's places, but they wanted to be at their side" instead of behind them. Marcus Garvey disputed the premise of the complaint, arguing that the UNIA was the "one organization that recognized women," and where women could be found on the Executive Council. Nevertheless, the resolutions were adopted, with slight amendments.[117]

While women were clearly underrepresented in leadership positions within the organization, they were nonetheless a notable presence. Women served as traveling organizers, regional commissioners, and presidents of divisions in Camden, Alabama; Calexico, Arkansas; Baxley, Georgia; and in Charleston, New Orleans, and Atlanta.[118] They dominated divisions in places like Worth County, Georgia, and Merigold, Mississippi; for a while, the most vocal and visible member of the New York local was Ethel Collins, who served as executive secretary of the Garvey Club, as acting secretary-general of the UNIA, and as a delegate to the convention in 1929.[119] Alaida Robertson, who was born in Bluefields, Nicaragua, was introduced to Garveyism while visiting New York in October 1920. Upon returning to her adopted home of New Orleans, she facilitated the organization of the New Orleans division, which elected her husband, S. V. Robertson, as its president, and grew into perhaps the most robust local division in the country. Alaida Robertson served as a field commissioner, and was nominated for the position of fourth assistant president general at the UNIA convention in 1922.[120]

Garveyite women also served in roles that placed them, at times, in positions second only to Marcus Garvey in terms of visibility, reputation, and importance. Henrietta Vinton Davis served the organization as international organizer, fourth president-general, second director of both the Black Star Line and the Black Cross Navigation and Trading Company, and as a member of the three-person delegation sent to Liberia in 1924 to establish a UNIA colony. In her speeches at Liberty Halls all over the Americas, and in her work as a contributor to the *Negro World*, Vinton Davis both extolled to virtues of Negro motherhood and celebrated the accomplishments of famous African American women in features on Harriet Tubman and

Sojourner Truth. For herself, she adopted a martial imagery that positioned her as the "Joan of Arc" of the race, an "Ethiopian Amazon" who could "never be accused of yielding a single inch of her rights."[121] In an article for the *Negro World*, Vinton Davis warned Garveyite men that the women were ready to take over if they proved unfit for the challenge. "The yellow man and brown man are rallying to their leaders," she wrote. If the black man did not follow Marcus Garvey, "then the women of the race must come forward, they must join the great army of the Amazons and follow a Joan of Arc who is willing to be burned at the stake to save her country. Africa must be saved!"[122]

Vinton Davis was surpassed by her protégée, Maymie Leona Turpeau De Mena, who emerged as a brilliant organizer and orator for the UNIA in 1925. After the Garveys were sent into exile in Jamaica, De Mena served as assistant international organizer, fourth assistant president-general, international organizer, and after the deposition of E. B. Knox, Garvey's official representative in America, the "Voice of Garvey." In 1932, De Mena penned the front-page editorial for the *Negro World*, making her the first editorialist to occupy that hallowed ground that had been reserved for Garvey since the paper's founding. In 1933, after the *Negro World* went out of print, De Mena briefly resuscitated it, and served as "Officer in Charge." From 1928, when she dominated the platform at Liberty Hall, through the organization of the refashioned Universal Negro Improvement Association, August 1929, of the World after the fractious convention of 1929, until the collapse of the *Negro World* and her move to Father Divine's Peace Mission, De Mena was the most visible officer of the UNIA in the United States.[123]

Like Vinton Davis, De Mena bolstered her image as a leader by draping herself in martial metaphors and symbolism. About to embark on a foreign trip, De Mena, who was suffering from a violent cold, told supporters in New York, "I do not know of another woman anywhere today in my condition whom you could get to lay their lives upon the altar of sacrifice for this Association and go out in the highways and hedges to bring them. . . . If I fall upon the battlefield I ask you to think of me as just one little drop of water that fell in the mighty sea, and that I fell doing my duty." At the UNIA convention in 1929, De Mena rode in the parade through the streets of Kingston, Jamaica astride a horse, a sword drawn. For a parade in Gary, Indiana in 1931, De Mena rode a white horse, dressed in full uniform, and again brandished a sword. It made for a stark contrast with the other featured woman in the parade, the splendidly gowned "Queen."[124]

In the *Negro World*, De Mena developed a strident defense for her own rise in the leadership of the movement, and for the rights of women within the organization. "Very little, if anything, is said of the women who form such a large percentage of the membership of this great movement," she noted. "For seven years we have been lauding our men through the press, on the platform ... while in reality the backbone and sinew of the Universal Negro Improvement Association has been and is the real women of the organization, who are laboring incessantly for the freedom of Negroes the world over." De Mena called on women in the UNIA "to line up for women's rights," to break out of their assigned "places" as Black Cross Nurses or as general secretaries of divisions. If women would make a real push, she argued, "the question of woman's sphere will soon become a myth, and woman's equality and not her inferiority, will be decided upon its merits."[125]

During the height of De Mena authority within the UNIA, it might perhaps be suggested that the organization enjoyed a brief "woman's era." As the organization's decline accelerated in the United States, women found themselves better represented in positions of authority, and better appreciated for their sacrifices and abilities.[126] Following an editorial by Marcus Garvey, in June 1930 in which he celebrated the leadership and fidelity of Vinton Davis and De Mena, while decrying the betrayals and failures of male leaders, a flurry of letters, articles, and editorials appeared in the *Negro World* demanding, as a Garveyite from Louisiana put it, "less of our oily, silver-tongued men and more of our loyal faithful women" in positions of authority. A male Garveyite from Brooklyn celebrated the fact that as people of color "climb the ladder of progress and aspire to places of world renown," Negro women were to be found "stepping out of the antiquarian wearisome path into the Realm of Freedom." De Mena's daughter Berniza penned an article declaring that in this new climate, "[t]he race ... can only look to the women for help," and argued that while men are "capable of leadership," they "generally lead in the wrong way." Mrs. B. Stephens, lady president of the Hartford Division, put everything in her title: "Ladies, Push Weak Men Up the Hill or Down the River."[127]

*

"What was the guiding star that has led these members safely this far?" asked Marie Trent at Liberty Hall in January 1926. "What made their rough traveling easier? What made them survive their losses and close their eyes to hardship? Because they saw the beckoning light, the hope of a redeemed Africa, the star of destiny."[128] In the years following the First World War, Garveyites constructed and nurtured a dazzling global narrative. Popularizing and sustaining a felicitous vision of world anticolonial revolution, and celebrating the penetration of their organization to the far corners of the earth, Garveyites marshaled a radical international discourse that invested their local work with a dramatic sense of purpose. This global metalanguage buffeted a difficult set of political circumstances during the 1920s, especially in the South. And it sustained the organization beyond the heady days of the Black Star Line, Liberian colonization, and the spectacular international conventions of 1920–24. This was to a great extent an "imagined" discourse;

UNIA officials were prone to wild overstatement, embellishment, and at times outright fantasy. But it was born from a sincere and sustained effort to connect diasporic subjects across the world in a shared purpose, an effort that bore significant fruit. And it was one that provided a platform for the negotiation of local identities, a fluid vehicle through which men and women might contest unequal relations of power, and a space for the development of political communities stretching across the country. It was a discourse within which Garveyites throughout the United States came to understand their actions.

Chapter Six

BROADCAST ON THE WINDS

ON NOVEMBER 25, 1923 in the heart of the Shire Highlands, the white settler region of colonial Nyasaland, four Angoni youths visited the store of
Osman Gani and asked about the price of cloth. When the shopkeeper
quoted a figure, the young men demurred, and provocatively explained
that they would wait until the next month, when Europeans and Indians
were gone from the country and the cloth could be acquired for free. On
the same day, on the nearby Glenbreck Estate, another Indian shopkeeper,
Hassam Osman, told a surprised white patron that he would prefer not
to install proper windows in his store ahead of a planned "native" rising.
Osman explained that throughout the week, "natives" had been complaining about the price of cloth, and threatening that they would soon obtain
the material for nothing. He had subsequently heard "strong" rumors that
members of the Watchtower movement, the independent African religious
sect, were preparing to ignite a rebellion, set to commence on December
15. Secret meetings, it was said, were being held nightly under the cover of
darkness along the road connecting Blantyre to the capital, Zomba. It could
only be imagined that at these meetings sinister plans for the rising were
being carefully drawn.[1]

Since May 1922, when members of the Watchtower movement had
been formally authorized to practice their faith in Nyasaland, a stream
of worried reports had been reaching colonial authorities. It was widely
believed—most pointedly by the Catholic missionaries of the Marist Mission and by white settlers—that the Watchtower were exploiting the misguided laxity of the colonial state, and using the veneer of religious worship as a cover for a political agenda with clear "pan-Ethiopian" objectives.[2]
What exactly that meant was not clear, but this was precisely the problem.
Africans were being recruited at an alarming pace, without regard to tribe
or origin, lifted out of the orbit of traditional rulers, beyond the surveillance arm of the colonial state, and into a shadowy world of African leadership, replete with widely reported illegal and completely unpreventable
secret meetings.[3] The information that was trickling through—a mixture

of rumor, hearsay, and innuendo—was hardly encouraging. Large centers of activity were reported near Portuguese East Africa (now Mozambique), from where Watchtower adherents were thought to be receiving inflammatory literature of the "bolshevic" and otherwise seditious sorts. Despite their questionable loyalty, Watchtower members were said to be employed in the King's African Rifles, in the police force, and by the local *boma* (administrative headquarters). They were said to hold chiefs and headmen in contempt.[4] In October 1923, a man who had left the Watchtower reported to authorities that all members had been told that war with Europeans was on the horizon, and that they must learn how to use spears. He also revealed that members secretly called their schools "John Chilembwe" schools, in reference to the martyred pastor who had risen against the state in 1915. This would have come as no surprise to members of the Marist Mission, who had years earlier warned authorities about Chilembwe, and who for the past year had been signaling the same alarm about the Watchtower movement, which they argued shared its essential features with Chilembwe's church. "The W.T. [Watchtower] movement is religious, and composed of fanatics," wrote Father Riviere in a long dispatch to intelligence authorities in Zomba. "[B]ut under the cloak of religion there is a secret political end, known to, and wished for by its leaders who, when they consider the time is ripe will utilize the fanaticism of their members for their political ends, which can be summed up in the phrase, 'Africa for the Africans.'" The Marists proposed drastic action, and suggested the inevitability of open rebellion if steps were not taken. The Planters' Association in Milalongwe also weighed in, expressing doubt that the government could credibly claim that their children were properly protected. The association advocated the recruitment of Africans from other colonies to serve as "mobile columns," and the stationing of KAR troops at Blantyre.[5]

On the morning of December 14, 1923 alarming reports that the insurrection was imminent spread quickly through Zomba. Indian storekeepers on the road between Zomba and Blantyre were said to be packing up their goods and decamping to more secure locations in Limbe; a few European planters and their families abandoned their estates to seek greater protection. KAR patrols were dispatched into districts of intense Watchtower activity, and police were advised to stand by. The alarm reached a fevered pitch on December 15 after false rumors circulated that two Indians had been murdered at Chiradzulu, just north of Blantyre. European estates emptied. The patrols waited. But nothing happened. In the days after the alarm, Watchtower leaders and adherents were called in for questioning and warned. All claimed their loyalty, and investigations uncovered no evidence of sedition. The governor captured the episode best when, trying to explain the alleged December 15 plot to the secretary of state for the colonies, he admitted "[i]t has been impossible to ascertain definitely what actually gave rise to the alarm."[6]

The phantom rising of 1923 comprises an instructive illustration of colonial anxieties on what I call the "Garveyist frontier." The Watchtower[7] movement extended across southern and central Africa in the years following World War I, reaching deep into Nyasaland, Northern Rhodesia (Zambia), Southern Rhodesia (Zimbabwe), and Portuguese East Africa, and disseminating a dynamic discourse of African religious independence that presented a formidable challenge to colonial governments throughout the region. As the 1920s wore on, Watchtower prophets increasingly joined their emphasis on apocalyptic liberation, drawn from the liturgy of the American-based Watch Tower Bible and Tract Society, with a powerful mythology that had filtered north from South Africa, predicated on the redemptive power of black Americans, who were prophesied to arrive shortly in Africa with the means—in the form of battleships, or airplanes, or heavy artillery—to drive Europeans from the continent. This mythology was a dramatic side effect of the persistent and remarkable efforts of Garveyite organizers and supporters to spread the word of Garveyism across large parcels of Africa.

The relationship between the Watchtower movement and Garveyism has been suggested by scholars, but never explored in a sustained way.[8] There is good reason for this: The historical record not only reveals little that would suggest a tangible connection between Watchtower prophets and Garveyite organizers, but demonstrates a rivalry between the two groups. As Garveyites in central Africa worked patiently and cautiously to construct the foundation for their liberation—as the next chapter will explore—they looked on in dismay as Watchtower dissidents organized audacious revivals that provocatively conflated the millennium with the bloody end of European rule.[9]

Yet by participating in this discourse, Watchtower prophets drew on an alternative tradition that had its own roots in Garveyite organizing. As the hyperbolic language of Garveyist redemption was carried across South Africa after the war, it was translated into what became a widely believed "myth of the black American liberator," a powerful symbolism that sparked a series of millennial revivals from one end of the continent to the other, from the Belgian Congo to the Eastern Cape. As the myth of the black American liberator was transmitted north, along the crisscrossing routes of labor migrancy connecting the vast region of central-southern Africa, it was adopted time and again by Watchtower prophets, filtered through a rich regional history of diasporic contact, reorganized in the context of local religious and political traditions, and projected in a fashion in which the Garveyite faithful in the United States could hardly have imagined. Following the transmission of Garveyist discourse here, to its outer limits, to the "Garveyist frontier," suggests the extent to which Garveyism was able to penetrate the consciousness of colonial Africa—a unique and unmatched accomplishment for a pan-African movement with its organizational roots primarily outside of the continent.

In charting the resonance of Garveyist discourse in a series of religious movements in southern and central Africa, this chapter owes a debt to the lively historiography of African religious expression. For decades, this literature was shaped by a series of polarities, constructed in the hopes of grasping a semblance of order out of an impossibly chaotic and diverse field. Historians and anthropologists writing during the period of nationalist triumph, in the 1950s and 1960s, wondered if African independent religious movements might constitute, as Georges Balandier suggested, "the pre-history of modern nationalism," or if they were better characterized as a mode of irrational escapism. Later scholars wondered if these movements should be framed as political, or religious, or politico-religious; whether they were impelled by global systems or local agency; whether they evinced nascent class formation or dynamic cultural production that confounded Marxist analysis; whether they reflected innovations during the colonial period or deeper trajectories of religious practices that predated European rule.[10]

In the end, the path out of the chaos looped back into the brambles of diversity that scholars had so long resisted. Rather than restricting African religious practices to particular frames, scholars instead began to view them as situationally constituted: diffuse and eclectic systems that were forged from a particular set of circumstances, adopted by historical actors for a particular set of reasons, and transformed by the collision of action and reaction, agency and constraint. In other words, religion, like all other social, cultural, and discursive complexes, provided the raw material with which people forged their lives. It was no longer a question of whether religious practices were political; rather, the question was, to what uses? As Jean and John Comaroff have demonstrated, religious observance in Africa offered a point of contact, a system of shared beliefs, a "long conversation" wherein colonial subjects might negotiate and contest their relationships with each other and with the colonial state. Neither the direction nor the outcome of these conversations was determined by the particular essence of religious expression. As Karen Fields has suggestively argued, religious ideas "are opiates at some times and stimulants at others. In themselves, they cause nothing but dreams." Rather, religious practices acquired a radical visage, an anticolonial posture, at those moments when they offered a viable means of articulating a conflict, a lingua franca within which both colonizer and colonized might revisit the terms of their relationship.[11]

For millennial revivals in southern and central Africa, Garveyism provided this very device. Garveyites sustained, facilitated, and amplified a
diasporic field of mythmaking that across the region had the unintended
effect of offering African prophets and proselytizers a means to claim their
independence, to project power, and to articulate their visions of a renewed
Africa. Revivalists challenged the authority of the state by linking their millennial visions of deliverance to fantastical rumors about the arrival of African American liberators, who would drive Europeans from the continent
and institute a peaceful era of black rule. Terence Ranger has cautioned that
the "parano[a]ic fears" of colonial agents—whose perspectives dominate
the historical record, and who at times worried excessively about the sinister influence of outside agitators—casts doubt upon the extent to which
independent religious movements were aligned with pan-African activists.[12]
But it was precisely these fears, the concern that the war had set a series
of forces loose upon the world, that pan-African sentiment was increasing,
that a rising tide of color would swallow a wounded white civilization, that
gave the "myth of the Americans" such force. Unable to credibly, or logisti-
cally, suppress independent African religious expression, colonial administers carefully policed the boundary between religion and politics, dwell-
ing obsessively upon creeping evidence of intertribal and extra-territorial
consciousness. Yet in practice religion and politics could not be neatly disentangled; arbitrary and punitive limits to free expression were codified.
In demarcating a line of sedition at the confluence of a contradiction, the
colonial state ensured that the line would be transgressed again and again.

"Ama Melika ayeza" (The Americans Are Coming): The Rising Tide of Color in South Africa

In the United States, Garveyites' embrace of the narrative of a "rising tide
of color" projected the focus of their aspirations abroad. In southern Africa, Garveyist assurances of a racial Armageddon in Africa, and promises of
aid from Africans-in-exile in the conflict, offered an electric and audacious
discursive vehicle for black political expression. This was particularly true
because it broadcast so precisely the specter that white administrators in
Africa feared the most. During the war, the mixing of black peoples from
across the continent and abroad had led to widespread concerns that the
carefully delineated boundaries of tribal administration had been undermined, that Africans were newly receptive to the doctrine of "Africa for
the Africans" mobilized to such explosive effect by John Chilembwe.[13] After
the conflict, there was much hand-wringing by commentators worried that
the war had shattered the prestige of Western civilization, revealing its vulnerability at the very moment that Europe lay in ruins, enfeebled militarily

and materially. Everywhere was evidence of a creeping race consciousness, spurred by wartime congress, exacerbated by postwar dislocations and deprivations, facilitated by improvements in postal and transportation technologies, and inflamed by the "flood" of propaganda entering the continent from nationalist sources in India and Egypt and from the "extreme section of American Negroes."[14]

Viewed through this prism, it is unsurprising that Garveyism shook the confidence of colonial governments and elicited a swift and sustained response. By the end of 1922, the *Negro World* had been officially banned throughout much of Africa—with the notable exception of South Africa—or was otherwise "strictly controlled."[15] Marcus Garvey's movements were closely monitored, his legal troubles gleefully reported, and his failures in Liberia celebrated. When Garvey announced plans to visit Africa as part of a world tour in 1923, the response from British authorities to block his entry was swift and coordinated.[16] Garvey's "seditious propaganda" kept others out as well. African American missionaries wishing to work in British West Africa were asked to demonstrate their loyalty by producing signed documents of guarantee from the Foreign Missions Conference of North America.[17] Rumors of Garveyist-engineered uprisings, alliances with Bolshevists and Pan-Islamists, and sundry conspiracies enlivened colonial fears.[18] And yet officials were unable to stem the flow of transatlantic information that carried news of the movement to Africa. Garveyite organizers continued to surface on the colonial radar, traveling from port towns in British West Africa, South Africa, and Portuguese East Africa to points along the coastline and deep into the interior. The *Negro World* continued to arrive, smuggled in mattresses and hidden inside the covers of other journals.[19]

For their part, Garveyites in the United States enthusiastically encouraged colonial apprehensions. Marcus Garvey assured that official suppression had not slowed the organization's African agents, working secretly, building support, and taking advantage of the indigenous practice of "drum wireless" to spread literature and information across the continent. "Africa has got the program of the UNIA," he boasted to his supporters in New York. "And even though they have suppressed the *Negro World* in French Africa, in British Africa, in Italian Africa, and Portuguese Africa, the Africans are conveying the propaganda of the Universal Negro Improvement Association through their own methods of communication." After the French prohibited the circulation of the *Negro World* in their colonies, Garvey taunted that the ban had come too late, and that not only had French West Africa been organized, but so too had Senegalese troops on the Rhine. "Today the *Negro World* stands out as the accepted voice of an awakened race," wrote Samuel A. Haynes in 1927. "It is translated into scores of dialects twenty-four hours after arrival in Africa, and carried by fleet runners into the hinterland, up the great lakes of Southeast Africa, and the uncharted reaches of the Nile, the Congo, the

Zambesi and the Niger, where millions of our fellowmen wait in silence for its arrival." In Asia was heard the cry of "China for the Chinese" and "India for the Indians"; the UNIA was laying the groundwork for a similar awakening in Africa. Garveyite orators like Haynes were fond of metaphors that all led back to the same place: the tide had turned; the writing was on the wall; the torch of liberty had been lit and could not be extinguished. The age of white world supremacy was passing from the stage.[20]

South African Garveyites readily confirmed this expansive view of the UNIA's influence. ANC activist Moses Mphahlele, writing to the *Negro World* from Johannesburg, reported that "[t]he spirit of Garvey is being carried throughout the continent and is taking possession of the hearts and minds of the native population." A Garveyite from Cape Town was heartened that the movement was growing stronger throughout the continent every day, that in "Zulu Land, Basuto Land, Bechuana Land, East, South, and West Africa, the cry is ever the same, 'Africa for the African.'" For South African Garveyites the work of the UNIA was connected, as Garveyist propaganda made clear, to the worldwide anticolonial struggle. In calling for the pardon of Garvey in 1927, the pro-Garvey paper *Abantu Batho* compared his persecution to those of Zaghlul Pasha in Egypt, Terence MacSwiney in Ireland, and Gandhi in India. "In less than ten years," the paper remarked, "the preachments of Marcus Garvey have, politically and economically, morally and educationally, awakened the slumbering race consciousness of black, brown, and yellow races to action, and no amount of diplomatic imperial intimidation will extinguish the burning fire of determination implanted in the bosoms of teeming millions of black, brown and yellow races of the globe."[21]

No one was more responsible for projecting this discourse in South Africa than James Thaele, the influential president of the African National Congress (Western Province), who used the platform of his newspaper, the *African World*, to promote an internationalist politics that positioned Garveyism as the primary vehicle for an emerging and inexorable Negro racial consciousness. In the paper's inaugural edition, Thaele declared the UNIA "the biggest thing today in Negro modern organizations," and deemed it essential that Africans at home seek cooperation with their brethren abroad. The UNIA, he argued, was to Negroes scattered around the globe what the League of Nations was to European governments; the *Negro World* was the "Bible" that would facilitate "the inevitable practicability of the African Empire." Along with an assimilation of the UNIA program, Thaele instructed South Africans to embrace Garveyites' celebration of creeping global color consciousness, suggesting that they learn lessons from Gandhian nonviolence, Japan's ascendance to world power, Éamon de Valera's "manly stand" in Ireland, and the "psychology and traits" of Zaghlul Pasha.[22] In August 1925, the *African World* reprinted an editorial by Amy Jacques Garvey

FIGURE 6.1. Southern and Central Africa.

entitled "Yellow and White Races Prepare for Future Armageddon—Mr. Black Man, What About You?," which appealed to Negroes to note the rising of Abd-el Krim in Morocco, agitation in China and Mexico, and the militarization of Japan, and to view them in the context of Marcus Garvey's preachments and prophecies. The article was accompanied by a promise to reproduce and translate the article into African dialects, and to send it to traditional African monarchs and dignitaries throughout the region.[23]

The prestige of the UNIA in southern Africa filtered into popular consciousness, and created for many Africans an impending, and undetermined, sense of event. As one Garveyite put it, "there's a huge bright Planet of Hope rising east from America. Its color is black. Its indication is a marvel. Its size is unknown. The world's greatest astronomers cannot calculate its distance nor its exact position." South African Garveyites like William O. Jackson, president of the Cape Town Division, contributed to this expectation by declaring that not only were American Negroes preparing to return to Africa, armed with the advanced knowledge of American civilization, but that such an event was prophesied in scripture. Beginning in 1920, UNIA propaganda throughout the region fueled persistent rumors about the impending arrival of a black fleet armed to do battle with whites. The moderate South African educator and activist, Davidson Don Tengo Jabavu, complained in 1922 that mistreatment by white employers after the war had "rendered the Natives . . . easy victims to the belief in Marcus Garvey, whose Black Republic propaganda promises such great things," including "the expulsion of the white man and his yoke of misrule." The attractiveness of the program, wrote Jabavu, had "made a deep impression on our illiterate people, so that even from backwoods hamlets rings the magic motto, 'Ama Melika ayeza' (The Americans are coming)."[24]

The so-called "myth of the American liberator" that grew up around the Garvey movement in southern Africa sprouted from fertile ground. By the early postwar period, an "American" presence—a collection of West Indian and African American migrant workers, sailors, and missionaries—had been well established in South Africa, dating back to the earlier part of the nineteenth century and quickening after the discovery of diamonds around Kimberley and gold on the Witwatersrand. The widespread belief that American Negroes had acquired what were for Africans unattainable levels of success and prestige in the New World was bolstered by the spectacular popularity of the Virginia Jubilee Singers, who toured South Africa three times between 1890 and 1899 and projected a dazzling visage of sophistication. This belief also lent authority to the narrative of providential destiny that Garvey had adapted from nineteenth-century black nationalists like Edward Wilmot Blyden and Alexander Crummell, and which cast the return of "civilized" and Christianized blacks to Africa as part of God's cosmic plan to redeem the race. Members of the South African mission elite sent their children to colleges in the United States and enthusiastically embraced the successes of Booker T. Washington. Mangena Mokone's Ethiopian Church, which splintered from the Wesleyan Methodist Missionary Society in 1892, merged in 1896 with the American Methodist Episcopal Church (AME), drawn at least in part by the prestige associated with African American Methodism. The great bishop of the AME Church, Henry McNeal Turner, traveled to South Africa for six weeks in 1898 to institutionalize the merger, and embodied for many a prototype of future black leadership and authority. Turner, long an advocate of Negro emigrationism, preached sermons from the Cape to the Transvaal, lending, as always, his immense skills as a motivator to a message of providential destiny adapted from Blyden and Crummell and a doctrine of race pride evocative of Martin Delany. When South Africans first learned of Garveyism, much of the content undoubtedly sounded familiar, and Garvey had Turner and the AME Church to thank. As James T. Campbell has suggested, "Garveyism flowed through channels first carved by independent Christianity."[25]

To this legacy Garveyism added its rich vocabulary of New Negro insurgency and international anticolonial mobilization. For many southern Africans, Garvey's marriage of providential design and postwar apocalyptic prophecy offered a spectacular vision of their destiny. It suggested an alternative framework of political and spiritual power beyond the authority of the white state. In popular African belief, political authority in the natural world was contingent on the ability of rulers to tame the spiritual authority of the supernatural world. Political legitimacy resulted in natural and spiritual harmony; illegitimacy augured disintegration, suffering, evil. The construction of a diasporic framework of power and authority, confirmed by scripture, bolstered by South African views about black Americans, offered an appealing and subversive vessel for Africans disillusioned with the capacity of the current regime to provide a judicious and harmonious equilibrium. Such a vehicle was especially potent in the aftermath of war and influenza, and amidst inflation, spiking taxes, labor shortages, drought, and repressive labor and land policies. As Garveyism was carried throughout the region, it offered Africans a discursive means to imagine new governing structures, to explore new reservoirs of political and religious independence.[26]

Most dramatically, Garveyism was deployed in the form of rumor and myth by a series of religious and political revivals in the Eastern Cape. Beginning with the religious sects guided by the prophets Enoch Mgijima and Nontetha Nkwenkwe in the early 1920s, and exploding by the end of the decade in the rural politics of the Wellington Movement and the Industrial and Commercial Workers' Union (ICU), activists in the region used news of the UNIA—and later popular beliefs about its potency—to bolster their own claims of authority, and to lend credibility to their own vehicles of dissent.[27]

Perhaps the most colorful of these revivals was led by the charismatic herbalist, organizer, and pan-Africanist Wellington Butelezi, who developed a robust following in the rural reserves of the Transkei that reached a peak in 1926 and 1927. Butelezi may have been first introduced to Garveyism while a student at the Lovedale Institution in the Eastern Cape in 1921, where at weekly forums with teachers and students the UNIA was a popular subject. Or perhaps he acquired an interest in Garveyism while living briefly with James Thaele in Cape Town in 1924.[28] What is clear is that in 1925, when Butelezi moved his herbalist practice to Qachas Nek, Basutoland, he found himself in the midst of extensive Garveyite organizing, spearheaded by the West Indian-born Ernest Wallace and other "black Americans" who had moved to Basutoland to establish UNIA divisions. Butelezi met Wallace, and conducted joint meetings with him in the nearby Matatiele district. He was inspired. As Butelezi traveled through the region selling his medicines, he began organizing the African peasantry under the banner of his own brand of homegrown Garveyism.[29]

Ernest Wallace, as the next chapter suggests, joined the bulk of his fellow African Garveyites in advocating a tactical and cautious program of racial cooperation, consciousness raising, and uplift designed to sustain the movement during a period of political inopportunity.[30] Butelezi took a less subtle tack. Under the assumed identity of Dr. Butler Hansford Wellington, Butelezi claimed to have been born in Chicago, to be the holder of an American medical degree, and to be the personal representative of Marcus Garvey in South Africa. To sell his persona, he spoke only in English, dressed in academic robes, and toured the Transkei in a Dodge sedan, for which he hired a personal driver. From the stump, Dr. Wellington implored Africans to abandon their tribal grievances, to unite under the banner of "Africa for the Africans," and to pursue the aim of independence by building an infrastructure of black-owned churches and schools free from the corrosive influence of white control. "I want you to do away with the European Government and as well as all the white people," he commanded during an address in Hershel, in August 1928. Blacks found themselves segregated and disempowered in European churches, excluded from representation in the House of Assembly, taxed heavily, and pressed together on inadequate plots of land. The only path forward was to "[leave] the whitemen": to begin the process of self-government.[31]

To lend added authority to his program of school and church building, the doctor assured his audiences that help was on the way. Drawing on the millennial revivalism of Mgijima and Nontetha, and evoking popular beliefs about Garveyism and black Americans, Wellington developed a breathtaking narrative of liberation.[32] On the day of judgment, a liberating army of black Americans, led by "General Garvey," would arrive in airplanes and rain balls of burning charcoal on whites and on non-believers. To distinguish themselves from doubters and thus assure their safety, Wellington's followers were advised to paint their houses black. More lucratively for Wellington, his followers were asked to purchase red, black, and green membership badges, at a cost of 2s. 6d., which would also shield them against the fire raining from above.[33] As Wellington's fame grew through the Transkei, peasants flocked to his cause by the thousands; mission schools reported decreasing attendance numbers, while Wellington's "American" schools flourished. It was widely believed that Wellington possessed magical powers, and that he was feared by whites. Such was the awe and enthusiasm of his followers that they rarely stuck to the membership fee and eagerly parted with twice, ten, or thirty times the amount. "[I]n all my life I have never seen so much money, either in coins or notes," recalled one follower. "The table was so full high up." The day of reckoning never came, and in March 1927, Wellington was banished from the Transkei by the South African government, effectively cut off from his base of support. Nevertheless, Wellington continued his campaign from adjoining regions, until he vanished from the record during World War II. His schools and churches were sustained in the Transkei through the 1930s. And his efforts to spread his particular brand of homegrown Garveyist politics were continued by loyalists who remained in the region, worked to organize UNIA divisions, and sustained his claims of approaching American liberation.[34]

The largest and most successful purveyor of millennial mythmaking in the Eastern Cape was the ICU. By mid-decade, Clements Kadalie's organization had shifted the bulk of its efforts away from urban unionism and toward the mobilization of the African peasantry. As the ICU spread into rural communities across the Eastern Cape, Natal, the Orange Free State, and the Transvaal, covering the eastern half of the country, the organization was shaped as much from below—by local conditions and discourses—as it exerted its own influence. The result was what Helen Bradford calls a "flexible nationalist ideology," which allowed organizers to join elements of socialism and class-based solidarity with strands of separatist Christianity, Garveyist pan-Africanism, and millennial prophecy.[35] The results were spectacular. Up to 1925, the ICU had organized over two dozen branches, the majority in cities in the Cape, and claimed 30,000 adherents; by the end of 1927, over one hundred branches existed, the majority based in small villages and in the hinterland, and the membership had ballooned to somewhere between 150,000 and 250,000.[36]

Garveyism had an important formative influence on the ICU—in 1920, Kadalie confided that his "essential object [was] to be the great African Marcus Garvey"—and despite Kadalie's subsequent paranoia that the Union would be swallowed into a UNIA auxiliary, dense layers of connections joined the two organizations throughout the 1920s.[37] In the countryside, ICU organizers quickly discovered the benefits of accenting this association. By the mid-1920s Garveyist ideas and rumors had blanketed the region; in Pondoland, just east of Wellington Butelezi's organizing heartland in Griqualand East, educator W. D. Cingo remarked on the common belief in a "mighty race of black people" living in America, manufacturing their own "mighty weapons of war," and feared by European nations.[38] When they could, ICU officers highlighted their familiarity with America, or boasted "American Negro" accents, or presented themselves as "Ambassadors from America."[39] They also sought to blur the line between their organizing efforts and the work of the UNIA. If the ICU formally promoted class-based solidarity alongside racial solidarity, and cited unionism as the key to breaking down tribal barriers, by the late 1920s its advocacy of racial awakening, organizing, and solidarity was indistinguishable from the advocacy of the UNIA. The iconography of the ICU—its red membership cards, red flag, and green badges—matched the UNIA's red, black, and green, and Helen Bradford has suggested that ICU organizers consciously exploited the similarity. ICU organizers were not adverse to the cry, "Africa for the Africans!"[40] Nor were they adverse to evoking the name of Marcus Garvey in the cause of unity, black self-consciousness, and self-help. It is unsurprising, as one South African remembered, that "[m]any country people thought that the ICU leaders were American Negroes who had come to deliver them from slavery."[41]

ICU workers seem to have eagerly adopted the myth of the American liberator.[42] Nowhere was this more true than in the volatile and depressed region of Pondoland, where Union organizers reached in mid-1927. By the end of the year, an elaborate discourse of millennial prophecy had grown up around the ICU's membership drive. The Union's red membership ticket—like Wellington's red, black, and green badges—became invested with a host of talismanic powers, most importantly the ability to distinguish the faithful on the day of reckoning, when American-steered airplanes would fly low over the country and rain fire upon the whites and upon the faithless. By August, ICU organizers were advocating the slaughter of pigs and the destruction of pig fat—traditionally thought to protect Mpondo from lightning. In sum, the ICU promised a vision of African liberation premised on an approaching African American beacon from across the sea, and dependent on the ability of ICU organizers on the ground to mobilize Africans around a set of common goals. In a time of great suffering and uncertainty, it offered to replace an old spiritual protection—pig fat—with a new one—red membership cards—which had come to embody a hybrid system of beliefs borrowing from nationalist, pan-Africanist, and traditional and Christian reservoirs.[43]

Making this dialogue legible—as it did for millennial revivals across the region—was the steady stream of Garveyist propaganda filtering through the country, and the successful efforts of Garveyite activists to invest their organization, and diasporic Africans more broadly speaking, with immense industrial and spiritual power. By the end of the 1920s, Garveyism, both in its organizational and mythical form, was identifiable to large sections of the South African people, projecting an eclectic and malleable discourse of deliverance, dispersed widely and widely understood. "The mad dreams and literature of Marcus Garvey . . . were broadcast on the winds," wrote W. D. Cingo in 1927. "Hopes for political and economical emancipation were revived and to-day the word America (*i Melika*) is a household word symbolic of nothing else but Bantu National freedom and liberty."[44]

This mythical translation of Garveyism was not long contained within the borders of South Africa. In central Africa, beliefs like the ones described by Cingo offered an explosive symbolism for a dynamic movement of independent Christianity that came to be known across the region simply as "Watchtower."

WATCH TOWER AND WATCHTOWER: MILLENNIAL PAN-AFRICANISM IN CENTRAL AFRICA

The Watch Tower Bible and Tract Society (WTBTS) was incorporated in 1884 by Charles Taze Russell, a former haberdasher from Allegheny, Pennsylvania. Russell interpreted scripture to reveal that Christ had returned invisibly to earth in 1874, in advance of Armageddon, which would occur in 1914. He encouraged his followers to spread the news and baptize converts while eschewing politics, adopting pacifism, and preparing for the portentous final battle, which would inaugurate the millennium for the faithful. Under the leadership of Joseph F. Rutherford, who assumed control of the WTBTS after Russell's death in 1916, Watch Tower prophecy pushed Armageddon into the near future, and declared 1914 as the moment Satan had descended to the earth to unleash his chaos. Until this truth was revealed, the Watch Tower must continue their work as ambassadors for Christ, "diplomats in an alien world" unbeholden to the trifles of misguided secular authority.[45]

In 1906, Russell was visited in Allegheny by Joseph Booth, and convinced to expand his field of missionary activity to Africa. With Russell's blessing, Booth returned to South Africa in 1907 and, using his extensive network of contacts, disseminated news and literature of the movement widely through the region. The marriage of Russell's millennial and antistatist prophecy to Booth's principled advocacy of African independence was, predictably, explosive. In 1908, one of Booth's converts at Cape Town, Elliott Kamwana, traveled home to the western shore of Lake Nyasa (Lake Malawi) and caused a sensation, baptizing between ten and twelve thousand people before his removal from the region in 1910. Kamwana prophesied the end of the world, in October 1914, and garnished news of the coming millennium with an explicitly anticolonial, pan-Africanist strain. Taxes would be abolished. Whites would be driven away. Africans would be restored to authority, and would—in Christ's kingdom—"build [their] own ships, make [their] own powder, and make or import [their] own guns." Kamwana's revival struck a chord with Nyasalanders, exposed to the preaching of the European missions, but denied its promises of salvation by stringent membership guidelines, long probationary periods, and limited access to positions of leadership. Kamwana offered something quite different: black leadership, baptism for all, and confirmation of the lingering feeling that European missionaries were concealing important parts of the Truth. Under the tutelage of Booth, influenced by the particular frustrations and needs of northern Nyasaland, Kamwana brought the Watch Tower into central Africa and transformed it into "Watchtower," a vehicle of African independent worship joining the conviction of Christ's imminent reign on earth with the belief that the millennium would make manifest a peaceful era of black rule.[46]

Kamwana's arrest, and subsequent deportation to the Seychelles, halted the momentum of the Watchtower movement in Nyasaland.[47] It was not long, however, before a second—and more subversive—wave of Watchtower revival washed over the neighboring district of Tanganyika, in Northern Rhodesia. The spark this time was World War I. The ferocious East Africa Campaign had administered a relentless series of plagues upon the region. Needing a massive recruitment of porters to transport supplies over long stretches of roadless territory, administrators raised taxes to compel service and ordered chiefs to mobilize workers. When these recruitment strategies proved inadequate to meet demand, the state turned to less subtle tactics: forcible conscription, hostage taking, hut burning, and other devices of terror. To this chaos was added the poverty, displacements and miseries of wartime, exacerbated by the confiscation of villagers' goods and provisions. The end of the war brought some relief, but also massive inflation and the worldwide influenza plague. As one administrator remarked, "Natives cannot reconcile the rise in prices with the great victory which they are told has been won by the allies."[48]

Into this tinderbox came seven Watchtower preachers, natives of the Tanganyika District, all trained at the Mwenzo mission, who had been forcibly expelled from the mines of Southern Rhodesia in 1917 for disseminating subversive doctrines. One of the men, Hanoc Sindano, quickly acquired a large following in his home district, building a headquarters and several churches, and recruiting a cadre of evangelists to spread his message and teachers to organize villages once converts had been won. Sindano had spent two years training at the headquarters of the WTBTS in Cape Town but, like Kamwana, his ministry combined elements of Watch Tower prophesy with an explosive doctrine of African independence catering to local expectations and needs. Sindano announced the coming millennium, and told followers to disassociate themselves from a corrupted secular world by refusing to work for the government or pay taxes, rejecting chiefly power and authority, and ceasing the cultivation of their crops in expectation of the end of days.[49] Central to Sindano's message was the accusation that Europeans, in their zeal to reap financial gain from Africa, had purposively betrayed the will of God by withholding His truth from Africans, and that Europeans were to be punished for their misdeeds. As he was recorded preaching by an undercover detective:

> Long ago the Europeans did not know God same as we, but some other people came to their country and taught them, and God helped them and gave them wis[dom] and all things, the Europeans did not know about our country (Africa), but God made them know and sent them with goods and ma[n]y things we see to come and give us free, and teach us about God, and when they get into this country, they hide everything, and teach us very little about God, they teach us how to write but they did not tell us what God sent them here for, and they could not give us the things free what God gave them to give us. They make us to work very very hard and give us [little] for the work we have done for them, therefore if we pray to God very hard with all our hearts, God will hear our prayer and will clear all the Europeans back home to England and everything will be ours, and we will be rich as they are.[50]

According to Father Tanguy of the White Fathers mission, Sindano also declared, "tous les hommes sont égaux, le noir et égal au blanc. Soyons nos propres maîtres: L'Europe à l'Européen, l'Afrique à l'Africain." Blacks are equal to whites. Let us be our own masters. Europe for the Europeans and Africa for the Africans.[51]

The confrontation between Watchtower adherents and the colonial state reached a climax toward the end of 1918, after a raid of German African troops into Northern Rhodesia left in ruins the bomas at Fife and Kasama, along with two Catholic mission stations, and was widely interpreted as an affirmation of Watchtower prophesy. Under the leadership of Shadrach Sinkala, who had joined Sindano north on the trek from Southern Rhodesia, hundreds were baptized. As the movement escalated, Sinkala struck a blow at the edifice of chiefly power by entering the village of Musamansi and destroying the headman's ancestor shrine, the visible manifestation of his spiritual authority. Then, at a meeting called by the district commissioners of Fife, Abercorn, and Chinsali with local chiefs and headmen to discuss the building crisis of chiefly—and, by extension, colonial—legitimacy, five hundred Watchtower adherents disrupted the proceedings with praying and singing, and—when confronted—openly resisted arrest. When Charles Draper, the District Commissioner of the Fife sub-district, sent boma messengers to detain Sinkala and his followers, Sinkala sent them away, declaring, "If you come back bring a [M]axim gun. Talk will not move me." Finally, Sinkala was captured, and in January 1919 British troops were dispatched to Kapililonga Hill to confront Sindano and hundreds of his supporters, arresting over a hundred resistors and banishing the leadership from the province. The suppression of the revival offered only partial comfort. As Draper reported, the Watchtower had created "a spirit of open defiance such as one has never dreamt of in this part of the world."[52]

"THE NEW NATION WILL BE AMERICA": THE WATCHTOWER MOVEMENT AND THE GARVEYIST FRONTIER

Beginning around 1924, as the deportees from the revival of 1917–19 were released and began to trickle back into Northern Rhodesia, the Watchtower enjoyed a renaissance that dispersed the movement broadly into rural villages, mine compounds, and urban centers across the colony.[53] Unlike the revivals of Kamwana, Sindano, and Sinkala, which escalated into dramatic confrontations with the colonial state, Watchtower preachers entered into an uneasy stalemate with colonial officials who recognized their inability to prevent the growth of the movement, and sought instead to demarcate a line of seditious behavior across which Watchtower adherents could not safely cross. Yet because Watch Tower liturgy was premised on the coming millennium, and because in its African translation the millennium was often synonymous with the forceful expulsion of Europeans from the continent, sedition remained an ever-present subtext. And because it was incumbent on Watchtower preachers to demonstrate to followers that their spiritual power and authority promised a superior alternative to the protections of the colonial state, forceful anticolonial language became a common feature of revivals. To evoke prophetic authority, Watchtower preachers widely turned to the myth of the American liberator, garnished with colorful local detail and dramatic personal flourishes. Diasporic discourse facilitated by Garveyism's wide and garbled dissemination circulated through Northern Rhodesia as a new pivot of Watchtower and state relations: simultaneously a means for Watchtower preachers to express their command over their flock, and a means for the state to exert its tenuous command over the Watchtower.

The emergence of this third wave of subversive Watchtower revivalism first caught the attention of authorities in the Southern Rhodesian urban hub, Bulawayo, where in 1923 George Kunga, a discipline of Bennett Siyasia, the leading figure in the Watchtower movement in Nyasaland, began forecasting the triumph of the "black races" over the powerful, white "Goliath."[54] By 1924, "rumors and wild talk" of missionary duplicity, boma corruption, and imminent liberation from white rule were being promulgated widely in the districts along the Northern Rhodesian rail line, which stretched north from Livingstone toward the nascent Copperbelt and the Katanga Province of the southeastern Congo. The transfer that year of the colony from the stewardship of the British South Africa Company to the Colonial

Office lent credibility to Watchtower claims about the dissolution of white rule and the prophesied arrival of black Americans.[55] In 1925, the infamous Tomo Nyirenda, whose witch-cleansing revival resulted in the drowning of dozens of people in the eastern region of Northern Rhodesia and in the Katanga Province, declared that he had been sent by the Americans to cleanse the country, and that when the Americans arrived all of the white men would be driven away, leaving vast sums of wealth along with white women, who would be made slaves.[56] In Ndola, that same year, Watchtower preachers forecast that in 1926 the black races would be emancipated by a "huge army of American Negroes."[57] By the early 1930s, the belief that American Negroes would soon liberate the country had spread among the villages throughout the Luapula Valley, and was reported in Fort Jameson to the east, in the Katanga Province to the north, and in the Mazabuka District to the south.[58]

As George Shepperson has suggested, the facilitation of this mythology in central Africa was at least in part spurred by the tour of the Ghanaian educator James E. K. Aggrey through Nyasaland and Southern Rhodesia in 1924 as a representative of the Phelps-Stokes Commission on African Education, an event that was cast in millennial terms and widely interpreted as the harbinger of an American invasion.[59] But even Aggrey himself—who was widely mistaken for an African American, and a Garveyite—was cast by popular perception in the framework of Garveyist organizing.[60] Word of Garveyism had reached Northern Rhodesia by 1923, when smuggled copies of the *Negro World* were discovered entering the colony.[61] And as the movement spread across South Africa and into neighboring colonies, it was carried through central Africa by workers traversing the vast circuits of labor migration that joined mines, European farms, and urban centers in a single network of shared information.[62] Watchtower members were drawn from nearly every segment of African society—men and women, educated and uneducated, clerks and laborers—but the movement was heavily represented by men who had received some education, and who traveled widely throughout the region in search of employment.[63] If their exposure to education and Christianity alienated them from the so-called "traditional" customary order of village life, their lack of education, and lack of Christian training, left them shut out of respectable positions in the "detribalized" society of the towns.[64] In the labor compounds of Southern Rhodesia, Portuguese East Africa, and South Africa, on their way to or from Northern Rhodesia, these migrants found in Watchtower a new means to leadership. And they discovered in Garveyism a new language of diasporic prophecy with which to express that authority.

There are mere whispers of tangible evidence connecting Watchtower to Garveyism.[65] Yet, as with millennial revivals in South Africa, Garveyism was less important in this context as an organizational vessel than as an abstract vehicle for the transmission of rumor, a malleable mythology of liberation from across the sea. Away from the hub of the European-controlled WTBTS, in Cape Town, and at sites of intense Garveyist organizing, especially in Portuguese East Africa, Watchtower acquired an unmistakably "Ethiopian" visage; and from this access point literature, information, and people streamed into the English colonies of central Africa.[66] Like the vampire stories that Luise White has so brilliantly mined, rumors of African American liberators emerged as a "genre" with recognizable outlines, adaptable to local particularities and needs.[67] On the Garveyist frontier they articulated the central point of confrontation between Watchtower adherents and colonial agents, offering for both whites and blacks, as Karen Fields has suggested, "a luxuriant symbolic language in which to think about African liberation."[68] In the same manner that World War I offered a context and a discourse for the projection of Watchtower radicalism, in the 1920s and 1930s rumors of diasporic deliverance emerged as a framing language for ambitious preachers eager to infuse their ministries with spiritual and secular fonts of power, a language that proved resilient because it so effectively articulated—and pushed—the "boundaries of attack and subversion" at which African dissidents and colonial agents met.[69]

Officials in British Central Africa had little interest in permitting Watchtower adherents to freely practice their faith. Although opinions varied about the degree of the threat the movement posed, there was general agreement on the point that, as C. A. Cardew wrote to the head of the colonial police force in Nyasaland, "the movement is not merely religious; it is Ethiopian and aims at the ideal of 'Africa for the Africans' and at the eventual expulsion of Europeans from Nyasaland."[70] The problem was twofold. Government observers were convinced that the greatest danger of the movement was its secrecy, its dreaded night time meetings at which, away from the watchful eyes of colonial observers, Watchtower leaders could poison credulous African minds with pernicious anti-European rhetoric. To suppress the movement would merely drive it further underground, to martyr its adherents, to give it the endorsement of colonial illegitimacy.[71] At the same time, colonial officials worried about their own legitimacy. Try as they might, there was no practical way to regulate or suppress African-controlled missions without opening the Pandora's box of religious persecution.[72] This was dangerous territory. In practical terms, colonial state apparatuses, spread thin on the ground, charged with conducting affairs on the cheap, lacked the resources to control independent African religious observance. To confront the Watchtower movement on religious grounds was to undermine the central legitimizing claim of the colonial enterprise: the gift of beneficent Western civilization, of which Christianity comprised a central plank. To confront the Watchtower movement and fail threatened to do worse: to bring into plain sight the fragility of state power.

Apart from brief lapses in nerve, the colonial government in Nyasaland handled the Watchtower movement with great intelligence and foresight.[73] Aiming to bring the movement into the open, to remove the prestige of colonial opposition, and to drive a wedge between Africans interested in the strict observance of religious faith and those with subversive and political aspirations, the colony formally authorized Watchtower preaching in May 1922. Representatives of the WTBTS were invited into the colony, although the European-controlled church met with meager success and comforted itself by fulminating against the perversions of their creed by the African Watchtower. Authorization was conditional. Watchtower church representatives were required to submit the names of their followers to district officers; night meetings were disallowed; and the church was compelled not to interfere with other missions, or to establish schools without colonial consent.[74] In general, officials seemed to understand that anti-European language, separated from the context of illegality, amounted to empty menace. The resident at Blantyre went further. Noting that colonial conquest had been eased by the ability of Europeans to exploit African ethnic divisions, he suggested that—at a moment when it was feared ethnic barriers were receding in favor of racial, or pan-African solidarities—the Watchtower offered a means to channel nascent nationalism within a decentralized religious body, and into a "multiplicity of creeds and sects." The Watchtower, to the resident's thinking, was "a source of strength not of weakness," an opportunity to attract "hotheads" into a movement with niche appeal and limited growth potential.[75]

Government policy was less effective in Northern Rhodesia, perhaps owing to the impracticality of control over such a vast colony, perhaps the result of vacillation and uncertainty. Colonial authorities could not quite bring themselves to offer the movement recognition, or to prescribe means of legitimate worship.[76] Unwilling to work with the WTBTS, which for their part condemned the Northern Rhodesian Watchtower for propagating "foolish and fanatical doctrines,"[77] unable to devise a means to suppress independent Christian worship, the state settled on an ambiguous policy of "toleration," based on the principle of noninterference in the absence of sedition "likely to lead to civil disturbance." Chiefs and headmen, native commissioners and intelligence officers, were expected to keep a close watch on Watchtower activity, to guard against creeping signs of insubordination.[78] In practice this placed a monumental burden on these authorities to demonstrate their discernment between religious worship and seditious behavior. That boundary was never clear when it came to Watchtower. But by the mid-1920s, both officials and Watchtower preachers seemed to have arrived at an agreement about what constituted anticolonial behavior. The deployment of the myth of the American liberator by Watchtower proselytizers signaled to authorities a malicious intent. It signaled to Watchtower converts a preacher with the spiritual mettle to defy the state. On the Garveyist frontier, the evocation of diasporic communion became the mobilizing vehicle of anticolonial defiance.

One of the most eloquent purveyors of the myth of the American liberator was the Watchtower preacher Jeremiah Gondwe. Gondwe was born in the Isoka District around 1890, a Muhenga with roots in Nyasaland. His early life was characterized, to a remarkable extent, by the types of experiences and tribulations that led many Northern Rhodesians to the Watchtower movement. Gondwe received some education, as a private pupil of David Kaunda, but was denied the advantage of mission training. During the war, he was forcibly conscripted into the army and, during his time as a military porter, was exposed to the revival of Hanoc Sindano. Like many young men of his generation, Gondwe migrated restlessly from one labor center to the next, working in Southern Rhodesia, the Belgian Congo, and across the Copperbelt region of Northern Rhodesia as a domestic servant, labor recruiter, brickmaker, petty trader, and as a participant in the construction of the Mulungshi dam. Near the end of the 1923, in the labor compound of Broken Hill, Gondwe was converted to Watchtower by Isaac Nyasulu, one of Elliott Kamwana's original students, and quickly emerged as a leading preacher. In 1924 reports emerged out of Broken Hill that Watchtower preachers were declaring the end of the white man's rule and the arrival of American Negroes. The British South Africa Company, on the eve of its transfer of the colony over to the Colonial Office, sent troops to Broken Hill as a warning. Gondwe was convicted of the minor crime of preaching without a permit, and was sentenced to three months in prison.[79]

In 1926 Gondwe emerged again on the colonial radar as the leading Watchtower preacher in the mining town of Ndola. By this time Gondwe had embroidered his prophesy of the coming millennium with a vivid imagery that built on Hanoc Sindano's preaching, while adding elements of the narrative of American liberation. As one of Gondwe's preachers, William Kalukelo, was recorded explaining:

> God the Father instructed Christ to give wealth to whitemen and to tell them to give some of this wealth to the blackmen—not to grudge them at all. This was done by Christ. But the whitemen did not carry out these instructions given them through Christ. When they brought the wealth to the blackmen they said we will not give them enough but will give them little by little. This has been done for many years—but this year Jesus Christ has said the people are troubled—I will divide the country between the two in order for both of them to live comfortably. We have seen the Aeroplanes coming to our country—it was Jesus Christ who sent the Americans to find out if the blackmen were clothed—the Americans have gone back and reported negative. They

have said the blackmen have no wealth and moreover they are greatly distressed. Then this year Jesus Christ sent the Americans with one Aeroplane with anger to again about it—and told them not to perch on the aerodromes. This Aeroplane dropped a red book to Jeremiah [Gondwe]—which cannot be lifted by one man but two. Nobody saw where this aeroplane landed—but went back to Jesus Christ. He will come before the reaping of the present Kaffir Corn Crops. He will line us all up—asking where we were washed—and how many Gods there are—we will say we were washed in Jordan—One God—God the Father, Son and Holy Spirit. After this he will divide us into two—those that were not washed will take part with the whitemen—those that were washed with Christ. Then He will [say] to the whitemen I gave you wealth which you did not divide between yourselves and the blackmen—and because you did not this I have taken away from you your kingdom and have given it to the blackmen. . . .

Gondwe carefully instructed his followers to withhold from outsiders the more inflammatory aspects of his message, and it took several months for investigators to compile enough evidence to arrest him. In 1927, while preaching around the Bwana Mkubwa Mine, authorities finally moved in, arresting Gondwe's head pastor, Zebediya Kachali. Before Gondwe could be detained, he fled to the Belgian Congo, where he had an established base of supporters.[80]

Gondwe spent the next two years as a fugitive, preaching his interpretation of Watchtower scripture in both the Belgian Congo and Northern Rhodesia. Rejecting the authority of the WTBTS, which he charged had abandoned their mission in Northern Rhodesia in shame after failing to reveal the Truth, Gondwe nurtured an explicitly pan-African doctrine that hinged at times on the redemptive power of black Americans, at others on a combination of white and black believers from across the sea. In one sermon, Gondwe declared white people in Africa "snakes" and "Satans," as well as those foolish enough to accept European religion. Gondwe advised his followers to plant large amounts of food in their gardens in preparation for the arrival of their "relatives with black skins," who would arrive in airplanes carrying vast amounts of wealth. Soon, Gondwe assured, the last would be first and the first would be last. Their "elder brothers" from America had learned of their benighted condition—a contravention of God's will—and were mobilizing resources to help. "These white people who are here now will go away to their own country," he preached, and a "new nation will come to live with us here. . . . The new nation will be America."[81]

Gondwe's peak years of preaching, from 1926 to 1929, coincided with the boom in Northern Rhodesian mining, which transformed the Copperbelt into a major hub of industrial production and brought thousands of

African laborers into its orbit.[82] For authorities, this cast Gondwe's popularity and success in an even more sinister light. "The pernicious doctrines of Jeremiya [are] liable to be broadcast throughout the whole country by natives returning to their homes from the local Mines," warned a colonial detective. "His presence in this District [Ndola] is a distinct menace to the good relations between the Europeans and the natives." Gondwe was finally captured in 1929, sentenced to one year of imprisonment, and then exiled to his home village for another two. He was allowed to return to Ndola in 1932 and to reunite with his followers under close control and supervision. There is no further evidence that Gondwe returned to the myth of the American liberator. To the contrary: in 1941 Gondwe established his own village for peaceful worship, which thrived for several years.[83]

The dissolution of Jeremiah Gondwe's radical ministry was followed closely by the rise to prominence of another Watchtower preacher, Joseph Sibakwe, who began organizing in and around Lusaka in 1931 and by early 1932 had emerged as "the biggest Watch Tower man" in the colony. If Gondwe's success was partially owed to the rapid expansion of the mining belt, Sibakwe's was built amidst staggering decline. The Great Depression was joined by drought and a plague of locusts; several mines closed, reducing employment from 30,000 in 1930 to 7,000 in 1932, a shock that was exacerbated by the closing of several European farms. Rather than return to their villages, many laborers stayed in the mining and urban compounds, or organized informal squatter compounds. The result was an unstable combination of poverty, overcrowding, and idle time; a scenario ripe, as the secretary for Native Affairs observed, for "subversive preaching" and "agitators."[84]

Sibakwe added to this moment of opportunity his own, impressive talents as an organizer. Relying on his extensive network of contacts, he smuggled banned copies of WTBTS literature into the colony and coordinated his activities with Watchtower leaders working in the Southern Rhodesian mines, particularly at the Wankie colliery. To facilitate the organization of Lusaka Town, he divided the African compounds into sections, devised a chain of leadership and command for his pastors, and developed discreet means to spread word of meetings beyond the purview of unsympathetic ears. By April 1932, it was reported that "over 75% of the native population" in Lusaka believed Sibakwe's forecast of a great war between whites and blacks, out of which only the Watchtower would survive, and had enrolled in the movement. Sibakwe's fame was also reported to have spread west through Mumbwa, north to Broken Hill, and east through Mkushi.[85]

In April, Sibakwe felt reasonably emboldened to directly defy colonial authority. After being warned not to preach antigovernment doctrines by the district commissioner, Sibakwe told his followers that he would preach his usual sermon, that he would not be arrested for his defiance, and that the episode would preview the coming war between the faithful and the non-believers that would restore Africans to power. When Sibakwe was not arrested his prestige grew, and numerous doubters joined his ranks. As colonial control began to slip away, J. Moffat Thomson, the secretary of Native Affairs, proposed a demonstration of "one or two machine gun practices by the military company" to reassert order. Before this could happen, however, an African detective traveled into the villages surrounding Lusaka and, with great difficulty, was able to secure damning testimony. Sibakwe preached that taxes had once been collected by a black man named Nimrod, who had used the money for the benefit of Africans. King George had then stolen the money from Nimrod and usurped him; thereafter Africans had been mistreated and denied access to true worship. In July the End would be inaugurated. The trains would stop running on the rail line, and whites and blacks would return to their homes. American Negroes would come, sparking a war between white and black from which the Watchtower faithful would emerge victorious.[86] It is unclear if colonial officials recognized the symbolism of Sibakwe's evocation of Nimrod, the Hamitic king, which may have suggested that Sibakwe was possessed of a broader pan-African understanding of his faith.[87] Either way, authorities had enough with which to work. Sibakwe was arrested on May 10, founded guilty of preaching sedition two days later, and sentenced to six months imprisonment.

The danger to colonial order inherent in the preaching of both Jeremiah Gondwe and Joseph Sibakwe can perhaps be glimpsed in the strikes and disturbances that erupted across the Copperbelt in 1935. On May 20, word spread through the mine at Mufulira that tax rates were scheduled to be raised. For workers already subjected to Depression-era wages, an industrial color bar that prevented their advancement in the mining hierarchy, overcrowded and unsanitary living quarters, and abusive treatment from European compound bosses, the news lit a spark. Large crowds gathered around the offices of the compound manager and the district officer, and mine authorities braced for violence—which never came—for several days. Reports of the confrontation quickly spread to nearby mining compounds, carried by rumor and runners, and posted on trees along the roads connecting one mine to the next.[88] On May 27, roughly one-third of the miners at Nkana left their posts in organized protest, but the situation quieted after the arrival of troops. The real showdown occurred at Luanshya on May 29, where two thousand workers at the Roan Antelope Mine Compound faced off with members of the military police, leaving six workers dead and twenty-two injured. The next day mine employees were joined by other workers at Luanshya in a general strike. Workers armed themselves with sticks, and rumors swirled about plans to burn the town's oil stores, to cut telephone lines, to interfere with the railway track. Order was finally restored on May 31, with the assistance of the Northern Rhodesia Police, the British South Africa Police, an air force platoon, and reinforcements from Southern

Rhodesia, and with the arrest of a large number of Africans. Among those detained was Jeremiah Gondwe, who had been proselytizing in and around Ndola, situated at the confluence of the three sites of labor disturbance.[89]

If the strikes were not immediately precipitated by Watchtower intrigue, they must be understood in the context of intensive Watchtower organizing in and around the mines.[90] Sibakwe's preaching was followed by years of steady proselytizing in urban centers and throughout the Copperbelt, including the sustained efforts of Watchtower leaders, under the direction of Manasseh Nkoma, to create a central Watchtower organizational structure along the rail line and in the mines.[91] Less than two weeks before the strike in Mufulira, Nkhoma hosted a meeting that brought 370 Watchtower leaders—including several from the Copperbelt—to Lusaka for a three-day conference. One of the attendees, Fred Kabombo, was convicted after the strikes for encouraging the non-payment of taxes among Copperbelt residents.[92] Another Watchtower preacher, Henry Chibangwa, who had been advocating for workers' rights on the mines since 1933, held meetings at all three sites, preaching that the troubles on the Copperbelt were a sign of the approaching Armageddon. Then there was the portentous note, posted at the Nkana Beer Hall on April 5, calling for workers to stay home on April 29 to protest poor wages and poor treatment, including arbitrary arrests for "loafing" and beatings in the mines. The author asked "all ... Africans men and women" to place their faith in God, and assured them that they were supported by "wisers who are far away and able to encourage us." The note was headed "B.M.R. Americas," a reference that every worker on the mines would have understood as the imprint of the Watchtower.[93]

This is not to suggest that members of the Watchtower movement carefully engineered the confrontations of late May. But as with a series of strikes that roiled the Southern Rhodesian mines in the 1920s, the Watchtower movement had carved a space for the expression of anticolonial frustrations leading up to the confrontation and—in the absence of an established labor movement—offered a vehicle of organization and mobilization, and a resource for spreading information from one mine to another once the showdown had begun.[94] Unlike labor unions, which colonial administrators could forbid, the Watchtower movement operated under the protection of its religious convictions. Attempting to prevent proletarianization, the state nonetheless allowed an organized space for the expression of dissent. The reevaluation of British labor policy that followed the Copperbelt strikes must be viewed at least in part as a triumph of Watchtower advocacy, which presented in clear detail the risk of a circulating, temporary labor force, and the value of stabilized industrial relations.[95] The strikes, cheered C.L.R. James, transcended the limits of a mundane labor dispute and suggested "a summons to relentless struggle with moral enemies." They demonstrated that "[s]hould world events give these people [Africans] a chance, they will destroy what has them by the throat as surely as the San Domingo [Saint Domingue] blacks destroyed the French plantocracy."[96]

*

On the Garveyist frontier, in the absence of a clear path to political activism Watchtower preachers adopted an anticolonial posture time and again, predicating their authority on the imminent arrival of black Americans, and the inauguration of a millennium forecasting an Africa restored to the Africans. This mythology was forged by years of devoted Garveyite organizing in South Africa and the Portuguese territories, and transmitted north along well-traveled paths in the form of rumor and prophesy. For thousands of labor migrants in Northern Rhodesia, the Watchtower movement offered the comfort of religious faith. And in so doing it disseminated a diasporic vision of the future both inseparable and discrete from the work of Garveyite activists, mobilizing in Northern Rhodesia and throughout much of the continent.

Chapter Seven

THE VISIBLE HORIZON

IN THE middle of May 1923, Isaac Clements Katongo Muwamba, a government clerk working in Lusaka, Northern Rhodesia (Zambia), approached the colony's Chief Secretary, Donald Mackenzie-Kennedy, with a proposal to establish a "Native Improvement Association" in the town compound. "[S]ince February . . . I have been observing . . . the constant week-end quarrels, differences and disrespectfulness among the African workers that consist of many tribes now living in the Lusaka area due no doubt to hatred, lies and jealousy," explained Muwamba. Such circumstances not only encouraged breaches of justice; they were "barriers against civilisation and improvement." They threatened to return Africans living in Lusaka to "barbarism." An improvement association, Muwamba suggested, would counter these impulses by fostering inter-ethnic harmony. It would instill in local Africans a respect for the "civilised law and order" that life in a "village of the whitemen" demanded.[1]

Muwamba's presentation to the chief secretary was obsequious, and the substance of his argument suggested nothing more than an interest in establishing a cautious, accommodationist organization dedicated to furthering the goals of the colonial administration by cracking down on disruptive behavior such as illicit beer making and petty crime. Muwamba was the son of a former chief, educated at the prestigious Livingstonia mission, and a veteran of the First World War. He had demonstrated his loyalty to the colonial state on one occasion by bringing to the notice of the native commissioner the surreptitious activities of an independent and officially undesirable African religious sect, the Church of Zion. Muwamba declared himself a "British subject," with an interest only in "helping [his] own people towards civilization." Disavowing the "foolish" path of radicals like Watchtower prophet Elliott Kenan Kamwana, he pledged to conduct his business in the open, and within the circumscribed barriers to African political participation demanded by the state. The historian Karen Fields, noting Muwamba's subsequent opposition to the Watchtower movement, has deemed him an "Anglophile."[2]

Nevertheless, Mackenzie-Kennedy had good reason to be suspicious. A month earlier, it had been discovered that Muwamba was receiving copies of the *Negro World* posted from Cape Town. Around the same time, Northern Rhodesian officials had intercepted correspondence between Muwamba and two of his nephews, Ernest Alexander Muwamba, a government clerk at Ndola, on the northern end of the rail line, and Clements Kadalie, general secretary of the Industrial and Commercial Workers' Union (ICU) in South Africa, that suggested a broader ambition for Muwamba's project. Using careful language, the three men considered strategies for ascending "to the loftiest pinnacle" and most effectively serving the interests of the race. Kadalie and Isaac Clements discussed arrangements for a proposed trip to America that would allow them to further their education and "culture [themselves] in the whiteman's modern government," making them more effective advocates. Recognizing that the political climate of Northern Rhodesia precluded the fiery and confrontational approach of his own organization, Kadalie expressed approval that "[i]n the meantime" Ernest Alexander and Isaac Clements were busy "planning to devise ways and means . . . to make representation" to the government. If theirs was not a solidarity of means, it was certainly a solidarity of aims.[3]

Mackenzie-Kennedy understood enough about this correspondence to know that authorization for the association was out of the question. Political organizations were barred in Northern Rhodesia, let alone ones connected even tangentially to the UNIA or the ICU. But he lacked the social vocabulary to properly contextualize Muwamba's contradictions. Mackenzie-Kennedy was privately convinced that it was only a matter of time before clerks and other educated men in the colony were approached by the UNIA to contribute to its project of African liberation. But for the chief secretary, as it was for his fellow administrators posted across the continent, the arrival of Garveyism portended disturbance, disobedience, and defiance. Muwamba may have received copies of the *Negro World*, but his declarations of admiration for the wisdom of British administrators and British policy suggested that the contact had been ephemeral, insubstantial. The moment of reckoning had yet to arrive. With sympathetic treatment, he concluded, Muwamba might remain an asset, might repay the administration with "loyalty and honest dealing" down the road.[4]

Muwamba was fortunate to evade punishment, for in truth he had already begun to participate in the networks of communication that would facilitate the spread of Garveyism across the continent.[5] But he was fortunate by design. If, as the previous chapter documents, Garveyite organizing in Africa could have explosive—and unexpected—consequences, it was disseminated with the greatest of care, under cover, and with long-range goals in mind. This chapter examines the efforts of a cadre of clerks, ministers, traders, and workers in the central African colonies of Nyasaland

(Malawi) and Northern Rhodesia to nurture the movement behind a guise of cautious reformism and under the watchful eyes of the state. Inhabiting a power structure that viewed them with suspicion, and a political climate in which demonstrations of independence and initiative were viewed with alarm, this group of mobile, politically ambitious, mission-educated men founded "Native Welfare Associations"[6] and independent churches, ostensibly apolitical vessels through which to assist the colonial governments in their project of African "civilization" and "uplift." Behind this mask of patriotic accommodationism they communicated with the UNIA and the ICU, distributed their literature, and filtered news of anticolonial politics throughout the region. By participating in the silent work of organization, they joined Garveyites across the continent in exploring the limits of—and opportunities for—African political expression during the dark years of the interwar period. They invested their hopes in Garveyism not because it offered a panacea, or even immediate relief, but because it invested their parochial politics with a diasporic identity and a global vision—with the promise of a far-reaching network of compatriots, growing powerful, patiently mobilizing, and laying the groundwork for a meaningful assault upon intractable European empires.

Race Men: Welfare Associations in Nyasaland and Northern Rhodesia

Educated Africans in Nyasaland and Northern Rhodesia faced formidable constraints in the 1920s and 1930s, their opportunities sharply circumscribed by the articulation—and ultimately the formal implementation—of indirect rule.[7] The brainchild of Frederick Lugard, indirect rule proposed a bifurcated structure of governance in which customary powers and local control were vested in "traditional" rulers, who had authority insofar as they maintained the day-to-day machinery of the colonial state, the broader operations of which remained in the hands of European administrators.[8] Lugard argued that Africans had been exposed to the light of civilization prematurely, and were unprepared for the excesses and complexity of Western mores. Indirect rule would allow them the opportunity to continue their development toward civilization and self-government on their own terms, and at a suitable pace. For the "visible horizon," African chiefs and headmen would be afforded scope for initiative and responsibility, while directed "in certain well-defined directions" by the "protecting Power." If indirect rule devolved certain political responsibilities, wrote Lugard, it recognized "that the subject races of Africa are not yet able to stand alone, and that it would not be conducive to the happiness of the vast bulk of the people—for whose welfare the controlling Power is trustee—that the attempt should be made."[9]

Buffeting the colonial state in Africa was its recourse to overwhelming, violent force, a reality not lost on anyone involved in the project.[10] Indirect rule offered a complimentary edifice of control. It solved the problem of legitimacy—as Mahmood Mamdani puts it, the problem of stabilizing the alien rule of an unwelcome minority—and solidified the colonial state's tenuous hold on discursive power.[11] On the one hand, indirect rule invested state-appointed African authorities with a significant stake in the exercise of colonial power, one that rested, as Karen Fields points out, on a "cushion of culture" that "distribute[d] power upward."[12] At the same time, by Balkanizing power along so-called tribal lines, the state established a "politically enforced system of ethnic pluralism" that discouraged potentially dangerous types of majoritarian political formations. State-sanctioned tribal boundaries were codified, legitimate channels of political participation defined entirely within the jurisdiction of chiefly rule. Trans-ethnic politics, or any form of African initiative that threatened to unsettle this balance of locally constituted authority, was subject to intense scrutiny and suspicion, and was often conflated with radicalism. As Mamdani writes, "[c]ontrol and representation were two sides of the same coin."[13]

The logic of indirect rule necessitated the marginalization of an emerging group of "new men" in Nyasaland and Northern Rhodesia, former students of the famed Livingstonia mission and graduates of the mission's prestigious Overtoun Institute, men eager to participate in colonial politics but suspicious of tribal boundaries and authority.[14] "During recent years a new advanced class of native has sprung up which is quite unknown to native society as hitherto recognized composed of 'Christians,' Clerks, Artisans, Store assistants, Tailors, and domestic servants consisting mainly of natives from North East Rhodesia and Nyasaland but with a sprinkling from tribes from other parts of this territory," reported the governor of Northern Rhodesia in 1922. "It is a class that will never fit in with the present tribal society system of Government through hereditary Chiefs and Headmen." Any influence vested to these men, argued Lugard, "would be antagonistic . . . to that of the native rulers and their councils—which are the product of the natural tendencies of tribal evolution." By educating himself, the "detribalized" African had turned himself, in the words of Sir Donald Cameron, into "a bad imitation of a European," an unrepresentative anomaly existing between two worlds and unable to effectively speak for, or fully understand, either. "In present conditions in Africa," wrote Lugard, "the numerous separate tribes, speaking different languages, and in different stages of evolution, cannot produce representative men of education." The Europeanized African had been "separated from the rest of the people by a gulf which no racial affinity can bridge. He must be treated—and seems to desire to be treated—as though he were of a different race."[15]

Official concerns about the lasting consequences of the Great War further circumscribed the opportunities of educated Africans in the immediate postwar period. Thousands of men, women, and children had died on behalf of the war's East African Campaign; the remaining suffered from the hardships of army work, food shortages, epidemics, lack of medical supervision, forced dislocations and, after the war, soaring commodity prices.[16] The memories of John Chilembwe's rebellion in Nyasaland and radical Watchtower revivalism in Northern Rhodesia were fresh, and engendered a climate of hostility and suspicion. Officials worried that the war had opened a Pandora's box, that it had irrevocably damaged white prestige and filled the minds of Africans with dangerous new ideas. Most troubling were reports that tribal, colonial, and regional barriers were dissolving, that Africans had discovered a common suffering and a common identity around camp fires and in the trenches during the conflict. Amidst swirling rumors of conspiracies and insurrections, colonial agents redoubled their efforts to confine African social formations to fixed tribal bounds. In Nyasaland, independent churches were disbanded, and former members either jailed or carefully monitored. When news of Garveyism reached the colony in 1922, the *Negro World* was promptly banned and district residents warned to keep a "sharp and constant watch" for any manifestations of the spirit of "Africa for the Africans."[17]

Welfare Associations offered "new men" in Central Africa a useful vessel through which to navigate these treacherous waters. At the close of the war in Nyasaland, and by the late 1920s in Northern Rhodesia, Livingstonia graduates like Levi Z. Mumba, Yesaya Z. Mwasi, Charles C. Chinula, Earnest Alexander Muwamba, and Isaac Clements Muwamba established associations catering to Central Africa's elite-in-exile, founded on the principle that educated Africans had an essential role to play in the day-to-day operation of the colonial state, both as interpreters of the public will and as adjuncts for the government's "civilizing mission."[18] Welfare Associations held frequent meetings to gauge local conditions and needs, and appealed to government officials for redress on a wide variety of grievances ranging from hostage taking and forced labor to issues of sanitation and cleanliness, from police brutality and ID cards to excessive beer drinking and restrictions on the planting of trees. Even at their most strident, association men couched their criticisms in a language of unyielding loyalty to the British Crown and a commitment to the long term aims of the colonial state. Like European administrators, they sought, in the words of the founding constitution of the West Nyasa Native Association (WNNA), to make their fellow Africans "understand the necessity and value of Order, and the importance of becoming law-abiding citizens, the value and importance of industrious

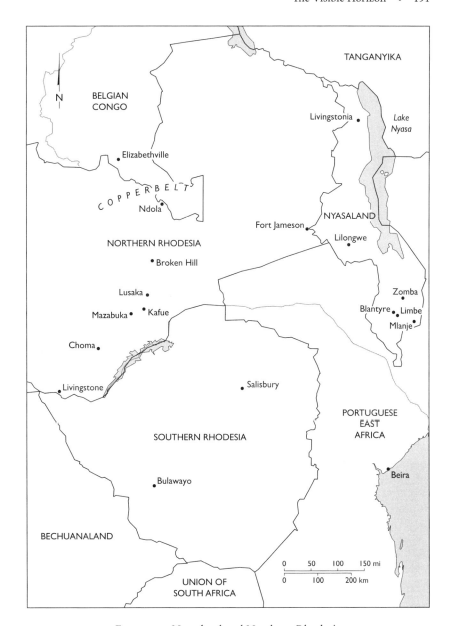

FIGURE 7.1. Nyasaland and Northern Rhodesia.

labour—and in short the value of Civilization against Ignorance, Laziness, Disloyalty and Anarchy."[19]

Welfare Associations have been dismissed by scholars as "ineffective instruments" of protest. Roger Tangri accuses association men of a kind of trade-union consciousness, interested in the immediate amelioration of petty and local grievances rather than the larger and more daring projects of self-government and independent statehood. "They operated ... like pressure groups on behalf of their members, politely and mildly attempting to exert influence upon government within the framework of the colonial situation," he writes. "At no time did they seek the political kingdom but instead resorted to constitutional methods in their attempts to persuade Government to better African conditions." Robert Rotberg similarly scolds Welfare Associations for seeking "concessions, compromises, and recognition from government," and dismisses them as elite-driven, unrepresentative, and engaged in nothing more than "gentle skirmishes" that were "essentially futil[e]." "They patiently awaited the happy day when the government would begin to deal justly with Africans and their self-appointed representatives," he concludes.[20]

Scholars have not been wrong to suggest the timidity of Welfare Association politics; rather, they have made the mistake of accenting the wrong details: actions instead of consciousness, stance instead of context, dramatization instead of unstated desire. As James C. Scott has demonstrated in his groundbreaking work on peasant resistance, to reduce subaltern politics to rebellion and grand gestures of insubordination is to miss the "prosaic but constant struggle" between the powerful and the weak, the "vital arena for ordinary conflict" in which multiple groups make claims to physical and discursive resources and in which the terrain of subsequent contestations is shaped. Rather than speaking truth to power, subalterns engage with the powerful using a "public transcript" that they have limited ability to shape, the use of which constitutes not submission to power but an unstated affirmation of its reality. Scott's work suggests the need to look beyond the public pronouncements of disempowered peoples, to search for unspoken or deflected meaning and to understand the complexities of the historical moment. It also suggests the need to look less at the form and structure of ideas and political associations than at the context in which they are assembled and the meaning with which they are populated by participants and opponents. Concepts like "uplift" or "civilization" or "Welfare Association" are not fixed signifiers but malleable and contested fields of meaning, shaped from multiple sides and understandable only in the moment of their articulation. They are historically specific. They tell us less about the desires of their standard bearers and more, as Frederick Cooper puts it, about "the range of possibility and constraint facing different political actors at any present moment, and the different trajectories of possibility and constraint that follow upon acting in one's own time."[21]

Association men inhabited a power structure that viewed them with suspicion, and a political climate in which their demonstrations of independence and initiative, especially those that suggested defiance, were viewed with alarm by the colonial state. They understood their awkward position. "We must cultivate patience, moderation of expression and above all we must be loyal," stressed Levi Z. Mumba, the leading light of the North Nyasa Native Association (NNNA). "That is the only way we can hope to win the confidence of the white people."[22] Mumba and his associates recognized the discomfort with which colonial officials viewed their actions; but they also remained keenly aware that so long as associations could not be seen to threaten public security, so long as their conversations were not demonstrably seditious, the state was compelled, in the interests of appearance, to recognize "the obligations of Christian civilization." For a government mandated to lift its black subjects out of "barbarism," it was rather impolitic to bar the efforts of associations dedicated to the project of mutual betterment.[23] Eager to carve out a space for organized politics, association men adopted an unsatisfying posture, engaging with the colonial state in an obsequious dialogue wherein the act of articulating their grievances, rather than the specific substance of those grievances, provided the subversive thrust of their efforts.

*

From the perspective of the Welfare Associations, this work was not merely "parochial," but part of a broad effort of pan-African mobilization facilitated by the global transmission of Garveyism.[24] In Central Africa, public evocations of Garveyism were out of the question. Nevertheless, "new men" in Nyasaland and Northern Rhodesia participated in the development of a particular form of African Garveyism that took root among educated colonial subjects across the continent.[25] Recognizing that little could be done under current conditions to directly challenge European regimes, Garveyites downplayed or eliminated the more strident political demands of the UNIA platform and seized on the organization's emphasis on self-help, mutual aid, and economic development. Adopting this posture afforded a tenuous space for the practice of diasporic politics. By supporting the UNIA financially, spreading the gospel of Garvey, and encouraging Africans to replace ethnic and regional identities with pan-African ones, African Garveyites worked tirelessly to build an indigenous foundation for the day of deliverance.

Support for the UNIA was by no means uniform among African activists. Opposition was perhaps fiercest in West Africa, where it developed from two complementary impulses. Many were wary about associating with an

organization that they believed to be situated, as Herbert Macauley suggested, "perilously near the border line of treason and sedition."[26] This mis-
calculation on the part of the UNIA was believed to speak to a broader
African American ignorance about African mores, customs, and political
strategies, an ignorance that disqualified Garvey and his associates from
positions of true leadership in the anticolonial struggle. At the founding
conference of the National Congress of British West Africa (NCBWA), in
March 1920, Gold Coast writer, pan-Africanist, and NCBWA Vice President
J. Casely Hayford argued that the new organization should welcome the
spirit of the UNIA, and especially its potential as a node for economic cooperation, just so long as it was remembered that "they have no idea of
our local circumstances and conditions," and that they may seek "to get
in touch with us by some channels that are not the right ones." The UNIA
must be reminded that "we who remained on this soil have known better
and understand the relations that exist between the Government and the
governed, so that if they desire to come back and enjoy the milk and honey
of their native land they may do so in a right and constitutional manner."
The Gold Coast nationalist Kobina Sekyi was more direct. "The salvation
of the Africans in the world cannot but be most materially assisted by the
Africans in America," he wrote, "but must be controlled and directed from
African Africa and by thoroughly African Africans."[27]

Neither of these charges were especially fair. If American Garveyites embraced a loud anticolonial posture, African UNIA divisions—tenuously
established in those colonies where Garveyism was nominally tolerated—
cultivated a carefully nonconfrontational visage. The Lagos division in
southern Nigeria hosted concerts and meetings, and dedicated itself to a
program of mutual aid and educational and industrial uplift.[28] The Luderitz
division, in coastal South West Africa (Namibia), promoted its local advocacy, including its work caring for the ill, its efforts to reduce criminal of-
fender roles, and its program of sickness and death benefits.[29] Even the surreptitious Dakar division, which was quickly discovered and suppressed by
French authorities in Senegal, emphasized its work toward assisting needy
members by providing interest-free loans, legal aid, and employment assistance. A frustrated French official noted that "[t]he written statutes of the
Dakar branch do not disclose [radical] aims, and instead suggest a mutual
aid society."[30] It was an impression that Garveyites throughout the region
were eager to confirm. Applying for permission to construct a hall for the
UNIA division in Windhoek, leading South West African Garveyite Fitz
Herbert Headly explained to the magistrate that the aims of the movement
were "Humanitarian; Charitable; Educational; Social Friendly; Constructive; and Expansive Organization that Encircles the Universe."[31]

Indeed, Garveyism, stripped of its immediate political aims, enjoyed
widespread support among intellectuals throughout British West Africa.

The Black Star Line, which promised West Africans an exhilarating means to pursue transatlantic commercial arrangements at a moment when European trading firms were consolidating and squeezing out African exporters and middlemen, was met with a tremendous amount of enthusiasm.[32] Editorialists in newspapers from the Gold Coast (Ghana) and Sierra Leone reacted to the news of the Black Star Line with jubilation. The *Times of Nigeria*, which dismissed Garvey's vision of a pan-African empire as "obviously ridiculous," considered the notion of a black-owned and black-operated steamship line as "a great and even sublime conception for which everybody of African origin will bless the name of Marcus Garvey."[33] For many West Africans, the promise of Garveyism was the promise of economic opportunity. Supporters wrote to the parent body in New York eager to learn how they could extend the infrastructure of the Black Star Line and the UNIA's industrial arm, the Negro Factories Corporation, into their regions.[34] Organizers traveled up and down the coast marketing the UNIA as a means to seize agency in the struggle to sustain local markets and build commercial ties.[35] Akinbami Agbebi, the UNIA's Black Star Line agent in Lagos, urged the parent body to concentrate its attention "firstly . . . [on] West African trade," rather than the "original plan of reaching all negro communities in the world."[36]

Marcus Garvey has not received enough credit for recognizing the extent to which the project of African liberation must be decentralized, built from local nodes of political organization and resistance that could most effectively cater to local conditions and opportunities. The goal of UNIA propaganda, he argued, was primarily to "bring . . . to the natives of Africa a consciousness of themselves and a desire on their part to free themselves from the thralldom of alien races and nations." The redemption of the continent would "not mean so much fighting from without as the rising of the people from within with a new consciousness of their power."[37] Garveyite agents relayed this message on the ground. Ernest Wallace, who organized a UNIA division in Basutoland (Lesotho), explained at a meeting in Matetiele that Africa was being asked to "cook her own pot." UNIA agents were not deputized "to tell what the negroes in America do . . . but to ask them to work out their own salvation." John Mungunda, the president of the UNIA division in Windhoek, South West Africa, likewise explained during an organizing meeting in the interior that "[t]he society has been formed through American ideas, but Americans only explained it but will not do the work—we must do that." The appeal of the movement, observed a supporter in Nigeria, was that it did not demand uniform action. "It is for the branches organized in British Colonies to arrange their own plan to suit their respective conditions," he wrote. In Lagos, where the political agenda "seems impracticable," the UNIA had taken up the work of "general improvement."[38]

As the last chapter made clear, the transmission of Garveyism to Africa encouraged wild rumors about the arrival of black American liberators, and transformed the movement into a potent symbol for a series of millennial religious revivals in central and southern Africa. This was not the intention of the "new men" drawn to the Garveyist program, who internalized instead Garvey's call for "silence and proper organization": a program of consciousness-raising, race-building, and patience.[39] African Garveyites were emboldened by the news broadcast across the continent by the *Negro World* that, as Fitz Herbert Headly put it, "Garveyism [had] flown to the four parts of Mother Africa," that blacks throughout the diaspora were cautiously mobilizing for freedom. But until Africans discovered their common destiny, they must obey the laws of the government and abide by the constitution. Until they worked together with a "united purpose" their adversaries would be too powerful. "Few now in numbers, there is strength in our ranks and we should strive to expand and bring to this branch our many friends and associates, who surely have a part of this universal pull for an African Republic," exclaimed John Henry Farmer at a meeting of the Dakar division. "If we cannot do much here under French Colonial Administration, we can do our utmost to further the universal aims of the association by our moral and financial support." The aim was the "entire emancipation of the negro race." But the moment required modesty. First Africans must be awakened from their slumber. They must coalesce around shared aims. They must prepare for a more felicitous moment.[40]

Like their brethren in western and southern Africa, association men in Nyasaland and Northern Rhodesia imagined their modest work in the context of racial awakening, nation-building, and eventual emancipation. Garveyist literature and ideas entered central Africa from the south, carried through the region's creative networks of informal communication, and along the massive labor migration network that brought educated Nyasalanders and Northern Rhodesians into steady contact and conversation with Africans from Southern Rhodesia (Zimbabwe), the Congo, Portuguese East Africa (Mozambique), and South Africa. The District Commissioner at Karonga, complaining about what he felt was an "intolerance of Europeans" and a growing race consciousness among Nyasaland's mission-educated Africans, noted "[t]here is a continuous contact with South Africa and leading native members of the [Livingstonia] Mission here are kept well informed concerning native labour organisations and political organisations in that country."[41] Copies of the *Negro World* entered central Africa throughout the 1920s, joined by literature from the ICU, particularly the *Workers' Herald*, which broadcast a message of racial unity and awakening that, as the last chapter suggests, often blended imperceptibly with Garveyite discourse. In a period when the gains of white power were further solidified in Central Africa, and a political climate in which association men were not only considered unsuitable for positions of authority, but counterproductive to the entire project of colonial rule, the premise of diasporic organization— the faith in a far-reaching network of compatriots, some powerful, and some mobilizing against otherwise intractable conditions—was infused with potent meaning. "In those days . . . we read Marcus Garvey's newspapers and learned that many American Negroes would be carried back to Africa in ships," remembered association member Charles Chinula. "We believed that Garvey was a great man and that he was there to help all of us."[42]

The project of establishing public, politically acceptable vehicles for the facilitation of Garveyist ideology required great nuance. Loose tongues and careless behavior might imperil the entire enterprise; or, as the secretary of the Livingstone Native Welfare Association (LNWA) put it, "one false brick may cause the fall of the whole building." Sam Mwase, acting chairman of the LNWA, and onetime correspondent of Marcus Garvey, warned that change would not come immediately, that progress would happen "gradually and very carefully." Mwase, like every association man, expressed unyielding loyalty to the imperial project.[43] Colonial authorities were not entirely fooled by this posture, but they were somewhat outmaneuvered. "We have to take notice of the fact that no suppression can prevent the natives from discussing political and other subjects and the characters of individual Europeans in the country round their camp fires at night, and they do so often, with a shrewdness and accuracy which would be disconcerting were it known to the parties concerned," wrote Robert Laws, head of the Livingstonia mission, to Nyasaland's chief secretary. To sanction the Associations was to invite the risk that a "hot-headed demagogue" might take advantage of the latitude, but better that such a risk be managed, that organizational activities be conducted above ground rather than in secret, that they adhere to oversight and regulation.[44]

With association men constrained from pursuing an openly Garveyite program and colonial officials constrained from banning Welfare Associations altogether, associational activity evolved as a carefully choreographed tug-of-war.[45] Associations were approved provided they confined their scope to the "non-political interests of detribalised natives resident in the various townships as such persons were outside the sphere of the Native Authorities who attended to the general welfare of the population in the tribal areas." If meetings were held, the local district resident must be informed, and copies of the minutes must be sent to both the resident and the provincial commissioner—a flawed safeguard that some officials recognized to be of limited effectiveness.[46] When association men overstepped the boundaries of political possibility, officials were within their authority to suspend operations, but generally chose—or felt pressure—to assert control in more subtle ways. In 1927, after firebrand clerk, independent trader, and suspected Garveyite George Simeon Mwase established the Central Province

Universal Native Association, officials demanded that he remove the appel-
lation "Universal" from the title, liable as it was to conjure associations with
the UNIA. Mwase, whom it was discovered read the *Workers' Herald* and
had held a subscription to the *Negro World* for at least a year prior to the
establishment of the association, was considered a menace and a potential
threat, but the administration did not want to turn him into a "martyr," and
desired to keep his activities in the open.[47]

Within this fluid space, Welfare Associations in Nyasaland and Northern Rhodesia set about disseminating a vision of awakening, race pride,
self-help, and unity that mirrored the work of African Garveyites across
the continent. Adopting the Garveyite rhetoric of racial competition and
civilizationism, association men acknowledged the work performed by the
bearers of "European Civilization" toward removing Africans from "barbarism," but argued that the next steps must be taken by Africans themselves.
"Europeans have opened ways for [natives] to march forward to civilization," explained Ernest Alexander Muwamba, leading light of the Welfare
Association at Ndola, Northern Rhodesia. "It is [now] those that help themselves that should expect other people's or God's help." Leaders must be
developed that could advocate more effectively for the needs of the people
than either the missions or the colonial government, both of which had
proven themselves unwilling to allow Africans to ascend to the next stage of
development. Invoking the Garveyite discourse of racial rebirth, Isaac Phiri
challenged his fellow association men at a meeting in Mazabuka to "try and
help ourselves to rise up from the present state of darkness." "We are now
still asleep," he declared, "let us wake up[.] We must not expect someone to
lift us up." Daniel Soko, of the LNWA, was even more succinct. "[The] time
has come," he thundered, "for Africans to uplift Africa."[48]

Important in this project of nation building was development of a powerful black identity. From the perspective of association men, this required a
new and more effective industrial, educational, and legal infrastructure. The
current system stifled the development of independent trade, emphasized
religious—rather than industrial—training, deprived Africans of the "good
government" and constitutional rights to which they had been introduced,
and generally "[cut] the African Natives off from the path of education and
civilisation."[49] Also required was a renewed commitment to the defense of
racial purity which, in the well-grooved tradition of national identity formation, fell heavily on the "respectability" of African womanhood. Welfare
Associations dwelled obsessively on a double standard in the penal code,
which severely punished African men from engaging in "unlawful carnal
connection" with white women, but did not so penalize white men for
engaging and housing African women. Applying antimiscegenation laws
equally would protect and restore to dignity "our poor Native women,"

argued George Mwase. It would be "for the good of both races," and give encouragement to "true race men and women."[50]

More than anything else, Welfare Associations extolled the benefits of unity. The primary lesson of European supremacy in Africa was that white peoples had learned to work together. It was a lesson reinforced by the "Negroes of America," who had "made wonderful progress" because they were "united." Africans must forget tribal differences. They must unite the young and the old, the educated and the non-educated, Christians and non-Christians, urban laborers and reserve dwellers. Welfare Associations teach "every native to know that every black person is his brother regardless of tribe," wrote Isaac Nyirenda and Godwin Mukubesa, leaders of the LNWA. This was more than a colony-wide appeal. Association men modeled their work on the example of the African National Congress in South Africa, and measured their educational facilities in comparison to other African colonies. Even more provocatively, they cast their eyes across the Atlantic, demanding the same opportunities afforded their "brother-negroes" in America. "If we kill [one] hundred people to-morrow, do you think that Europeans will free us?" asked Charles Muchena at a large public meeting in Livingstone in 1932. Emancipation depended not on the spear of violence but the "spear [of] Unity." Freedom, argued Nyirenda, would be achieved by "understand[ing] the new life," adhering to the aims and objects of the Association, and "do[ing] what is good for Africans." It resided, explained LNWA member Twembuchi Nasando, in teaching their children "to love different tribes belonging to this Cont[in]ent and beyond the seas."[51]

Although officially confined to pursuing association work in their discrete locations, association men in both Nyasaland and Northern Rhodesia endeavored to construct the edifices of national political organizations. From the beginning, according to Levi Z. Mumba, Welfare Associations mobilized with "a view to amalgamation." In Nyasaland, Mumba established the Representative Committee of Northern Province Native Associations (RCNPNA), an umbrella group that would advocate for African rights from the capital, Zomba, while forging a "United Power" between associations in Karonga, Chinteche, and Mombera. In Northern Rhodesia, the Livingstone Native Welfare Association was viewed as the "parent body," and associations spread north along the artery of rail in Choma, Mazabuka, Lusaka, Broken Hill, Ndola, and Luanshya "branches." The Livingstone Association, perhaps more than any other body, demonstrated the futility of official attempts to Balkanize the consciousness of educated Africans into discrete units. Educated African workers in Livingstone's Maramba compound had been connected to channels of diasporic communication since at least 1924 thanks to the efforts of Nyanja church elders Andrew and Duncan Funsani, who received smuggled copies of the *Negro World* from Southern Rhodesia wrapped inside editions of the *Bulawayo Chronicle*, and offered their church as a safe haven for early political meetings. Like most residents in Maramba, association leaders had traveled widely and forged pan-regional connections. R. Isaac Nyirenda, who became chairman of the LNWA, and was involved in Isaac Muwamba's 1923 campaign to establish his "Native Improvement Association," was born in Nyasaland and had worked in Feira, Salisbury, and Bulawayo. Sam Mwase, who also led the association for a brief period, was also born in Nyasaland, had traveled extensively through Northern Rhodesia, and had made personal contacts with both Marcus Garvey and Clements Kadalie. Both men, along with other members of the LNWA's executive committee, were trained at the Livingstonia mission and privy to the information network connecting Overtoun graduates throughout the southern and central African region.[52]

The drive for a national organization in Northern Rhodesia reached its climax in 1933, when members of the Lusaka African Welfare Association, headed by Isaac Muwamba, called for a meeting of all associational branches to coordinate opposition to the proposed amalgamation of the Rhodesias. Representatives of the Livingstone, Lusaka, and Mazabuka associations attended a two-day conference at Kafue, which was open to the public and attended by a large number of nonmembers. Delegates agreed to form the United African Welfare Association of Northern Rhodesia, which would amalgamate all existing branches. Even more ambitiously, as Nelson Namumango of the LNWA suggested, the new organization would aspire to extend beyond the rail line and "stretch out in the villages for the common good for the people." The United African Welfare Association would not merely represent the interests of mission-educated clerks and workers scattered across labor compounds and urban centers, but would unite in common cause all people of black skin.[53]

It was one provocation too far. Association men had overstretched. Associations "have been repeatedly informed that they were approved by the Governor in respect only to the townships within which the members resided, but recently the tendency of the Associations has been to discuss matters outside the scope of the activities for which they were formed," Donald Mackenzie-Kennedy wrote, referring to Kafue. For Welfare Associations to claim to speak for the tribal areas was to question the legitimacy of chiefly authority and—by extension—the linchpin of British rule. Recent actions had left no doubt that the activities of the associations were political, their scope national, argued Mackenzie-Kennedy. Amalgamation was out of the question. And while Welfare Associations were allowed to survive, African employees of the government—the clerks that dominated the leadership ranks of the movement—were debarred from membership in the organizations, and prohibited from speaking at meetings or writing letters on their behalf.[54]

Welfare Associations suffered a similar fate in Malawi. Colonial authorities had long attempted to marginalize associational activities by promoting local district councils, conservative bodies dominated by chiefs and headmen, as proper bodies for the expression of public opinion. With the formal imposition of indirect rule in 1933, associations lost the ability to directly petition government entirely. "Since the inception of the policy of native local government the proper medium between the natives and Government is the Native Authority," explained Keith Tucker, the acting chief secretary, to the RCNPNA. "For this reason Government is not prepared to take any action on resolutions passed by native associations unless they have been submitted through or adopted by a Native Authority." Association men were encouraged to attend meetings of the Native Authority, take part in discussions, and assist the Council of Chiefs as best they could. But their work could only achieve legal status if conducted through the Authority, the official "spokesmen of the people." The RCNPNA waged a spirited battle in opposition. Isaiah Murray Jere, the association's secretary, pointed out that before colonial rule chiefs were checked in their authority by advisors and independent councils, as "is the case . . . in all civilized countries including the British Empire." Levi Mumba compared the Native Authority to the House of Lords and Native Associations to the House of Commons, arguing that they served different and complementary functions. It was to no avail. By 1935, association politics, for all intents and purposes, were moribund.[55]

From the Welfare Associations of Nyasaland and Northern Rhodesia emerged the types of cautious, ameliorative, and ostensibly conservative politics that scholars have suggested. From them also emerged a powerfully articulated vision of pan-ethnic, pan-African identity. Association men communicated and strategized endlessly with each other, and sought to transcend state-dictated tribal barriers by establishing multiethnic, national advocacy organizations. They reached out to their compatriots abroad, in Southern Rhodesia, Portuguese East Africa, and South Africa, and forged alliances with other African advocacy groups, particularly the ICU, that organized around the same set of goals but presented their demands in a more militant, direct manner. They read the *Negro World*, communicated with Garvey and UNIA agents, and imbibed the language and philosophy of Garveyism: rebirth, education, silent organization, unity, and cultural pride. Their direct appeals to the colonial state were rarely strident, and were always couched in a discourse of unflinching loyalty to the imperial project. But the very performance of those appeals, in the context of indirect rule, posed a subversive challenge to the logic of colonial domination, one that authorities could not long ignore. And their internalization of, and traffic in, a diasporic "hidden transcript" projected their local and seemingly myopic struggles against an unyielding, dominant power onto a broad canvas of

world-historical racial emancipation, offering a radical subtext to their behavior and linking their efforts to their equally marginalized, if differently
situated, brethren in the African world.

CHRISTIANITY OF THE SOIL: THE INDEPENDENT CHURCH MOVEMENT IN NYASALAND

The decline of Welfare Association politics in Nyasaland shifted the attention of educated Africans to another form of political expression. By the
late 1920s, a number of association men had begun to explore the organizational possibilities of the independent church. The church was an appealing
vessel because of the protection it afforded for the creation of black coun-
terpublics otherwise curtailed by the strong arm of the state. Independent
churches tended to be spearheaded by men suspected of anti-European behavior, men connected to subversive political movements in Nyasaland and
abroad, men linked to both the UNIA and the ICU in their correspondence
and in their deeds. Even absent these concerns independent churches—like
all African-controlled organizations—were subject to intense scrutiny, suspicion, and mistrust. Yet religious liberty, as one official noted in frustration,
was "one of the axioms of British administration." So long as activities were
confined to a religious sphere, so long as they could not be linked directly
to political behavior, recognition must be reluctantly granted. The curtail-
ment of religious expression, top officials in London pointedly reminded
their agents on the ground, "savor[ed] of racial distinction" and was "incon-
sistent with the general policy of His Majesty's Government."[56]

Religious organization was also appealing because it cut across the logic
of indirect rule. The churches that emerged in Nyasaland in the late 1920s
and early 1930s offered trans-ethnic, trans-regional edifices through which
to promote expansive visions of shared racial consciousness. Their commitment to proselytization was not a ruse, but neither was it innocent of the
political motivations that authorities suspected. For the leaders of independent Christianity in the protectorate, association men raised on the political imagination of Garveyism, the pursuit of Afrocentric Christianity could
not be easily disentangled from secular expectations of redemption. Like
American Garveyites, they viewed the worship of a black god, under the
direction of black leadership, as a precursor to the "resurrection" of the race
and the liberation of Africa. By promoting a project of racial pride, self-help,
and institution building, and by articulating visions of African Christianity
forged in the merger of Western and local cultures, independent church
leaders organized dynamic vehicles through which to augment and continue the work of Welfare Associations, and to carry the torch of Garveyite
pan-Africanism.[57]

The ecclesiastical underpinnings of the independent church movement in Nyasaland were articulated in a thoughtful article published by Levi Z. Mumba in the *International Review of the Missions* in 1930. The argument was twofold. First, Mumba defended the "religion of [his] fathers" by meditating on the universal quality of faith. Far from exceptional, the worship of Christ comprised an attempt by Europeans to realize "the Supreme Being in everyday life" that was common to Muslims, Hindus, and animist worshipers across Africa. Far from a simplistic muddle of superstition and savagery, Bantu religions shared at their core the same search for meaning pursued by Abrahamic peoples before the coming of Christ—an argument Mumba demonstrated by citing parallels between Bantu beliefs and verses from the Old Testament. But if faith had a universal quality, its transmission relied on particularities. Christianity could not be brought to Africans in the same manner as it was brought to Europeans. And it could not be successfully imparted by outsiders. The successful transmission of the faith to the continent depended on the work of those with a respect for the past rather than a contempt for African tradition, and it must be grounded in the existing social fabric rather than predicated on its destruction.[58]

Mumba applied these principles when composing the constitution for the newly organized African National Church (ANC). Founded in 1927 or 1928, and officially recognized in 1929, the church revolved around the ecclesiastical work of association men and former Livingstonia students, many of whom had been excommunicated from the Presbyterian Church for practicing polygamy or otherwise offending the strictures of the European mission.[59] The ANC, argued Mumba, offered a vehicle for the uplift of Africans en masse, welcoming into its ministry those deemed unsuitable for the rigors of Christian worship by the European mission: polygamists, beer drinkers, the old and uneducated. More than this, it offered a model of African worship that—while acknowledging the "brotherhood of man regardless of colour and creed"—embraced God's particular vision for Africa. The traditions, laws, and customs of African religion, far from the impediments to civilization that European missionaries assumed, were the very foundation of African civilization, instituted by God himself "so that the African may realize Him by their observance." Implicit in this rendering, cloaked in the language of religious observance, was a declaration of independence. If civilization and uplift must emanate from African traditions as well as European ones, if they must be ushered in by teachers and leaders versed in both worlds, the logic of European rule disappeared. Members of the ANC interviewed by Terence Ranger in the 1960s remembered the church as a voice of African nationalism before the rise of political parties.[60]

The leader of the ANC most closely connected to the broader currents of anticolonial politics was Robert Sambo, manager of the church's Central School at Deep Bay. Sambo was born in Nyasaland's Karonga District, and educated at Livingstonia. While working in Southern Rhodesia, he became Assistant General Secretary of the Gwelo Native Welfare Association, a front organization for ICU and Garveyite propaganda, and was expelled from the colony in 1927 after attempting to secretly organize a branch of the ICU in Bulawayo. In 1926, Sambo spent six months in Nyasaland, where he made contacts with "leading men" and "tried to shake those sleeping people" into a political alliance with their "country-men" to the south. In an anonymous letter to the *Workers' Herald*, Sambo pledged to work for the ICU "until the matches [Kadalie had] lit ablaze run like veld fire from South Africa to Nyasaland and thence to East Africa." He also wrote to the famed African educator, James E. K. Aggrey, seeking means to procure the help of "our 15,000,000 [black] friends and brethren in America." After migrating to Durban, South Africa, and joining the local ICU, Sambo ran afoul of the law again, and was deported back to Nyasaland in 1929. There he joined the African National Church, which offered a new and more protective platform through which to work for the "development of the African Continent."[61]

Perhaps the most compelling figure of the independent church movement was Yesaya Zerenji Mwasi, a talented preacher and revivalist who ascended through the ranks of the Livingstonia mission and was ordained as one of the mission's first African ministers.[62] Even as he achieved personal success, Mwasi chafed at the paternalistic attitudes among both white missionaries and colonial officials that restricted the development and autonomy of African converts. By the late 1920s, Mwasi had emerged as the leading figure in the West Nyasa Native Association (WNNA), through which he developed the most sustained and far-reaching critique of colonial rule of any association man in the protectorate. Acknowledging that Africans owed a debt to the white man for his gifts of religion, good government, and schools, Mwasi excoriated the means by which they remained "cheap and degraded" by the execution of colonial rule. Rather than being encouraged in their "racial increase," Africans had seen their land alienated by a series of questionable treaties and handed to white settlers. They faced compulsory labor practices that amounted to little more than "slavery in disguise." And they suffered generally from poor wages, poor worker housing, poor oversight, and poor educational facilities that constrained them within a "disgusted Colour Bar stage."[63] Mwasi viewed the WNNA as a prototype for what would eventually become a national organization in service of the race. Perhaps with this in mind, he communicated with his nephew Clements Kadalie, read the *Negro World*, and entered into a long correspondence with Marcus Garvey. In 1926, the parent body of the UNIA in New York sent Mwasi an application form that authorized him to head a clandestine UNIA division in Nyasaland. Later that year, authorities intercepted a large parcel headed for Mwasi's village, containing several copies of the *Negro World*, numerous copies of a UNIA pamphlet that described the history of the organization and outlined Garvey's aims, and fifty envelopes bearing the printed address of the UNIA's secretary general. There is no evidence that Mwasi officially consummated the relationship, but his long flirtation with the UNIA clearly shaped his view of the struggle. As he worked patiently within the limitations of Nyasaland's restrictive colonial arrangement, he warned officials that "[t]he modern world is full of turmoils in sympathy with the native," a gesture to the Garveyite view of a "rising tide of color" and a suggestion of the global perspective with which he continued to mark his relatively modest work.[64]

By 1933, the WNNA neutered by the new strictures of indirect rule, Mwasi threw himself into the independent church movement. From the pulpit at Sanga, Chinteche, he announced his break from the Livingstonia mission and the formation of the Blackman's Church of God which is in Tongaland. The European missions, declared Mwasi, had failed the African. They had spread "the erroneous idea that God is more in foreign missionaries, lands, languages institutions, thoughts words and actions but is less or not in the native Christianity . . . that God loves white colour and hates black colour. In short that white man on account of his good surroundings is nearer to God than a black man who lacks such environments." Rather than train Africans to assume control of their own churches, missions sought to make them "perpetual subjects under their permanent control." Worse, missions had not worked for the "unification of the race," but had fractured Africans with denominationalism, thwarting efforts to "nationalize" the people. "I wish to avoid unjust persecution by my fellow countrymen that I am proclaiming strange Gods to them," said Mwasi, "that I am a lucrative preacher employed by foreigners for the sake of money to uproot native customs and traditions—hence I am exposed to their just censure that I am a traitor to my country."[65]

Instead, Mwasi called for a "Christianity of the soil," the worship of an "indigenous and personal God" through which African customs and traditions may be allowed to breathe. The European missions were mere placeholders; the true work of uprooting evil customs, of conquering Africans for Christ, could only be completed by an African Moses, an African Luther, an African Calvin. The universality of the Christian message could be reached only through regional and cultural particularity, narrowly defined in racial terms. We are of "the African race in Africa," explained Mwasi. "[T]o erase nature, locality or race of Africa for foreign denominations is worse than useless, and in fact it is sin against God and His Church." Mwasi sought to "naturalize and nationalize God," to build a Christian movement allowed to "grow out of its own soil, having its own customs and traditions purified by the Gospel of Christ." Like the ANC's constitution, Mwasi's demand for a "purely indigenous Church" implied the demand for a broader political freedom down the road. Evoking the UNIA's spiritual-religious liturgy, Mwasi declared the black man's right to worship a black god, to "start his own ministry out of the Bible," and—by extension—work for the "Redemption of . . . [the] race."[66]

If the Blackman's Church of God appeared to be modeled on Garvey-ite principles, so too did the Nyasaland Blackman's Educational Society (BES), Mwasi's ambitious scheme to establish an African college guided by the ethics of racial independence, cooperation, and self-improvement. The proposed school would be neither denominational nor particular to a single tribe in Nyasaland but "National and Coextensive with [the] Black-man as a race within and outside Nyasaland." It would strive to "Improve or Develop the Impoverished Condition of the Blackman religiously, morally, economically, physically and intellectually." To build a fund-raising base, Mwasi traveled to Northern and Southern Rhodesia, acquiring verbal support and contributions from Nyasaland workers in mines and town compounds abroad. At Livingstone, Mwasi met with Atonga migrants from Chinteche and the adjoining districts, and recruited Isaac Clements Mu-wamba at Lusaka and Thom Manda at Broken Hill to leadership positions. Workers would form committees and invest money at the Standard Bank at Blantyre on behalf of the BES; the money raised would fund the establishment of the school, teacher training, the erection of school buildings, dormitories, hospitals, and clothing and food expenses for student boarders and patients. Mwasi believed the money would be raised because of the stakes involved. "The education in question does not concern a single man or woman," he wrote. "The idea of this Comprehensive Scheme is to make every man and woman, both great and small, to feel and bear this Essential Responsibility—personally and individually . . . by undertaking the function of a redeemer of his or her own black race from so fearful, lamentable, impoverishing, deadly, age-long and total blindness due to Intellectual Ignorance."[67]

The Blackman's Church of God was afforded reluctant authorization, but the BES was too much. Publicly, officials found the scheme impractical, and cited the bitter opposition of the Council of Atonga Tribal Chiefs; privately, they worried about Mwasi's motives, and stressed the need to keep him away from "more gullible natives."[68] His grandest dream stalled, Mwasi turned to the work of building a national religious organization. In 1935, the Blackman's Church of God merged with two similarly oriented independent denominations—Charles Chinula's Eklesia Lanangwa (Christianity of Freedom) and Yaphet Mkandawire's African Reformed Presbyterian Church—to form Mpingo wa Afipa mu Africa (Church of the Black People of Africa).[69] The church grew steadily and by 1938 boasted nearly 3,400 members, operated a modest school at Deep Bay, and was preparing to begin operations on another school in the Kota Kota District.[70] It was in this more humble guise that Mwasi continued to adhere to Garvey's call for silent and peaceful work in the interests of African redemption.

JOHN CHILEMBWE'S CHRISTIANS: THE REBIRTH OF THE PROVIDENCE INDUSTRIAL MISSION

Predating both the African National Church and the Blackman's Church of God in the project of ecclesiastical nation-building was the resurrected Providence Industrial Mission (PIM), John Chilembwe's church, which had been disbanded after Chilembwe's abortive rebellion in 1915. The effort was spearheaded by the Reverend Dr. Daniel Sharpe Malekebu, a former student at PIM and one of Chilembwe's first converts. As a boy Malekebu caught the attention of Emma B. DeLany, an African American missionary working at PIM under the auspices of the Foreign Mission Board of the National Baptist Convention (NBC). After DeLany returned to the United States, in 1905, Malekebu decided to join her. Stealing away from his family, Malekebu set out for the coast, nearly three hundred miles away, traveling by foot, sleeping in trees, building large fires to keep wild animals at bay. In Beira, he secured employment on a steamship, working his way first to London, then to Ellis Island. Over the next decade, with the support of the NBC, Malekebu studied theology and medicine in North Carolina, Illinois, and Tennessee, earning three degrees, culminating in an MD from Meharry Medical College in Nashville in 1917.[71]

By the end of the First World War Malekebu had begun laying plans for his return to Nyasaland. Immersed in African American missionary culture and fluent in the language of "providential destiny," Malekebu had developed a clear self-understanding of the role that he had been chosen to play in the restoration of Africa. The spread of Christianity and civilization on the continent, he believed, had been stalled by the failure of European missionaries to properly communicate the faith. The "vital spot in the heart of the heathens" could only be reached by one familiar with the "customs and thinking" of the people, one who himself had "come out of the Darkness," one who, like Malekebu, had been trained abroad, learned the arts of Western civilization, and was prepared to carry the Gospel home. "I believe the salvation of Africa rests upon the African sons and daughters," Malekebu declared in a fundraising pamphlet in 1918. By rebuilding PIM, the "finest church in the whole Central Africa," he would do just that.[72]

It would not be easy. Malekebu's first attempt to return to Nyasaland was aborted in 1920, when he was detained by police, accused of harboring a radical political agenda, and sent into exile in Liberia.[73] Indeed, the very idea of resurrecting John Chilembwe's mission was an act of defiance, and was understood to be so by the group of men and women—Andrew Mkulichi, Isaac Chambo, Ruth Lawrence, Wallace Kampingo—who nurtured the tattered remains of the church during its dark period and boldly referred to themselves as "John Chilembwe's Christians."[74] To restore PIM on the same plot of land, with the same name, and with the help of men, like Mkulichi, Chambo, and Kampingo, who had been imprisoned for their involvement in the rebellion, broadcast a provocative signal to those chafing at the colonial version of events.[75] And the memory of Chilembwe was very much up for grabs. Watchtower adherents, who awaited the millennium that would drive Europeans out of Africa, secretly referred to their schools as "John Chilembwe" schools. Rumors proliferated among former PIM followers that Chilembwe was not dead, that he had escaped to America, and that he would return to liberate the country. George Mwase composed a revisionist account of the rebellion, recasting Chilembwe as a latter-day John Brown, a martyr to a future cause. And Clements Kadalie inspired his staff by relating to them stories of Chilembwe's exploits, and sought to obtain more information about the rebellion for the "future history of Africa," worried that "the white men will not preserve [the] genuine history of the black man."[76] By restoring PIM, Malekebu and his adherents were providing a public face and an institution around which to construct these alternative histories. They were not openly challenging European rule, but they were investing themselves in the types of identity building—of nation building—practiced by the ANC and Mpingo wa Afipa, imaginings that did not include the long-term presence of European rulers.

In this context it is perhaps unsurprising that the effort to reconstitute the Providence Industrial Mission became interwoven with the most sustained attempt in the interwar period to establish a Garveyite beachhead in Nyasaland. Spearheading the conspiracy was not Daniel Malekebu but his brother-in-law, Isa Macdonald Lawrence, who was employed as a clerk in Portuguese East Africa. With Malekebu in exile, Lawrence had emerged by 1921 as a crucial middle man in the effort to resurrect PIM, appealing to the Foreign Mission Board in Philadelphia for financial and diplomatic aid, coordinating with Malekebu in Liberia, and relaying instructions to supporters in Nyasaland via correspondence with his wife Ruth Lawrence and other members of the old mission.[77] He had also become a point man for the dissemination of Garveyism and other subversive material into British Central Africa. By early 1923, Lawrence was in contact with the UNIA's parent body in New York, and by early 1924 he had made entreaties to Clements Kadalie, who asked him to organize the dockworkers in Beira for the ICU. Through 1926, when PIM finally won reinstatement, Lawrence continued to distribute copies of the *Negro World* and the *Workers' Herald* throughout Nyasaland and Northern Rhodesia, concealed inside other, government-approved, papers. When Lawrence was seized by police that August, as he returned to Nyasaland to assume a senior position with the mission, he was discovered carrying copies of both the *Negro World* and the *Workers' Herald*, along with a copy of the UNIA's "Constitution and Book of Laws."[78]

For Lawrence and his brother John B. Chattah Lawrence the work of reestablishing the mission became increasingly associated with the global project of African redemption. John, a clerk in PEA, a steady reader of the *Negro World*, and an ardent supporter of both Garvey and Kadalie, viewed Malekebu as Nyasaland's "Moses," the man best equipped to carry the continent-wide, UNIA- and ICU-led project of liberation home. "[N]early [one] thousand . . . Nyasalanders are busy abroad training for the 'NE-GROES' SECOND BLOW,'" he boasted to his cousin Alex Sisseo in Blantyre, requesting that Sisseo and his brethren organize an association, presumably modeled on the UNIA, that might represent the interests "of our black race." He promised to send copies of the *Negro World*, the *Workers' Herald*, and James Thaele's Garveyite *African World* so that Sisseo might "preach well." Isa Macdonald who, like John, viewed the rebuilding of PIM as the building of a new Jerusalem, likewise understood the gravity of the "gigantic work" that he was preparing to launch. Months before PIM's reopening, he transcribed a poem from the *Negro World* and mailed it to Ruth:

Oh Africa my native land
As in thy golden sun I stand
And throw across the bitter sea
The broken whip of Simon Legree
And view my own my shining shore
Where the white devil dominates no more.

O Africa my native land
I owe my soft, dark skin to thee
And they can strip it from my bones,
If that will set my country free,
My lustrous eyes should love their light,
And all my blood flow out for thee.
Amen! Amen! Amen.[79]

With Isa Lawrence detained in prison, John never made the journey back to PIM, and little came of their audacious scheming. John campaigned vigorously for his brother's release, writing the editors of the *Negro World* and the *Workers' Herald* and casting Isa as a Christlike figure, crucified by the "imaginary fears" of the government. Kadalie appealed to the Colonial Secretary in London, noting that the *Workers' Herald* was "the official organ of a legitimate Trade Union," and that the sentence "proves the atrocities being perpetrated upon the African communities under British Rule in Africa." The ICU began a Macdonald Lawrence Fund, and the case was debated in the House of Commons. The *Negro World* declared Lawrence "a martyr to a great cause—the cause of Africa for the Africans," and predicted that his imprisonment "will help to spread the light among the natives of Nyasaland and of South Africa, who will clamor all the more and louder for justice and fair play in their own land."[80]

Meanwhile, the mission at Chiradzulu carried on. Despite intense surveillance efforts, colonial authorities could uncover no evidence that Malekebu was involved in the plot.[81] To the contrary, the Chief Commissioner of Police approvingly noted Malekebu's "excellent burnt brick house," and the education inspector, with praise rarely reserved for African-controlled schools, suggested that PIM's school at Chiradzulu "should become a powerful educational influence on the community."[82] Malekebu involved himself in associational work, founding the Chiradzulu District Native Association (CDNA) in 1929, but the CDNA pursued modest and uncontroversial aims and appeared to act as little more than an outreach organization for the church.[83] Perhaps this was by design. As John Lawrence explained, to "carry the message of the Lord in Nyasaland, amongst powerful enemies, with their well organized armies," required that Malekebu "avoid evil acqua[i]ntances." The most important thing was not to "draw back the Mission work." For his part, Malekebu, well aware that his every move was being monitored, counseled patience. He would not be another Chilembwe, would not strike a blow and die. After all, as he explained to Isa Lawrence in 1925, "any thing that is worth while takes time and we all must learn to wait."[84]

Despite limited support from the Foreign Mission Board and the colonial government, by the end of the 1930s PIM boasted over 5,000 members in Nyasaland, and Dr. Malekebu had expanded his mission from its headquarters in Chiradzulu to branches in eight other districts, and had opened outposts in Southern Rhodesia and Portuguese East Africa. The mission's first hospital was established in 1927, as was its Central School, and in 1933 work was completed on its impressive New Jerusalem Temple.[85] Malekebu gave his life to the mission and to the task of educating African students for a new day to come. That PIM adopted a nonconfrontational stance perhaps speaks less to Malekebu's politics than to the intense pressures of the surveillance state, pressures which limited the terrain of the politically possible in Malekebu's day. Perhaps it reflected Malekebu's calculation that his missionary work—the signal aim of his life—was only feasible if it projected the benign face of accommodationism. By washing his hands of the more radical politics percolating to the south and across the Atlantic, PIM was afforded the space to perform the work that Garveyism asked of it: the work of silent and peaceful penetration, the work of uplifting African souls, of preparing the groundwork for a more auspicious day. Daniel S. Malekebu embodied the paradox of diasporic politics in Central Africa, never directly tied to Garveyism and yet inextricably linked to its pan-African project of racial emancipation.

*

In interwar Central Africa, Garveyism's diasporic reach offered Welfare Associations and independent churches an organizational impetus upon which to imagine the exigencies of local political struggles. Taking cues from the south and across the sea, association men built a locally situated diasporic politics that, rather than seeking to defy the stifling boundaries of representation, offered a set of tools for the task of building within it.[86] The articulation of a powerful, transnational identity—the New Negro— offered an organizational structure and an underlying logic for resistance and defiance against the colonial state. It projected an unapologetic pan-Africanism, predicated on the idea of an awakening diaspora, stirring its neighbors and preparing—from the various corners of the world—for a day of greater opportunity. When that opportunity emerged after World War II, the new organizations were dominated by the leaders of the 1920s and 1930s, men whose political educations bore the imprint of the silent struggles of the past decades.[87] When Isa Macdonald Lawrence, the first treasurer-general of the Nyasaland African Congress, told his colleagues that "[w]ithout unity we cannot . . . lay good foundations for our future generations," he was drawing on a vocabulary that reached backwards as it projected forwards. It was a vocabulary impossible to understand without Garveyism. As Harry Mwaanga Nkumbula, then president-general of the African National Congress of Northern Rhodesia, put it, Mr. and Mrs. Garvey "create[d] the nucleus for the freedom and independence of . . . Africa."[88]

Chapter Eight

MUIGWITHANIA (THE RECONCILER)

IN THE beginning of things, Mogai (*Ngai*, God) took the man Gikuyu (Kikuyu) to the top of Mount Kenya and bequeathed to him the bountiful land below. Mogai provided Gikuyu with a wife, Moombi (Mumbi), and they had nine daughters. When the daughters had grown, Mogai provided them with nine husbands, and together they prospered and had many children of their own. After the passing of Gikuyu and Moombi, the nine daughters divided their families into separate *mbaris*, or clans, and spread across the land of their father. To sustain kinship ties and preserve bonds of unity, they organized themselves under a common tribal identity—*Rorere rwa Mbari ya Moombi*, or Children of Mumbi. After a time, a system of generational bonds—*riika*, or age grading—was established to ensure cooperation in times of need, and to sustain harmony in political, social, religious, and economic life. The people living below Mount Kenya became known as Kikuyu.

This story appears near the beginning of Jomo Kenyatta's classic work of anthropology and cultural representation, *Facing Mount Kenya*.[1] Published after Kenyatta had spent nearly a decade in Europe, a period during which he had sought alliances with—and absorbed lessons from—an eclectic group of liberals, communists, Marxists, and pan-Africanists, *Facing Mount Kenya* nevertheless sustained the project of group identity and nation building that Kenyatta had embarked upon as a young man in Kenya. As Bruce Berman and John Lonsdale have brilliantly illustrated, Kenyatta—joined by a group of mission-educated colleagues in the Kikuyu Central Association (KCA), the forebear of the Kenya African Union—worked to discursively resolve the internal contradictions of Kikuyu ethnic community ("moral ethnicity") in favor of an outward-looking posture ("political tribalism") that simultaneously renegotiated the relationship between Kikuyu and Western traditions, projected a harmonious unity of group interests, and bolstered Kenyatta's own claim to political representation in the altered landscape of colonial rule. If the logic of indirect rule ceded Kenyan politics to white settlers and their imperial enablers, and the preservation of local African "custom" to a group of government-appointed chiefs, Kenyatta and his colleagues would construct a new platform from which to project a competing authority. Faced with a tribal history of porous boundaries and competing moralities, their embrace of the story of Gikuyu and Moombi became an act of cultural nationalism.[2]

The outlines of this story—not to mention the broader narrative of Kenya's independence struggle of which it is a part—have been well drawn. Nevertheless, in viewing the politics of Kikuyu "invented tradition" through the prism of local and national frames, scholars have missed an opportunity to explore the extent to which interwar Kikuyu nationalism was forged in the context of broader African rhythms. In particular, interwar Kikuyu activists joined their brethren throughout the continent in pursuing contacts with Garveyist and other pan-Africanist organizers, absorbing the lessons of African Garveyism, and implementing those lessons in conversation with their particular needs, grievances, and opportunities. After the brief and explosive attempt to organize a pan-African insurgency under the leadership of Harry Thuku in 1921–22, Kikuyu activists pursued a more cautious strategy of fictive unity, consciousness raising, self-help, and separatist institution building that both mirrored the political activism of Garveyism in other parts of the continent and reconstituted it as tribal politics. Their outreach in 1935 to the Garveyist religious leader, Archbishop Daniel William Alexander of the African Orthodox Church, both sustained the tradition of Kenyan Garveyism and demonstrated the extent to which Kikuyu activists, engaged in the intensely local politics of central Kenya, were simultaneously participating in a more expansive project.

The Kikuyu Central Association and the Politics of Garveyist Tribalism

It was nearly a decade after the Thuku massacre before a second wave of crisis hit central Kenya. The controversy that enveloped the colony surrounding the Kikuyu rites of initiation (*irua*), in particular the practice of female circumcision, has received a considerable amount of scholarly attention.[3] In 1929, frustrated by years of half measures and enraged by the forcible circumcision of a fourteen-year-old girl who was seized from her dormitory at the Gospel Missionary Society's (GMS) Kambui mission, John W. Arthur of the CSM led the bulk of the Protestant missions in Kikuyu country on a righteous crusade to stamp out the custom among Kikuyu Christians. Heavy-handed tactics, in particular demands that church members declare oaths of loyalty to "Church law" and foreswear the practice of female circumcision, precipitated a massive backlash across Kikuyu society, led by the Kikuyu Central Association (KCA), an organization founded by young,

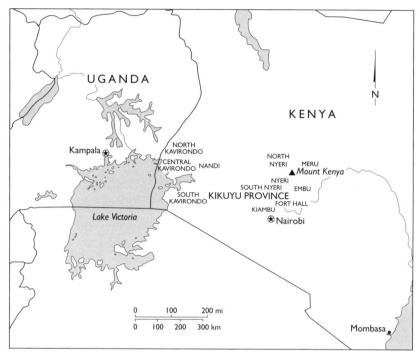

FIGURE 8.1. East Africa.

mission-educated men intent on continuing with greater circumspection the work of the East African Association. KCA activists blanketed Kikuyu Province and the settler farms, holding meetings, collecting funds, arguing that Arthur's attack on circumcision was part of a larger, government-sponsored campaign to eliminate the custom among all Kikuyu, Christian and non-Christian. By the end of the year, the CSM had lost nine-tenths of its membership, and mission schools across the province had been abandoned or seen their attendance sharply drop. Once again, as with the Thuku troubles, Arthur wrote to Oldham concerned about the possibility of "serious revolution and blood shed."[4]

Arthur was not alone in voicing this concern. By October 1929, students at the National Industrial Training Depot in Kabete had developed a menacing forum for protest in form of *muthirigu* dances, which—as Arthur complained—showcased "all the sensual rhythms and movements of the old Kikuyu dances," and added song verses that assaulted and taunted government officials, chiefs, missionaries, and uncircumcised women.[5] By the end of December the *muthirigu* had spread to Kikuyu across the reserves and on the farms, often bringing together huge crowds, and at times threatening to turn violent.[6] The district commissioner for Kiambu observed that the "notable difference in the demeanour of natives" was spreading from the veiled dissent of the dances into normative interactions between whites and blacks. The governor, Sir Edward Grigg, was convinced that the movement was "primarily and consciously nationalist," engaged in a program of "'Africa for the African' and the elimination of the European." By this time, rumors were circulating among both Europeans and Africans about a coming racial confrontation.[7] The brutal attack on Hilda Stumpf, a missionary working at a remote AIM outpost who was set upon in her home, forcibly circumcised, and suffocated to death, seemed to confirm the worst fears of white settlers, who in the words of one, were "surrounded by so many Kikuyus" on their large and lonely estates. Unconvinced by settler paranoia, the colonial government nevertheless worked quickly to stem the tide of unrest, banning the *muthirigu*, legally curtailing the freedom of the KCA to raise money and hold meetings, and arresting dozens of dissenters, including Joseph Kang'ethe, the KCA's president. By March 1930 the governor could report with confidence that order had been restored.[8]

Both missionaries and government officials viewed the KCA's championing of the circumcision issue as a cynical attempt to attack the Church, to curry favor with non-Christians as well as Christians, and to pursue their subversive program of antigovernment and anti-white agitation behind a veneer of cultural anxiety.[9] In this view they have been joined by several historians who have labeled the issue an "immediate excuse," a movement of "contrived" outrage, and a "convenient platform" on the march from local politics to nationalist aspirations.[10] These perspectives downplay the extent to which the European missions' campaign against Kikuyu initiation rites struck at the heart of the KCA's own claim to political, ideological, and moral leadership of the Kikuyu people. In the aftermath of Thuku's audacious, pan-African assault on European rule, and the violent and determined response of the state, Kikuyu activists found a more stable platform in the politics of ethnicity, the project of nation building within the parameters of their own tribal boundaries. Crucial to this ostensible retreat into reserve politics was the ability of Kikuyu representatives more broadly, and KCA activists specifically, to control the discourse of Kikuyu morality and agency. If an assault on the realms of European authority and administration was beyond their immediate reach, it became essential that in the reserves, the realm at least rhetorically reserved for African leadership, European views about Kikuyu social development be replaced by those of the "children of the soil." Missionaries in this context, with their own views about the proper exercise of African "morality," emerged as an existential threat to Kikuyu self-determination.

In embarking on this project, KCA activists believed themselves to be laying the groundwork for their liberation. To do so, as Edward Grigg insightfully noted, they pursued a strategy of "Africa for the African" by aiming for "local independence," by reconstituting Thuku's radical pan-Africanism within the more cautious parameters of tribal representation.[11] This did not mean abandoning the pan-African project. In the years after the fall of the East African Association, KCA leaders sustained their ties to black activists in Europe, and remained connected to the streams of Garveyist information and instruction that continued to flow through Africa. More dramatically, they adopted a long-range strategy of unity, self-help, education, and Kikuyu pride that both mirrored Garveyist ideology and tactics and rendered them for more local and limited uses. Deploying these devices, KCA activists constructed the edifice of Kikuyu—and, to a large extent, Kenyan—nationalism. The influence of Garveyism in this process has seldom been acknowledged.

*

In the aftermath of the Thuku massacre, colonial authorities worked to curtail political radicalism along two tracks. On the one hand, administrators took measures to bolster the channels through which "responsible" Africans might pursue their political grievances. At a *baraza* held in Kiambu mere days after the shooting, attended by Kikuyu chiefs, missionaries, and representatives of the KA, the chief native commissioner lauded the restraint of people who were not led astray by "this foolish agitation," and reaffirmed the government's commitment to native societies conducted along "proper" lines, and willing to respect and work within the appropriate channels of colonial bureaucratic procedure. To this end, in 1924 the government authorized the establishment of Local Native Councils (LNCs), a mechanism that allowed for a measure of popular representation at the local level and provided a forum for younger Africans otherwise excluded from the mechanisms of indirect rule to participate in colonial politics. The deck was stacked: government nominees—chiefs, headmen, missionaries—held a majority over elected representatives; meetings were chaired by district commissioners, who were instructed to suppress criticism of government policy; and while LNCs were empowered to allocate funds, European officials retained absolute veto power. The LNCs, in short, offered the spectacle of political theater without demanding accountability from the colonial state. As the acting governor, Sir Edward Brandish Denham, gushed at the first meeting of the Kiambu LNC, the new system offered the "gift" of participation in a drama that had already been written—an opportunity for Africans to "help . . . in the work that is being done for [their] benefit."[12]

At the same time, East African authorities took measures to quarantine Africans from the poisonous influence of African American propagandists. An investigation into Thuku's operation, which uncovered evidence of the circulation of the *Negro World* in Kenya and revealed Thuku's correspondence with Garveyites in New York, confirmed officials' worst fears about the dreaded spread of international race consciousness. The *Negro World* was banned, and steps were taken—as R. T. Coryndon, the governor first of Uganda, then Kenya, put it—to "discourage as far as possible the connection which is gradually becoming established between East Africa and the Southern States of America." Although not in theory adverse to the "best type of negro missionary (e.g., the 'Tuskegee' type) entering Kenya," the risk of "undesirable propaganda of the Marcus Garvey type" entering the region through this channel was too great, and government agents and missionary councils in England and the United States colluded to ensure that African American missionaries were unofficially barred from East Africa. At the same time, Coryndon moved to suppress the growing trickle of Ugandan students making their way to Tuskegee and other colleges in the United States, worried that UNIA activists would seize the opportunity to open new lines of communication with impressionable young Africans. Coryndon ordered all passport requests to the United States be denied. Kenneth King has convincingly suggested that concerns about the influence of black agitators in the United States spurred the establishment of Makerere College in Kampala in 1922; in the words of one administrator, "to prevent young men going abroad for education, at any rate to Alabama."[13]

For their part, members of the EAA worked to sustain the flame of political activism. In the years following Thuku's arrest and his subsequent deportation to Kismayu (a port city in modern Somalia), representatives continued to meet in secret in Fort Hall, raising money to petition for Thuku's release, maintaining a skeleton framework of the organization with branches, elected delegates, and traveling propagandists, and emerging periodically to hold mass meetings and to forward telegrams to the Colonial Office. Uncovering evidence of a local branch of the EAA near his mission station at Kahuhia, in August 1923, H. D. Hooper was impressed by the passion and determination with which organizers were setting out to learn political and administrative theory. "There can be no return to the status quo," he reported to Oldham. "[T]he more intelligent natives are determined to have a finger in the pie of their destinies."[14]

In 1924, EAA leaders met in Nairobi and reconstituted themselves as the Kikuyu Central Association. Beginning with a cadre of two hundred to three hundred young, mission-educated men from Fort Hall, the KCA spread persistently and impressively across Kikuyu Province. By the end of the decade, the organization had established branches in every Kikuyu reserve, and across the farms of the Rift Valley, claiming a membership in the thousands.[15] Its reach was extended by the inauguration of *Muigwithania* (the Reconciler), a monthly journal published by the KCA in the Kikuyu vernacular, which debuted in 1928 and quickly attained great influence over a wide area, reaching an audience that stretched into Tanganyika

(Tanzania).[16] At first dismissed by the district commissioner at Fort Hall, R. G. Stone, as a small collection of semi-educated malcontents, by 1928 Stone was forced to admit that the KCA included in its ranks "some of the most progressive and educated young men," in the district, and that the organization had begun to emerge as a truly representative body, gaining "an increasing influence on the council of elders."[17]

In founding the KCA, Kikuyu activists did not plan a break from the ideological or political foundations established by the East African Association. Members dated the founding of the organization to 1921, to the founding of the EAA, not 1924, the date of its rebranding.[18] Despite the difficulty of communicating with Thuku, who was carefully watched, leaders like James Beauttah were able to correspond with him periodically, considered him their leader-in-exile, and devoted considerable energy and expenses to effect his release.[19] The KCA adopted many of its operational tactics from the EAA, including its emphasis on oath taking, and its rigorous methods of decision making and communication between delegates. M. A. Desai remained a surreptitious advisor, as did other Indian friends.[20] Although the KCA developed an explicitly tribal focus, at moments of political ferment, such as during the circumcision crisis, it pursued trans-ethnic cooperation, and at times it presumed to speak for Kenyan Africans as a whole.[21] And although the KCA remained carefully removed from explicit expressions of support for pan-Africanist causes, leaders remained connected to diasporic currents that continued to flow through the colony, including dispatches from Garveyites.[22] Asked several years later what the KCA had sought to accomplish, a former member responded, "We wanted only to make the Europeans go from the country."[23]

What was new about the KCA was its tone. The violence of the government's response to the peaceful protests of 1922, joined by the swift deportation of Thuku and two of his associates without trial or recourse, served, as the historians Carl G. Rosberg Jr. and John Nottingham have written, as "a dramatic illustration of the limits within which the new politics could be conducted."[24] KCA activists replaced Thuku's vocal disdain for the legitimacy of colonial government with repeated and disciplined declarations of loyalty.[25] Though nearly uniformly convinced that the KCA was engaged in the worst expressions of race consciousness, and devoted to an antigovernment, anti-mission, and anti-settler agenda, white observers in Kenya searched in vain for evidence of sedition.[26] Behind the curtain, KCA leaders developed a sophisticated network of oral transmission through which to devise, communicate, and implement strategy, and organized an "intelligence" service that reached into police and government circles. In Mombasa, James Beauttah organized *Kiamba kia Kunyamara* (Society of the Destitute), a social and welfare society that operated—beyond government purview—as a KCA front organization in Kenya's busiest port. Although the spread of the *muthirigu* dances proved an overreach, they demonstrated the extent to which KCA activists endeavored to project expressions of dissent behind the masks of performance—or, if in written form—parable. Even here, KCA leaders were careful to remain in the background during meetings at which the *muthirigu* was performed. And, after the dance was banned, it continued underground as a source of inspiration.[27] Frustrated whites were left grumbling about the Kikuyu's love of "concealment" and allegory, his "secretive disposition."[28]

Central to this strategy of "loyal" resistance was the KCA's decision to work within—rather than outside—the rules established by the colonial occupation. Acknowledging the authority of the state, KCA activists endeavored to establish legitimacy and representative clout within the context of reserve politics. This strategic concession to British sovereignty acknowledged the opportunities provided by indirect rule, in particular the government's deference to African agents and missionaries on matters of "tradition" and culture. Rather than positioning themselves against a powerful and intractable colonial government, KCA activists confronted the more pliable bureaucracies of the reserves—the LNCs and the missions—seeking to construct an alternative space within which to arbitrate Kikuyu grievances, needs, morality, education, and a host of local concerns.

It was in this space that organizers fashioned an unmistakably Garveyist politics, albeit repackaged in the container of "political tribalism." If Harry Thuku's strident confrontation with the colonial state grew in part from the enthusiasm generated by Garveyism's early transmission to East Africa, KCA activists joined later African Garveyites in accepting the more strategic and cautious logic of "silent organization." Like Garveyist association men in Central Africa, they embraced a rhetorical platform of unity, preparation, and self-help that projected obeisance to the colonial project while surreptitiously nurturing the construction of an anticolonial alternative. In the same manner that Garveyites constructed a unified Negro culture, and evoked the Negro's glorious fictive past in Egypt and Ethiopia, KCA activists exalted Kikuyu culture and nurtured their own historical mythology. Like Garveyites, they matched this appeal to primordial kinship and racial purity with a celebration of European modes of pedagogy, language, religion, medicine, and hygiene. As Marcus Garvey invented a Negro race and elevated himself to provisional president, so KCA activists set to work inventing a Kikuyu nation, the logic of which supported their own claims to leadership.

The KCA's embrace of a Garveyist discourse and approach suggests, at the very least, a shared vision of African politics that linked the UNIA and Kenyan nationalists in a manner that is hinted at by scattered evidence. According to Jomo Kenyatta, the foundation of associational politics in Kenya was strongly influenced by the Kikuyu encounter with Garveyism. "[I]n 1921 Kenya nationalists, unable to read, would gather round a reader of

Garvey's newspaper, the *Negro World*, and listen to an article two or three times," he later told C.L.R. James. "Then they would run various ways through the forest, carefully [*sic*] to repeat the whole, which they had memorized, to Africans hungry for some doctrine which lifted them from the servile consciousness in which Africans lived."[29] Despite the efforts of the colonial government to isolate its Kenyan subjects from Garveyist currents in the years following the Thuku massacre, Garveyist materials continued to enter the colony, if in reduced numbers. Kenyatta, who emerged as the KCA's General Secretary and de facto leader in 1927, sustained a fascination with Garvey that matched his commitment to Garveyist politics. According to Tony Martin, the black, red, and green flag of Kenyatta's Kenya African Union—which emerged in the 1940s following the suppression of the KCA during World War II—paid tribute to the UNIA's red, black, and green colors. In 1967, the now President Kenyatta told Reverend Clarence W. Harding that he had met Garvey while living in London in the 1930s, heard him speak many times, and considered himself to be a member of the UNIA.[30]

The primary vehicle for the articulation of KCA aspirations was the association's official organ, *Muigwithania*, founded by Jomo (then Johnstone) Kenyatta in 1928. Taken as a whole, *Muigwithania* is a fascinating document, a diverse collection of editorial opinion, foreign news, local political reporting, allegorical fables, and Kikuyu proverbs that comprise an impressively unified, and profoundly Garveyist, roadmap for Kikuyu uplift and emancipation. In a similar fashion to *Negro World* propagandists, *Muigwithania* contributors argued that the Kikuyu "race" had become despised and disparaged by other races and nations, and was threatened with "extermination." The primordial unity of the tribe had been lost: Kikuyu were "scattered amongst foreigners," divided by district, religion, education, and age. The old traditions, and the morality inherent to them, had been neglected. As a result of this disorganization, the Kikuyu had fallen behind the other "black race[s]" in their march to "civilization." While they slept, others had come together and were making progress. Lacking common focus and common purpose, Kikuyu men and women were by contrast becoming poor imitations of Europeans, corrupted by their pernicious influence and without a sense of how to marshal their successes toward the advancement and glory of their own people.[31]

The solution, argued *Muigwithania* writers, was twofold. First, the Kikuyu must look to the past and awaken to a sense of their ancient and God-given unity. Kikuyu, they stressed, had sprung from a common ancestor, shared a common language, and had been blessed with a common land. To rebuild "Kikuyu nationality" required a rededication and commitment to their virtuous, pre-colonial traditions, to the Kikuyu language, and particularly to the land, which must be preserved, restored, and properly cultivated, revered as a foundational source of wealth, identity, and—with the development of both—salvation. It meant setting aside petty disputes between elders and young men, parents and children, Christians and non-Christians, and it meant learning to speak with a common voice.[32] Anticipating Benedict Anderson by several decades, *Muigwithania* writers self-consciously cheered their own contribution to this work. "[N]ow many people will see how their country . . . progresses," wrote the KCA's president Joseph Kang'ethe. "[T]hose who have opinions of value will see similar opinions in *Muigwithania*. And, furthermore, those also who have no opinions will come to have them, because *Muigwithania* will come to a man wherever he may be, and if it is really *Muigwithania* [the Unifier] the paper will bring to his ears important matters such as will enable a man to exalt his country, in his own Kikuyu speech."[33]

As they were honoring their past, Kikuyu must also learn from the example of black peoples who had already awoken to their modern condition. Europeans had brought them the necessary materials for their economic, political, and moral uplift; now it was time to forego tutelage for self-reliance. "The people of America when they were like us considered that if they failed to advance by their own efforts they would be of no account," explained one contributor. "When they considered this, they jumped up and decided to teach themselves." Here more than anywhere else *Muigwithania* writers suggested the ways in which their tribal progress was connected to global pan-African currents. Writers celebrated news of black achievement in West and South Africa, and cast an envious eye to the work being done in neighboring Uganda and Tanganyika. Through his correspondence with leaders of the West African Student Union (WASU), in London, Kenyatta acquired news of the opportunities for educational attainment and political advocacy in the imperial capital, and launched a campaign to send Kikuyu students to England to receive training as lawyers, doctors, and other "superior branches of knowledge" for the benefit of the nation. "[T]he time is approaching when we Kikuyu should help ourselves as regard our tasks and our needs," Kenyatta explained. "The time for being helped is coming to an end, and unless we are diligent to help ourselves and to prosecute our tasks in earnest, and without decrying one another and without queering one another's pitches, you should know that we shall be hindering the advancement of our country."[34]

What this two-step program amounted to, in other words, was a careful blending of old and new. Mirroring Garvey's evocation of the New Negro, KCA activists positioned themselves as leaders of a coming age, committed to uniting a scattered flock by reclaiming the dignity of the past, performing the work of tribal self-help by steering the Kikuyu from their "adolescence" toward a new and more dynamic maturity.[35] *Muigwithania* writers exalted the virtues of custom while encouraging Kikuyu to wear European clothes, build European-style homes, study in European schools, and adopt

European methods of cultivation. They decried the pernicious "jargon of foreigners" that threatened their own vernacular while encouraging Kikuyu to learn to read, write, and speak in English. None of this was viewed as contradictory; the task, argued one contributor, was to effectively arbitrate between the past and the present, "to eliminate the customs that involved evil and change the bad parts, supplying good words." It was a task for which KCA activists—as both children of the soil and educated spokesmen—were uniquely qualified to shoulder. If missionaries were more accomplished arbiters of European culture and education, their separation from—and disdain for—African tradition and innovation disqualified them from moral leadership. So too the existing hierarchy of chiefs, elders and headmen, the wisdom of whom did not stretch adequately beyond the reserves, and the power of whom was framed by the parameters of colonial—rather than popular—authority.[36]

Also disqualified from leadership in this nationalist project, unsurprisingly, were women.[37] In both constructing a fictive Kikuyu unity and projecting a path to nationhood, *Muigwithania* writers participated in a profoundly gendered discourse. If young men were to be empowered to work for the future, to train in the modern arts, young women were to return to the stern discipline of that past, to timelessly preserve the talisman of racial purity. Like so many nationalisms, including Garveyism, the mastery of the land began with the masculinist prerogative of familial control.[38] For *Muigwithania* writers, the "Kikuyu seed" had been scattered and imperiled not only by the loss of the country, but by the reckless behavior of Kikuyu women, who had had their heads turned by mission education and modern accoutrements, rejected the authority of their husbands and fathers, and found themselves in the markets of Nairobi, either in rebellion or for economic necessity, where they were "harassed and tormented by other nations," or willing participants in the capital's burgeoning prostitution industry.[39] From the participants' perspective, all of these actions— seeking education, pursuing sexual and economic independence—could be viewed as complex and often dynamic engagements with the new opportunities and limitations created by European rule: performing the same type of work, in other words, as KCA activists. Indeed, Kikuyu women did not passively accept the gendered imbalances inherent in the KCA's program, participating in the organization from the beginning, and leveraging their way into formal membership in 1933.[40] To *Muigwithania* writers, however—including its rare women contributors—the "respect" of the nation rested on the capacity of its men to "protect" a vulnerable and careless womanhood, to police reproduction, to exalt female purity. If men were to build a new nation, women must be anchored to its past.[41]

As they rhetorically established their claim to leadership, KCA activists set themselves to the work of representation. Activists could not directly challenge the authority of the colonial state without facing serious repercussions. Yet here, as with association men in Central Africa, KCA activists understood that the form of their actions—the demonstration of representation itself—carried its own subversive logic. Following the tradition established by the Kikuyu Association and the East African Association, the KCA submitted formal petitions to Nairobi and London in 1925, 1929, 1930, and 1934, presented grievances in less formal meetings with colonial agents, particularly between 1926 and 1929, and presented memoranda and testimony before the Hilton Young Commission in 1928–29, the Joint Committee on the Closer Union of East Africa, 1931–32, and the Morris Carter Kenya Land Commission in 1932–34. In these appeals, the KCA demanded the right to representation in the colonial legislature, the right to grow cash crops like coffee, which was prohibited in the reserves, the right to free association, and the right to elect a paramount chief to preside over a single Kikuyu administrative unit (rather than the five districts that existed). They lodged complaints against the *kipande* system, requested better medical, educational, and sanitary facilities in the reserves, and doggedly sought the return of Harry Thuku until his release in 1931. Most persistently and passionately, they demanded the return of—or compensation for—Kikuyu lands alienated for white settlement, along with formal titles of ownership that would protect existing Kikuyu lands from further encroachment. These demands reached a head with the publication of the report by the Kenya Land Commission in 1934, which "solved" extant claims by Kikuyu *mbari* (clans) in a manner that formalized an untenable status quo: a growing Kikuyu population, inadequate and overused lands in the reserves, and an increasingly homeless and redundant squatter population. In other words, the framework for the explosions of the 1950s.[42]

More subversively, the KCA pursued a rather scattershot series of tactics, including mass meetings, tax evasion, and petty acts of vandalism, aimed to both mobilize Kikuyu under their banner and to build an atmosphere of mistrust surrounding the activities of missionaries, settlers, and the colonial government.[43] KCA activists spread rumors that experimental agricultural gardens organized at mission outstations were part of a broad conspiracy to test the quality of reserve land and prepare for a new round of alienations, a campaign that led to the uprooting of trees and crops.[44] Beginning in early 1928, the KCA organized a large and coordinated campaign to convince squatters on European farms to refuse to sign new contracts, claiming that the new agreements would bind them to their employers for life. Squatters demonstrated their solidarity against the new contracts by engineering slowdowns at work and by providing a myriad of excuses for their suddenly poor productivity. They allowed weeds to grow unabated, and left large tracts un-hoed. One white farmer reported hearing the names of Thuku and Kenyatta rising from the chatter in the fields, and suggested that KCA leaders hoped that massive crop failure would precipitate the exit of white settlers from the country and the return of the country to the Africans. Government officials wondered whether activists hoped to return squatters to the reserves to highlight with greater vividness the land pressures facing their people.[45]

In a more sustained manner, KCA activists endeavored to patiently establish through their organization an alternative framework of leadership and representation. As will be discussed below, KCA activists organized independent schools and churches, supported by their own bureaucracies and central bodies. To coordinate and formalize *mbari* claims to present to the Kenya Land Commission, the KCA organized the Kikuyu Land Board Association (KLBA) in 1932, raising large sums of money and drafting printed, standardized petitions for Kikuyu clients.[46] And in 1937 the KCA created the Kikuyu Food Department, a collective designed to safeguard food supplies to mitigate the risk of famine, and to engage in cooperative trade in foodstuffs.[47] According to James Beauttah, the very performance of KCA debate and decision making was calibrated to foster an atmosphere of cooperation and participation within a sophisticated organizational hierarchy.

> At one of our monthly meetings, in Nairobi, someone like me would pass a resolution which would then be discussed and voted upon. If it was approved, the leaders who were available would go out into the various parts of Central Province [Kikuyu Province], usually outside the towns, and hold meetings in the houses of trusted members. Here, we would tell the people about the resolutions, listen to their views, and then move on to the next area. It was a time consuming process, but through it we learned what was going on in the various parts of Central Province and in addition, we made our members feel that they were playing an important part in our organization. After such a tour, the leaders would return to Nairobi to present their findings to our Central Committee.... Normally, this Committee would confirm the people's decision and then draft a resolution putting it into words. The next step was to find someone who would translate it into proper English for presentation to the Government.

The affect was conscious. As Beauttah observed about the KLBA, "[i]ts leaders were certain that the KCA appeal for the return of land taken by Europeans was hopeless, but ... they wanted to show the people that there was an African organization that could help them in protests against the Government."[48] The work of advocacy, rather than the immediate result, was the objective. As Kenyatta argued in *Muigwithania*, "later comes the struggle." Now was a time for "careful preparation" and "proper humility."[49]

Perhaps the KCA's most successful performance of representation was its decision to send Kenyatta to London to directly petition the Colonial Office and to serve as a liaison between central Kenya and the center of the empire. In *Muigwithania*, Kenyatta had forcefully argued for the need to send talented Kikuyu men to Europe to receive the education denied them in Kenya. Now, as he explained to his readers in February 1929, he would embark on that "long Journey in the interests of the soil of the Kikuyu." Koinange wa Mbiyu, the leading figure in the Kikuyu Association, warned that any money invested in such an endeavor would be in vain, and counseled KCA activists to remain patient and to work through the channels of local administration. But Kenyatta clearly had a broader vision in mind. Adopting the mantle of "Muigwithania" for himself, he would physically illustrate the potency of the KCA's claim to leadership by sidestepping local politics and performing the work of the paramount leader his organization sought, making direct representations to the British government in the name of a united and aggrieved Kikuyu people. The theatrics were impressive; according to the KCA leader Johana Kunyiha, "the trip gave the KCA the first grip it had on the people." Preceding the circumcision crisis by only a few months, "Muigwithania's Journey," as Kenyatta coined his trip, turned the KCA into a popular fundraising force.[50]

Except for a six-month return to Kenya between September 1930 and April 1931, and two periods in the Soviet Union, Kenyatta remained in England until 1946. During that time, as Bruce Berman and John Lonsdale have wonderfully demonstrated, Kenyatta's search for allies, for an education, and for an effective means to pursue Kikuyu grievances pulled him toward an eclectic group of reformers and radicals, from sympathetic missionaries and Labour Party representatives to Communists, Trotskyists, and pan Africanists, and into the intellectual orbit of the famed Polish-born anthropologist Bronislaw Malinowski. During his first months in London, Kenyatta met the Trinidadian Communist George Padmore, whom he followed to Moscow in August 1929, and later—after both men's disillusionment with the Soviet Union—joined in the creation of the International African Friends of Abyssinia in 1934, and the International African Service Bureau (IASB), in 1937, along with West Indians C.L.R. James and T. Ras Makonnen, and I.T.A. Wallace-Johnson from Sierra Leone.[51] Released from the stifling censorship imposed on colonial subjects at home, and exposed to new vistas of discourse and dissent, Kenyatta's writings during his London years reflected his broadening and deepening political consciousness. In a short piece written for Nancy Cunard's anthology, *Negro*, in 1934, Kenyatta comfortably used the language of capitalist exploitation and imperial domination to advocate that Kenyans unite and claim their birthright. By the eve of his return to Kenya, Kenyatta was warning the British that a failure to recognize the need for "a fundamental change in the present political, economic, and social relationship between Europeans and Africans," would augur violence. "Africans are not hostile to Western civilization as such; they would gladly learn its techniques and share in the intellectual and material benefits which it has the power to give," wrote Kenyatta.

> But they are in an intolerable position when the European invasion destroys the very basis of their old tribal way of life, and yet offers them no place in the new society except as serfs doomed to labour for bare existence. There is not one of the boastful blessings of white civilization in which has yet been made generally available to the Kenya Africans.... [T]he Africans make their claim for justice now, in order that a bloodier and more destructive justice may not be inevitable in time to come.[52]

Yet even as he maintained a physical distance from the work of the KCA in Kikuyu country, and even as he embraced a more strident political advocacy, Kenyatta remained connected to, and committed to, the patient work of nation building that he had embarked upon as the editor of *Muigwithania*. Intellectually, this set him apart from his colleagues in the IASB. Through his time in London, Kenyatta remained wedded to a model of "political tribalism"—or a bourgeois nationalism that was anathema to black radicals like Padmore and James. Rather than pursue "world revolution" like Padmore, or even African liberation in a broad and abstract sense, Kenyatta turned to anthropology as a felicitous vehicle to continue the politics of representation. In the context of interwar Kikuyu politics, Kenyatta's work of history, culture, mythology, and identity, *Facing Mount Kenya*, is a revealing document, a reflection of both Kenyatta's growing intellectual sophistication and of the work to which Kenyatta remained connected through frequent correspondence with activists at home. To his friends in London, however, it rang hollow. From Makonnen's perspective, Kenyatta "was simply concerned to get certain things known about his people." James praised Kenyatta for remaining "in constant touch with people from Kenya," but sardonically observed that "he kept [his brains] to himself."[53]

As with *Muigwithania*, the extent to which *Facing Mount Kenya* mirrors Garveyist sensibilities has yet to be acknowledged. The ambivalence of Kenyatta's friends in the IASB toward the work makes sense in this context; Padmore, Makonnen, and James had an especially contentious relationship with Garvey and his politics.[54] Yet the available evidence seems to suggest that Kenyatta felt differently during his London period. As a young man, the *Negro World* had inflamed his imagination. Then, when he first arrived in London, he either stayed with—or maintained close contact with— Ladipo Solanke, founder of the West African Students' Union, who, according to his daughter, introduced Kenyatta to the expression, "African Nationalism," and maintained contact with Garvey for several years. According to London police, both Solanke and Kenyatta were representatives of the Universal Negro Improvement Association, an implausible suggestion that may have stemmed from the fact that Garvey gave WASU a house in London to use for a proposed student hostel.[55] Solanke, like many West African intellectuals, rejected the stridency of Garvey's demand for African liberation. Nevertheless, his support for the politics of racial pride and self-help, and his admiration for Garvey's work "arous[ing] in us in a material way our race-consciousness," connected him, at least ideologically, to Garvey's more pared back approach to African politics after 1924.[56] So too Kenyatta. According to Amy Jacques Garvey, during his time in London Kenyatta remained an admirer of Marcus Garvey, and a proponent of Garveyism.[57]

Facing Mount Kenya presents a more focused and sophisticated version of the argument made by *Muigwithania*, developing a claim to Kikuyu self-government that relies on a Garveyist blend of cultural pride, self-reliance, and Westernized reform. Like *Muigwithania*, *Facing Mount Kenya* invents a harmonious Kikuyu past, charts the disintegration of Kikuyu culture and society under European rule, and proposes a path forward that is navigable only for one authentically "Kikuyu" and Western trained. (Lest there be any confusion about who Kenyatta had in mind, he uses his preface to illustrate his own capacity to "speak as a representative" of his people in both Western and "tribal" forums, adding for good measure a picture of himself adorned in a monkey-fur robe and grasping a spear.) In Kenyatta's telling, Kikuyu people sprang from a common ancestor and grew to acquire the lands around Mount Kenya by clearing the forests or by legal sale. They developed a form of tribal organization that both allowed for private *mbari* ownership and united the group through a system of *riika* (age grading) that connected generations of boys and girls in common purpose and stabilized political, social, religious, and economic life. European colonizers had come to Kenya with a series of "progressive" tools—ideas of material prosperity, of medicine and hygiene, and literacy—but rather than share these gifts with the African they had "rob[bed] him of his government, condemn[ed] his religious ideas, and ignore[d] his fundamental conceptions of justice and morals, all in the name of civilization and progress." Rather than having an alien system imposed on them, the Kikuyu must be "left in peace on their own lands." This self-sufficiency would in turn allow them the autonomy and freedom to preserve the things of value and integrity from their own traditions while choosing "what parts of European culture could be beneficially transplanted, and how they could be adapted." It was a task not suited to false arbiters of African culture, but to a generation of future leaders among whom Kenyatta was most distinguished.[58]

The crux of Kenyatta's argument is contained within his remarkable chapter on male and female initiation, in which he sets out to explain why clitoridectomy, a custom viewed as barbaric by European audiences, was defended by the most educated and intelligent Kikuyu. "The real argument lies not in the defence of the surgical operation or its details, but in

Figure 8.2. Jomo Kenyatta, in *Facing Mount Kenya*. (Secker and Warburg, 1938)

the understanding of a very important fact in the tribal psychology of the Gikuyu (Kikuyu)," writes Kenyatta. Initiation was viewed as a necessary bridge between childhood and adulthood, was inextricably bound to the "moral code of the tribe," and indeed embodied the very unity of the tribe, creating bonds of association through age grouping, sustaining oral traditions marked by the names given to these groups, and thus preserving the history and origin of the people. Because clitoridectomy "is still regarded as the very essence of an institution which has enormous education, social, moral, and religious implications," and because "[f]or the present it is impossible for a member of the tribe to imagine an initiation without clitoridectomy," the abolition of the surgical element was ill-advised; it meant to the Kikuyu "the abolition of the whole institution." In a sweep Kenyatta both defended the cultural integrity of Kikuyu custom and pointed to a way forward. In rejecting the immediate abolition of female circumcision he both allowed for the criticism of the surgery and segregated the surgery (bad custom) from the practice of initiation itself (vital custom). And in thus performing his own act of surgery, Kenyatta demonstrated his own claim to leadership.[59]

In the years surrounding the publication of *Facing Mount Kenya*, Kenyatta also thrust himself into the arena of Kikuyu educational politics, petitioning sympathetic members of Parliament on behalf of one of the two independent school associations to emerge out of the circumcision crisis, the Kikuyu Karing'a Education Association (KKEA). In 1946, after he returned to Kenya, Kenyatta visited over two hundred independent schools and, along with Peter Mbiyu Koinange, the son of Chief Koinange, worked to raise funds for the Kenya Teachers College at Githunguri, which had been organized by Mbiyu Koinange beginning in 1938.[60] Like Kenyatta, Mbiyu Koinange had received a privileged education abroad, his in the United States, at Hampton Institute in Virginia, then Ohio Wesleyan University, in Delaware, Ohio. And like Kenyatta, Mbiyu Koinange had made at least brief contact with Garveyites while abroad.[61] The two men returned to lead an educational movement that had nurtured a Garveyist politics in Kikuyu country throughout the 1930s, engaged in a long game that proposed unity, self-help, consciousness raising and institution building as the predicates for a successful assault on European rule. It was a movement that had found a useful ally in an archbishop from South Africa engaged in his own cautious project of African Garveyism. And it was a movement that would propel Kenya into the troubled era of Emergency when, as Kenyatta had forewarned, Kikuyu rebels would seek their bloody claims to justice, and the brutal underpinnings of British rule would be brought to their logical and murderous conclusions.

Institutional Independency: The Kikuyu Independent Schools Movement and the African Orthodox Church

The first two independent schools in central Kenya were founded in 1922, nurtured by future KCA leaders and collaborators. They grew out of disputes with European missionaries, who until then had held a monopoly over the instruction of African boys and girls in the colony.[62] It was the circumcision crisis of 1929–30, however, and the mass exodus of Kikuyu dissenters from the missionary sphere that created the opportunity, the necessity, and the framework for the emergence of educational and religious independency in Kikuyu country. By November 1929, a flood of applications for the approval of African-run schools were being submitted to nervous local administrators in Kiambu and Fort Hall. In September 1933 Kikuyu education activists met to discuss the formation of an administrative body to standardize and coordinate the growth and operation of independent schools in southern Kiambu, organizing the Kikuyu Karing'a Educational Association. The next year, a more ambitious project to merge a group of existing school committees stretched across Fort Hall, Kiambu, Nyeri, and Embu led to the creation of the Kikuyu Independent Schools Association (KISA). By the end of 1937, KKEA controlled ten schools, and KISA ran more than fifty. By the declaration of the Emergency in 1952, and the decision by the state to suppress the independent schools movement as a subversive breeding ground for revolutionary behavior, 158 schools were in operation, serving more than 39,000 children.[63]

The independent schools movement was comprised of a dizzying array of local projects and personal schisms. It was also divided by two oversight committees—KISA and KKEA—between which real friction and disputes existed. Still, the movement was united by a fundamental theory of Kikuyu nationalism pursued through local control, institution building, and consciousness raising within the context of broader colonial domination. Recognizing the liberatory potential of European-style education, but bound by a colonial orthodoxy that conspired to train Africans to be effective laborers rather than effective leaders,[64] independent school activists leveraged the opening provided by the missions' hard-line stance on female circumcision into a reengineered foundation for African education legitimately oriented toward an era of African rule.[65] This project, like much of the work that flowed out of the KCA in the 1920s and 1930s, was pursued in the language of accommodation; indeed, according to Johana Kunyiha, member of the EAA, KCA, and the first president of KISA, KCA and KISA leaders met in secret and signed "a work division agreement" intended to protect KISA from being implicated in KCA political activities. Framed by an innocuous set of rules and regulations that proposed to "further the interests of the

Kikuyu . . . and to safeguard the homogeneity of interests of the Kikuyu nation such as spiritual, economic, social and educational matters," independent school activists, as Derek Peterson has argued, pursued a bureaucratic and administrative competency that would presage their liberation, and a curriculum that, as James Arthur Wilson has demonstrated, pursued a vision of cultural nationalism that anticipated Jomo Kenyatta's political project of *harambee* (pull together).[66] It was an arrangement, in other words, that freed Kikuyu independent schools to pursue the same brand of educational and—in short order—religious uplift being pursued cautiously by Garveyite activists throughout the continent.

This relationship was explicitly consummated by the alliance forged between independent school leaders in Kenya and Daniel William Alexander, archbishop of the Garveyist African Orthodox Church (AOC) in South Africa. The church was the brainchild of George Alexander McGuire, chaplain-general of the Universal Negro Improvement Association, who founded the AOC in New York in 1921 as a mechanism to pursue the project of African redemption through the work of spiritual uplift. Born in Antigua, McGuire had arrived in the United States in 1894, rising to the highest position held by a black man within the Episcopal Church before growing weary of the structural barriers to black leadership erected by white Christianity.[67] McGuire argued that rather than being reduced to beggars within the white Church, the Negro must establish his own claim to leadership in his own ecclesiastical bodies; as AOC minister and Garveyite Reverend Fred A. Toote put it, Negroes must "no longer 'lust after the flesh-pots of Egypt,'" but rather "steadfastly pursue the line of duty dictated by both natural and divine revelation that all races must accomplish their own destiny." The call to spiritual independence, unity, and organization directed explicitly and uniformly religious means toward the realization of political ends. "We have a God to serve, an aim to pursue, a destiny to achieve," explained McGuire in the inaugural edition of the AOC's official organ, *The Negro Churchman*. "And since no people can build a permanent social, industrial or political superstructure except upon a religious and spiritual foundation, we call upon the Negro ministry of an awakened Race to stretch out their hands to the Everlasting God." Princes would come out of Egypt, assured McGuire. But only once Ethiopia had first stretched forth her hands unto God. The African Church "must prepare the way for African Nationhood."[68]

Like Garvey, McGuire at first conceived his project in the most grandiose organizational terms; under the auspices of the UNIA, McGuire would preside over a "Church Ethiopic," a sort of religious League of Nations that would unify under a single tent the splintered denominations of black faith—Methodists, Baptists, Presbyterians, Catholics, Muslims—while sustaining a diversity of worship and denominational self-governance.[69] It was a vision not warmly received by Garveyites jealous of their religious independence, nor by Garvey himself, who recognized the danger of involving his organization in an ecclesiastical turf war. McGuire was asked to resign from his post as chaplain-general, then was expelled from the UNIA, inaugurating a personal feud between McGuire and Garvey that at times became bitter.[70] Nevertheless, McGuire never strayed from his belief that Garveyism represented the only solution to the race problem, and by the end of 1923 the two men had reconciled.[71] By this time, McGuire had scaled back his personal ambition. The lofty goal of African redemption remained, but it was to be pursued through the more modest work of denomination building. Like Garveyism itself, the spirit of the cause of African Christianity would flow through a decentralized project of consciousness raising and institution building better calibrated to the complexities and disjunctures of "Negro" life and the constraints of interwar white supremacy. In this guise, the AOC spread across the Americas. By the Second World War, the church had established work throughout the United States, and in Canada, the Bahamas, Cuba, Trinidad, Jamaica, Barbados, British Guiana (Guyana), and Nicaragua.

On August 1, 1924 McGuire delivered a thunderous sermon at the opening of the UNIA's Fourth International Convention. With an eye to the new mood that had swept over the UNIA in the wake of the breakdown of talks with the Liberian government, and presaging Garvey's declaration of the end of the organization's "radical" period by a few months, McGuire constituted Garveyism a "spiritual movement," propelled not by "[b]lind courage" or "material force" but by a "spiritual force" that transcended the fallibility of both the UNIA and its leader. This elevation of Garveyism to a metaphysical level, and above the declining fortunes of its organizational beachhead, was consistent with both Garvey's evolving view of the role of the UNIA in the diasporic movement for African liberation, and McGuire's belief that spiritual freedom must come first, that it must be "the basis of all other freedoms." Accusing white missionaries of "defil[ing] the religion of Jesus Christ" and making it "the harlot of their lust, avarice and ambition," McGuire implored Negroes to refuse "the white man's catechism," and to embrace the Negro pastors and bishops who could be the "only . . . true Shepherds of Negroes." By the reformation of black religion and the growth of black religious freedom, Garveyism might be made a spiritual movement "not only in verbal characterization but in actual operation." Political momentum would flow not through the impatience of material confrontation but through the dawning appreciation of Garveyism's prophetic logic. "The Jews made of Zionism a spiritual movement and today the goal is achieved, the fact accomplished," argued McGuire. "Africanism must become a spiritual movement among Negroes."[72]

The text of McGuire's sermon was printed in the *Negro World* and carried across the Atlantic, eventually finding its way to the desk of Daniel William Alexander in Kimberley, South Africa.[73] Alexander was born in 1883 in Port Elizabeth, South Africa to parents who had emigrated from the Caribbean. An ambitious man in search of a platform, Alexander had served as a chaplain in the Anglican Church, secretary of the Pretoria branch of the colored political association, the African Political Organization (APO), and grand true secretary of the Independent Order of True Templars, another influential colored organization, before gravitating toward independent black Christianity and joining the African Church.[74] Alexander returned to religious work after reading Booker T. Washington's *My Larger Education*, which, as Alexander later reflected, made him "determined to settle my mind on some definite object, and then strive to attain the height of that objective."[75] News of the African Orthodox Church, and of McGuire's expansive view of its charge, struck Alexander like a lightning bolt. He immediately wrote to McGuire, and without waiting for a reply, led 450 clergy and laypeople out of the African Church and into the African Orthodox Church of South Africa. Joseph Masogha, the local agent of the *Negro World* in Kimberley, attended the preliminary meeting of the church on October 6, 1924, and told Alexander that he was assuming a "heavy load" and would succeed only with "patience and forebearance." It was a task for which Alexander had been preparing his whole life.[76]

Like McGuire, Alexander viewed the work of the AOC as a restoration project. If European missionaries had done much to spread the work of Christ through sub-Saharan Africa, they were unable to view the black man as anything other than "perpetual hewers of wood and drawers of water," and conspired not to elevate Africans to their true potential but to retard their development. The task of salvation must as a result fall to black leaders, working in their own institutions, training their own clergy, performing their own missionary work among the "backward people" of the African interior. This was the discourse of providential design. By patiently raising a respectable, Western-style church, Alexander—a descendent of slaves in the Americas, returned to the continent to lead his people to civilization—would restore the "ancient glory" of Africa.[77]

In examining the ministry of Daniel William Alexander, scholars have drawn misleading distinctions between Alexander's institutional and ecclesiastical work and the UNIA's political activism.[78] This impression has been reinforced by Alexander's careful efforts to protect the work of his church from the hint of political participation. It was a concern that sparked a bitter personal feud between Alexander and his second-in-command, Reverend John Scota Likhing, after Likhing's election as a provincial president of the African National Congress, and precipitated Likhing's excommunication from the church in 1933.[79] Rather than position the AOC in opposition to the machinery of the state, Alexander worked tirelessly to convince a skeptical South African government of the church's fundamental disinterest in politics. He applied to the Native Affairs Commission for government recognition in 1926, 1929, and 1935, each time unsuccessfully. "The fact that a Church is a Separatist body and is not under European control should not of itself debar the Church from registration," he argued. "The sole condition for registration should be that the Church is a stable organization and that its ministers are responsible persons fit to exercise the civil duties of Ministers of religion."[80]

Yet if, as Michael O. West has suggested, Alexander believed his primary duty to be the development of his church, "narrowly defined," he viewed this work in the manner that McGuire—and Garvey—intended it, as a necessary precondition to political emancipation. The nonconfrontational stance that Alexander brought to his work, as the AOC spread through the Transvaal and Cape Province, and then north into Southern Rhodesia, Uganda, and Kenya, was a pragmatic acknowledgment of the terrain upon which Garveyist politics could function on the continent. As McGuire warned, in his early correspondence with Alexander, the work of the church in South Africa must be "adjust[ed] . . . to the conditions" of white governance in Africa. For this reason, McGuire applauded Alexander's efforts to work in the open and through official channels, and stressed the importance of distancing the South African Orthodox Church from its Western brethren—a source of inevitable suspicion—by organizing it as an autonomous body with only loose ties of affiliation. Behind this tactical separation, however, was an understanding that the work on both sides of the Atlantic was "exact[ly] parallel." And this meant spreading the word of Garveyism under an ecclesiastical cover. "We are not officially connected with the UNIA," McGuire explained to Alexander, "but are all of us individually members of the Organization as we are one in sentiment, political and Religious."[81]

Despite Alexander's best efforts, no one was really convinced that the AOC in South Africa was anything other than a Garveyist beachhead. South African and British authorities, relying on a questionable mix of innuendo and conjecture, believed that Garvey had provided the funds for the construction of the AOC's central church building at Beaconsfield, a suburb of Kimberley; that Alexander was secretly conspiring with Josiah T. Gumede, president of the ANC, Communist, and admirer of Garvey, to drive the whites out of Africa; and that Alexander's consecration by McGuire was part of an effort to spread dissension through the British colonies, and to establish a channel through which to send Garveyist ministers between the United States and Africa.[82] Those attracted to the AOC from outside of South Africa viewed its objectives in a similar manner. In April 1925, an ambitious Baganda man named Reuben Spartas read McGuire's convention sermon in the *Negro World* and penned two letters to the United States, one to McGuire, asking for advice on how to properly preach, and one to Amy Jacques Garvey, in which he vowed "to go to hell, jail or die for the redemption of Africa." In April, 1929, Dick Dube, an aspiring Garveyite living in Bulawayo, wrote to Alexander explaining his desire to establish an AOC branch in Southern Rhodesia, not to learn theology but to study the "problem of race which is the race problem, so as to [be] able to organize my people under the name African Communities League [UNIA]."[83] Even Alexander himself, who was far more cautious than Spartas or Dube, was a consistent reader of the *Negro World*, and maintained direct ties with the UNIA at least until 1927, when he addressed Garveyite meetings during his visit to New York to receive his official consecration as archbishop. Nor did he shy away from the propagandistic value of his association with the American church. As Likhing remarked in 1932, "the backbone of the many members and would be members are [*sic*] the hope of the link or closer cooperation with the church in America."[84]

The confusion rested in the contradictions of African Garveyism, which promised a radical overthrow of existing institutions while demanding of its adherents a disciplined deference to the status quo. Alexander would have surely welcomed the ends of the activities conjured by white authorities, but certainly not the means. And while he embraced the project of Garveyist missionary work to the north, this work must be couched in the most careful terms. After connecting with Spartas in 1928, Alexander helped establish the AOC in Uganda, but only after both men assured Ugandan authorities of their disinterest in politics. He organized the AOC in Southern Rhodesia, but not before ensuring that the church was led by a man with a "good record," Reverend James Poyah, and not Dube or Poyah's rival, James Mphamba, who had ties to the ICU. Like other Garveyist churchmen in Africa, Alexander sold a philosophy of Negro redemption that replaced political declarations of African liberation with a spiritual discourse that proposed the same result. "We need Race pride, respect for each other, and the ambition to achieve for ourselves that which is constructive and substantial, so that when we are asked to recite what we have done for ourselves, we may point with satisfaction to our quota in the world's progress in the sciences of medicine, philosophy, agriculture, as well as in the realm of commerce and finance," wrote Alexander. This project of uplift, joined with a "martyrdom of faith and zeal," would bring the princes out of Egypt. Until then, as Alexander put it in a revealing poem, the Negro must "Work and Wait" for his Empire: "Work! For His law is good and just; / Wait! Truth can never die."[85]

To this discourse of Garveyist preparation, leaders of the AOC added an ecclesiastical twist. By his consecration into the Historic Episcopate as archbishop, George Alexander McGuire had reclaimed the Catholic tree of Apostolic Succession for the Negro, a conferral that, as Alexander remarked, had been denied for centuries by the "petty jealousy" of white clergy members.[86] And yet God had found a channel, through the AOC, to restore the honor to the race, to repair the ancient connections bridging early black Christians and modern ones. It was from this seed, from this sacred font of authority, that a scattered race might be drawn together, might build its own institutions and nurture its own leadership. Alexander's consecration as archbishop in 1927 had brought this promise of ecclesiastical independence to Africa. It was a gift that Alexander hoped to carry to every corner of the continent. "Africa is awakening, the morning is breaking for her; her children's eyes are no more close[d] in sleep," he boasted of the work being done in Uganda. "[W]ould that more of our brethren, both here and in America, dare to be freemen in their own vineyard, only then will we be able to build a vast Catholic Church governed entirely by Negroes, covering every land in which they reside."[87]

In September 1931, Alexander traveled to Uganda, where he assisted Reuben Spartas in the work of establishing the AOC in the colony.[88] On his way home in 1932, Alexander spent ten days in Mombasa, and was introduced to leaders of the Kenyan independent schools movement, who explained to him their eagerness to join the schools with an "Independent National African Church," but that they lacked a mechanism to secure ordination for the clergy of an African-controlled religious body.[89] Before Alexander sailed back to South Africa, James Beauttah asked him to return:

> I took him down to Kilindini Pier, gave him sh. 20, saying, "This money is not mine, although I am giving it to you. It belongs to the Kikuyu people. Do you agree that if they need you you will come back and help them to reform their own church?" He said that he would, and I promised that we would send for him and pay his way back.

Three years later, during which time Alexander had remained in contact with Kikuyu activists, sufficient funds had been raised, and Johana Kunyiha, KISA's president, forwarded the balance to Beaconsfield. "Our people are at the beginning of modern civilization, so it is our duty to educate them spiritually and economically to the best of our ability," Kunyiha wrote. "We . . . hope that your visit to Kenya will be an enjoyable time and that your work will be a nucleus in which [the] Negro Race will set an example to the world indicating what the race can do itself without any assistance of another race."[90]

Alexander worked in Kenya from November 1935 to July, 1937, during which time he baptized "8,000 souls," including 646 in one day, ordained four African clergymen, and established the nucleus for a sustained and viable infrastructure of religious independency.[91] In the process his mission revealed and exacerbated extant fissures within the independent schools movement, and within the realm of Kikuyu nationalism more broadly speaking. Disagreements between members of KISA and KKEA led to a schism shortly after Alexander's departure, and the creation of the African Independent Pentecostal Church (AIPC), aligned with KISA.

Once again, however, Alexander's work revealed the political possibilities of Garveyist race first politics, a politics that had been embraced by Kikuyu activists for several years. Shielding his message behind careful expressions of loyalty, Alexander implored his students to doubt the capacity of European missionaries to properly represent their spiritual interests, and to embrace the movement toward a network of Negro leadership that spanned the African diaspora. KISA leaders, who continued to view Alexander as their "Spiritual father" after their break with the AOC, explained that while the church "admits to membership and other privileges persons of all races, it seeks particularly to reach out to the millions of African descent in both hemispheres and declares itself to be perpetually autonomous and controlled by negroes entirely. It is a Church (of the Africans, governed by the Africans and for the Africans) to make daily supplications to Almighty God led by Priests who have the welfare of Africans at heart." Beauttah never forgot the day he sent the funds to Alexander for his visit. "I had such confidence that he would bring us a new religion which would be ours alone, which would spread throughout the country and all through East Africa," he remembered. "His arrival would bring us religious freedom and I was certain that political independence would eventually follow."[92]

AFTERWORD

THE BUSTLING streets of modern Nairobi are inscribed with the history of Kenya's anticolonial struggle. Kenyatta Avenue runs along Uhuru Park and through the heart of the city's downtown, past Koinange Street, past Kimathi Street and a memorial to the executed rebel, Dedan Kimathi, and ending at Tom Mboya Street. Harry Thuku Road starts out toward the affluent Westlands before abruptly halting; Joseph Kangethe Road runs to the north of the Kibera slums. Alongside these monuments to national liberation are gestures to a broader narrative of pan-Africanism: Haile Selassie Avenue and Menelik Road, an ode to Ethiopia; Nkrumah Lane, Banda Street, and Kaunda Street, tributes to the first leaders of independent Ghana, Malawi, and Zambia, and a gesture to the momentous Fifth Pan-African Conference in Manchester, England, which all three attended. George Padmore, who secretly traveled to Kenya in 1933, is honored, as is Ralph Bunche, who visited a few years later.[1] To the west of the downtown, a block from where I briefly rented a room, lies Marcus Garvey Road.

Road naming, like nation building, requires imagination; like all memorials to the past, it encourages both remembrance and forgetfulness. As President, Kenyatta's project to reconcile the messy fissures of his new state with the demands of national administration continued the work of invented tradition that he had begun as a member of the KCA. Only now, he was the victor. The work of identity, behind which dissident Kenyans—and Africans across the continent—mobilized successfully, was to be exposed to the harsh reality of multiple identities, of multiple claims, of competing and powerful aspirations. The triumph of the nationalist moment was fleeting.

The story told by Nairobi's cartography is of Kenyans at home intersecting with Africans abroad. When the new generation of African leaders considered the heroic past, they often viewed it in these terms. Thus in the moment of national independence was the Universal Negro Improvement Association, assumed to have passed with Garvey, returned briefly to the stage. William Sherrill, the UNIA's president-general, was invited to attend the lavish celebrations staged by Kwame Nkrumah in Ghana in 1957, where Sherrill was assigned a new car, a driver, and an aide-de-camp, and generally treated like royalty. Sherrill was surprised and overwhelmed by the high regard held for his organization. Nkrumah publicly declared that "his life and work had been largely influenced by the Philosophy of Marcus Garvey and the UNIA," and encouraged Sherrill in a long private conference to continue the struggle for freedom outside of Africa as he was to continue the work throughout the continent. Several "African Chiefs and Nationalist leaders" expressed their praise for the UNIA, many telling Sherrill that they had been members of the organization in their youth. Sherrill met with

Harry M. Nkumbula, president-general of the African National Congress of Northern Rhodesia, and T.D.T. Banda, president-general of the Nyasaland African Congress, both of whom expressed an interest in affiliating their work with the UNIA. Banda later wrote to Sherrill, "Most of my people in Nyasaland have read and heard quite a lot about the philosophy of your Founder and the 'Aims and Objects' of your great and wonderful association and we are all very happy that we have come to see each other at last."[2]

In 1967, the UNIA's High Commissioner to Africa, Reverend Clarence W. Harding, was invited to Addis Ababa to meet with Diallo Telli, secretary-general of the Organization of African Unity (OAU), to discuss the future role that the UNIA might play in Africa. Harding left his office in Monrovia on October 13 and reached Kinshasa two days later, where he was feted by President Joseph Mobutu and Congolese dignitaries. Mobutu declared himself a "staunch admirer" of Marcus Garvey, and welcomed Harding to establish UNIA divisions in the country whenever he was prepared. From the Congo, Harding traveled to Nairobi, where he was met by Jomo Kenyatta and Tom Mboya, and again assured of support and encouraged to establish divisions in the country. In Addis Ababa, Harding addressed the representatives of fourteen African nations, appealing for support, outlining the aims and history of the UNIA and describing the organization's current vision for Africa. All agreed to welcome the UNIA to their countries, and the UNIA was granted a non-voting position in the OAU's General Assembly, and promises of financial support after an observation period. "[W]e made history," Harding reported to Thomas W. Harvey, the new president-general of the UNIA. Yet even as he celebrated the victory, Harding sensed that a powerful nostalgia had overtaken any reasonable expectation for his organization's future role. "It is just too bad that this could not have been done when we have millions of dollars," he remarked wistfully.[3]

The UNIA's triumphal era of ascent—of transatlantic shipping lines and magnificent conventions, of overflowing coffers and strident demands for political upheaval—comprised a brief moment in its organizational history, and a briefer moment still in the long struggle toward African liberation. A preoccupation with the spectacle of these early years has left us with an unsatisfying understanding of precisely what was accomplished, precisely what Garveyism wrought. Just as the UNIA provided a vivid symbol of nostalgia in post-colonial Africa, it offered a powerful ideological and political vehicle for African activists during the dark years of interwar European rule. This was true both because Garveyite propagandists relentlessly broadcast on the winds a hopeful language of diasporic mobilization and emancipation, and because Garveyites—after it became clear that the UNIA would not be the vehicle of pan-African liberation—turned their attention to the mundane and patient work of consciousness raising, institution building, and preparation.

The success of Garveyism in the United States during the interwar period was also premised on a careful assessment of the limits and possibilities of the moment. As in Africa, the efforts of American Garveyites to construct vibrant organizational containers during an inauspicious decade resonated through the years. After the decline of the UNIA in the late 1920s, when many Garveyites gravitated away from the organization, they resurfaced in the Congress of Industrial Organizations, the Communist Party, and the Brotherhood of Sleeping Car Porters. E. B. "Britt" McKinney, an important organizer for the Garvey movement in rural Arkansas, became an important organizer for the Southern Tenant Farmers' Union, bringing many former Garveyites into the organization with him. James Nimmo, a Miami Garveyite, became one of the most important figures in the city's labor movement in the 1940s. "Queen Mother" Audley Moore, a member of the UNIA in New Orleans in the early 1920s, mentored the Revolutionary Action Movement in Detroit, which in turn provided inspiration for the Black Panther Party in Oakland. Elijah Muhammad was a Garveyite, as was Earl Little, who sometimes took his young son, Malcolm (X), to UNIA meetings. Septima Clark watched the first ship of the Black Star Line dock in Charleston; Student Non-Violent Coordinating Committee organizer Ivanhoe Donaldson grew up in a UNIA household, as did pioneering scholar St. Clair Drake. A number of Garveyite women distinguished themselves with their political activism in other forums, including Sylvia Woods, Charlotta Bass, and Mittie Maud Lena Gordon, president-general of the Peace Movement of Ethiopia. M.L.T. De Mena published a journal in support of Father Divine's Peace Movement, the *World Echo*, on the old printing presses of the *Negro World*. Amy Ashwood Garvey, Garvey's first wife and cofounder of the UNIA, served as a member of the Council on African Affairs, and helped organize the Fifth Pan-African Congress. Amy Jacques Garvey spoke alongside Kwame Nkrumah in Ghana, and at the historic Asian-African Conference in Bandung, Indonesia, in 1955.[4]

In the Caribbean, the return of labor radicalism in the mid-1930s both eclipsed established modes of Garveyist political association and boasted a leadership that had been nurtured within the Garvey movement.[5] The fiery leader of Trinidad's bloody strikes of 1937, Tubal Uriah "Buzz" Butler, opened his labor meetings with rousing renditions of "From Greenland's Icy Mountains," a hymn that had gained great notoriety for its use at the opening of UNIA meetings.[6] Garveyism continues to resonate across the landscape of Caribbean politics, religion, and culture. The movement had a formative influence on the emergence of Rastafarianism, whose adherents view Garvey as a prophet, a John the Baptist to Ras Tafari—the Emperor Haile Selassie, and the second coming of Christ.[7] The influence of Garveyism on reggae music has been equally profound. In 1976, Robert A. Hill, a young Jamaican scholar, sent Bob Marley his recently completed collection of Garvey's last journal, *The Black Man*. Hill would later become the editor of the Marcus Garvey Papers Project and the world's foremost Garvey scholar. Marley, a Rastafari, would borrow a passage from a speech reprinted in Hill's volume to use in "Redemption Song," the final track of his final album: "Emancipate yourself from mental slavery; / None but ourselves can free our minds . . ."[8]

In 1966, the UNIA was granted 2,000 acres of land by the Paramount Chief of Tchien, in Liberia. Opening the First International Convention of the Negro Peoples of the World, in 1920, Garvey had celebrated his plan to remove the headquarters of the UNIA to Monrovia as the first salvo in the rebuilding of a liberated Africa. Now, Garvey's dream finally realized, the goals were more modest. Beset by financial difficulties, Clarence Harding had by the end of the decade nevertheless established a medical clinic, a thriving agricultural farm, and a broadsheet, the *African World*, distributed to embassies across the continent. Along with three "bush" schools, the Garvey Memorial Institute was opened in 1969, serving 530 elementary and high school students in its first year. That same year Harding hosted a General Conference attended by representatives from Ghana, Mali, Congo, Côte d'Ivoire, Senegal, and Sierra Leone. It was a fitting, and decidedly unspectacular, tribute to years of patient activism. "We are at last doing the work that our beloved founder the late Hon. Marcus Garvey wanted us to do," wrote Thomas W. Harvey. "[S]o let us be true to our purposes."[9]

ABBREVIATIONS

AOC: Papers of the African Orthodox Church, Pitts Theological Library, Emory University

ATOR: *African Times and Orient Review*

BFMA: Belgian Foreign Ministry Archives, Brussels

KNA: Kenya National Archives, Nairobi

MGP: *Marcus Garvey and UNIA Papers*, ed. Robert A. Hill (Berkeley: University of California Press, 1983–2011)

NA: National Archives, College Park, MD

NAM: National Archives of Malawi, Zomba

NAZ: National Archives of Zambia, Lusaka

NW: *Negro World*

PCEA: Presbyterian Church of East Africa Papers

PRO: Public Records Office, London (National Archives of England)

SC-NYPL: Schomburg Center, New York Public Library

SOAS-IMC: School of Oriental and African Studies, London, International Missionary Council Papers

UNIA: Universal Negro Improvement Association Papers, Manuscript, Archives and Rare Book Library, Emory University

NOTES

INTRODUCTION

1. Report of Madison Square Garden Meeting, 3 August 1920, MGP, 2:497–508.

2. Tony Martin, *Race First: The Ideological and Organizational Struggles of Marcus Garvey and the Universal Negro Improvement Association* (Westport, CT: Greenwood Press, 1976), 164.

3. C.L.R. James, "From Toussaint L'Ouverture to Fidel Castro," in *The Black Jacobins: Toussaint L'Ouverture and the San Domingo Revolution* (New York: Vintage Books, 1963), 396.

4. Statement by John E. Bruce, c. January 1918, MGP, 1:236; Emmett J. Scott, "Report on UNIA," 11 December 1918, NA, RG 165, File 10217–61: Interviews with Du Bois and Owen by Charles Mowbray White, 20–22 August 1920, MGP, 2:609–11, 620–21; A. Philip Randolph, "Garveyism," *Messenger* 3, no. 4 (1921), 248–52.

5. Edmund David Cronon, *Black Moses: The Story of Marcus Garvey and the Universal Negro Improvement Association* (Madison: University of Wisconsin Press, 1955), 203; Judith Stein, *The World of Marcus Garvey: Race and Class in Modern Society* (Baton Rouge: Louisiana State University Press, 1986), 6; David Levering Lewis, *W.E.B. Du Bois: The Fight for Equality and the American Century, 1919–1963* (New York: Henry Holt, 2000), 39, 70–75.

6. Martin, *Race First*, ix.

7. See, for example, Emory Tolbert, *The UNIA and Black Los Angeles: Ideology and Community in the American Garvey Movement* (Los Angeles: Center for Afro-American Studies, UCLA, 1980); Mary G. Rolinson, *Grassroots Garveyism. The Universal Negro Improvement Association in the Rural South, 1920–1927* (Chapel Hill: University of North Carolina Press, 2007); Claudrena N. Harold, *The Rise and Fall of the Garvey Movement in the Urban South, 1918–1942* (New York: Routledge, 2007); Steven Hahn, *The Political Worlds of Slavery and Freedom* (Cambridge, MA: Harvard University Press, 2009), 115–62; Robert Trent Vinson, *The Americans Are Coming!: Dreams of African American Liberation in Segregationist South Africa* (Athens: Ohio University Press, 2011).

8. Steven Hahn, *The Political Worlds of Slavery and Freedom* (Cambridge, MA: Harvard University Press, 2009), 117–20.

9. Stephen Tuck, *We Ain't What We Ought to Be: The Black Freedom Struggle from Emancipation to Obama* (Cambridge, MA: Harvard University Press, 2010), 163.

10. Colin Grant, *Negro with a Hat: The Rise and Fall of Marcus Garvey* (Oxford: Oxford University Press, 2008); Wilson Jeremiah Moses, *Creative Conflict in African American Thought: Frederick Douglass, Alexander Crummell, Booker T. Washington, W.E.B. Du Bois, and Marcus Garvey* (Cambridge: Cambridge University Press, 2004), 231–32.

11. Wilson Jeremiah Moses, *The Golden Age of Black Nationalism, 1850–1925* (Hamden, CT: Archon Books, 1978), 197–98.

12. For example, see Tolbert, *UNIA*, 109–10; Harold, *Rise and Fall*, 2–3; Rolinson, *Grassroots*, 15.

13. Frederick Cooper, *Colonialism in Question: Theory, Knowledge, History* (Berkeley: University of California Press, 2005), 3.

14. George Shepperson, "The African Abroad, or the African Diaspora," in *Emerging Themes of African History: Proceedings of the International Congress of African Historians*, ed. T. O. Ranger (Nairobi: East Africa Publishing House, 1968), 153, 170; Brent Hayes Edwards, "The Uses of Diaspora," *Social Text* 66 (Spring 2001): 52.

15. Kim D. Butler, "Defining Diaspora, Refining a Discourse," *Diaspora* 10, no. 2 (2001): 193; James Clifford, "Diasporas," *Cultural Anthropology* 9, no. 3 (1994): 306, 315; J. Lorand Matory, *Black Atlantic Religion: Tradition, Transnationalism, and Matriarchy in the Afro-Brazilian Candomblé* (Princeton, NJ: Princeton University Press, 2005), 273.

16. Clifford, "Diasporas," 306; Frank Guridy, *Forging Diaspora: Afro-Cubans and African Americans in a World of Empire and Jim Crow* (Chapel Hill: University of North Carolina Press, 2010), 7.

17. Earl Lewis, "To Turn as on a Pivot: Writing African Americans into a History of Overlapping Diasporas," *American Historical Review* 100, no. 3 (1995): 765–87.

18. Matory, *Black Atlantic*, 290; Edwards, "Uses," 64; Jacqueline Nassy Brown, *Dropping Anchor, Setting Sail: Geographies of Race in Black Liverpool* (Princeton, NJ: Princeton University Press, 2005), 6. For a theoretical discussion of the implication of "roots" and "routes," see Paul Gilroy, *The Black Atlantic: Modernity and Double-Consciousness* (Cambridge, MA: Harvard University Press, 1993).

19. I follow George Shepperson in drawing a distinction between "Pan-Africanism"—the discrete political movement associated with the Pan-African congresses of W.E.B. Du Bois (1919, 1921, 1923, 1927, 1945) and later embraced by George Padmore and Kwame Nkrumah—and "pan-Africanism," which Shepperson views as a more defuse and undefined "cultural" tradition. It was out of the pan-African tradition, I argue, that Garveyism emerged. It was pan-Africanism—during the interwar period—that Garveyism came to embody. And it was Garveyism's groundwork during this period that played a large and still largely unacknowledged role in generating a mass base of support for the Pan-Africanism that emerged as a viable political vehicle after the Second World War. See George Shepperson, "Pan-Africanism and 'Pan-Africanism': Some Historical Notes," *Phylon* 23, no. 4 (1962): 346–58.

20. The phrase "portable eschatology" is borrowed from Clifford, "Diasporas," 321.

21. Guridy, *Forging Diaspora*, 64; Michelle Ann Stephens, *Black Empire: The Masculine Global Imaginary of Caribbean Intellectuals in the United States, 1919–1962* (Durham, NC: Duke University Press, 2005), 79–81.

22. Speech by Garvey, 16 November 1924, MGP, 6:42–46.

CHAPTER ONE

THE EDUCATION OF MARCUS MOSIAH GARVEY

1. Gad Heuman, '*The Killing Time': The Morant Bay Rebellion in Jamaica* (London: Macmillan, 1994), 3–14; Edward Bean Underhill, *The Tragedy of Morant Bay: A Narrative of the Disturbances in the Island of Jamaica in 1865* (London: Alexander

and Shepheard, 1895), 58–59; Thomas C. Holt, *The Problem of Freedom: Race, Labor, and Politics in Jamaica and Britain, 1832–1938* (Baltimore: Johns Hopkins University Press, 1992), 263, 295–302.

2. Underhill, *Tragedy*, 59–65; Holt, *Problem of Freedom*, 302–3.

3. Frederick Cooper, Thomas C. Holt, and Rebecca J. Scott, *Beyond Slavery: Explorations of Race, Labor and Citizenship in Postemancipation Societies* (Chapel Hill: University of North Carolina Press, 2000), 22.

4. W.E.B. Du Bois, *The Souls of Black Folk* (Chicago, A.C. McClurg & Co., 1904), 4.

5. Ethiopianism was the nineteenth-century, religiously grounded project of black unity and African redemption, inspired by Psalm 68:31.

6. Eddie S. Glaude Jr., *Exodus! Religion, Race, and Nation in Early Nineteenth-Century Black America* (Chicago: University of Chicago Press, 2000), 20.

7. Michael O. West and William G. Martin, "Contours of the Black International: From Toussaint to Tupac," in *From Toussaint to Tupac: The Black International since the Age of Revolution*, eds. Michael O. West, William G. Martin, and Fanon Che Wilkins (Chapel Hill: University of North Carolina Press, 2009), 11.

8. Underhill, *Tragedy*, xiii–xviii; 12–29; Mimi Sheller, *Democracy After Slavery: Black Publics and Peasant Radicalism in Haiti and Jamaica* (Gainesville: University Press of Florida, 2000), 190–92; Holt, *Problem of Freedom*, 263–79; Heuman, *'Killing Time,'* 86–77.

9. Holt, *Problem of Freedom*, 180–261.

10. Ronald Rainger, "Race, Politics, and Science: The Anthropological Society of London in the 1860s," *Victorian Studies* 22, no. 1 (Autumn 1978): 51–70; James Hunt, "On the Negro's Place in Nature," in *Memoirs Read Before the Anthropological Society of London, 1863–1864*, vol. 1 (London: Trubner and Co., 1865), 51–60; [James Hunt], "On the Negro Revolt in Jamaica," *The Popular Magazine of Anthropology* 1, no. 1 (January 1866), 14–16; Editorial in *The Times* [London], Saturday, November 18, 1865, 8.

11. James Anthony Froude, *The English in the West Indies; or, The Bow of Ulysses* (1887; New York: Charles Scribner's Sons, 1900), 235, 261–87, 364.

12. Froude, *English*, 252–344.

13. Matthew J. Clavin, "American Toussaints: Symbol, Subversion, and the Black Atlantic Tradition in the American Civil War," *Slavery and Abolition* 28, no. 1 (2007): 87–113; Sara C. Fanning, "The Roots of Early Black Nationalism: Northern African Americans' Invocations of Haiti in the Early Nineteenth Century," *Slavery and Abolition* 28, no. 1 (2007), 61–85; T. Lothrop Stoddard, *The French Revolution in San Domingo* (Boston: Houghton Mifflin Company, 1914), vii; J. A. Hobson, *Imperialism: A Study* (London: James Nisbet & Co., 1902), 129.

14. Mahmood Mamdani, *Citizen and Subject: Contemporary Africa and the Legacy of Late Colonialism* (Princeton, NJ: Princeton University Press, 1996), 74–76; E. A. Ayandele, *Holy Johnson: Pioneer of African Nationalism*, 1836–1917 (New York: Humanities Press, 1970), 102–6, 161–88, 228.

15. Michael O. West and William G. Martin, "Haiti, I'm Sorry: The Haitian Revolution and the Forging of the Black International," in West, Martin, and Wilkins, *From Toussaint to Tupac*, 92–93; David Walker, *Walker's Appeal in Four Articles* (Boston, 1830), 34 (italics removed).

16. *Report from the Select Committee on Africa (Western Coast)* (London: House of Commons, 26 June 1865), iii.

17. James Africanus Horton, *West African Countries and Peoples* (1868; Edinburgh: Edinburgh University Press, 1969), v–vii, 65–68, 59, 246–49.

18. George Shepperson, "Introduction," in *West African Countries*, xiii.

19. Ayandele, *Holy Johnson*, 42–45, 65, 72, 105.

20. Edward Wilmot Blyden, *Christianity, Islam, and the Negro Race*, (London: W.B. Wittingham, 1887), 276–77, 65; Hollis R. Lynch, "Edward W. Blyden: Pioneer West African Nationalist," *Journal of African History* 6, no. 3 (1965): 377–80.

21. P. J. Cain and A. G. Hopkins, *British Imperialism 1688–2000*, 2nd ed. (Harlow, England: Longman, 2002); Ronald Ronaldson and John Gallagher with Alice Denny, *Africa and the Victorians: The Climax of Imperialism* (Garden City, NY: Anchor Books, 1968); Rudolf Hilferding, *Finance Capital: A Study of the Latest Phase of Capitalist Development*, trans. Morris Watnick and Sam Gordon (London: Routledge & Kegan Paul, 1981); Jane Brubank and Frederick Cooper, *Empires in World History: Power and the Politics of Difference* (Princeton, NJ: Princeton University Press, 2010), 312–15; C. A. Bayly, *The Birth of the Modern World, 1780–1914: Global Connections and Comparisons* (Malden, MA: Blackwell Publishing, 2004), 229–30; Hobson, *Imperialism*, 224–34.

22. Bayly, *Birth*, 230; John Morrow Jr., *The Great War: An Imperial History* (New York: Routledge, 2004), 7–8.

23. Charles Darwin, *The Descent of Man and Selection in Relation to Sex*, 2 vols. (New York: D. Appleton and Company, 1871), 1:154–70.

24. I. A. Newby, *Jim Crow's Defense: Anti-Negro Thought in America, 1900–1930* (Baton Rouge: Louisiana State University Press, 1965), 12–16.

25. Sir Harry Johnston, *A History of the Colonization of Africa by Alien Races* (1899; Cambridge: Cambridge University Press, 1905), 91, 101–2.

26. Frederick Cooper, "Conditions Analogous to Slavery: Imperialism and Free Labor Ideology in Africa," in *Beyond Slavery*, 113–16; Hobson, *Imperialism*, 242.

27. Ayandele, *Holy Johnson*, 175, 189.

28. Eric Foner, *Forever Free: The Story of Emancipation and Reconstruction* (New York: Vintage, 2005), 64–112; W.E.B. Du Bois, *Black Reconstruction in America, 1860–1880* (1935; New York: Atheneum, 1969), 55–83; Steven Hahn, *The Political Worlds of Slavery and Freedom* (Cambridge, MA: Harvard University Press, 2009), 55–101.

29. The best study of southern black politics in the nineteenth century remains Steven Hahn, *A Nation Under Our Feet: Black Political Struggles in the Rural South from Slavery to the Great Migration* (Cambridge, MA: Harvard University Press, 2003). See also Rayford W. Logan, *The Negro in American Life and Thought: The Nadir, 1877–1901* (New York: Dial Press, 1954).

30. Foner, *Forever Free*, 164–65; Steven Hahn, *The Roots of Southern Populism: Yeoman Farmers and the Transformation of the Georgia Upcountry, 1850–1890* (Oxford: Oxford University Press, 1983), 171–203; Frederick Douglass, "I Denounce the So-Called Emancipation as a Stupendous Fraud" (1888), in *Frederick Douglass: Selected Speeches and Writings*, ed. Philip S. Foner (Chicago: Lawrence Hill Books, 1999), 715–19.

31. Glenda Elizabeth Gilmore, *Gender and Jim Crow: Women and the Politics of White Supremacy in North Carolina, 1896–1920* (Chapel Hill: University of North

Carolina Press, 1996), 92–118; Edward Ayers, *The Promise of the New South: Life After Reconstruction* (Oxford: Oxford University Press), 289–309; Foner, *Forever Free*, 190–94.

32.   Foner, *Forever Free*, 194–210; Hahn, *Nation*, 427; Jacqueline Dowd Hall, "The Mind that Burns in Each Body: Women, Rape and Racial Violence," in *Powers of Desire: The Politics of Sexuality*, eds. Ann Snitow, Christine Stansell and Sharon Thompson (New York: Monthly Review Press, 1983), 330; Maurice Smethurst Evans, *Black and White in the Southern States: A Study of the Race Problem in the United States from a South African Point of View* (London: Longmans, 1915), 68–69.

33.   Ida B. Wells, *A Red Record* (Chicago, 1894); Hall, "Mind that Burns," 330; Leon Litwack, *Trouble in Mind: Black Southerners in the Age of Jim Crow* (New York: Vintage, 1998), 280–325.

34.   Hall, "Mind that Burns," 334–35; Wells, *Red Record*, 12; Vardaman, quoted in Thomas F. Gossett, *Race: The History of an Idea in America* (1963; Oxford: Oxford University Press, 1997), 271.

35.   Foner, *Forever Free*, 97.

36.   Lee D. Baker, *From Savage to Negro: Anthropology and the Construction of Race, 1896–1954* (Berkeley: University of California Press, 1998), 87.

37.   Gossett, *Race*, 310–69; Theodore Roosevelt, "Fourth Annual Message to Congress," in *A Compilation of the Messages and Papers of the Presidents*, vol. 16 (New York, 1897), 6922–23.

38.   Booker T. Washington, *Up from Slavery* (1901; New York: Signet Classic, 2000), 152–56.

39.   Washington, *Up from Slavery*, 18–29, 74.

40.   Andrew Zimmerman, *Alabama in Africa: Booker T. Washington, the German Empire, and the Globalization of the New South* (Princeton, NJ: Princeton University Press, 2010), 41–44; General Samuel C. Armstrong, "The Founding of the Hampton Institute" (1890), in *Old South Leaflets*, vol. 6, no. 149 (New York: Burt Franklin, 1966), 521–32.

41.   Washington, *Up from Slavery*, 177–78, 199, 218–20; Louis R. Harlan, "The Secret Life of Booker T. Washington," *Journal of Southern History* 37, no. 3 (1971): 394.

42.   Howell is quoted in *Up from Slavery*, 156.

43.   Zimmerman, *Alabama in Africa*, 42, 113–72; Frank André Guridy, *Forging Diaspora: Afro-Cubans and African Americans in a World of Empire and Jim Crow* (Chapel Hill: University of North Carolina Press, 2010), 33–34; Kenneth James King, *Pan-Africanism and Education: A Study of Race, Philanthropy and Education in the Southern States of America and East Africa* (Oxford: Clarendon Press, 1971), 47–53; Michael O. West, "The Tuskegee Model of Development in Africa: Another Dimension of the African/African-American Connection," *Diplomatic History* 16, no. 3 (1992): 382–86.

44.   Zimmerman, *Alabama in Africa*, 173–97; James Campbell, *Middle Passages: African American Journeys in Africa, 1787–2005* (New York: Penguin, 2006), 147

45.   Booker T. Washington, "Industrial Education in Africa," in *The Booker T. Washington Papers*, ed. Louis R. Harlan (Urbana: University of Illinois Press, 1972), 8:549–50; Harlan, "Secret Life," 393–416; Louis R. Harlan, "Booker T. Washington and the White Man's Burden," *The American Historical Review* 71, no. 2 (1966): 452.

46.   Guridy, *Forging Diaspora*, 44–45.

47. For the historical resonance of racial destiny routed through the Book of Exodus, see Glaude, *Exodus!* For the politics of respectability, see Evelyn Brooks Higginbotham, *Righteous Discontent: The Women's Movement in the Black Baptist Church, 1880–1920* (Cambridge, MA: Harvard University Press, 1993).

48. Guridy, *Forging Diaspora*, 35–36.

49. West, "The Tuskegee Model," 380–82; Thomas C. Howard, "West Africa and the American South: Notes on James E.K. Aggrey and the Idea of a University for West Africa," *Journal of African Studies* 2, no. 4 (1975/1976): 445–65; R. Hunt Davis Jr., "John L. Dube: A South African Exponent of Booker T. Washington," *Journal of African Studies* 2, no. 4 (1975/1976): 497–528.

50. Zimmerman, *Alabama in Africa*, 185–87; "The Negro Conference at Tuskegee Institute," *ATOR* 1, no. 1 (1912): 10–12; Guridy, *Forging Diaspora*, 22–23.

51. James T. Campbell, *Songs of Zion: The African Methodist Episcopal Church in the United States and South Africa* (Oxford: Oxford University Press, 1995), 101–37, 249–50.

52. Jacqueline Anne Rouse, "Out of the Shadow of Tuskegee: Margaret Murray Washington, Social Activism, and Race Vindication," *Journal of Negro History* 81, no.1/4 (1996): 40.

53. Marika Sherwood, *Origins of Pan-Africanism: Henry Sylvester Williams, Africa, and the African Diaspora* (New York: Routledge, 2011), 39–44; David Levering Lewis, *W.E.B. Du Bois: Biography of a Race, 1868–1919* (New York: Henry Holt, 1993), 162, 168–70.

54. Imanuel Geiss, *The Pan-African Movement: A History of Pan-Africanism in America, Europe and Africa*, trans. Ann Kemp (New York: Africana Publishing Co., 1974), 179–80; Sherwood, *Origins*, 50. Among the luminaries involved in the African Association and the conference were James F. Holly and Benito Sylvain of Haiti; Henry M. Turner and Alexander Walters, and Anna Julia Cooper of the United States; Mojola Agbebi, James Johnson, C. W. Farquhar, and Otonba Payne of West Africa; and John Tengu Jabavu of South Africa.

55. Geiss, *Pan-African Moment*, 187; Sherwood, *Origins*, 83; W.E.B. Du Bois, "To the Nations of the World," in *W.E.B. Du Bois: A Reader*, ed. David Levering Lewis (New York: Henry Holt, 1995), 639–40.

56. Rev. Mojola Agbebi, "Inaugural Sermon" (1902), in *Ideologies of Liberation in Black Africa, 1856–1970: Documents on Modern African Political Thought from Colonial Times to the Present*, ed. J. Ayo Langley (London: R. Collings, 1979), 76.

57. J. E. Casely Hayford, *Ethiopia Unbound: Studies in Race Emancipation* (1911; London: Frank Cass & Co., 1969), 168–70, 183–97; Hayford, "Gold Coast Land Tenure and Forest Bill," *ATOR* 1, no. 2 (1912), 57; Hayford, *The Truth about the West African Land Question* (1913; New York: Negro Universities Press, 1969), 3–13, 100–117.

58. "Report of the First Universal Races Congress," *ATOR* 1, no. 1 (1912): 27–28; W.E.B. Du Bois, "The First Universal Races Congress," in *Du Bois: A Reader*, 44–47; Dusé Mohamed Ali, "Forward," *ATOR* 1, no. 1 (1912), iii.

59. Hayford, *Ethiopia Unbound*, 207–8.

60. Ali, "A Word to Our Brothers," *ATOR* 1, no. 1 (July 1912): 2. For an example of the ATOR's expansive reach, see Ali's list of correspondents in "Forward," *ATOR* 1, no. 1 (NS) (March 24, 1914): 1.

61. Ali, "Yesterday, Today, and Tomorrow," *ATOR* 1, no. 5 (1912): iii; Ali, "A Merry Christmas to You All," *ATOR* 2, no. 17–18 (1913): 181–82; Ali, "Yesterday, Today, and Tomorrow," *ATOR* 1, no. 7 (NS) (May 5, 1914): 145–47.

62. Tony Martin, *Marcus Garvey, Hero: A First Biography* (Dover, MA: The Majority Press, 1983), 13; Sheller, *Democracy After Slavery*, 238; Marcus Garvey, "The British West Indies in the Mirror of Civilization" (1913), MGP, 1:30.

63. Colin Grant, *Negro with a Hat: The Rise and Fall of Marcus Garvey* (Oxford: Oxford University Press, 2008), 13–18; Amy Jacques Garvey, "The Early Years of Marcus Garvey," in *Marcus Garvey and the Vision of Africa*, ed. John Henrik Clarke (New York: Vintage, 1974): 32–33; Rupert Lewis, *Marcus Garvey: Anti-Colonial Champion* (Trenton, NJ: Africa World Press, Inc., 1988), 44–46.

64. Lewis, *Marcus Garvey*, 25–34; "UNIA Memorial Meeting for Dr. J. Robert Love," MGP, 1:97.

65. See Winston James, *Holding Aloft the Banner of Ethiopia: Caribbean Radicalism in Early Twentieth-Century America* (London: Verso, 1998), 14–30; Ronald N. Harpelle, *The West Indians of Costa Rica: Race, Class, and Integration of an Ethnic Minority* (Montreal & Kingston: McGill-Queen's University Press, 2001), 13–17; Laura Putnam, "Eventually Alien: The Multigenerational Saga of British West Indians in Central America, 1870–1940," in *Blacks & Blackness in Central America: Between Race and Place*, eds. Lowell Gudmundson and Justin Wolfe (Durham, NC: Duke University Press, 2010), 278–82.

66. Grant, *Negro with a Hat*, 44–49; Garvey, "The British West Indies in the Mirror of Civilization," MGP, 1:31.

67. Garvey, "The Negro's Greatest Enemy" (1923), MGP, 1:5.

68. Garvey, "A Talk with Afro-West Indians" (1914), MGP, 1:55–62.

69. MGP, 1:103–5, 113–17, 128, 132–36, 177–83.

CHAPTER TWO

THE CENTER CANNOT HOLD

1. George Smith to His Excellency, The High Commissioner of South Africa, 25 May 1915, PRO, CO 525/61/30044; Leroy Vail and Landeg White, "Tribalism in the Political History of Malawi," in *The Creation of Tribalism in Southern Africa*, ed. Leroy Vail (London: James Currey, 1989), 166; Robert I. Rotberg, *The Rise of Nationalism in Central Africa: The Making of Malawi and Zambia, 1873–1964* (Cambridge, MA: Harvard University Press, 1965), 15–43; Landeg White, "Tribes and the Aftermath of the Chilembwe Rising," *African Affairs* 83, no. 333 (1984): 516–17.

2. Rotberg, *Rise of Nationalism*, 6–7; George Shepperson and Thomas Price, *Independent African: John Chilembwe and the Nyasaland Rising of 1915* (1958; Blantyre, Malawi: Christian Literature Association, 2000), 39.

3. Testimony of Dr. A. Hetherwick, Church of Scotland Mission, Blantyre, 29 June 1915; Testimony of Rev. Harry Kambwiri, Church of Scotland Mission; Testimony of Joseph Bismarck, Blantyre, 14 July 1915; Written Statement by M. M. Chisuse, Native of Church of Scotland Mission, Blantyre. In PRO, CO 525/66/18136.

4. Testimony of Dr. A. Hetherwick, Church of Scotland Mission, 29 June 1915, PRO, CO 525/66/18136; "The Sabbath Evangelizing and Industrial Association, No. 2: Advantages of the Industrial Mission," NAM, 56/SDB; Joseph Booth, *Africa for the African* (1897; Blantyre, Malawi: Christian Literature Association in Malawi, 1996), 10, 13–14, 39–40, 90–93; Shepperson and Price, *Independent African*, 26.

5. Shepperson and Price, *Independent African*, 37, 48; Booth to Chilembwe, 10 December 1911, PRO, CO 525/61/30044.

6. Shepperson and Price, *Independent African*, 85–93, 112–17; John Chilembwe, "Prospectus for the American Development Society" (n.d.), NAM, 56/SDB.

7. Governor Smith to the High Commissioner of South Africa, 25 May 1915 (Attachment: Joseph Booth), PRO, CO/525/61/30044; Shepperson and Price, *Independent African*, 138–46, 174; Landeg White, *Magomero: Portrait of an African Village* (Cambridge: Cambridge University Press, 1987), 131.

8. Shepperson and Price, *Independent African*, 146–47, 166–67; White, *Magomero*, 123. The AIS was founded in 1909 as the Native Industrial Union, and became the AIS in 1911. See also Joey Power, *Political Culture and the Nationalism of Malawi: Building Kwacha* (Rochester, NY: University of Rochester Press, 2010), 17.

9. Shepperson and Price, *Independent African*, 189–96; White, *Magomero*, 111–20, 131.

10. According to testimony collected after Chilembwe's rising, Chilembwe continued to impart Booth's doctrine of Africa for the Africans at PIM. See Testimony of Rev. Harry Kambwiri, Church of Scotland Mission, PRO, CO 525/66/18136.

11. Melvin E. Page, *The Chiwaya War: Malawians and the First World War* (Boulder, CO: Westview Press, 2000), 12–13; John Chilembwe, "The Voice of African Natives in Present War," (1914, unpublished), NAM, S10/1/6.

12. Testimony of Mr. L.T. Moggridge, District Resident, Blantyre, 28 June 1915; Testimony of Bishop Anneau, 28 June 1915. In PRO, CO 525/66/18136.

13. White, "Tribes," 520.

14. Jane Linden and Ian Linden, "John Chilembwe and the New Jerusalem," *Journal of African History* 12, no. 4 (1971), 638–47; Page, *Chiwaya War*, 12, 17; Testimony of Dr. A Hetherwick, Church of Scotland Mission, Blantyre, 29 June 1915, PRO, CO 525/66/18136.

15. Robert I. Rotberg, *Strike a Blow and Die: A Narrative of Race Relations in Colonial Africa by George Simeon Mwase* (Cambridge, MA: Harvard University Press, 1970), 36.

16. V. I. Lenin, *Imperialism, the Highest Stage of Capitalism* (Peking: Foreign Language Press, 1970), 6.

17. Erez Manela, *The Wilsonian Moment: Self-Determination and the International Origins of Anticolonial Nationalism* (Oxford: Oxford University Press, 2007), 4.

18. Harris is quoted in Melvin E. Page, "Introduction: Black Men in a White Men's War," in *Africa and the First World War*, ed. Melvin E. Page (New York: St. Martin's Press, 1987), 19.

19. For Nyasaland recruits, see Page, *Chiwaya* War, 35, 52. For Indian, African, and Chinese figures, see Jane Burbank and Frederick Cooper, *Empires in World History: Power and the Politics of Difference* (Princeton, NJ: Princeton University Press, 2010), 375; and Manela, *The Wilsonian Moment*, 11. For French African and African American enlistment numbers, see Chad L. Williams, *Torchbearers of Democracy:*

African American Soldiers in the World War I Era (Chapel Hill: University of North Carolina Press, 2010), 6, 151. For the West Indies, see Winston James, *Holding Aloft the Banner of Ethiopia: Caribbean Radicalism in Early Twentieth-Century America* (London: Verso, 1998), 52.

20.   W.E.B. Du Bois, "The African Roots of the War" (1915), in *W.E.B. Du Bois: A Reader*, ed. David Levering Lewis (New York: Henry Holt, 1995), 650; Adriane Lentz-Smith, *Freedom Struggles: African Americans and World War I* (Cambridge, MA: Harvard University Press, 2009), 208.

21.   David Killingray, "The War in Africa," in *A Companion to World War I*, ed. John Horne (Malden, MA: Blackwell Publishing, 2010), 115; Gregory Mann, *Native Sons: West African Veterans and France in the Twentieth Century* (Durham, NC: Duke University Press, 2006), 16–17; James, *Holding Aloft*, 56; Albert Grundlingh, "The Impact of the First World War on South African Blacks," and Page, "Introduction," in *Africa and the First World War*, 55, 12–13.

22.   Joe Harris Lunn, "Kande Kamara Speaks: An Oral History of the West African Experience in France, 1914–1918," and Page, "Introduction," in *Africa and the First World War*, 30–33, 4.

23.   The four communes in Senegal—Saint-Louis, Dakar, Rufisque, and Gorée—were small colonies established by the French in the eighteenth century. Their inhabitants, the *originaires*, were endowed with the rights of citizens but governed civilly under Islamic law. See Burbank and Cooper, *Empires in World History*, 376–77.

24.   The *indigénat* was the governing colonial law code of French West Africa, conferring the legal status of subject—and the requisite taxation, labor, and legal requirements of subjecthood—rather than citizen.

25.   Alice L. Conklin, *A Mission to Civilize: The Republican Idea of Empire in France and West Africa, 1895–1930* (Stanford, CA: Stanford University Press, 1997), 155; Mann, *Native Sons*, 69–70; Myron Echenberg, *Colonial Conscripts: The Tirailleurs Sénégalais in French West Africa, 1857–1960* (Portsmouth, NH: Heinemann, 1991), 44–45. Diagne is quoted in Lunn, "Kande Kamara Speaks," 43.

26.   Dusé Mohamed Ali, "Our War Loan," *ATOR* 4, no. 4 (1917), 67–68; Ali, "Today," *ATOR* 4, no. 1 (1917), 1–2; Ali, "India and Africa," *ATOR* 4, no. 3 (1917): 45; Grundlingh, "Impact of the First World War," 64; Wilson J. Moses, *The Golden Age of Black Nationalism, 1850–1925* (Hamden, CT: Archon Books, 1978), 231–33; Burbank and Cooper, *Empires*, 375.

27.   Mark Ellis, *Race, War, and Surveillance: African Americans and the United States Government during World War I* (Bloomington: Indiana University Press, 1978), 4; Jeanette Keith, *Rich Man's War, Poor Man's Fight: Race, Class, and Power in the Rural South during the First World War* (Chapel Hill: University of North Carolina Press, 2004), 119.

28.   Robert R. Moton, Open Letter to President Wilson, in *Crisis* 14, no. 1 (1917): 37; "Negro Loyalty," *ATOR* 4, no. 6 (1917): 122; Bruce Grit [John E. Bruce], "The Attitude of the American Negro Towards the War," *ATOR* 5, no. 4 (1917): 85; "Resolutions of the Washington Conference," *Crisis* 14, no. 2 (1917): 59–60.

29.   "Resolutions of the Washington Conference," *Crisis* 14, no. 2 (1917): 60; Statement Issued by AME Preachers of Norfolk, VA, 2 October 1917, NA, RG 16, PI-191, Entry 17, Box 1; P. J. Bryant, et al., Atlanta, to Hon. Thomas W. Gregory, Attorney General, 5 March 1918, NA, RG 60, Central Files, Straight Numerical Files,

File 158260, Box 1276; "Letter by Prof. Kelly Miller," 65th Congress, 1st Session, *Congressional Record* 55 (September 12, 1917): 6991.

30. Manela, *Wilsonian Moment*, 21–52. Lansing is quoted in Robert A. Hill, "Racial and Radical: Cyril V. Briggs, *The Crusader* Magazine, and the African Blood Brotherhood, 1918–1922," introduction to *The Crusader*, ed. Cyril V. Briggs (New York: Garland, 1987), xv.

31. Morton Sosna, "The South in the Saddle: Racial Politics during the Wilson Years," *Wisconsin Magazine of History* 54 (Fall 1970): 30–49; Thomas J. Knock, *To End All Wars: Woodrow Wilson and the Quest for a New World Order* (Princeton, NJ: Princeton University Press, 1992), 25–84.

32. Laurent Dubois, *Avengers of the New World: The Story of the Haitian Revolution* (Cambridge, MA: Harvard University Press, 2004), 3–7; Steven Hahn, *The Political Worlds of Slavery and Freedom* (Cambridge, MA: Harvard University Press, 2009), 55–101.

33. "Europe's Obligation to Africa," reprinted in *ATOR* 5, no. 7 (1918): 136–37; Dusé Mohamed Ali, "To-day," *ATOR* 5, no. 7 (1918): 129–30; W.E.B. Du Bois, "Flaming Arrows," *Crisis* 17, no. 1 (1918): 7.

34. See, for example, Lajpat Rai, *Young India: An Interpretation and a History of the Nationalist Movement from Within* (New York: B.W. Huebsch, 1917), 63–64, 222–23; Benjamin Brawley, *Africa and the War* (New York: Duffield & Company, 1918), 30–45.

35. W.E.B. Du Bois, "The Black Soldier," *Crisis* 16, no. 2 (1918): 60; Du Bois, "World War and the Color Line," *Crisis* 9, no. 1 (1914): 29–30.

36. W.E.B. Du Bois, "Our Special Grievances," *Crisis* 16, no. 5 (1918): 216–17.

37. Ellis, *Race*, xvi–xvii, 101–5, 131–34; Keith, *Rich Man's War*, 135. Johnson is quoted in William Jordan, "'The Damnable Dilemma': African-American Accommodation and Protest during World War I," *Journal of American History* 81, no. 4 (March, 1995): 1575.

38. W.E.B. Du Bois, "The Perpetual Dilemma," *Crisis* 13, no. 6 (1917): 271.

39. Hubert H. Harrison, "The Liberty League of Negro-Americans: How It Came to Be," and "Resolutions Passed at First Liberty League Meeting," in *A Hubert Harrison Reader*, ed. Jeffrey B. Perry (Middletown, CT: Wesleyan University Press, 2001), 86–89.

40. Williams, *Torchbearers*, 31–32; Keith, *Rich Man's War*, 58–74, 48; Remarks by Sen. Caraway, "Intellectual and Spiritual Preparedness," 64th Congress, 1st Session, *Congressional Record* 53 (August 15, 1916): 12688–89; Sen. James K. Vardaman, "Recent Disturbances in East St. Louis, Ill.," S. Res. 10, 65th Congress, 1st Session, *Congressional Record* 55 pt. 6 (August 16, 1917), 6063.

41. Williams, *Torchbearers*, 64–65; Bulletin No. 35, 92nd Division, Camp Funston, Kansas, 28 March 1918, NA, RG 65, File 10218;–G. B. Perkins, Chief, Military Morale Section, to Emmett J. Scott, 27 September 1918, NA, RG 65, File 10218–209.

42. Williams, *Torchbearers*, 108–21.

43. Letter from Colored Soldier, Camp Sherman, OH, to Emmett J. Scott, 12 Sept 1918, NA, RG 165, File 10218–226; RG 165, Letter sent by sister in Chicago, 4 Dec. 1918, File 10218–270; "The War," *The Crisis*, 16, no. 1 (May, 1918): 22; Letter from Soldier at Camp Lee, VA, to Emmett J. Scott, 17 Sept 1918, NA, RG 165, File 10218–234; "Negro Soldiers of the 19th Regiment, Camp Jackson, to I.F. Simmons, Hampton, VA, 5 Nov 1918, RG 165, File 10218–201.

44.   James, *Holding Aloft*, 53, 56; W. F. Elkins, "A Source of Black Nationalism in the Caribbean: The Revolt of the British West Indies Regiment at Taranto, Italy," *Science and Society* 34, no. 1 (Spring 1970): 99–100; Eyre Hutson to Viscount Milner, 31 July 1919, PRO, CO 123/295/48750; Report of the Riot Commission, Appendix O, CO 123/296/65699.

45.   Page, *Chiwaya War*, 37–52, 96–110, 132–36; David Killingray and James Matthews, "Beasts of Burden: British West African Carriers in the First World War," *Canadian Journal of African Studies* 13, no.1/2 (1979): 17; Page, "Introduction," 12–14.

46.   For the numerous complaints made by black soldiers and compiled by the MIB, see NA, RG 165, File 10218. In particular, see Report on Camp Conditions (Camp Sevier) by Major W. H. Loving, 19 Nov 1918, RG 165, File 10218–271.

47.   Investigation of Military Camps by Major Loving, 24 Nov 1918, NA, RG 165, File 10218–279; Anonymous Letter from Camp Devens, MA, to Emmett Scott, 28 Sept 1918, RG 165, File 10218–239; Negro Soldiers of the 19th Regiment, Camp Jackson, to I. F. Simmons, Hampton Institute, 5 Nov 1918, RG 165, File 10218–201; Report on Camp Conditions by Major Loving, RG 165, File 10218–271.

48.   Ellis, *Race*, 86–87; "Lynching Record for the Year 1918," *Crisis* 17, no. 4 (1919): 180–81.

49.   Walter F. White, "The Work of a Mob," *Crisis* 16, no. 5 (1918): 221–23.

50.   Ellis, *Race*, 31–32; Martha Gruening and W.E.B. Du Bois, "The Massacre of East St. Louis," *Crisis* 14, no. 6 (1917): 219–38; Herbert W. Horwill, "A Negro Exodus," *Contemporary Review* 114 (July/Dec. 1918): 303; "The Riot in East St. Louis," *Crisis* 14, no.4 (1917): 175–78.

51.   Williams, *Torchbearers*, 27–28.

52.   "The Riot in East St. Louis," and "Roosevelt," *Crisis* 14, no. 4 (1917): 177–78, 164; "Recent Disturbances in East St. Louis, Ill.," 65th Congress, 1st Session, *Congressional Record* 55 (July 16, 1917): 5151–5152; James K. Vardaman, "Recent Disturbances in East St. Louis, Ill.," S. Res. 10, 65th Congress, 1st Session, *Congressional Record* 55, pt. 6 (August 16, 1917): 6061.

53.   For numerous examples of these types of reports see the Military Intelligence Division's enormous "Negro Subversion File," NA, RG 165, 10218.

54.   Lt. Col. Van Deman to Major Loving, 20 Oct 1917, NA, RG 165, File 10218–37; G. B. Perkins to A. H. Fleming, 27 August 1918, RG 165, File 10218–200; "Possible Pro-German Feeling Among Negroes," Lexington, KY, 4 Dec 1917, RG 165, File 10218–61; Bolton Smith, "Notes on the Negro Problem," June 1918, RG 165, File 10218–178.

55.   Echenberg, *Colonial Conscripts*, 43–44; "The Black Peril—Appalling Idea of a Vaster World War Outlined by General Smuts," *ATOR* 4, no. 6 (1917), 119; Captain J.E. Phillips, "Africa for Africans and Pan-Islam," 1917, PRO, WO/106/259.

56.   Conklin, *Mission to Civilize*, 147–49; Mann, *Native Sons*, 68; Page, "Introduction," 7; James K. Matthews, "Reluctant Allies: Nigerian Responses to Military Recruitment, 1914–1918," in *Africa and the First World War*, 100–102; Mahir Şaul and Patrick Royer, *West African Challenge to Empire: Culture and History in the Volta-Bani Anticolonial War* (Athens: Ohio University Press, 2001), 1–3.

57.   Elkins, "Source of Black Nationalism," 99–102; James, *Holding Aloft*, 57–63.

58.   For example, between 1914 and 1918, the price of both flour and rice in Panama rose from 5 cents a pound to 12.5 cents. J. R. Murray, British Consulate,

Colón, to Sir Claude C. Mallet, 3 February 1919, PRO, CO 318/350/19715. See also J. R. Chancellor, Governor of Trinidad and Tobago, to Secretary of State for the Colonies, 7 December 1919, PRO, CO 295/523/69892; CO/318/352/72908: Labour Unrest and Wages Question, 1919; "Report of the Riot Commission," Belize, British Honduras, 21 October 1919, CO, 123/296/65699.

59.   O. Nigel Bolland, *The Politics of Labour in the British Caribbean: The Social Origins of Authoritarianism and Democracy in the Labor Movement* (Kingston, Jamaica: Ian Randle Publishers, 2001), 192–95; Glen Richards, "Leeward Islands" in MGP, Volume 11:ccxxix–ccxxxvi; J. A. Nathan to Walter Long, 19 April 1918, PRO, CO 152/359/29043; Circular Letter from Dillon C. Govin, Secretary, Association of Loyal Negroes, Montreal, 22 July 1918, in MGP, 11:102–103.

60.   Jeffrey B. Perry, "Introduction," in *Harrison Reader*, 2; Patricia Sullivan, *Lift Every Voice: The NAACP and the Making of the Civil Rights Movement* (New York: The New Press, 2009), 41–100; Oswald Garrison Villard, et al., "A Call to Action" (1909), in *From Bondage to Liberation: Writings by and about Afro-Americans from 1700–1918*, ed. Faith Berry (New York: Continuum, 2001), 455–57; "NAACP, Sixth Annual Report, 1915," *Crisis* 11, no. 5 (1916), 255; "New Branches and More Members," *Crisis* 17, no. 3 (1919), 122; "NAACP: Results of the Drive," *Crisis* 16, no. 4 (1918), 173–74; "The Crisis," *Crisis* 18, no. 5 (1919): 235.

61.   "NAACP: The Tenth Anniversary," *Crisis* 18, no. 4 (1919): 190.

62.   Steven Tuck, *We Ain't What We Ought to Be: The Black Freedom Struggle from Emancipation to Obama* (Cambridge, MA: Harvard University Press, 2010), 145; Ellis, *Race*, 23; W.E.B. Du Bois, "The Migration of Negroes," *Crisis* 14 no. 2 (1917): 63–66.

63.   Irma Watkins-Owens, *Blood Relations: Caribbean Immigrants and the Harlem Community, 1900–1930* (Bloomington: Indiana University Press, 1996), 13–18; James, *Holding Aloft*, 7; Laura Putnam, "Eventually Alien: The Multigenerational Saga of British West Indians in Central America, 1870–1940," *Blacks & Blackness in Central America: Between Race and Place*, eds. Lowell Gudmundson and Justin Wolfe (Durham, NC: Duke University Press, 2010), 281–85; Frank André Guridy, *Forging Diaspora: Afro-Cubans and African Americans in a World of Empire and Jim Crow* (Chapel Hill: University of North Carolina Press, 2010), 7.

64.   Jeffrey B. Perry, *Hubert Harrison: The Voice of Harlem Radicalism, 1883–1918* (New York: Columbia University Press, 2009), 5–8, 272–78; Hubert Harrison, "Two Negro Radicalisms," in *Harrison Reader*, 103.

65.   Lentz-Smith, *Freedom Struggles*, 82; Williams, *Torchbearers*, 7. See also Michele Mitchell, *Righteous Propagation: African Americans and the Politics of Racial Destiny after Reconstruction* (Chapel Hill: University of North Carolina Press, 2004).

66.   Hubert Harrison, "The White War and the Colored Races," in *Harrison Reader*, 206–7.

67.   Harrison, "The New Policies for the New Negro," "Our Professional Friends," and "Declaration of Principles, Liberty League," in *Harrison Reader*, 139–40, 144–47, 90–92.

68.   "Resolution Adopted by Negro Improvement Association . . ." *Gleaner*, 17 September 1914; "UNIA Farewell to the Jamaica War Contingent," *Jamaica Times*, 13 Nov 1915, in MGP, 1:70–71, 163; "Article in the *Gleaner*," Jamaica, 25 October 1915, in MGP, 11:79. For Garvey's difficulties in Jamaica, see Colin Grant, *Negro with*

a Hat: The Rise and Fall of Marcus Garvey (Oxford: Oxford University Press, 2008), 54–71.

69. Marcus Garvey, "The Negro's Greatest Enemy" (1923); "Article by Marcus Garvey in *Champion Magazine*," January 1917, in MGP, 1:7, 198; Grant, *Negro with a Hat*, 83.

70. Perry, *Hubert Harrison*, 294; Printed Address by Marcus Garvey on East St. Louis, 8 July 1917, in MGP, 1:212–18.

71. Hubert H. Harrison, "The East St. Louis Horror" and Diary, May 24, 1920, in *Harrison Reader*, 94–95, 190. Jeffrey Perry catalogues the numerous points of overlap between Garvey and Harrison in his introduction to the *Harrison Reader*, 19.

72. Resolutions by the UNIA and African Communities League, 10 Nov 1918, in MGP, 11:117–18.

73. "Nyasaland and the War" (unpublished), NAM, S1/946/19; George Smith, Governor, to Secretary of State for the Colonies, 3 February 1915, PRO, CO 525/61/12753; Power, *Political Culture*, 19.

74. Shepperson and Price, *Independent African*, 239; Robert I. Rotberg, "Psychological Stress and the Question of Identity: Chilembwe's Revolt Reconsidered," in *Rebellion in Black Africa*, ed. Robert I. Rotberg (London: Oxford University Press, 1971), 142; Linden and Linden, "John Chilembwe," 632.

75. *Report of the Commission Appointed by His Excellency the Governor to Inquire into . . . the Native Rising within the Nyasaland Protectorate* (Zomba: Government Printer, 1916), in NAM, S1/1494/19; Shepperson and Price, *Independent African*, 221; Statements by Mrs. Alyce Roach and Mrs. Livingstone, 30 January 1915, NAM, S10/1/2.

76. Governor George Smith, Zomba, to Secretary of State for the Colonies, 3 February 1915, PRO, CO 525/61/12753; *Report of the Commission*, NAM, S1/1494/19.

77. Booth to Chilembwe, 10 December 1911, and George Smith to High Commissioner of South Africa, 25 May 1915, PRO, CO 525/61/30044; "African Repatriation Society," *Sabbath Recorder*, 20 January 1903, in NAM, 56/SDB.

78. Shepperson and Price, *Independent African*, 150–55.

79. Peter Nyambo, Harry Kanduna, et al., "The Rhodesia-Nyasaland Appeal of May 1914," in NAM, S2/68/19; Joseph Booth, "The British African Congress, Preamble," Basutoland, 4 July 1915, in PRO, CO 525/68/48172.

80. Misc. Document on J. Chilembwe, n.d., NAM, 56/SDB; Booth to John Chilembwe, 1 October 1911, Booth to Chilembwe, 10 December 1911, and Booth to Chilembwe, 29 July 1914, in PRO, CO 525/61/30044; Shepperson and Price, *Independent African*, 28, 356–58.

CHAPTER THREE
AFRICA FOR THE AFRICANS!

1. Joyce Cary, *The Case for African Freedom* (London: Secker & Warburg, 1941), 16–17.

2. Barbara Foley, *Spectres of 1919: Class and Nation in the Making of the New Negro* (Urbana: University of Illinois Press, 2003), 66.

3. Robert A. Hill, "Introduction," in MGP, 11:lxii. See also Hill, "Boundaries of Belonging: Essay on Comparative Caribbean Garveyism," *Caribbean Studies* 31.1 (2003): 10–33; Lara Putnam, "Nothing Matters but Color: Transnational Circuits, the Interwar Caribbean and the Black International," in *From Toussaint to Tupac: The Black International since the Age of Revolution*, eds. Michael O. West, et al. (Chapel Hill: University of North Carolina Press, 2009), 110.

4. Cyril Briggs, "Our Far-Flung Challenge," *Crusader* 2, no. 1 (1919): 8.

5. "Strike Influenza," *The Messenger*, November, 1920, 5; Clements Kadalie, *My Life and the ICU: The Autobiography of a Black Trade Unionist in South Africa* (New York: The Humanities Press, 1970), 41–45; Alice L. Conklin, *A Mission to Civilize: The Republican Idea of Empire in France and West Africa, 1895–1930* (Stanford, CA: Stanford University Press, 1997), 159; Ibrahim Abdullah, "Rethinking the Freetown Crowd: The Moral Economy of the 1919 Strikes and Riot in Sierra Leone," *Canadian Journal of African Studies* 28, no. 2 (1994): 197–218.

6. W. A. Domingo, "A New Negro and a New Day," *Messenger* 2, no. 10 (1920): 144.

7. Erez Manela, *The Wilsonian Moment: Self-Determination and the International Origins of Anticolonial Nationalism* (Oxford: Oxford University Press, 2007), 4–13; Jane Burbank and Frederick Cooper, *Empires in World History: Power and the Politics of Difference* (Princeton, NJ: Princeton University Press, 2010), 380–90.

8. Lothrop Stoddard, *The Rising Tide of Color against White World Supremacy* (1920; New York: Charles Scribner's Sons, 1922), 173–76, 219–20; Hubert Harrison to Lothrop Stoddard, 24 June 1921, Hubert H. Harrison Papers, Columbia University, Rare Book and Manuscript Library, Series 1, Box 2.

9. Foley, *Spectres*, 8–9; Chad L. Williams, *Torchbearers of Democracy: African American Soldiers in the World War I Era* (Chapel Hill: University of North Carolina Press, 2010), 223–34; "The Real Causes of Two Race Riots," *Crisis* 19, no. 2 (1919), 56–58; Nan Elizabeth Woodruff, "African-American Struggles for Citizenship in the Arkansas and Mississippi Deltas in the Age of Jim Crow," *Radical History Review* 55 (Winter 1993): 41–42; Paul Ortiz, *Emancipation Betrayed: The Hidden History of Black Organizing and White Violence in Florida from Reconstruction to the Bloody Election of 1920* (Berkeley: University of California Press, 2005), 172–222.

10. W. E. Hawkins, "When Negroes Shot a Lynching Bee into Perdition," and "Chicago Rebellion . . . State Street Hindenburg Line," *Messenger* (September 1919): 29, 32; James Weldon Johnson, "The Riots: An NAACP Investigation," *Crisis* 18, no. 5 (1919): 242–43.

11. A. Philip Randolph, "A New Crowd—A New Negro," *Messenger* (May–June, 1919): 26–27.

12. *The World Forum*, Organ of the ILDP, 1, no. 1 (1919), DNA, RG 165, File 10218–296; "Synopsis of UNIA Meeting," 29 March 1919, MGP, 1:393.

13. BOI Report, 10 July 1919, MGP, 1:454–55; Report by Agent Davis, 20 August 1919, DNA, RG 165, File 10218–261; "Negro Mass Movement," *Messenger* (May–June, 1919): 8–9; Hubert H. Harrison, "Two Negro Radicalisms," in *A Hubert Harrison Reader*, ed. Jeffrey B. Perry (Middletown, CT: Wesleyan University Press, 2001), 104.

14. Editorial by Garvey, 30 November 1918, and BOI Report, November 12, 1918, in MGP, 1:302–3, 288; Eliezer Cadet to Marcel Herard, 2 December 1918, DNA, RG 165, File 10218–261.

15. Petition by Garvey, 21 February 1919; Speech by Garvey, 11 July 1920; Speech by Garvey, 21 October 1919; "Race First," 26 July 1919; Editorial by Garvey, 31 January 1919. In MGP, 1:367–68, 351–52, 468–69, 2:414–16, 2:92–93.

16. Bruce to Loving, 13 January 1919; Newspaper Report, 27 April 1919; Editorial by Garvey, 27 April 1920. In MGP, 1:349, 411, 11:631.

17. Speech by Garvey, 5 April 1919, MGP, 1:397.

18. Editorial by Garvey, 22 June 1920, and Editorial by Garvey, 7 September 1920, in MGP, 2:391, 3:8–10; Tony Martin, *Race First: The Ideological and Organizational Struggles of Marcus Garvey and the Universal Negro Improvement Association* (Westport, CT: Greenwood Press, 1976), 43.

19. Sunday Night Meeting, 8 August 1920, and Report of Meeting, 25 April 1920, in MGP, 2:559, 294.

20. Report of Meeting, 29 April 1920, MGP, 2:301–2.

21. Report of Meeting, 25 October 1919; Speech by Eason, 30 September 1919; "Editorial by Garvey," 22 October 1919. In MGP, 2:117, 38, 99.

22. Address by Garvey in Brooklyn, 28 February 1919; Speech by Garvey in the *Afro-American*, 28 February 1919; Speech by Garvey, 21 October 1919. In MGP, 1:375–76, 2:91

23. Address by Garvey in Brooklyn, 28 February 1919, and Report by Special Agent P-138, 6 November 1920, in MGP, 1:377, 3:71.

24. W. F. Elkins, "Marcus Garvey, the *Negro World*, and the British West Indies: 1919–1920," in *Garvey: Africa, Europe, and the Americas*, eds. Rupert Lewis and Maureen Warner-Lewis (Kingston, Jamaica: Institute of Social and Economic Research, 1986), 48–49.

25. Putnam, "Nothing Matters but Color," 107–24; Frank André Guridy, *Forging Diaspora: Afro-Cubans and African Americans in a World of Empire and Jim Crow* (Chapel Hill: University of North Carolina Press, 2010), 7–9; Hill, "Introduction," in MGP, 11:lxvi–ii; Ronald Harpelle, "Cross Currents in the Western Caribbean: Marcus Garvey and the UNIA in Central America," *Caribbean* Studies 31, no. 1 (2003): 38; Winston James, *Holding Aloft the Banner of Ethiopia: Caribbean Radicalism in Early Twentieth-Century America* (London: Verso, 1994), 88, 134.

26. A division of the UNIA had been established in Panama, by December 1918, and in Belize, British Honduras, and Kingston, Jamaica by April 1919. See Censored letter from Edgar McCarthy, Secretary, Colón Branch, UNIA, to Cecil Hope, Secretary General, UNIA, New York, 8 March 1919, DNA, RG 165, File 10218–261; UNIA; "Military Intelligence Report," 5 April 1919, MGP, 1:402; Carla Burnett, "'Are We Slaves or Free Men?': Labor, Race, Garveyism and the 1920 Panama Canal Strike" (PhD diss., University of Illinois at Chicago, 2004), 67. See also Memo from War Office, Whitehall, 5 November 1918, DNA, RG 165, File 10218–261.

27. Charles O'Brien, Governor, Barbados, to Viscount Milner, 14 July 1919, MGP, 11:231; Henry A. Baker to Secretary of State, 9 December 1919, and Baker to Secretary of State, 6 December 1919, DNA, RG 59, File 844G.

28. The *Negro World* was prohibited from entering British Honduras, Trinidad, British Guiana (Guyana), St. Vincent, Grenada, Jamaica, the Bahamas, and Costa Rica, under a wave of seditious publications ordinances. In Barbados, prohibition was considered, but ultimately rejected.

29.   Marcus Garvey to D. B. Lewis, 1 November 1918, DNA, RG 165, File 10218–261; Testimony of Captain William Caile Price, interviews conducted by the Riot Commission, Belize, PRO, CO 123/296/65699; Eyre Hutson, Governor, British Honduras, to Secretary of State for the Colonies, PRO, FO 371/4467/A5761.

30.   Stewart E. McMillin to Robert Lansing, 21 Dec 1919, MGP, 11:471.

31.   Eyre Hutson to Secretary of State for the Colonies, 10 May 1920, PRO, FO 371/4467/A5761.

32.   Article in the *West Indian*, 23 March 1919, MGP, 11:188–89; J. R. Ralph Casimir in the *Negro World*, Roseau, Dominica, 26 April 1920, MGP, 11:621–22; Report of Speech by Garvey at Liberty Hall, 7 January 1920, and transcription of remarks by George Tobias, in "Negro Agitation," M.I.1.C, New York, Report No. 232 (3), PRO, FO 371/4467/A443.

33.   W.M. Gordon to Viscount Milner, 29 July 1919, and Report by May, Inspector General, 29 July 1919, PRO, CO 295/521/50043; Testimony of Captain William C. Price and Lieutenant-Colonel James Cran, Riot Commission Interviews, PRO, CO 123/296/65699.

34.   "Race Riots in the United Kingdom," *Belize Independent*, 16 July 1919, 11; Report by Hugh Burgess, Inspector, CID, c. November 1919, PRO, CO 318/352/66887; Eyre Hutson to Viscount Milner, 31 July 1919, PRO, CO 123/295/48750; Report by Hugh Burgess, Inspector, CID, c. November 1919," PRO, CO 318/352/66887.

35.   "The Riots Once More," *NW*, 11 October 1919, in PRO, CO 23/285.

36.   Ramla M. Bandale, *Black Star: African American Activism in the International Political Economy* (Urbana: University of Illinois Press, 2008), 111.

37.   Article in the *Dispatch*, Panama, c. 11 October 1919, and Article in the *Workman*, Panama City, 20 December 1919, in MGP, 11:368–69, 460–61.

38.   R.E.M. Jack to the Barbados *Weekly Illustrated Paper*, 12 October 1919, MGP, 11:374–75; "Monster Mass Meeting," *West Indian*, 5 May 1920 ; Eyre Hutson, Governor, British Honduras, to Viscount Milner, 31 July 1919, CO 123/295/48750; Casimir in the *Negro World*, 26 April 1920, MGP, 11:626–27.

39.   Testimony of Tubal Uriah Butler, *Rex v. Butler*, PRO, CO 295/608/5.

40.   Lieutenant-Colonel Robert Deane to Wilfred Bennett Davidson-Houston, 21 February 1920, MGP, 11:562.

41.   Burnett, "Are We Slaves," 120–23, 148–51; "Marshall" to James Wilson, 1 March 1920, MGP, 11:572.

42.   Report of the Riot Commission, 21 October 1919, and testimony of Captain Henry Melhado, Joseph Lewis, Captain Matthews, and Samuel G. Humphrey, PRO, CO 123/296/65699.

43.   W. F. Elkins, "Black Power in the British West Indies: The Trinidad Longshoremen's Strike in 1919," *Science and Society* 31, no. 1 (Winter 1969): 71–75.

44.   G. H. May to Colonial Secretary, 5 August 1919, CO 295/522/50042; Report by Major H. de Pass, 12 March 1920, and Report by L. H. Elphinatono, 12 March 1920, PRO, CO 295/527/17716.

45.   Elkins, "Black Power," 71; Martin, "Marcus Garvey and Trinidad, 1912–1947," in *Garvey: Africa, Europe and the Americas*, 54–69; Bridget Brereton and Melisse Thomas-Bailey, "Trinidad and Tobago," in MGP, 11:cclxv.

46.   Robert A. Hill and Gregory Pirio, "'Africa for the Africans': the Garvey Movement in South Africa, 1920–1940," in *The Politics of Race, Class and Nationalism in*

Twentieth-Century South Africa, eds. Shula Marks and Stanley Trapido (London: Longman, 1987), 243.

47. Alan Gregor Cobley, "'Far from Home': The Origins and Significance of the Afro-Caribbean Community in South Africa to 1930," *Journal of Southern African Studies* 18, no. 2 (June 1992), 365; Robert Trent Vinson, *The Americans are Coming!: Dreams of African-American Liberation in Segregationist South Africa* (Athens: Ohio University Press, 2011), 73.

48. Henry J. Lenton to Secretary of the Interior, 12 June, MGP, 10:184.

49. Fitz H. Headly, "Conditions of Life Among Our Race in the Protectorate," *NW*, February 25, 1922, 11; Moulin to Henri Jaspar, 16 March 1923, MGP, 10:30; Z. M. to the *Negro World*, 4 August 1924, MGP, 10:224–25; Letter from Joseph Masagha, *NW*, September 27, 1924, 12; "Letter from J. Barnard Belman," *NW*, October 24, 1925, 10; Report of Speech by Ernest Wallace in the *Matatiele Mail*, Basutoland, in MGP, 10:351; Report from South West Africa, 15 February 1929, MGP, 10:501.

50. Record of Lawrence Trial, 22 Sept 1926, NAM, S2/50/23; First Monthly Report on Watch Tower Activities, 12 October 1923, NAM S2/98/23; Helen Bradford, *A Taste of Freedom: The ICU in Rural South Africa, 1924–1930* (New Haven, CT: Yale University Press, 1987), 5; Garvey at Liberty Hall, 8 April 1923, *NW*, April 14, 1923, 2.

51. H .F. Worley and C. G. Contee, "The Worley Report on the Pan-African Congress of 1919," *The Journal of Negro History* 55, no. 2 (April 1970): 141; "Letter from 'Dorn,'" *NW*, March 26, 1921, 4; A. H. Venn, "An African Letter," *NW*, February 21, 1931, 4; R. L. Okonkwo, "The Garvey Movement in British West Africa," *Journal of African History* 21, no. 1 (1980), 107–10; A. Agbebi to John E. Bruce, Lagos, 15 May 1920, SC-NYPL, John Edward Bruce Papers, Group B, Box 2, Item 258.

52. A. W. Wilkie to J. H. Oldham, 8 December 1920, quoted in Arnold Hughes, "Africa and the Garvey Movement in the Interwar Years," in *Garvey: Africa, Europe and the Americas*, 2.

53. Evidence of Garveyist organizing has been found in Senegal, Gambia, Sierra Leone, Côte d'Ivoire, Liberia, the Gold Coast, Togo, Dahomey (Benin), Nigeria, and Cameroon. See Fred W. Toote, Freetown, Sierra Leone, to John E. Bruce, 12 January 1922, John Edward Bruce Papers, Reel 1, Group A, Folder 7, H, 1–15, SC-NYPL; "Speech by John Farmer and Toasts at Farewell Banquet for John Kamara," MGP, 9:467–68; R.C.F. Maugham, Consul-General, Dakar, to Secretary of State for Foreign Affairs, 17 August 1922, PRO, FO 115/2766: Embassy and Consulary, United States: Negroes; "Report on John Smith, from Office of the Governor-General of French West Africa," Dakar, 25 June 1924, MGP, 10: 199.

54. Rev. J. K. Macgregor to J. H. Oldham, 10 February 1923, SOAS-IMC, Calabar Missionary Correspondence, 1911–1923; *NW*, April 9, 1923, 2; *NW*, February 4, 1922, 3; W. F. Gowers to Hon. Secretary to the Government, Lagos, 28 March 1922, PRO, CO 583/109; Hughes, "Africa and the Garvey Movement," 117.

55. Nnamdi Azikiwe, *My Odyssey: An Autobiography* (London: C. Hurst & Co., 1970), 31–35; Lieutenant Governor of Côte d'Ivoire to Martial-Henri Merlin, 4 Dec 1921, MGP, 9:251–56; Article from *Cape Argus*, 5 January 1923, reprinted in *NW*, February 24, 1923, 10; Hermann Norden, *Fresh Tracks in the Belgian Congo: from the Uganda Border to the Mouth of the Congo* (London, 1924), 64.

56. Robert Trent Vinson, "'Sea Kaffirs': 'American Negroes' and the Gospel of Garveyism in Early Twentieth-Century Cape Town," *Journal of African History* 47 (2006): 281.

57. Gregory Pirio, "The Role of Garveyism in the Making of Namibian Nationalism," in *Namibia 1884–1984: Readings on Namibia's History and Society*, ed. Brian Wood (London: Namibia Support Committee, 1988), 261; C. Lewis Warner to Secretary for South West Africa, 20 March 1922; Report by P.K.K. Atlogbe, ca. 10 September 1921; Letter from R.S. Cope to J.F. Herbst, 21 December 1921; Acting Magistrate, Swakopmund, to Secretary for South West Africa, 18 May 1922; South West Africa Police Report on UNIA Activities, 10 November 1922. In MGP, 9:204, 279, 386–87, 425, 673–74.

58. "Divisions of the UNIA, 1925–1927," Records of the Universal Negro Improvement Association, Central Division, New York, 1918–59, Box 2, a16 [microform].

59. Cobley, "Far from Home," 357–66; Vinson, "Sea Kaffirs," 285–89; R. L. Okonkwo, "Garvey Movement," 112.

60. Helen Bradford, *Taste of Freedom*, 214.

61. For the interconnecting relationships between the UNIA, the ANC, and the ICU, see Vinson, *Americans Are Coming!*, 82–101; Hill and Pirio, "'Africa for the Africans,'" 215–36; Bradford, *Taste of Freedom*, 123–43, 214–38. For Hayford and the NCBWA, see Supporting Speech by Hon. Casely Hayford, British West African Conference, March 1920, PRO, CO 554/54/1512; J. Ayodele Langley, *Pan-Africanism and Nationalism in West Africa, 1900–1945* (London: Oxford University Press, 1973), 125–33; Hayford to John E. Bruce, 24 November 1923, SC-NYPL, John Edward Bruce Papers, Reel 1, Group A, Folder 7, H, 1–15.

62. See, for example, MGP, 9:315; 10:134–35, 342, 705–7, 718.

63. Robert Edgar, "Garveyism in Africa: Dr. Wellington and the American Movement in the Transkei," *Ufahamu* 6.3 (1976): 33; Hill and Pirio, "Africa for the Africans," 234; Frederickson, *Black Liberation*, 162.

64. Matshoba is quoted in Robert Edgar, "The Prophet Motive: Enoch Mgijima, the Israelites, and the Background to the Bulhoek Massacre," *International Journal of African Historical Studies* 15, no. 3 (1982): 420–21.

65. Frederick Hale, "Fear and Support of an African Independent Church: Reactions to the Bulhoek Massacre of 1921," *Fides et historia: offical publication of the Conference on Faith and History* 26, no. 1 (Winter 1994): 77; "Article in *Christian Express* (Lovedale, South Africa)," 1 July 1921, in MGP, 9:54; Bradford, *Taste of Freedom*, 215.

66. *Interim and Final Reports of the Native Affairs Commission . . . relative to 'Israelites' at Bulhoek and Occurrences in May, 1921* (Cape Town: Government Printers, 1921), 3–10; Robert Edgar, *Because they Chose the Plan of God: The Story of the Bulhoek Massacre* (Johannesburg: Ravan Press, 1988), 1; Raymond Leslie Buell, *The Native Problem in Africa*, vol. 1 (1928; London: Frank Cass & Co., Ltd., 1965), 121–22.

67. For useful histories of Kimbanguism, see Efraim Andersson, *Messianic Popular Movements in the Lower Congo* (Uppsala: Almqvist & Wiksells Boktryckeri, 1958), 48–67; Wyatt MacGaffey, *Modern Kongo Prophets: Religion in a Plural Society* (Bloomington: Indiana University Press, 1983), 33–41.

68. R. Lanyon Jennings and A. W. Hilliard to The Missionary Staffs of BMS Stations, 19 May 1921, PRO, CO 536/138/10282; Rapports 165 et 171 du 19 et 20.6.21 de A. T. Luozi à C.D.D. Boma, in *L'Administration et le Sacré: Discours Religieux et*

Parcours Politiques en Afrique Centrale (1921–1957), eds. Paul Raymaekers and Henri Desroche (Brussels: Académie Royale des Sciences d'Outre Mer, 1983), 68–69; Cecilia Irvine, "The Birth of the Kimbanguist Movement in the Bas-Zaire 1921," *Journal of Religion in Africa* 6, no. 1 (1974): 43–44; Andersson, *Messianic*, 65; Article in *L'Avenir Colonial Belge*, 17 July 1921, in MGP, 9:98.

69. Martial-Henri Merlin to Albert Sarraut, 27 July 1921, MGP, 9:111; Cartier to Jaspar, 29 June 1921, BFMA, Quatre Bras, Brussels, AF-1–17 (1921); G. Ashie-Nikoi to General Agent, Black Star Line, 18 February 1922, PRO, CO 583/109; A. Earnsure Johnson, "The New Belgian Congo," *NW*, October 14, 1922, 6.

70. Lettre confidentielle du le Substitut, Colin, Lisala, à Monsieur le Procureur du Roi, 5 October 1920, BFMA, AF-1–17 (1884–1920); Vice Governor General to the Minister of the Colonies, 2 August 1921, and Report by Governor General, 2 August 1921, in BFMA, AI (A15) 1405 bis II/Q/3.

71. Vice Governor General to Minister of the Colonies, 2 August 1921, BFMA, AI (A15) 1405bis II/Q/3.

72. AT Léon Morel to the Vice Governor General, 22 September 1921, BFMA, AI (A15) 1405 bis II/Q/3 (translation mine); W. Reynolds, quoted in Andersson, *Messianic*, 254.

73. Report by C.D.D. Adj./ Thysville, 2 July 1921, in Irvine, "Birth," 47; Letter from Vice-Governor General to the Governor General of the Congo, 14 August 1921, in BFMA, AI (A15) 1405 bis II/Q/3; "Article in *Congo*," November 1921, in MGP, 9:247–48; Rev. Thomas Moody, quoted in *NW*, October 27, 1923, 2; Aurélien Mokoko Gampiot. *Kimbanguisme et Identité Noire* (Paris: L'Harmattan, 2004), 61; J. C. Van Cleemput, "Mouvement prophetique au Bas-Congo," 14 Sept 1921, BFMA, AI (A15) 1405 bis II/Q/3.

74. "Conference of Negroes," *East African Chronicle*, November 6, 1920, 11.

75. Arthur to Oldham, "Political Developments in Kenya Colony," 19 March 1922, in SOAS-IMC, Box 236, File D.3.

76. In 1920, the East African Protectorate was reclassified as a Crown colony, Kenya.

77. In the Kikuyu (or Gikuyu) language, *Gigikuyu*, the Kikuyu people are referred to as *Agikuyu* (singular: *Mugikuyu*). For the purposes of clarity, I will use "Kikuyu" here to refer to all.

78. Caroline Elkins, *Imperial Reckoning: The Untold Story of Britain's Gulag in Kenya* (Cambridge, MA: Harvard University Press, 2005), 1–7; Carl G. Rosberg Jr. and John Nottingham, *The Myth of "Mau Mau": Nationalism in Kenya* (New York: Meridian, 1966), 7–16. For a concise account of the epidemics of the 1890s, see Luise White, *The Comforts of Home: Prostitution in Colonial Nairobi* (Chicago: University of Chicago Press, 1990), 29–32.

79. Frederick B. Welbourn, *East African Rebels: A Study of Some Independent Churches* (London: SCM Press, 1961), 113; Rosberg and Nottingham, *Myth*, 16–18, 106–10.

80. Cora Ann Presley, *Kikuyu Women, the Mau Mau Rebellion, and Social Change in Kenya* (Boulder CO: Westview Press, 1992), 43–47; Elkins, *Imperial Reckoning*, 5–17; White, *Comforts of Home*, 29–50.

81. Johnstone Kenyatta, "Kenya," in *Negro: An Anthology*, ed. Nancy Cunard (1934; New York: Continuum, 1996), 454.

82. Norman Leys to Secretary of State for the Colonies, 7 February 1918, SOAS-IMC, Box 248, File A.

83. Rosberg and Nottingham, *Myth*, 28–29; Presley, *Kikuyu Women*, 49; H. D. Hooper, "Kenya Colony," (unpublished manuscript), SOAS-IMC, Box 247, File A; Norman Leys, *Kenya* (1924; London, Frank Cass, 1973), 303; Arthur to Secretary of Foreign Missions Committee, Church of Scotland, October, 1920, in Welbourn, *East African Rebels*, 125.

84. Leys to Secretary of State for the Colonies, 7 February 1918, SOAS-IMC, Box 248, File A.

85. See, for example, C. W. Hobley, *Bantu Beliefs and Magic: with Particular Reference to the Kikuyu and Kamba Tribes of Kenya Colony Together with some Reflections on East Africa after the War* (London: H.F. & G. Witherby, 1922), 287.

86. See, for example, "Self Determination," *East African Standard*, 1 May 1920, PRO, WO 106/259.

87. H. D. Hooper, "A Dilemma and an Experiment in B.E.A.," n.d., in SOAS-IMC, Box 247, File A.

88. Welbourn, *East African Rebels*, 122; Harry Thuku, *An Autobiography* (Nairobi: Oxford University Press, 1970), 19.

89. Northey, quoted in Audrey Wipper, "Kikuyu Women and the Harry Thuku Disturbances: Some Uniformities in Female Militancy," *Africa* 59, no. 3 (1989), 308; Welbourn, *East African Rebels*, 124–26. Presley, *Kikuyu Women*, 50–52, 110.

90. Thuku, *Autobiography*, 21–22; H. D. Hooper, "Development of Political Self-Consciousness in the Kikuyu Native," c. 29 March 1922; Memorandum of Grievances: Important Discussion between Officials and Kikuyu Association, 24 June 1921, in SOAS-IMC, Box 236, File D.2.

91. Thuku, *Autobiography*, 14–15; K. J. King, "The Nationalism of Harry Thuku: A Study in the Beginnings of African Politics in Kenya," *Transafrican Journal of History* 1, no. 1 (1971): 40–42.

92. Letter from H.D. Hooper, 5 January 1922, SOAS-IMC, Box 236, File D.2.

93. Sana Aiyar, "Empire, Race and the Indians in Colonial Kenya's Contested Public Political Sphere, 1919–1923," *Africa* 81, no. 1 (2011): 132–54; Keith Kyle, "Gandhi, Harry Thuku and Early Kenya Nationalism," *Transition* 27 (1966): 16–22.

94. Thuku, *Autobiography*, 16–20; J.C.R. Sturrock, PC Buganda, to Chief Secretary, 27 September 1921, PRO, CO 537/949/55782; R. T. Coryndon, Governor, Uganda, Confidential Report, 28 June 1922, PRO, CO 533/279/40275.

95. Thuku, *Autobiography*, 22–23; Kyle, "Gandhi," 18; Harry Thuku to Acting Colonial Secretary, 19 July 1921, and "Resolutions of the East African Association," in SOAS-IMC, Box 236, File D.2.

96. Rotberg and Nottingham, *Myth*, 47–48.

97. Ula District Council Meeting, Machakos, 22 March 1922, KNA, DC/MKS/5/1/2.

98. Thuku to Matthew Njeroje, 23 December 1921, PRO, CO 533/275/10273; John Spencer, "James Beauttah: Kenya Patriot" (manuscript, 1972), in KNA, MSS 35/1.

99. Thuku, *Autobiography*, 29; Hooper, "Development of Political Self-Consciousness in the Kikuyu Native," SOAS-IMC, Box 236, File D.2.

100. John Spencer, "The Kikuyu Central Association and the Genesis of the Kenya African Union," *Kenya Historical Review* 2, no. 1 (1974): 68.

101. Letters from H. D. Hooper, 5 January 1922, and 24 January 1922, in SOAS-IMC, Box 236, File D.2; Arthur to Oldham, 14 March 1922, SOAS-IMC, Box 247, File D.

102. Thuku to Matthew Njeroje, 23 December 1921, PRO, CO 533/275/10273; Statement of Jacob wa Makeri, 27 February 1922; Statements of Warohuja wa Kungu and Wamarema wa Kimani, 16 March 1922; Statement of Koinange wa Mbui, Kiambu, 17 February 1922. In PRO, CO 533/280/40279; Thuku, *Autobiography*, 84, 39; Rotberg and Nottingham, *Myth*, 48.

103. Northey to Churchill, 16 July 1922, PRO, CO 533/280/40269; Letter from H.D. Hooper, 5 January 1922, SOAS-IMC, Box 236, File D.2; C.F. Andrews, "Kikuyu African Rising," *The Modern Review* 31.4 (April 1922), 513; King, "Nationalism," 44–46; Statement of Wamarema wa Kimani, 16 March 1922, PRO, CO 533/280/40279.

104. M. A. Desai, "The Arab Association," *East African Chronicle*, July 9, 1921, A, in PCEA, I/G/12; "Faith in the Imperial Government," *East African Chronicle*, August 27, 1921, 4.

105. "Negro Congress," *East African Chronicle*, August 27, 1921, 5.

106. King, *Pan-Africanism*, 58–77.

107. Thuku to Kamulegeya, 9 September 1921, PRO, CO 533/277/25950; Thuku to Secretary, Tuskegee Institute, 8 September 1921, reproduced in King, *Pan-Africanism*, 261–62.

108. H. D. Hooper to Jesse Jones, 10 August 1922, SOAS-IMC, Box 247, File A; King, *Pan-Africanism*, 77; Interview in *Sekanyolya* with Daudi Basude, SOAS-IMC, Box 241, File C.

109. Hooper to Oldham, 4 March 1922, SOAS-IMC, Box 236, File D; Translation: Prayers compiled for Christians and Non-Christians Alike of Village of Kahuhia, 9 March 1922, PRO, CO 533/276/22644; Statement by Munene wa Kagwanja, 13 March 1922, and Statement by Karuiki wa Waruingi, 12 March 1922, PRO, CO 533/280/40279.

110. According to Mrs. Harry Thuku, Mary Nyanjiru worked with Thuku in the EAA, and was in his room when the police came to arrest him. See Presley, *Kikuyu Women*, 112. Muchuchu's recollections are recorded in Rotberg and Nottingham, *Myth*, 51–52.

111. Rotberg and Nottingham, *Myth*, 51–53; Acting Commissioner, Kenya Police, to Colonial Secretary, 16 March 1922, PRO, CO 533/276/226644.

112. Excerpts from Speech by Garvey, MGP, 9:377–82; Hooper, "Development of Political Self-Consciousness in the Kikuyu Native," 29 March 1922, SOAS-IMC, Box 236, File D.2; Arthur to Oldham, 14 March 1922, SOAS-IMC, Box 247, File D; Arthur to Oldham, 19 March 1922: "Political Developments in Kenya Colony," SOAS-IMC, Box 236, File D.3.

CHAPTER FOUR
"THE SILENT WORK THAT MUST BE DONE"

1. "Convention Parade of the UNIA" and "Article in the *Negro World*," MGP, 3:566–69.

2. Robert A. Hill, "Introduction," MGP, 3:xxxiii–iv; Ramla M. Bandale, *Black Star: African American Activism in the International Political Economy* (Urbana: University

of Illinois Press, 2008), 107; Ronald Harpelle, "Cross Currents in the Western Caribbean: Marcus Garvey and the UNIA in Central America," *Caribbean Studies* 31, no. 1 (2003): 58–61.

3. Articles in the *NY World*, MGP, 4:352; W.E.B. Du Bois, "Back to Africa," *Century Magazine* 105 (Feb. 1923), 543–47.

4. Robin D. G. Kelley, *Freedom Dreams: The Black Radical Imagination* (Boston: Beacon Press, 2002).

5. *NW*, February 9, 1924, 3.

6. Judith Stein, *The World of Marcus Garvey: Race and Class in Modern Society* (Baton Rouge: Louisiana State University Press, 1986), 129; Alice L. Conklin, *A Mission to Civilize: The Republican Idea of Empire in France and West Africa, 1895–1930* (Stanford, CA: Stanford University Press, 1997), 157–88; P. J. Cain and A. G. Hopkins, *British Imperialism 1688–2000*, 2d ed. (Harlow, England: Longman, 2002), 406–7.

7. John Higham, *Strangers in the Land: Patterns of American Nativism, 1860–1925* (1955; New Brunswick, NJ: Rutgers University Press, 2002), 222; Nancy MacLean, *Behind the Mask of Chivalry: The Making of the Second Ku Klux Klan* (New York: Oxford University Press, 1994), xii, 5–18, 177; Mae M. Ngai, "Nationalism, Immigration, Control, and the Ethnoracial Remapping of America in the 1920s," *OAH Magazine of History* (July 2007): 11–15; Thomas F. Gossett, *Race: The History of an Idea in America* (1963; Oxford: Oxford University Press, 1997), 407.

8. Erez Manela, *The Wilsonian Moment: Self-Determination and the International Origins of Anticolonial Nationalism* (Oxford: Oxford University Press, 2007), 22–43; John H. Harris, "Native Races and Peace Terms," *Contemporary Review* 109 (January/June 1916), 751–52; F. D. Lugard, *The Dual Mandate in British Tropical Africa* (Edinburgh: William Blackwood and Sons, 1922), 62–63.

9. L. S. Woolf, *Economic Imperialism* (London: Swarthmore Press, 1920), 104–11; E. D. Morel, *The Black Man's Burden* (Manchester: National Labour Press, 1920), vii; Harry H. Johnston, *The Black Man's Part in the War* (London: Simpkin, Marshall, Hamilton, Kent & Co., 1917), 103–4; Johnston, *The Backwards Peoples and Our Relations with Them* (London: Oxford University Press, 1920), 61.

10. Frederick Cooper, "Conditions Analogous to Slavery: Imperialism and Free Labor Ideology in Africa," in Frederick Cooper, Thomas C. Holt, and Rebecca J. Scott, *Beyond Slavery: Explorations in Race, Labor and Citizenship in Postemancipation Societies* (Chapel Hill: University of North Carolina Press, 2000), 123–25; Lugard, *Dual Mandate*, 91, 193–207, 615–18.

11. Mahmood Mamdani, *Citizen and Subject: Contemporary Africa and the Legacy of Late Colonialism* (Princeton, NJ: Princeton University Press, 1996), 68–95; Andrew Zimmerman, *Alabama in Africa: Booker T. Washington, the German Empire, and the Globalization of the New South* (Princeton, NJ: Princeton University Press, 2010), 201–2.

12. Cooper, "Conditions," 125–26. See also Eric Hobsbawm and Terence Ranger, eds., *The Invention of Tradition* (Cambridge: Cambridge University Press, 1983).

13. Kenneth James King, *Pan-Africanism and Education: A Study of Race, Philanthropy and Education in the Southern States of America and East Africa* (Oxford: Clarendon Press, 1971), 21–43, 50–56; Michael O. West, "The Tuskegee Model of Development in Africa: Another Dimension of the African/African-American Connection,"

Diplomatic History 16, no. 3 (1992): 383–85; Lugard, *Dual Mandate*, 425; Sir F. D. Lugard, "The Colour Problem," *Edinburgh Review* 233, no. 476 (1921): 283.

14.   For a discussion of the establishment of "crustaceous borders" in the era of high nationalism, see Ngai, "Nationalism," 12.

15.   Gossett, *Race*, 363–74.

16.   Lothrop Stoddard, *The Revolt against Civilization: The Menace of the Under Man* (New York: Charles Scribner's Sons, 1922), 30–44, 238–40; Johnston, *Backwards Peoples*, 37–45; Earnest Sevier Cox, *White America* (Richmond, VA: White America Society, 1923), 153–57; Seth K. Humphrey, *Mankind: Racial Values and the Racial Prospect* (New York: Charles Scribner's Sons, 1917), 105–6.

17.   Cox, *White America*, 299; Lothrop Stoddard, *The Rising Tide of Color against White World Supremacy* (1920; Charles Scribner's Sons, 1922), vi, 162–68, 218–21; Lugard, "Colour Problem," 280.

18.   Warren G. Harding, *Address of the President of the United States at the Celebration of the Semicentennial of the Founding of the City of Birmingham, Alabama, October 26, 1921* (Washington: Library of Congress, 1921).

19.   Theodore Kornweibel, Jr., *"Seeing Red": Federal Campaigns against Black Militancy, 1919–1925* (Bloomington: Indiana University Press, 1998), 100–106; Hoover to Ridgely, 11 October 1919, MGP, 2:72.

20.   Bandele, *Black Star*, 108–9, 130, 162.

21.   Bandele, *Black Star*, 107–13; Report from A. M. Brookfield, 30 September 1920, MGP, 3:36.

22.   Reports by Special Agent P-138, 6 November 1920, MGP, 3:71–72.

23.   Reports by Special Agent P-138, 17–19 October 1920 and 4 January 1921, in MGP, 3:52–59, 122–25.

24.   Report by Special Agent P-138, 11 February 1921, Hoover to Baley, 11 February 1921, and Hurley to McBride, 24 June 1921, in MGP, 3:177–78, 484; Tony Martin, *Race First: The Ideological and Organizational Struggles of Marcus Garvey and the Universal Negro Improvement Association* (Westport, CT: Greenwood Press, 1976), 184–86.

25.   Robert A. Hill, "Garvey's Gospel, Garvey's Game," in *The Philosophy and Opinions of Marcus Garvey*, ed. Amy Jacques Garvey (New York: Atheneum, 1992), xxv–xxvi; "UNIA Meeting at Carnegie Hall," 25 August 1919, and Speech by Garvey, 1 February 1921, in MGP, 1:506, 3:150–51.

26.   "Garvey in Jamaica," *Tribune*, 15 May 1921, in PRO, CO 318/364/34269; "Speeches by Marcus Garvey at Colón, 27 April 1921, MGP, 3:368–70; G. P. Chittendon to V. M. Cutter, United Fruit Company Records, Costa Rica, TLS, accessed April 2, 2011, http://bolt.lakeheadu.ca/~sojourners/diaspora/doc1.html.

27.   Revealing of his mindset, Garvey declared his intention for US citizenship upon his return. See MGP, 4:6.

28.   Speech by Garvey, 24 July 1921, and Garvey to the White Press of the World, January, 1923, in MGP, 3:549, 5:205.

29.   Report by P-138, 19 July 1921, MGP, 3:531.

30.   Article by J.W. Johnson, 24 September 1921; Article in the *NY Evening Post*, 7 September 1921; and Garvey to the White Press of the World, January, 1923. In MGP, 4:80, 4:45–46, 5:204–5.

31.   Speech by Garvey, 11 February 1921, MGP, 3:180–81.

32. Speech by Garvey, 4 September 1921, MGP, 4:25–27.

33. Editorial by Garvey, 27 June 1922, and Speech by Garvey, 13 February 1922, in MGP, 4:685, 503.

34. Speech by Garvey, 9 July 1922; Speech by Garvey, 7 September 1921; and Speech by Garvey, 4 September 1921. In MGP, 4:707–12, 4:27, 34.

35. Cyril Briggs, "Is Not This Treason?" and "Garvey Upholds Ku Kluxism!" in *Crusader* 5, no. 2 (1921): 8–9; W.E.B. Du Bois, "A Lunatic or a Traitor," *Crisis* 28, no. 1 (1924): 8–9; A. Philip Randolph, "Marcus Garvey! The Black Imperial Wizard Becomes Messenger Boy of the White Ku Klux Kleagle," *Messenger* 4, no. 7 (1922): 437; Martin, *Race First*, 321–26; "Enclosure," 15 January 1923, MGP, 5:182–86.

36. "Enclosure," 15 January 1923, MGP, 5:183–84; Du Bois, "Lunatic or Traitor," 9; Martin, *Race First*, 323.

37. Reports by James E. Amos and Mortimer J. Davis, January 23, 1923, and Report by Davis, 25 May 1923, in *Federal Surveillance of Afro-Americans (1917–1925): The First World War, the Red Scare, and the Garvey Movement*, ed. Theodore Kornweibel Jr. (microfilm, 25 reels, University Publications of America, 1986), Reel 2, Frames 482–83, and Reel 3, Frame 21.

38. Colin Grant, *Negro with a Hat: The Rise and Fall of Marcus Garvey* (Oxford: Oxford University Press, 2008), 355.

39. Article in *New Orleans Times-Picayune*, 2 January 1923, MGP, 5:161–62; Reports by Battle, 2 October 1922 and 28 February 1923; Gulley to Hoover, 16 January 1923; Report by Mortimer J. Davis, 19 June 1923. All in *Federal Surveillance*, Reel 4, Frame 34, 2:843, 2:471, 2:972.

40. Editorial by George W. Harris, MGP, 5:377–78.

41. Speech by Garvey, 16 November 1924, MGP, 6:42–46; William Sherrill in *NW*, August 15, 1925, 2–3.

42. Martin, *Race First*, 127–30; Grant, *Negro with a Hat*, 382–86.

43. Report by Lenon, 18 January 1921, MGP, 3:133–34; *NW*, August 20, 1921, 1; *NW*, June 21, 1924, 15; *NW*, November 29, 1924; *NW*, October 2, 1926, 7.

44. *NW*, February 6, 1926, 3; *NW*, March 17, 1923, 3–4; *NW*, February 20, 1926, 7.

45. *NW*, March 10, 1926, 4; *NW*, January 14, 1928, 8.

46. Harpelle, "Cross Currents," 41–46; Frank A. Guridy, "'Enemies of the White Race': The Machadista State and the UNIA in Cuba," *Caribbean Studies* 31, no. 1 (2003): 107–37; "Barbados," "British Guiana (Guyana)," and "Trinidad," in MGP, 11:cli–cliii, clxvii–clxxiii, cclxv–cclxvi; Rupert Lewis, *Marcus Garvey: Anti-Colonial Champion* (Trenton, NJ: Africa World Press, Inc., 1988), 209–12, 260–65; "Divisions of the UNIA, 1926–1927 (compiled from index cards)," Universal Negro Improvement Association Records of the Central Division (New York), 1918–59, SC-NYPL: microfilm, Reel 1, Series A, Box 2, Section A16.

47. Ibrahim Sundiata, *Brothers and Strangers: Black Zion, Black Slavery, 1914–1940* (Durham, NC: Duke University Press, 2005), 2. For a discussion of emigration movements, see James T. Campbell, *Middle Passages: African American Journeys to Africa, 1787–2005* (New York: Penguin, 2006).

48. Opening Speech of the Convention by Garvey, 1 August 1921, MGP, 3:577; *NW*, April 14, 1923, 2, 10; *NW*, May 2, 1925, 3.

49. *NW*, April 28, 1923, 10; *NW*, April 28, 1923, 2.

CHAPTER FIVE
THE TIDE OF PREPARATION

1. *NW*, March 26, 1927, 2; Sun Yat-sen, "Pan-Asianism," in Sun Yat-sen, *China and Japan: Natural Friends—Unnatural Enemies*, ed. T'ang Leang-Li (Shanghai: China United Press, 1941), 141–51.

2. *NW*, March 26, 1927, 6.

3. *NW*, March 26, 1927, 6.

4. Winston James, *Holding Aloft the Banner of Ethiopia* (London: Verso, 1998), 134–35.

5. Earl Lewis, *In Their Own Interests: Race, Class, and Power in Twentieth-Century Norfolk, Virginia* (Berkeley: University of California Press, 1991), 74–75; Harold, *The Rise and Fall of the Garvey Movement in the Urban South, 1918–1942* (New York: Routledge, 2007), 91, 96; Barbara Bair, "Renegotiating Liberty: Garveyism, Women, and Grassroots Organizing in Virginia," in *Women of the American South: A Multicultural Reader*, ed. Christie Anne Farnham (New York: New York University Press, 1997), 224

6. Harold, *Rise and Fall*, 30–37; Jahi U. Issa, "The Universal Negro Improvement Association in Louisiana: Creating a Provisional Government in Exile" (PhD diss., Howard University, 2005), 101–15; Rolinson, *Grassroots Garveyism*, 49, 86, 92–96.

7. Mary G. Rolinson, *Grassroots Garveyism: The UNIA in the Rural South, 1920–1927* (Chapel Hill: University of North Carolina Press, 2007), 49, 60–62; Issa, "Universal," 79–80, 95–97; Joe William Trotter Jr., *Coal, Class, and Color: Blacks in Southern West Virginia, 1915–1932* (Urbana: University of Illinois Press, 1990), 243–45; "Convention Report, Afternoon Session," 4 August 1924, MGP, 5:659–60; Harold, *Rise and Fall*, 65–66; Military Intelligence Division, Weekly Situation Survey, July 9, 1921, in *Federal Surveillance of Afro-Americans (1917–1925): The First World War, the Red Scare, and the Garvey Movement*, ed. Theodore Kornweibel Jr. (microfilm, 25 reels, University Publications of America, 1986), reel 17, frame 749; Emory Tolbert, *The UNIA and Black Los Angeles* (Los Angeles: Center for Afro-American Studies, UCLA, 1980), 96; Report of Japanese Activities, Week Ending June 10, 1922, in *Federal Surveillance*, reel 23, frame 700.

8. Rolinson, *Grassroots Garveyism*, 8, 96–98, 103, 204–13; Jarod Roll, *Spirit of Rebellion: Labor and Religion in the New Cotton South* (Urbana: University of Illinois Press, 2010), 52–75; Nan Elizabeth Woodruff, *American Congo: The African American Freedom Struggle in the Delta* (Cambridge, MA: Harvard University Press, 2003), 116–18.

9. Rolinson, *Grassroots Garveyism*, 86, 95, 98, 130.

10. Steven Hahn, "Marcus Garvey, the UNIA, and the Hidden Political History of African Americans," in *The Political Worlds of Slavery and Freedom* (Cambridge, MA: Harvard University Press, 2009), 118

11. My use of "metalanguage" is borrowed from Evelyn Brooks Higginbotham, who argues that technologies of race have manifested themselves in the United States as a metalanguage, exerting a "powerful, all-encompassing effect on the construction and representation of other social and power relations, namely, gender,

class, and sexuality." Higginbotham, "African-American Women's History and the Metalanguage of Race," *Signs* 17 (Winter 1992): 252.

12. Tolbert, *UNIA*, 110.

13. Samuel Alonzo Culmer, "Why I Am a Garveyite?" *NW*, November 6, 1926, 5. For "vocabularies of agency," see Eddie S. Glaude, Jr., *Exodus! Religion, Race, and Nation in Early Nineteenth-Century Black America* (Chicago: University of Chicago Press, 2000), 20.

14. Letter from J. B. Washington, *NW*, March 7, 1925, 10.

15. Letter from J. C. Wilson, *NW*, August 13, 1921, 9.

16. For example, see *NW*, January 21, 1922; *NW*, June 10, 1922.

17. "Report from British Military Intelligence, October 1919, in *Federal Surveillance*, reel 12, frames 20–21; Opening Speech of Convention, 1 August 1921, in MGP, 3:586–87.

18. Report of Japanese Activities, Week Ending 3 July 1922, and 18 March 1922 to 10 June 1922, in *Federal Surveillance*, reel 17, frames 49–50, reel 23, frames 686–700; J. J. Hannigan, to Director, Office of Naval Intelligence, 3 December 1921; Hannigan to Director, 27 December 1921; Hannigan to Director, 9 January 1922; Hannigan to Director, 4 February 1922, MGP, 4:233–37, 311–12, 339, 477.

19. *NW*, February 19, 1927, 8; *NW*, March 26, 1927, 2; *NW*, April 16, 1927, 8; *NW*, April 30, 1927, 8; *NW*, June 16, 1928, 2; *NW*, May 24, 1930, 4; *NW*, May 31, 1930, 4.

20. Letter from James Phillips, *NW*, October 17, 1925, 10. For similar comments by Garveyites, see *NW*, June 5, 1926, 8; *NW*, July 4, 1925, 10.

21. *NW*, November 26, 1921, 7.

22. *NW*, November 19, 1921, 2; Hubert Harrison, "The Line-Up of the Color Line," in *A Hubert Harrison Reader*, ed. Jeffrey B. Perry (Middletown, CT: Wesleyan University Press, 2001), 217–19; *NW*, October 6, 1928, 4.

23. Interview with Thomas W. Harvey, Philadelphia, 1975 and 1976, in *Footsoldiers of the Universal Negro Improvement Association* (Trenton, NJ: Africa World Press, 1989), 26; *NW*, August 4, 1923, 7; Letter from J. Baxter Logan, Boley, Oklahoma, *NW*, September 12, 1925, 10.

24. Letter from Mrs. S. M. Taylor, *NW*, May 19, 1923, 7; Letter from A.W. Fitz, *NW*, June 4, 1921, 2; Letter from Henry Sutton, *NW*, November 8, 1930, 4; Letter from James A. Teasley, *NW*, January 1, 1930, 4.

25. *NW*, November 13, 1926, 5.

26. Marcus Garvey, quoted in an article by Robert Minor for the *Daily Worker*, August 18, 1924, cited in MGP, 5:753.

27. *NW*, February 11, 1928, 2; Amy Jacques Garvey, "Africa Bides Her Time!" *NW*, February 5, 1927.

28. *NW*, March 31, 1928, 3.

29. Rolinson, *Grassroots Garveyism*, Appendix A.

30. Southern branch files of the NAACP during the interwar period evince an organization struggling to stay afloat in an unfavorable climate, and contain stories of remarkable leadership. For an example of both, follow the correspondence of Carrie L. Shepperson, secretary of the NAACP branch in Little Rock, Arkansas, from 1924 to 1926, in *Papers of the NAACP, Part 12: Selected Branch Files, 1913–1939; Series A: The South*. Branch Files (Little Rock, AR), Group 1, Series G, Box G-12, Reel 3, Frames 819–980.

31. Steven Hahn, *A Nation Under Our Feet: Black Political Struggles in the Rural South from Slavery to the Great Migration* (Cambridge, MA: Harvard University Press, 2003).

32. Letter from Mrs. Jimmie L. Dennis, *NW*, June 7, 1924; Rev. J. N. Bridgeman, "Garveyism: An Interpretation," *NW*, June 4, 1921, 9.

33. For Georgia and Mississippi, see Rolinson, *Grassroots Garveyism*, 171, 175. For Missouri, see Jarod Roll, "Road to the Promised Land: Rural Rebellion in the New Cotton South, 1890–1945" (PhD diss., Northwestern University, 2006), 142–47.

34. Rolinson, *Grassroots Garveyism*, 62, 141.

35. For West Virginia, see MGP, 5:659–60. Jarod Roll suggests that UNIA divisions in the Bootheel, which emphasized racial separation and productive farming, may have received protection from local planters in the KKK. Roll, "Road," 158. For Phillips County, see Rolinson, *Grassroots Garveyism*, 99.

36. William Pickens to Marcus Garvey, July, 1922, in *Papers of the NAACP*, Part 11: Special Subject Files, 1912–1939, Series A (Marcus Garvey), Group 1, Box 304, Reel 35, frames 781–82.

37. Speech by Marcus Garvey, July 9, 1922, in MGP, 4:712.

38. Convention Report, Wednesday Afternoon, August 6, 1924, in MGP, 5:671–73; *NW*, June 21, 1924, 3. Similar sessions were held at the conventions in 1920 and 1922.

39. Interview with Thomas W. Harvey, in *Footsoldiers*, 23–24.

40. Letter from Eugene Gavin, *NW*, October 17, 1925, 10; Letter from H. Harrison, February 20, 1926, 10; Letter from Harry Udell, *NW*, December 26, 1925, 8; Letter from B. F. Jones, *NW*, April 11, 1925; Letter from M. Harrold, *NW*, July 4, 1925, 10; Letter from J. H. Blackwell, *NW*, November 27, 1926, 2; Letter from A. J. Smith, *NW*, November 1, 1924, 16.

41. Report by High Commissioner Jacob S. Slappy, *NW*, March 17, 1923, 8; Mass Meeting in Newport News, Virginia, 4 May 1924, *NW*, May 17, 1924, 8; *NW*, August 23, 1924, 14; Letter from Amos H. Carnegie, *NW*, March 12, 1927, 10; Aurelia Aulston Haynes, "Why I Am a Garveyite?" *NW*, November 13, 1926, 5; James H. Robinson, quoted in Amy Jacques Garvey, *Garvey and Garveyism* (1963; New York: Octagon Books, 1978), 80.

42. Jacques Garvey, in Ula Yvette Taylor, *The Veiled Garvey: The Life and Times of Amy Jacques Garvey* (Chapel Hill: University of North Carolina Press, 2002), 3; Tolbert, *UNIA*, 110.

43. Michele Mitchell, *Righteous Propagation: African Americans and the Politics of Racial Destiny after Reconstruction* (Chapel Hill: University of North Carolina Press, 2004), 7.

44. "Race First," *NW*, July 26, 1919, MGP, 1:468–69; Garvey, "African Fundamentalism," *NW*, June 6, 1925, 1.

45. *NW*, February 24, 1923, 7.

46. For challenges facing interracial unionism, see Earl Lewis, *In Their Own Interests: Race, Class, and Power in Twentieth-Century Norfolk, Virginia* (Berkeley: University of California Press, 1991), 15–16, 28.

47. Estella Brown, Report of Easter Celebration by Philadelphia Division, *NW*, April 9, 1921; Louise J. Edwards, "The New Day Appears," *NW*, June 12, 1926, 7; William Sherrill at Liberty Hall, *NW*, October 20, 1923, 3; Letter from Harold Alexander Blackwell, *NW*, April 2, 1921.

48. St. Clair Drake, *The Redemption of Africa and Black Religion* (Chicago: Third World Press, 1970), 11, 74.

49. Randall Burkett, *Black Redemption: Churchmen Speak for the Garvey Movement* (Philadelphia: Temple University Press, 1978), 8.

50. J. N. Bridgeman, "Garveyism: An Interpretation," *NW*, June 4, 1921, 9.

51. Randall Burkett, *Garveyism as a Religious Movement: the Institutionalization of a Black Civil Religion* (Metuchen, NJ: Scarecrow Press, 1978), 111.

52. Burkett, *Black Redemption*, 9; Burkett, *Garveyism*, 112; Roll, "Road," 143; Rolinson, *Grassroots Garveyism*, 203.

53. Jacques Garvey, *Garvey and Garveyism*, 29; Wilson Henry Moses, quoted in Burkett, *Garveyism*, 121; Letter from Willina P. Hudson, *NW*, April 25, 1925, 5.

54. Speech by Garvey, Liberty Hall, 11 July 1920, in MGP 2:415.

55. Kimberley L. Phillips, *AlabamaNorth: African-American Migrants, Community, and Working-Class Activism in Cleveland, 1915–1945* (Urbana: University of Illinois Press, 1999), 170; James R. Grossman, *Land of Hope: Chicago, Black Southerners, and the Great Migration* (Chicago: University of Chicago Press, 1989), 157.

56. "Garvey Repudiated," *Norfolk Journal and Guide*, January 26, 1924.

57. *NW*, March 3, 1923, 5; Letter from A. Sewell, *NW*, July 9, 1921, 4; Letter from W.T. Johnson, *NW*, January 10, 1925, 12.

58. S. A. Haynes, "Spiritual Leaders Not Catering to Needs of a Struggling Race," *NW*, October 30, 1926, 5.

59. "Report from B. W. Wilson," *NW*, February 19, 1921, 5.

60. *NW*, April 2, 1921, 1; *NW*, December 3, 1921, 10; *NW*, April 16, 1921, 2.

61. *NW*, May 9, 1925, 3.

62. Speech by Garvey, 22 February 1921, MGP, 3:232.

63. Speech by Garvey, 16 April 1922, MGP, 4:601–3.

64. Burkett, *Garveyism*, 81–82.

65. Burkett, *Garveyism*, 7–8.

66. Address by Eason, 30 September 1919, MGP, 2:35.

67. *NW*, November 5, 1921, 11; *NW*, May 7, 1921, 3; *NW*, March 31, 1928, 3.

68. Amy Jacques Garvey, "Wanted—Missionaries for Africa," *NW*, February 21, 1925, 7; *NW*, April 2, 1921, 3.

69. *NW*, January 24, 1925, 7; *NW*, May 26, 1928, 3.

70. Glaude, *Exodus!*

71. William Ware in *NW*, April 4, 1925, 2, 6.

72. Mamie De Mena in *NW*, April 18, 1928, 3.

73. "Editorial Letter by Marcus Garvey in *NW*," 10 February 1925, in MGP, 6:97–98.

74. "Letter by N. H. Grissom," *NW*, November 8, 1930, 4; George McGuire, "UNIA Convention Opening, 1 August 1924," in MGP, 5:628.

75. Editorial by Garvey, 22 May 1923, in MGP, 5:313.

76. UNIA Convention Opening, 1 August 1924, MGP, 5:627; *NW*, August 20, 1921, 3.

77. Burkett, *Garveyism*, 67–71. Tony Martin points out that an early copy of the preamble to the UNIA constitution used the phrase "Christian" worship, and was revised to "spiritual" worship. See Tony Martin, *Race First: The Ideological Origins and*

Organizational Struggles of Marcus Garvey and the Universal Negro Improvement Association (Westport, CT: Greenwood Press, 1976), 74–75.

78. Letter from G. M. Moore, *NW*, July 5, 1924, 14.

79. George Fredrickson, *Black Liberation: A Comparative History of Black Ideologies in the United States and South Africa* (New York: Oxford University Press, 1995), 139; Grossman, *Land of Hope*, 130–57; Phillips, *AlabamaNorth*, 169–86. For the class-based (and gender-based) implications of the "politics of respectability," see Higginbotham, *Righteous Discontent: The Women's Movement in the Black Baptist Church, 1880–1920* (Cambridge, MA: Harvard University Press, 1993), 19–45.

80. Roll, "Road," 143–52.

81. See Mary Rolinson's helpful compilation of UNIA members' profiles in Georgia, Arkansas, and Mississippi, in *Grassroots Garveyism*, 203–10; Harold, *Rise and Fall*, 6, 37; Phillips, *AlabamaNorth*, 187.

82. Harold, *Rise and Fall*, 37, 64–65.

83. William Pickens, in *NW*, December 17, 1921, 9; Marcus Garvey, in *NW*, March 31, 1928, 1.

84. Fredrickson, *Black Liberation*, 159; Marcus Garvey, quoted in *NW*, November 17, 1923, 5.

85. Editorial by Garvey, 19 August 1924, MGP, 5:757.

86. Marcus Garvey, "A Talk with Afro-West Indians," in MGP, 1:55–56.

87. Letter from C. R. Urquhart, *NW*, January 19, 1924, 10; Letter from A. Sewell, *NW*, July 9, 1921, 4.

88. Letter from H.W. Harrison, *NW*, November 1, 1924, 16; Letter from R.H. Williams, *NW*, May 17, 1924, 12.

89. Report of a Meeting, Liberty Hall, 13 March 1920, in MGP, 2:250–52; E. L. Gaines at Liberty Hall, *NW*, April 9, 1921, 3; Editorial by Garvey, *NW*, November 17, 1923, 1.

90. Martin Summers, *Manliness and Its Discontents: The Black Middle Class and the Transformation of Masculinity, 1900–1930* (Chapel Hill: University of North Carolina Press, 2004), 18–21.

91. Martin, *Race First*, 35.

92. For Philadelphia, see *NW*, November 24, 1923, 7. For Detroit, see Interview with John Charles Zampty, Detroit, 1974, in *Footsoldiers*, 46–47. For New York, see *NW*, March 11, 1922, 5; Martin, *Race First*, 34–35. For Philadelphia and East Berlin, CT, see Article by William H. Ferris, 22 July 1922, MGP, 4:730–32. For New Orleans, see Convention Reports, Afternoon Session, Tuesday, August 8, 1922, 828. For a long list of Garveyite business ventures, see Theodore G. Vincent, *Black Power and the Garvey Movement* (Berkeley, CA: Ramparts Press, 1971), 166.

93. Jacques Garvey, *Garvey and Garveyism*, 96–97.

94. Judith Stein, *The World of Marcus Garvey: Race and Class in Modern Society* (Baton Rouge: Louisiana State University Press, 1986), 227; Article by William H. Ferris, 22 July 1922, MGP, 4:730; "News and Views, New Orleans," *NW*, January 21, 1928, 6; "News and Views," Detroit, *NW*, July 26, 1924, 9; Harold, *Rise and Fall*, 48; "News and Views, New Orleans," *NW*, May 14, 1927, 8; "News and Views, Pittsburgh," *NW*, January 17, 1925, 10; *NW*, October 20, 1923, 7; *NW*, October 27, 1923, 7.

95. Voluntary Committee of the UNIA to the Mayor of New Orleans, 16 February 1923, *NW*, March 24, 1923, 8.

96. "Speech by Garvey," 14 October 1919, in MGP, 2:97–98; *NW*, December 1, 1923, 3; A. H. Venn, "An African Letter," *NW*, February 21, 1931, 4; Marcus Garvey, "The Universal Negro Improvement Association: What It Aims At. Real Aristocracy of Race," *Jamaica Times*, January 16, 1915, in MGP, 1: 104–5.

97. Gail Bederman, *Manliness and Civilization: A Cultural History of Gender and Race in the United States, 1880–1917* (Chicago: University of Chicago Press, 1995); Elsa Barkley Brown, "Negotiating and Transforming the Public Sphere: African American Political Life in the Transition from Slavery to Freedom," *Public Culture* 7 (1994), 139–44; Summers, *Manliness*, 8–15, 67–109.

98. See, for example, Samuel Haynes in *NW*, September 1, 1928, 3. For constructions of women as the "atavistic and authentic body of national tradition" in nationalist discourse, see Anne McClintock, "'No Longer a Future in Heaven': Gender, Race and Nationalism," in *Dangerous Liaisons: Gender, Nation, and Postcolonial Perspectives*, eds. Aamir Mufti and Ella Shohat (Minneapolis: University of Minnesota Press, 1997), 91–92.

99. Barbara Bair, "True Women, Real Men," in *Gendered Domains: Rethinking Public and Private in Women's History*, eds. Dorothy O. Helly and Susan M. Reverby (Ithaca, NY: Cornell University Press, 1992), 155; Mitchell, *Righteous Propagation*, 222; Barbara Bair, "'Ethiopia Shall Stretch Forth Her Hands Unto God': Laura Kofey and the Gendered Vision of Redemption in the Garvey Movement," in *A Mighty Baptism: Race, Gender, and the Creation of American Protestantism*, eds. Susan Juster and Lisa MacFarlane (Ithaca, NY: Cornell University Press, 1996), 59.

100. For examples of this tendency, see Mitchell, *Righteous Propagation*, 222–39; Matthew Pratt Guterl, *The Color of Race in America, 1900–1940* (Cambridge, MA: Harvard University Press, 2001), 93–94; Clare Corbould, *Becoming African Americans: Black Public Life in Harlem, 1919–1939* (Cambridge, MA: Harvard University Press, 2009), 21–26, 37, 48–51.

101. Barbara Bair, "'Ethiopia Shall Stretch Forth Her Hands Unto God,'" 38. For a discussion of negotiations by female participants within nationalist and male-dominated movements, see Richard G. Fox, "Gandhi and Feminized Nationalism in India," in *Women Out of Place*, 39–40; Lois A. West, "Introduction: Feminism Constructs Nationalism," in *Feminist Nationalism*, ed. Lois A. West (New York: Routledge, 1997), xiv; Higginbotham, *Righteous Discontent*, 120–48.

102. See Taylor, *The Veiled Garvey*, 2, 64; Bair, "Ethiopia," 38–40; Kate Dossett, *Bridging Race Divides: Black Nationalism, Feminism, and Integration in the United States, 1896–1935* (Gainesville: University Press of Florida, 2008), 154–75.

103. For the black church, see Higginbotham, *Righteous Discontent*, 7–8. For the role of women in the civil rights movement, see Charles M. Payne, *I've Got the Light of Freedom: The Organizing Tradition and the Mississippi Freedom Struggle* (Berkeley: University of California Press, 1995), 266–67, 274–77; Belinda Robnett, *How Long? How Long?: African-American Women in the Struggle for Civil Rights* (New York: Oxford University Press, 1997).

104. Rolinson, *Grassroots Garveyism*, 121, 214; Bair, "Ethiopia," 44–45, 54; Bair, "Renegotiating Liberty," 225–26; James, *Holding Aloft*, 141.

105. Paule Marshall, "From the Poets in the Kitchen," *Callaloo* 18 (Spring-Summer 1983): 24–27.

106. Summers, *Manliness*, 93, 96, 125; Bair, "Ethiopia," 45.

107. "Woman," *NW*, June 9, 1923, 4.

108. See, for example, E. Almond, "A Feminine Conception of Woman," *NW*, December 10, 1921, 6.

109. Saydee E. Parham, "The New Woman," *NW*, February 2, 1924, 10; Eunice Lewis, "The Black Woman's Part in Race Leadership," *NW*, April 19, 1924, 10. See also Lavinia D. M. Smith, "What does the Garvey Movement Mean to Negro Womanhood?" *NW*, August 20, 1921, 5; Marie Trent, "The Negro Woman's Call to Duty," *NW*, November 15, 1924, 8.

110. Taylor, *Veiled Garvey*, 2.

111. *NW*, October 20, 1923, 2; *NW*, October 27, 1923, 2; *NW*, November 3, 1923, 2; Jacques Garvey, *Garvey and Garveyism*, 129–131. See also Taylor, *Veiled Garvey*, 55–56.

112. Amy Jacques Garvey, "The Hand That Rocks the Cradle," *NW*, July 5, 1924, 12; Jacques Garvey, "Our Women Getting into Larger Life," *NW*, July 12, 1924, 10; Jacques Garvey, "Women as Leaders Nationally and Racially," *NW*, October 24, 1925, 7; Jacques Garvey, "Woman's Function in Life," *NW*, December 19, 1925, 7; Jacques Garvey, "Black Women's Resolve for 1926," *NW*, January 9, 1926, 7.

113. Jacques Garvey, "Do Negro Women Want to Express Themselves?" *NW*, April 11, 1925, 7. For an extended discussion of the woman's page, see Taylor, *The Veiled Garvey*, 65–89.

114. The inaugural edition of "Our Women" (February 2, 1924), for example, carried articles on the Women's Party in New York; African ladies in fashion; the "New Mistress of 10 Downing Street"; recipes; suggestions for housewives; and Saydee Parham's article, mentioned above.

115. "Will the Entrance of Woman in Politics Affect Home Life?" *NW*, June 14, 1924, 12; "Does Education Keep Women from Marriage?" *NW*, March 14, 1925, 7; Article by Vida Horsford, *NW*, September 19, 1925, 7.

116. At the East Brooklyn Division, the Black Cross Nurses staged a debate with the resolution, "That Woman Has Contributed More to the Progress of the UNIA Than Men," with the women's side coming out on top, 19–18. *NW*, November 14, 1931.

117. Convention Reports, MGP, 4:1037–38.

118. Mrs. Lillian Willis, in *NW*, November 17, 1923, 3; "Convention Reports," MGP, 4:1038; Issa, "Universal," 163–64; Rolinson, *Grassroots Garveyism*, 121–22, 214–15; "News and Views, Atlanta," *NW*, January 15, 1927, 8; *NW*, June 2, 1928, 4.

119. Rolinson, *Grassroots Garveyism*, 121–22. For Ethel Collins, see *NW*, April 7, 1928, 3; *Negro World*, April 6, 1929, 2. For a brief biography of Collins, see MGP, 6:573.

120. Harry D. Gulley to J. E. Hoover, 26 January 1923, in *Federal Surveillance of Afro-Americans*, reel 2, frame 474; "Convention Reports," MGP, 4:1003, 1038; Harold, *Rise and Fall*, 22.

121. See *NW*, February 26, 1921, 3; Henrietta Vinton Davis, "A Brief Sketch of the Work of Harriet Tubman," *NW*, January 3, 1925, 8; Vinton Davis, Article on Sojourner Truth, in *NW* January 17, 1925, 8; *NW* March 19, 1921, 3.

122. Henrietta Vinton Davis, "The Exigencies of Leadership," *NW*, October 17, 1925, 7.

123. *NW*, December 5, 1931, 3; *NW*, January 23, 1932, 1; *NW*, April 15, 1933, 2; *NW*, April 7, 1928, 3. See also Bair, "Renegotiating Liberty," 228–29. See also the helpful biography of M.L.T. De Mena in MGP, 6:117–18.

124. *NW*, October 16, 1926, 2; Speech by Marcus Garvey at the 1929 UNIA Convention, MGP, 7:317; *NW*, August 15, 1931, 3. See also Bair, "Renegotiating Liberty," 229.

125. M.L.T. De Mena, "Part Women Must Play in the Organization," *NW*, January 23, 1926, 7; De Mena, "Our Women," *NW*, October 31, 1925, 7.

126. As Winston James has noted, the decline of the UNIA was matched by an increase in female representation. At the Convention of 1921, only 12.8% of delegates were women; in 1924, the number had risen slightly, to 19.4%. But 1929, in contrast, women delegates represented 39.5% of the attendees, and by 1938, the number had grown to 49.1%. See James, *Holding Aloft*, 154.

127. Marcus Garvey, "Negro Women Most Loyal, Men Often Betray," *NW*, June 7, 1930, 1; Letter from T.E.C. Smith, *NW*, August 16, 1930, 4; "Letter from Samuel C. Clarke," *NW*, August 16, 1930, 4; Berniza De Mena, "Negro Women Teach Loyalty to Men!" *NW*, June 14, 1930, 6; Mrs. B. Stephens, "Ladies, Push Weak Men Up the Hill or Down the River," *NW*, August 16, 1930, 3.

128. *NW*, January 16, 1926.

CHAPTER SIX
BROADCAST ON THE WINDS

1. L. E. Skinner to Acting Chief Secretary, 8 January 1924, NAM, S2/98/23.

2. Report by A. A. Fenn, 10 October 1922, NAM, S2/72/23; M. Riviere to Assistant Superintendent, CID, 20 September 1923, NAM, S2/98/23; Meeting of the Milalongwe Planters' Association, 30 September 1923, S2/94/23.

3. R. Rankine to Lord Duke of Devonshire, 14 November 1923, NAM, S2/94/23.

4. Meeting of the Milalongwe Planters' Association, 30 September 1923, S2/94/23; Governor Bowring, Nyasaland, to Governor, Northern Rhodesia, 16 April 1924, NAM, S2/17/24; R.M. Antill to Williams, Resident, Neno, 8 October 1923 and Resident, Neno, to Chief Secretary, 9 October 1923. NAM, S2/20/23 Part 1; Report by Resident, Ncheu, 24 October 1923, NAM, 1/18/15.

5. Resident, Neno, to Chief Secretary, 9 October 1923. NAM, S2/20/23 Part 1; Report by A. A. Fenn, 10 October 1922, NAM, S2/72/23; M. Riviere to Assistant Superintendent, CID, 20 September 1923, NAM, S2/98/23; Meeting of the Milalongwe Planters' Association, 30 September 1923, S2/94/23.

6. Governor Bowring, Nyasaland, to Governor, Northern Rhodesia, 16 April 1924, NAM, S2/17/24; Governor, Nyasaland, to Lord Duke of Devonshire, 17 December 1923, NAM, S2/115/23.

7. "Watchtower" here refers to the independent African religious sect that splintered from—and operated independently of—the American-based Watch Tower Bible and Tract Society. Members of the African Watchtower have been referred to, variously, as "Watchtower" and as "Watch Tower." In the interest of clarity, in

this chapter I refer to the independent African movement as Watchtower, and the American- and South African-based movement as Watch Tower.

8.   George Shepperson, "Nyasaland and the Millennium," in *Millennial Dreams in Action: Studies in Revolutionary Religious Movements*, ed. Sylvia L. Thrupp (New York: Schocken Books, 1970), 153–54; Karen E. Fields, *Revival and Rebellion in Colonial Central Africa* (Princeton, NJ: Princeton University Press, 1985), 11–12.

9.   Sam K. K. Mwase, "Memorandum on Education, Watch Tower, and Market," NAZ, Sec2/436, vol. 1; Police Inspector's Report, 20 April 1933, NAZ, Sec2/434, vol. 1.

10.   Terence Ranger, "Religious Movements and Politics in Sub-Saharan Africa," *African Studies Review* 29, no. 2 (June, 1986): 1–69.

11.   William Beinart and Colin Bundy, *Hidden Struggles in Rural South Africa: Politics and Popular Movements in the Transkei and Eastern Cape, 1890–1930* (London: James Currey, 1987), 261; Jean Comaroff and John Comaroff, *Of Revelation and Revolution, Volume I: Christianity, Colonialism, and Consciousness in South Africa* (Chicago: University of Chicago Press, 1991), 17–18; Karen Fields, "On War: The Watchtower Episode of 1917–1919 in Colonial Northern Rhodesia," *The Journal of the Historical Society* 1, no.2/3 (Winter 2000/Spring 2001), 7.

12.   Ranger, "Religious Movements," 17.

13.   Captain J. E. Phillips, "Africa for Africans and Pan-Islam," 1917, PRO, WO/106/259.

14.   "Reuters Article," reprinted in *NW*, March 11, 1922, 10; Rudolf Asmis, "Africa—a World Problem," *NW*, March 18, 1922, 4; "Strong Anti-White Wave Sweeps Continent of Africa," *NW*, April 15, 1922, 3; Sir H. H. Johnson, "Our Rule in East Africa: A Grave Indictment; The Nduru Outrages; Stains on the British Record; Alienating the Negro," *Observer* 15 August 1920.

15.   The *Negro World* was banned throughout French West Africa on January 14, 1922. It was banned in Nyasaland (Malawi) on March 24, Nigeria in June, the Gambia in September, and the Gold Coast in December, all in 1922. In Sierra Leone, the paper was "strictly controlled," and only a few copies were allowed to circulate. In the Belgian Congo, officials were informally empowered to suppress Garveyite materials in mid-June, 1921; the *Negro World* was officially suppressed in April, 1922.

16.   See PRO, CO 533/294/32018; Nyasaland Register of Correspondence, 15 May 1923, CO 703/7; Register of Correspondence, Gold Coast, 17 May 1923, CO 343/28; Nigeria Correspondence, CO 583/118/34197; Acting Governor to Duke of Devonshire, Freetown, Sierra Leone, CO 267/600/28912.

17.   Governor, Sierra Leone, to Winston S. Churchill, 4 October 1922, PRO, CO 267/597/51419.

18.   Arnold Hughes, "Africa and the Garvey Movement in the Interwar Years," in *Garvey: Africa, Europe, and the Americas*, eds. Rupert Lewis and Maureen Warner-Lewis (Kingston, Jamaica: Institute of Social and Economic Research, 1986), 116; Tony Martin, *Race First: The Ideological and Organizational Struggles of Marcus Garvey and the Universal Negro Improvement Association* (Westport, CT: Greenwood Press, 1976), 114–16.

19.   For methods of smuggling the *Negro World* into colonies where it was banned, see Casely Hayford to J. E. Bruce, 24 November 1923, John Edward Bruce Papers, Group B, Box 2, Item 258, SC-NYPL; Casely Hayford to J. R. Ralph Casimir,

10 January 1925, in J. R. Ralph Casimir Papers, Sc MG 110, Box 1, Folder 8, Manuscripts, Archives and Rare Book Division, SC-NYPL; Report by Pierre Didelot, Saint-Louis to Governor-General of French West Africa, c. August 1922, MGP, 2:582.

20. Marcus Garvey at Liberty Hall, *NW*, April 14, 1923, 2; Speech by Marcus Garvey, July 23, 1922, in MGP 4:745; S. A. Haynes in *NW*, August 20, 1927, 4; Marcus Garvey at Liberty Hall, *NW*, April 14, 1923, 2, 10; S. A. Haynes at Liberty Hall, *NW*, September 15, 1928, 4.

21. Letter from Moses Mphahlele, *NW*, January 20, 1926, 8; Letter from Frank Mothiba, *NW*, July 11, 1925, 10; *Abantu Batho*, March 17, 1927, reprinted in *Negro World*, April 30, 1927, 2.

22. Letter from the Editor, *African World*; Article by James Theale in the *African Voice*, 22 September 1923; Editorials in the *African World*, 23 May 1925 and 13 June 1925. In MGP, 10: 119, 308–9, 312–13.

23. "Editorial by Marcus Garvey, and Comment, in the *African World*," MGP, 10:331–34. The article appeared in the *Negro World* in the July 4, 1925 edition, and is misidentified as Marcus Garvey's by both the *African World* and the Marcus Garvey Papers.

24. Letter from F. J. Smith, *NW*, January 26, 1929, 1; Agent's Report on Meeting of the ANC, 8 June 1923, MGP, 10:73–74; Robert A. Hill and Gregory A. Pirio, "'Africa for the Africans': the Garvey Movement in South Africa, 1920–1940," in *The Politics of Race, Class and Nationalism in Twentieth-Century South Africa*, eds. Shula Marks and Stanley Trapido (London: Longman, 1987), 211; Vinson, "Sea Kaffirs," 288–90; D.D.T. Jabavu, "Native Unrest in Soiuth Africa," *International Review of Missions* 19, no. 42 (April, 1922): 250.

25. James T. Campbell, *Songs of Zion: the African Methodist Episcopal Church in the United States and South Africa* (New York: Oxford University Press, 1995), 81–83, 126–37, 301–2; Vinson, "Sea Kaffirs," 288–89.

26. Robert Edgar, "The Prophet Motive: Enoch Mgijima, the Israelites, and the Background to the Bulhoek Massacre," *International Journal of African Historical Studies* 15, no. 3 (1982): 419–20; Sean Redding, *Sorcery and Sovereignty: Taxation, Power, and Rebellion in South Africa, 1880–1963* (Athens: Ohio University Press, 2006), 20; Karen E. Fields, *Revival*, 6, 147; Sean Redding, "'Maybe Freedom Will Come to You': Christian Prophecies and Rumors in the Development of Rural Resistance in South Africa, 1948–1961," *Journal of Religion in Africa* 40 (2010): 164–69; Wyatt MacGaffey, *Custom and Government in the Lower Congo* (Berkeley: University of California Press, 1970), 250–58.

27. For Mgijima's Isrealite movement, see chapter Three. For the prophetess Nontetha, see Robert R. Edgar and Hilary Sapire, *African Apocalypse: The Story of Nontetha Nkwenkwe, a Twentieth-Century South African Prophet* (Athens, OH: Ohio University Center for International Studies, 2000).

28. Robert Edgar, "Garveyism in Africa: Dr. Wellington and the American Movement in the Transkei," *Ufahamu* 6.3 (1976): 34; Vinson, "Sea Kaffirs," 293.

29. Edgar, "Garveyism in Africa," 35–36.

30. Report of Speech by Ernest Wallace, 23 December 1925, MGP, 10:351–52.

31. Edgar, "Garveyism in Africa," 40–41; Robert Trent Vinson, *The Americans Are Coming! Dreams of African American Liberation in Segregationist South Africa* (Athens:

Ohio University Press, 2012), 103–4; Speech by Wellington, 15 August 1928, in MGP, 10:430.

32.   Wellington visited Nontetha in an attempt to win her adherents to his cause. See Clifton C. Crais, "Representation and the Politics of Identity in South Africa: An Eastern Cape Example," *International Journal of African Historical Studies* 25, no. 1 (1992): 117.

33.   Vinson, *Americans Are Coming!*, 108–9; Articles by Rev. J. G. Locke against Wellington Movement, 23 October—20 November, 1928, in MGP, 10:737–39.

34.   Edgar, "Garveyism in Africa," 41–42; Vinson, *Americans Are Coming!*, 109–18; Helen Bradford, *A Taste of Freedom: The ICU in Rural South Africa, 1924–1930* (New Haven, CT: Yale University Press, 1987), 217; Redding, *Sorcery*, 123–39.

35.   Bradford, *Taste of Freedom*, 62, 113.

36.   Bradford, *Taste of Freedom*, 8, 12–13; George Fredrickson, *Black Liberation: A Comparative History of Black Ideologies in the United States and South Africa* (New York: Oxford University Press, 1995), 171.

37.   Clements Kadalie, *My Life and the ICU: The Autobiography of a Black Trade Unionist in South Africa* (New York: The Humanities Press, 1970), 99–100, 220; Vinson, "Sea Kaffirs," 297–99.

38.   Quoted in Bradford, *Taste of Freedom*, 216.

39.   Bradford, *Taste of Freedom*, 126–27; W. D. Cingo to *Kokstad Advertiser*, 30 September 1927, in MGP, 10:407.

40.   Bradford, *Taste of Freedom*, 127, 93–94.

41.   For an explicit evocation of Garvey by an ICU organizer, see Alfred Mnika, cited in Beinart and Bundy, *Hidden Struggles*, 283; Gilbert Coka, cited in Hill and Pirio, "Africa for the Africans," 215.

42.   Robert Edgar, interview with Mary Jali, Ndindwa Location, Middledrift, 27 April 1974, in Edgar, "Garveyism in Africa," 37–38; Interview with Gqambuleni et al., 25 March 1977, quoted in Bradford, *Taste of Freedom*, 218.

43.   Bradford, *Taste of Freedom*, 214–37.

44.   W. D. Cingo to the *Kokstad Advertiser*, ca. 30 September 1927, MGP, 10: 407.

45.   For a discussion of Watch Tower beliefs, see Fields, *Revival*, 91–98; George Shepperson and Thomas Price, *Independent Africa: John Chilembwe and the Origins, Setting and Significance of the Nyasaland Native Rising of 1915* (Edinburgh: Edinburgh University Press, 1958), 151–52.

46.   Kamwana is quoted in Shepperson and Price *Independent African*, 156. See also Fields, *Revival*, 99–127; Sholto Cross, "The Watch Tower Movement in South Central Africa, 1908–1945" (PhD diss., Oxford University, 1973), 53.

47.   The movement did not disappear, however. See Cross, "Watch Tower," 75–81.

48.   Annual Report on Native Affairs for Northern Rhodesia, 31 March 1920, NAZ, Annual Reports, 1911–26, Box 1, Government Publications; Cross, "The Watch Tower Movement in South Central Africa," 192; Fields, *Revival*, 134–35; Karen Fields, "On War," 8.

49.   Fields, "On War," 3; Cross, "Watch Tower," 194; Fields, *Revival*, 138; P. E. Hall, "Memorandum," 13 March 1926, NAZ, RC/388.

50.   G. C. Latham to Chief Secretary, 4 April 1923, PRO, CO 795/1/32378.

51.   Father Tanguy, quoted in Cross, "Watch Tower," 197.

52. Summary of Events in Tanganyika District, c. 1919, and Draper to Administrator, Livingstone, 19 January 1919, NAM, S2/11/19; Annual Report of Native Affairs, 31 March 1919, NAZ, Annual Reports, 1911–26, Box 1, Government Publications; Fields, "On War," 3, 11–12; Cross, "Watch Tower," 197–200; Fields, *Revival*, 152–54.

53. Fields, *Revival*, 203–4.

54. Sholto Cross, "Watch Tower," 136. For Kunga, see also "Testimony of George Kunga," 16 May 1923, NAM, S2/54/23; T. O. Ranger, *The African Voice in Southern Rhodesia, 1898–1930* (Evanston, IL: Northwestern University, 1970), 200–201.

55. Memo to Taggart, SNA, 26 May 1924, NAZ, ZA 1/10; Report by D.M. Kennedy, 30 July 1931, NAZ, Sec2/434, vol. 1; Sholto Cross, "Social History and Millennial Movements: the Watch Tower in South Central Africa," *Social Compass* 24, no. 1 (1977): 175.

56. Testimony of Mubakasa, NAZ, KSM 3/1/1: "Enquiry, Watch Tower Activities in Mrushi Sub-District, 1925–1926"; J. Moffat Thomson, "Summary of Events," PRO, CO 795/11/4881; Fields, *Revival*, 163–92.

57. Extract from Patrol Report, Ndola, 24 September 1925, NAZ, ZA 1/10.

58. J. B. Thomson to Provincial Commissioner, 6 June 1931; "Quarterly Report, Mweru-Luapula Province," 10 June 1931; J.O. Talbot Phibbs, Report on Evidence of Watch Tower, Fort Jameson, 9 June 1932, all in NAZ, Sec 2/434, vol. 1; "Notes on the 'Kitawala' Movement in the Belgian Congo and Northern Rhodesia made by British Vice Consul, Elizabethville," January 1932, NAZ, ZA 1/15/M/1; John Hawkins, Assistant Inspector, Northern Rhodesia Police, 12 September 1935, NAZ, Sec2/436, Volume 2.

59. Shepperson, "Nyasaland," 145. See also Fields, *Revival*, 11, 194. Among the possessions of a group of Watchtower members from Moero-Luapula Province, deported from the Belgian Congo for spreading prophecies about the arrival of American Negroes and the throwing of whites in the sea, was a copy of Edwin W. Smith's *Aggrey of Africa*. See H. G. Willis, British Vice Consul, 9 January 1932, NAZ, ZA /15/M/1.

60. This was also the case when Aggrey visited South Africa at the behest of the Phelps-Stokes Commission. As his biographer, Edwin Smith, writes, "Aggrey was supposed by some to be the herald of an invading band of Negroes—they thought all Americans were Negroes—who would drive the whites of South Africa into the sea." Quoted in Hill and Pirio, "Africa for the Africans," 228–29.

61. Assistant Secretary to Chief Secretary, 26 June 1923, NAM, S2/71/23.

62. As Michael O. West, "The Seeds are Sown: The Impact of Garveyism in Zimbabwe in the Interwar Years," *International Journal of African Historical Studies* 35, no. 2/3 (2002): 338.

63. Provincial Commissioner, Southern Province, to Chief Secretary, 6 October 1923, NAM, S2/101/23; Report by the Resident, Ncheu, 24 October 1923, NAM, NC 1/18/15; Resident, Karonga, to PC, Northern Province, 24 November 1923, NAM, S2/1/24; Report by A. A. Fenn, 10 October 1922, NAM, S2/72/23.

64. See, for example, Keith, Acting Director of Education, to Chief Secretary, Mazabuka, 18 August 1931, NAZ, Sec2/434, vol. 1. A high proportion of these migrants were skilled and literate, and held relatively good jobs. See Cross, "Social History," 87–88.

65.   Lott Nondo, a prominent participant in the attempt to form a centralized Watchtower movement along the Northern Rhodesia rail line (see below), was believed to be receiving literature from, and in communication with, Marcus Garvey. B. Farrant to Assistant Superintendent in Charge, CID, 14 June 1933, and CID to Secretary of Native Affairs, 30 June 1933, NAZ, Sec2/1175.

66.   For Garveyist organizing, see Report by CID, Cape Town, 22 January 1923, and Report by Alberto Pais, Beira, 23 February 1923, NAZ, KDD 1/4/1; Acting Principal Immigration Officer to Acting Chief Secretary, 17 May 1923 and Confidential Report on Isa Macdonald Lawrence, NAM, S2/50/23. For Watchtower radicalism in PEA, see R. M. Antill to Williams, Resident, 8 October 1923, NAM, S2/20/23 Part I; Meeting of the Milalongwe Planters' Association, 30 Sept 1923, NAM, S2/94/23; M. Riviere to Asst. Superintendent, CID, Zomba, 20 September 1923, NAM, S2/98/23; Cross, "Watch Tower," 230.

67.   Luise White, *Speaking with Vampires: Rumor and History in Colonia Africa* (Berkeley: University of California Press, 2000), 6.

68.   Fields makes this wonderful suggestion, but does not explore its implications. See *Revival*, 12.

69.   White, *Speaking*, 63. See also Luise White, "Vampire Priests of Central Africa: African Debates about Labor and Religion in Colonial Northern Zambia," *Comparative Studies in Society and History* 35, no. 4 (October 1993): 746–72; Ann Laura Stoler, "'In Cold Blood': Hierarchies of Credibility and the Politics of Colonial Narratives," *Representations* 37 (Winter 1992): 151–89.

70.   C.A. Cardew to Major Stephens, 4 April 1923, NAM, NC 1/18/15.

71.   Memo from Governor, 21 October 1922, NAM, NC, 1/18/14; Cardew to Stephens, 4 April 1923, NAM, NC 1/18/15.

72.   Confidential Circular to All District Officials, 11 February 1926, NAZ, RC/715.

73.   In November 1923, as rumors of a native rising swirled, Governor Rankine proposed a "Native Missions Ordinance" that would either bring the Watchtower under European control or suppress the movement entirely. The proposal was rejected in London. R. Rankine, Acting Governor, to Lord Duke of Devonshire, Secretary of State for the Colonies, 14 November 1923, NAM, S2/94/23.

74.   Note by Governor, 21 October 1922; Note by Acting Provincial Commissioner, Lilongwe, 25 May 1922. NAM, NC 1/18/14; Report by Resident, Chiradzulu, 1 October 1923; Report by Resident, Zomba, 26 September 1923. NAM, S2/101/23; Thomas A. Walder to Chief Secretary, Cape Town, 21 August 1926, NAM, S2/12/25; H.J. Hudson to District Magistrate, Blantyre, April 1926, NAM, S2/8/24. By 1935, the WTBTS had less than four hundred recognized members in Nyasaland; unrecognized Watchtower members numbered in the thousands. See Report by F. T. Stephens, Commissioner of Police, Nyasaland, 22 November 1935, NAZ, Sec2/434.

75.   Confidential Report from the Resident, Blantyre, 20 September 1923, NAM, S2/101/23.

76.   Fields, *Revival*, 225.

77.   Thomas A. Walder to Tagart, 21 November 1925, NAZ, KDE 2/16/3; Letter from George R. Phillips, 14 September 1932, NAZ, RC/1247.

78.   Report of the Secretary for Native Affairs, Year Ending 31 March 1925, NAM, S2/4/26.

79. Cross, "Watch Tower," 271–79; Cecil Arnott to CID Livingstone, 14 September 1929, NAZ, Sec2/1172; J. Moffat Thomson to Chief Secretary, 29 February 1928, NAZ, RC/1216; Assistant Superintendent, Livingstone, to Commissioner of Police, 20 May 1933, NAZ, Sec2/1173.

80. Cecil Arnott to CID Livingstone, 14 September 1929, NAZ, Sec2/1172; Testimony relating to Watch Tower Activities, Ndola Sub-District, c. 1927, NAZ, Sec2/1174 Part 1.

81. Testimony relating to Watch Tower Activities, Ndola Sub-District, c. 1927, NAZ, Sec2/1174 Part 1; Sworn Testimony in the Case against Jeremiah Gondwe, NAZ, Sec2/1172.

82. See the annual Reports Upon Native Affairs in Northern Rhodesia, 1926–29, NAZ, Government Publications, Box 2: African Affairs, Annual Reports, 1927–34.

83. Cecil Arnott to CID Livingstone, 14 September 1929, NAZ, Sec2/1172; Assistant Superintendent, Livingstone, to Commissioner of Police, 20 May 1933, NAZ, Sec2/1175; Cross, "Watch Tower," 279; Sholto Cross, "A Prophet Not Without Honour: Jeremiah Gondwe," in *African Perspectives: Papers in the History, Politics and Economics of Africa Presented to Thomas Hodgkin*, eds. Christopher Allen and R.W. Johnson (London: Cambridge University Press, 1970), 172.

84. Police Inspector's Report on Watch Tower Preaching, Broken Hill, 20 April 1932, NAZ , Sec2/343, vol. 1; Reports Upon Native Affairs in Northern Rhodesia, 1931 and 1932, NAZ, Government Publications, Box 2: African Affairs, Annual Reports, 1927–34; Cross, "Watch Tower," 352–53, 361.

85. Provincial Commissioner, Lusaka, to Chief Secretary, 11 March 1932; Report by Jacob Ngulube, through Isaac Muwamba; Police Inspector's Report, Broken Hill, 20 April 1932. In NAZ , Sec2/343, vol. 1.

86. Police Inspector's Report, Broken Hill, 20 April 1932; Report by Native Detective Petros Mukamba, 15 April 1932. Both in NAZ , Sec2/343, Vol. 1; *Rex v. Joseph Sibakwe*, 1932, NAZ, Sec2/1174 Part 2.

87. Sibakwe certainly was not influenced by J. F. Rutherford or the WTBTS on this point. In Rutherford's *The Final War*, which Sibakwe carried with him, Nimrod is charged with building Babel under the supervision of Satan and in defiance of God, thus precipitating "the very inception of the Devil's earthly organization." See J. F. Rutherford, *The Final War*, pamphlet in NAZ, Sec2/434, vol. 4.

88. *Report of the Commission Appointed to Enquire into the Disturbances in the Copperbelt* (Lusaka: Government Printer, 1935), 19; Testimony of John Smith Moffat, *Evidence Taken by Commission Appointed to Enquire into the Disturbances in the Copperbelt, Northern Rhodesia*, 2 vols. (Lusaka: Government Printer, 1935), 284–85.

89. E. H. Goodall, Provincial Commissioner's Report on the Native Disturbances, NAZ, Sec1/1359 vol. 2.

90. *Report of the Commission*, 16, 49; Cross, "Watch Tower," 381–88; Ian Henderson, "Early African Leadership: The Copperbelt Disturbances of 1935 and 1940," *Journal of Southern African Studies* 2, no. 1 (October 1975): 90; Frederick Cooper, *Decolonization and African Society: The Labor Question in French and British Africa* (Cambridge: Cambridge University Press, 1996), 58.

91. Cross, "Watch Tower," 376–78; CID, Livingstone, to Secretary of Native Affairs, 30 June 1933, NAZ, Sec2/1175.

92. Report by DC, Fort Jameson, 18 June 1935; EBH Goodall to Dundas, 29 June 1935. Both in NAZ, Sec2/434, vol. 2; Cross, "Watch Tower," 385; *Evidence Taken by Commission*, 339–43, 398–405.

93. Testimony of Sam Kawinga Kamchacha Mwase, 2 September 1935; Testimony of Eliti Tuli Phili, *Evidence Taken by Commission*, 753–58; Letter posted at Nkana Beer Hall, 5 April 1935 (translated from Chiwemba), NAZ, Sec1/1359, Vol. 2; Cross, "Watch Tower," 386–88.

94. Ranger, *African Voice*, 141.

95. Cooper, *Decolonization*.

96. C.L.R. James, *A History of Negro Revolt* (London: Fact International, 1938), 81.

Chapter Seven
The Visible Horizon

1. Muwamba to Mackenzie-Kennedy, 16 May 1923, NAZ, S2/71/23.

2. Muwamba to Mackenzie-Kennedy, 16 May 1923, and D. Mackenzie, "Interview with Isaac Clements Muwamba," NAZ, S2/71/23; Isaac C.K. Muwamba to Chief Secretary, 25 January 1929, NAZ, S1/1180/28; Karen E. Fields, *Revival and Rebellion in Colonial Central Africa* (Princeton, NJ: Princeton University Press, 1985), 231.

3. Assistant Secretary to Chief Secretary, 26 June 1923, NAZ, S2/71/23; "Richard Goode to Sir Arthur Frederick," MGP, 10:61; Clements Kadalie to E. Alexander Muwamba, 29 April 1923, and Clements Kadalie to Isaac Clements Katongo II, 2 May 1923, NAZ, S2/71/23.

4. Assistant Secretary to Chief Secretary, 26 June 1923, and Mackenzie-Kennedy to Secretary, 31 May 1923, NAZ, S2/71/23.

5. Most evocative of this is Muwamba's fascinating, garbled account of the UNIA's activities during his interview with Mackenzie-Kennedy. D. Mackenzie-Kennedy to Secretary, 31 May 1923, NAZ, S2/71/23.

6. Native Welfare Associations were most commonly referred to in Nyasaland as simply "Native Associations," and sometimes as "African Associations." In the interests of consistency, below I will use "Welfare Association" to refer to Associations in both Nyasaland and Northern Rhodesia.

7. Indirect rule was formally implemented in Northern Rhodesia in 1930, and in Nyasaland in 1933, but official recognition merely codified existing colonial practice. See Fields, *Revival*, 39.

8. Scholars have, to say the least, disagreed with this judgment. For a cogent analysis of the ways in which colonial authorities reconstituted tribal hierarchies and authority in the interests of administrative efficiency and domination over the African peasantry, see Mahmood Mamdani, *Citizen and Subject: Contemporary Africa and the Legacy of Late Colonialism* (Princeton, NJ: Princeton University Press, 1996), especially Chapter 1.

9. Frederick Lugard, *The Dual Mandate in British Tropical Africa* (London: Frank Cass & Co., 1922), 197.

10. Mamdani, *Citizen*, 50.

11. Mamdani, *Citizen*, 3–4.

12. Fields, *Revival*, 59–60.

13. Mamdani, *Citizen*, 6, 90.

14. J. Van Velsen, "Some Early Pressure Groups in Malawi," in *The Zambesian Past: Studies in Central African History*, eds. Eric Stokes and Richard Brown (Manchester: University of Manchester Press, 1966), 381; Roger Tangri, "Inter-war 'Native Associations' and the Formation of the Nyasaland African Congress," *Transafrican Journal of History* 1 no. 1 (1971): 85–86; David J. Cook, "Influence of Livingstonia Mission upon Formation of Welfare Associations in Zambia, 1912–31," in *Themes in the Christian History of Central Africa*, eds. T. O. Ranger and John Weller (Berkeley: University of California Press, 1975); Robert I. Rotberg, *The Rise of Nationalism in Central Africa: The Making of Malawi and Zambia 1873–1964* (Cambridge, MA: Harvard University Press, 1965), 116.

15. NAZ, Annual Reports, 1911–26, Box 1, Government Publications, Annual Report, 31 March 1922; Lugard, *Dual Mandate*, 195, 81; Cameron, quoted in Mamdani, *Citizen*, 80.

16. Annual Reports on Native Affairs, 1918 and 1920, NAZ, Annual Reports, 1911–26, Box 1, Government Publications.

17. Captain J. E. Phillips, "Africa for Africans and Pan-Islam," 1917, PRO, WO/106/259; Acting Chief Secretary, to All Residents, 4 May 1922, NAM, S2/30/20. The *Negro World* was officially listed as a prohibited publication in March 1922.

18. "North Nyasa Native Association, 1919–1935," NAM, S1/1481/19. Founded in 1912, the NNNA held only three meetings before the outbreak of the war.

19. "Constitution of the West Nyasa Native Association," 15 January 1920, NAM S1/2065/19

20. James R. Hooker, "Welfare Associations and Other Instruments of Accommodation in the Rhodesias between the World Wars," *Comparative Studies in Society and History* 9, no. 1 (Oct. 1966): 56; Roger K. Tangri, "The Rise of Nationalism in Colonial Africa: The Case of Colonial Malawi," *Comparative Studies in Society and History* 10, no. 2 (1968): 48, 51; Rotberg, *Rise of Nationalism*, 123, 116.

21. James C. Scott, *Weapons of the Weak: Everyday Forms of Peasant Resistance* (New Haven, CT: Yale University Press, 1985), 29; Scott, *Domination and the Arts of Resistance: Hidden Transcripts* (New Haven, CT: Yale University Press, 1990), 14; Frederick Cooper, *Colonialism in Question: Theory, Knowledge, History* (Berkeley: University of California Press, 2005), 236.

22. Levi Z. Mumba, "Native Associations in Nyasaland," *Zo Ona* (Blantyre), 24 April 1924, 1.

23. See Report from East Luangwa Province, c. 1931, NAZ, Sec2/433; "An Ordinance to Regulate the Establishment and Operations of Missions in Nyasaland," 1925, NAM S2/30/24.

24. Rotberg, *Rise of Nationalism*, 9.

25. UNIA divisions attracted mission-educated clerks, traders, educators, journalists, and skilled workers from British Africa, and economically successful migrants from the West Indies. See, for example, G. O. Olusanya, "Notes Lagos Branch of the Universal Negro Improvement Association," *Journal of Business and Social Studies (Lagos)* 1 (1970): 135; R. L. Okonkwo, "The Garvey Movement in British West Africa," *The Journal of African History* 21, no. 1 (1980): 107–13.

26. G. H. Walker to Secretary, Southern Province, Lagos, 29 March 1922, PRO, CO 583/109/28194. See also Patriarch J. G. Campbell in the *Times of Nigeria*, 8 November 1920, in MGP, 10:709.

27. Exhibit "D": British West African Conference (March 1920), Supporting Speech by Hon. Casely Hayford, PRO, CO 554/54/1512; Kobina Sekyi, "The Parting of the Ways," MGP, 10:354, italics removed.

28. Okonkwo, "Garvey Movement," 114. Part of the appeal of Garveyism, explained a Nigerian supporter, was that the movement did not demand uniform action but rather allowed its divisions "to arrange their own plan to suit their respective conditions." In West Africa, this meant eliminating "impracticable" political stridency and favoring "works of general improvement." "Mr. Rambler" in the *Times of Nigeria*, 8 November 1920, MGP, 10:707.

29. "Letter from Fitzherbert Headly," *NW*, October 8, 1921, 11; Gregory Pirio, "The Role of Garveyism in the Making of Namibian Nationalism," in *Namibia 1884–1984: Readings on Namibia's History and Society*, ed. Brian Wood (London: Namibia Support Committee, 1988), 261.

30. Minutes of the Inaugural Meeting of Dakar Branch, UNIA, 7 May 1922, MGP, 9:418; Didelot to Governor General, FWA, 4 July 1922, MGP 9:506.

31. Headly to Hofmeyr, 2 February 1922, MGP, 9:348.

32. A. G. Hopkins, "Economic Aspects of Political Movements in Nigeria and in the Gold Coast, 1918–1939," *The Journal of African History* 7, no. 1 (1966): 133–36; Duffield, "Pan-Africanism, Rational and Irrational," 608–11; Alex Harneit-Sievers, "African Business, 'Economic Nationalism,' and British Colonial Policy: Southern Nigeria, 1935–1954," *African Economic History* 24 (1996): 25–30.

33. "Article in the *West African Mail and Trade Gazette*," 24 September 1921, in MGP, 10:718; J. Ayodele Langley, *Pan-Africanism and Nationalism in West Africa, 1900–1945* (London: Oxford University Press, 1973), 91–92.

34. "Right Oh!" to John E. Bruce, Lagos, 1 November 1920, SC-NYPL, John E. Bruce Papers, Group B, Box 2, Item 188; "Letter from Sierra Leone by 'Dorn,'" *NW*, March 26, 1921, 4.

35. "Report on Garveyite 'John Smith' in Cameroon," 9 July 1923, MGP, 10:93–95.

36. Agbebi to Bruce, 15 May 1920, SC-NYPL, John E. Bruce Papers, Group B, Box 2, Item 258.

37. *NW*, March 17, 1923, 1.

38. Report of Speech by Ernest Wallace, 23 December 1925, MGP, 10:351–52; Report by Native Corporal Jacob, MGP, 9:671; "Mr Rambler" in the *Times of Nigeria*, 8 November 1920, MGP, 10:707.

39. Marcus Garvey, "The Silent Work that Must be Done," 16 November 1924, MGP, 6:44; *NW*, April 14, 1923, 2.

40. Fitz H. Headley [*sic*], "Hon. Marcus Garvey Has Made Africans Think Black," *NW*, April 11, 1925, 2; Letter from Headly to Mr. Barnabas, 25 January 1922, MGP, 9:320; Intercepted Letter from Headly to Hailand, 14 November 1922, MGP, 9:684; Speech by John Farmer and Toasts, MGP, 9:467.

41. Terence O. Ranger, *The African Voice in Southern Rhodesia* (London: Heinemann Educational, 1970), 139; Sholto Cross, "The Watch Tower Movement in South Central Africa, 1908–1945" (PhD diss., Oxford University, 1973), 39–40.

"Subversive" newspapers and pamphlets were smuggled north, wrapped inside other papers, packed into crates by workers at wholesale stores, or carried through informal channels like the "bicycle mail service" uncovered by a priest that linked Blantyre and Limbe with Mlanje at the border of Portuguese East Africa. Record of Lawrence Trial, 22 Sept 1926, High Court Blantyre, NAM S2/50/23; Helen Bradford, *A Taste of Freedom: The ICU in Rural South Africa, 1924–1930* (New Haven, CT: Yale University Press, 1987), 5; First Monthly Report on Watch Tower Activities, 12 October 1923, NAM S2/98/23. For the spread of newspapers, see Confidential Letter, Downing Street to Under Secretary of State, Foreign Office, 27 August 1920; Acting Chief Secretary to All Residents, 4 May 1922. NAM, S2/30/20; Assistant Superintendent, CID, to PC CP, Lilongwe, 21 April 1926, NAM, NC 1/23/1; Assistant Secretary, Livingstone, Northern Rhodesia, to Chief Secretary, Zomba, 26 June 1923, NAM S2/71/23; DC, Karonga, to PC, Northern Province, 27 January 1931, NAM, S1/1481/19.

42. Chinula quoted in Kings Phiri, "Afro-American Influence in Colonial Malawi, 1891–1945," in *Global Dimensions of the African Diaspora*, 2nd ed., ed. Joseph E. Harris (Washington, DC: Howard University Press, 1993), 399–400, 407–16.

43. Speech by Godwin Mukubesa, 18 April 1931; P. R. Jamin Silavwe to Secretary of Native Affairs, 12 February 1931; Moffat Thomson to Chief Secretary, 18 February 1931. NAZ, Sec2/442.

44. Robert Laws to Acting Chief Secretary, 18 January 1920, NAM, S1/2065/19.

45. As James C. Scott as observed, "It is in this no-man's land of feints, small attacks, probings to find weaknesses, and not in the rare frontal assault, that the ordinary battlefield lies.... The limits of the possible are encountered only in an empirical process of search and probing." Scott, *Domination*, 192–93.

46. Donald Mackenzie-Kennedy to all Provincial Commissioners, 4 September 1933, NAZ, Sec2/433; C. H. Wade, Official Position Regarding Recognition of Native Associations, 13 November 1926, NAM, NC/1/3/5; Secretary of Native Affairs to Chief Secretary, 25 August 1930, NAZ, Sec2/442.

47. Resident, Lilongwe, to Provincial Commissioner, Central Province, 13 December 1927, NAM, NC/1/3/2; Central Province Annual Reports, 1928–30, NAM, S1/566/29; Assistant Superintendent, CID, to PC, Central Province, 21 April 1926; PC, Central Province, to Commissioner of Police, 23 March 1926, NAM, NC 1/23/1.

48. Minutes of the Second Meeting of the Choma Native Welfare Association, 15 August 1931, NAZ, Sec2/454; Minutes of the Meeting of the Lusaka Native Welfare Association, 3 June 1931, NAZ, Sec2/453; Ernest Alexander Muwamba and E. H. Chunga to DC, Ndola, 1 June 1930, NAZ, Sec2/443; Minutes of the Meeting of the Native Welfare Association, Mazabuka Branch, 8 July 1930, NAZ, Sec2/444; Minutes of a Public General Meeting, LNWA, 5 March 1932, NAZ, ZA 1/9/45/1.

49. Minutes of Meeting, LNWA, March 1931, NAZ, Sec2/442; Minutes of Meeting, Central Province Universal Native Association, 19 November 1927, NAM, NC/1/3/2; Record of Interview Granted by Acting Governor to the Lusaka African Welfare Association, 8 October 1932, NAZ, Sec2/453.

50. Petition from Isaiah Murray Jere, RCNPNA, 29 December 1930, NAM, S1/1481/19; Minutes of Meeting, Central Province Universal Native Association, 10 December 1927; George Mwase, CPUNA, to Provincial Commissioner, Central Province, 28 March 1928. NAM, NC 1/3/2.

51. Minutes of Public Meeting, LNWA, 24 December 1932, NAZ, Sec2/442; LNWA to His Highness The Paramount Chief Yeta III, 2 October 1931, NAZ, Sec2/442; "Nyasaland Notes," *The Black Man*, (August 1920): 4; Minutes of Meeting, Lusaka Native Welfare Association, 10 November 1931, NAZ, Sec2/453; Minutes of Public Meeting, LNWA, 11 August 1933, NAZ, KDB 4/2/2. To open at least one meeting Association men sung the hymn "Nkosi Sikelel' iAfrika," sung at ICU and ANC meetings and, since 1996, South Africa's national anthem. Minutes of Meeting, Choma NWA, 15 October 1932, NAZ, Sec2/454.

52. Mumba is quoted in Roger Tangri, "Inter-war 'Native Associations,'" 88; Petition from Isaiah Murray Jere, RCNPNA, 29 December 1930, NAM, NC 1/3/4; Minutes of Meeting of the Native Welfare Association, Mazabuka Branch, 8 July 1930, NAZ, Sec2/444; Cook, "Influence of the Livingstonia Mission," 112, 114–15.

53. Moffat Thomson, 25 August 1933: The First General Meeting of the Representatives of the United African Welfare Association of Northern Rhodesia, NAZ, Sec2/453; DM Kennedy to All PCs, 4 Sept 1933, NAZ, Sec2/433.

54. Kennedy to All PCs, 4 Sept 1933, NAZ, Sec2/433

55. Keith Tucker to RCNPNA, 28 March 1934; DC to Secretary, WNNA, 15 July 1933, NAM, NC 1/3/5; Isaiah Murray Jere to Senior PC, Blantyre, 21 July 1934; Note by Chief Secretary, 4 June 1935; Information about Native Associations in Existence, June 1935. NAM, NC 1/3/6.

56. DC, Chinteche, to PC, Northern Province, 10 November 1934, NAM S2/20/23; L.M.S. Amery, Secretary of State for the Colonies, to C. C. Bowring, Governor, Nyasaland, 13 July 1925; Downing Street to Conference of Missionary Societies, September 1924. NAM S2/30/24.

57. Randall Burkett, *Garveyism as a Religious Movement: The Institutionalization of a Black Civil Religion* (Metuchen, NJ: Scarecrow Press, 1978), 5–7.

58. An African [Levi S. Mumba], "The Religion of My Fathers," *International Review of the Missions* 19, no. 75 (1930), 363–76.

59. "The African National Church," September 1940, NAZ, Sec2/412; African National Church, Mission School Reports, 1936 and 1937, NAM, NNK 1/4/1; Monica Wilson, *Communal Rituals of the Nyakyusa* (London: Oxford University Press, 1959), 195.

60. "Beliefs and Constitution of the African National Church," NAZ Sec2/412.

61. "Letter from a 'prominent' African worker in Bulawayo, Southern Rhodesia," *Workers Herald*, 12 January 1927, 5; "ICU Penetrates to Southern Rhodesia," *Workers Herald*, 18 March 1927, 5; Memo: "The African National Church," September 1940, NAZ, Sec 2/412; Michael O. West, "The Seeds are Sown: The Impact of Garveyism in Zimbabwe in the Interwar Years," *International Journal of African Historical Studies* 35, no. 2/3 (2002): 351. Because of the tremendous impact of Garveyism in 1920s South Africa, and the perception that Aggrey was an African American, many Africans believed Aggrey—who toured Africa as a member of the Phelps-Stokes Commission, and was a vocal opponent of the UNIA—to be a Garveyite. See Bradford, *Taste of Freedom*, 215.

62. John Parratt, "Y.Z. Mwasi and the Origins of the Blackman's Church," *Journal of Religion in Africa* 9, no. 3 (1978): 193–97.

63. Minutes from Meeting, WNNA, 1–2 May 1929, NAM S1/2065/19; "WNNA Replies to Request of Government to substantiate its minutes of May Meeting," 29

October 1929, NAM S1/2065/19; Yesaya Mwasi, Welcome Letter to the New Governor, Sir Hubert Winthrop Young, 20 April 1933, NC 1/3/5.

64. Minutes of Meeting, WNNA, 9 February 1929, NAM, S1/2065/19; Stephens to Acting Chief Secretary, 5 May 1922, NAM, S2/30/20; Report, Native-Controlled Missions, 27 September 1926, NAM, S2/8/24; "Nyasaland Notes," *Black Man* (August 1920): 4; Rotberg, *Rise of Nationalism*, 150; Report on Watch Tower and Native-Controlled Missions, 16 November 1926. NAM, S2/50/23; "WNNA Replies to Request of Government to substantiate its minutes of May Meeting," 29 October 1929, NAM S1/2065/19.

65. Y. Z. Mwasi, "My Essential and Paramount Reasons for Working Independently," 1933, NAM, 84/BCAP/1/1 (a–d).

66. Mwasi, "My Essential and Paramount Reasons …" NAM, 84/BCAP/1/1 (a–d); Martin Chanock, "The New Men Revisited: An Essay on the Development of Political Consciousness in Colonial Malawi," in *From Nyasaland to Malawi: Studies in Colonial History*, ed. Roderick J. Macdonald (Nairobi: East African Publishing House, 1975), 251–52.

67. The Nyasaland Blackman's Educational Society, 18 August 1934; PC, Northern Province, Note, 13 December 1934; Report on Rev. Y. Mwase [*sic*], CID, Livingstone, Northern Rhodesia, Report on Rev. Y. Mwase, 21 February 1935. NAM, NN 1/19/4.

68. Note, PC, Northern Province, 13 December 1934; Hall, Chief Secretary, to PC, Northern Province, 29 January 1935. NAM, NN 1/19/4.

69. Charles Chinula to DC Mzimba, 5 July 1934, NAM, NN 1/19/4; DC, Karonga, to PC, Northern Province, 3 July 1934, NAM, NN 1/19/4; Chinula to DC Mzimba, 7 February 1935, NAM, NNM 1/13/2; Parratt, "Y.Z. Mwasi," 202.

70. Police Report, Native-Controlled Missions, 7 June 1938, NAM, S2/20/23 Part II; DC, Karonga, Report on Native-Controlled Missions, 18 Jan 1936; DC, Karonga, Report on NC Missions, 1937, NAM, NN 1/19/4

71. Daniel S. Malekebu, "A Plea for Africa," (unpublished, 1918), in NAM, S2/17/20; George Shepperson and Thomas Price, *Independent African: John Chilembwe and the Origins, Setting and Significance of the Nyasaland Native Rising of 1915* (Edinburgh: EdinburghUniversity Press, 1958), 127–42.

72. Malekebu, "Plea for Africa," NAM, S2/17/20.

73. Stephens to Chief Secretary, 28 July 1924, NAM S2/28/24.

74. Andrew Mkuliche, Jackson Chiwayula, and Isaac Chambo to Chief Secretary, 16 June 1924, NAM, S2/22/34. Isa M. Lawrence, writing to James East, suggested that the men had "risked their lives" by approaching the Chief Secretary and pleading with him to allow the reopening of PIM. Lawrence to Dr. D.S. Malekebu, July 1924, NAM, S2/28/24.

75. Police Report, 25 March 1932, NAM, S2/20/23; I.M. Lawrence to Dr. J.E. East, 22 December 1921, NAM, S2/50/23. Mkulichi, Chambo and Kampingo were all sentenced to death for their involvement in the Chilembwe rebellion, and all had their sentences subsequently commuted.

76. Resident, Neno, to Chief Secretary and PC, Blantyre, 9 October 1933 NAM, S2/20/23 Part I; Report made by Detective on Watch Tower Society in Lilongwe and Dedza Districts, 14 November 1922, NAM, NC 1/18/14; George Simeon Mwase, *Strike a Blow and Die: A Narrative of Race Relations in Colonial Africa by George Simeon*

Mwase, ed. Robert I. Rotberg (c. 1932; Cambridge, MA: Harvard University Press, 1970), 36; Clements Kadalie to Isa M. Lawrence, 4 April 1925, NAM, S2/8/24.

77.   I. M. Lawrence to Rev. J. E. East, 22 Dec 1921; Confidential Report on Isa Macdonald Lawrence, 1926, NAM, S2/50/23; Lawrence to Malekebu, July 1924; Stephens to Chief Secretary, 28 July 1924, NAM, S2/28/24.

78.   Confidential Report on Isa M. Lawrence, 1926, NAM, S2/50/23; Stephens to Chief Secretary, 28 July 1924, NAM, S2/28/24; Reports by Police, 1924–30, NAM, S2/8/24; Record of Lawrence Trial, 22 September 1926, NAM, S2/50/23.

79.   Police Report on Watch Tower and Native Missions, 1925; John B. Lawrence to I. M. Lawrence, 24 February 1925; J.B.C. Lawrence to Alex M. Sisseo, Quelimane, 16 April 1926; J.B.C. Lawrence to Sisseo, 11 January 1926; Kadalie to Lawrence, 4 April 1925; Police Report, 13 March 1926. NAM, S2/8/24.

80.   J.B.C. Lawrence to Isa M. Lawrence, c/o Ruth Lawrence, PIM, 16 Feb 1927, NAM, S2/8/24; Clements Kadalie to Colonel L.S. Amery, MP, Colonial Secretary, 15 March 1927 and 20 October 1926, NAM, S2/50/23; *Workers Herald*, 18 March 1927, 3; Editorial in the *Negro World*, in MGP, 10:385.

81.   As early as 1924, when it looked likely that Malekebu would return to Nyasaland, officials were noting the importance of watching his movements and actions carefully. Undercover agents attended PIM services, and Malekebu's movements were "unobtrusively observed." Despite the difficulty of keeping African detectives near Chiradzulu without coming under suspicion, the CID maintained a close watch on PIM for at least two years after its restoration. See "Report on Watch Tower and Native-Controlled Missions," 16 November 1926; Report on Native-Controlled Missions, 13 March 1926, NAM, S2/8/24; Confidential Report on Native-Controlled Missions, 13 April 1928. NAM, S2/20/23.

82.   Chief Commissioner of Police, Confidential Report on PIM, January–June, 1927, NAM, S2/20/23 Part I; Inspection Report, PIM, Chiradzulu, 27 November 1928, NAM, S1/1059/26.

83.   See "Chiradzulu District Native Association," 1929–35, NAM, NS 1/3/5.

84.   After Isa Macdonald's arrest, John Lawrence put it rather bluntly in a letter to Ruth Lawrence: "I don't write neither say anything to the Dr. because our mot[t]o is not to raise obstacles for the Doctor and the Mission." J.B.C. Lawrence to Ruth Lawrence, 20 December 1926, NAM S2/50/23; J.B.C. Lawrence, Quelimane, to I.M. Lawrence, Beira, 16 March 1925; J.B.C. Lawrence to D.S. Malekebu, 12 February 1927; Daniel S. Malekebu to Isa M. Lawrence, 1 January 1925. NAM S2/8/24.

85.   Patrick Makondesa, *The Church History of Providence Industrial Mission: 1900–1940* (Zomba: Kachere Series, 2006), 12; Stephens, Report on PIM, 1 Feb 1937, NAM, S2/22/34; Roderick J. Macdonald, "Rev. Dr. Daniel Sharpe Malekebu and the Re-Opening of the Providence Industrial Mission: 1926–39," in *From Nyasaland to Malawi: Studies in Colonial History*, ed. Roderick J. Macdonald (Nairobi: East African Publishing House, 1975), 230.

86.   I borrow this use of "representation" from Stuart Hall, "Cultural Identity and Diaspora," in Diaspora and Visual Culture, ed. Nicholas Mirzoeff (London: Routledge, 2000), 21.

87.   For example, James Frederick Sangala, prominent member of the Blantyre Native Association (BNA) and founding member of the Nyasaland African Congress (NAC); Levi Z. Mumba, founder and Secretary of the North Nyasa Native Association,

Chairman of the Representative Committee of Northern Province Native Associations, first president of the NAC; Charles C. Chinula, founder and Secretary of the Mombera Native Association, Vice-President of the NAC; Isa Macdonald Lawrence, member of the BNA and the first Treasurer-General of the NAC; George Simeon Mwase, founder of the Central Province Universal Native Association, Committee Member of the NAC.

88. Harry Mwaanga Nkumbula to William Sherrill, 26 July 1957. UNIA, MSS 1066, Box 6.

CHAPTER EIGHT

MUIGWITHANIA (THE RECONCILER)

1. Jomo Kenyatta, *Facing Mount Kenya: The Tribal Life of the Gikuyu* (1938; London: Secker and Warburg, 1953), 2–8.

2. Bruce Berman and John Lonsdale view "moral ethnicity" as the messy, contested, and internal politics of group identity, and "political tribalism" as a project of fictive unity analogous to nationalism. See *Unhappy Valley: Conflict in Kenya and Africa* (London: James Currey, 1992).

3. See, for example, Frederick B. Welbourn, *East African Rebels: A Study of Some Independent Churches* (London: SCM Press, 1961), 135–42; Cora Ann Presley, *Kikuyu Women, the Mau Mau Rebellion, and Social Change in Kenya* (Boulder, CO: Westview Press, 1992), 89–93; Carl G. Rosberg Jr. and John Nottingham, *The Myth of "Mau Mau": Nationalism in Kenya* (New York: Meridian, 1966), 105–25; Robert L. Tignor, *The Colonial Transformation of Kenya: the Kamba, Kikuyu, and Maasai from 1900 to 1939* (Princeton, NJ: Princeton University Press, 1976), 235–49.

4. Arthur to Oldham, 10 November 1929, SOAS-IMC, Box 247, File D. For first-hand accounts of the crisis, see J.W. Arthur, "Memorandum Prepared by the Kikuyu Mission Council on Female Circumcision" (Church of Scotland, 1931), Edinburgh University, Special Collections, John William Arthur Papers, Gen. 763, File 2; Interview between the Church at Kikuyu and its member, Johnstone Kenyatta, Church of Scotland Mission, Kikuyu, 5 November 1930, PCEA, I/B/BA/9–17; J. W. Arthur, "Factors Leading Up to the Present Crisis," 21 November 1929, and J. W. Arthur, "The Crisis at Kikuyu, No. 2," 15 December 1929, SOAS-IMC, Box 247, File D. For a useful summary of KCA tactics, see DC, Kiambu, to Senior Commissioner, Nyeri, 24 December 1929, KNA, PC/CP/8/7/1.

5. J. W. Arthur, "Factors Leading Up to the Present Crisis," 21 November 1929, SOAS-IMC, Box 247, File D.

6. Arthur, "The Crisis at Kikuyu, No. 2," 15 December 1929, SOAS-IMC, Box 247, File D; Reports by S. I. Luka and Kagwanarwa, CID, 28 October 1929, PRO, CO 533/392/1.

7. DC, Kiambu, to Senior Commissioner, Nyeri, 24 December 1929, KNA, PC/CP/8/7/1; Edward Grigg to SSC, 21 March 1930, PRO, CO 533/398/11; E. Huxley, *White Man's Country: Lord Delamere and the Making of Kenya*, 2 vols. (London: Macmillan and Co., 1935): 2:276.

8. "Murdered Missionary in Kenya," *The Times*, 17 February 1930, and Telegram from Grigg to Secretary of State for the Colonies, 22 January 1930, in PRO, CO 533/394/10. For a fascinating sense of settler anxieties, see their letters in early 1930,

collected in PRO, CO 533/398/11. For the government's response, see "The Governor Among the Kikuyu," *East African Standard*, March 1, 1930; "Young Kikuyu Leader's Appeal Fails," *East African Standard*, 7 May 1930; Johnstone Kenyatta to Secretary of State for the Colonies, 22 January 1930, and Telegram from Edward Grigg, 22 January 1930, PRO, CO 533/394/10.

9. John W. Arthur to Director of Education, 16 January 1930, KNA, PC/CP/8/1/1; Note by the Colonial Secretary, PRO, CO 533/394/10.

10. Welbourn, *East African Rebels*, 135; John Anderson, "Self Help and Independency: The Political Implications of a Continuing Tradition in African Education in Kenya," *African Affairs* 70, no. 278 (Jan., 1971): 13; James Arthur Wilson Jr., "The Untold Story: Kikuyu Christians, Memories, and the Kikuyu Independent Schools Movement, 1922–1962" (PhD diss., Princeton University, 2002), 4.

11. Edward Grigg to Secretary of State for the Colonies, 21 March 1930, PRO, CO 533/398/11.

12. "Account of Chief Native Commissioner's Speech," Kiambu, March 1922, SOAS-IMC, Box 236, D.3; Minutes of the First Meeting of the Kyambu Local Native Council, Kiambu, 17 July 1925, KNA, PC/CENT/2/1/4. For a useful description of the Councils, see Donald G. Schilling, "Local Native Councils and the Politics of Education in Kenya, 1925–1939," *The International Journal of African Historical Studies* 9, no. 2 (1976): 220–23.

13. Edward Northey to Winston Churchill, 4 May 1922, PRO, CO 533/277/25950; R. T. Coryndon, Confidential Report, 28 June 1922, CO 533/279/40275; J. H. Oldham to Fennel P. Turner, 27 March 1923, and Oldham to H. F. Batterbee, 4 May 1923, CO 533/305/16050; R. T. Coryndon to Secretary of State for the Colonies, 30 May 1922, CO 536/119/02501; K. J. King, "The American Negro as Missionary to East Africa: A Critical Aspect of African Evangelism," *African Historical Studies* 3, no. 1 (1970): 5; Kenneth James King, *Pan-Africanism and Education: A Study in Race Philanthropy and Education in the Southern States of America and East Africa* (Oxford: Clarendon Press, 1971), 72.

14. R. T. Coryndon to Duke of Devonshire, 10 January 1923, PRO, CO 533/292/6599; H. D. Hooper to J. H. Oldham, 1 August 1923, SOAS-IMC, Box 247, File A; K. J. King, "The Nationalism of Harry Thuku: A Study in the Beginnings of African Politics in Kenya," *Transafrican Journal of History* 1, no. 1 (1971): 53.

15. DC, Fort Hall, to Senior Commissioner, Nyeri, 2 January 1926, KNA, PC/CP/8/5/2; Rotberg and Nottingham, *Myth*, 137.

16. By the end of 1928, *Muigwithania* had achieved "a considerable circulation" according to the DC of Fort Hall. Annual Report, Kikuyu Province, 1928, KNA, PC/CP 4/1/2. See also J. W. Arthur, "Factors Leading up to the Present Crisis," 21 November 1929, SOAS-IMC, Box 247, File D; Rotberg and Nottingham, *Myth*, 137.

17. Kikuyu Province Annual Reports from 1926, 1927, and 1928, in KNA, PC/CP 4/1/2.

18. Henry M. Gichuiri, "Kikuyu's Lack of Repute," *Muigwithania* 1, no. 6 (October 1928): 7. Existing copies of *Muigwithania*, translated into English, can be found in KNA, DC/MKS/10B/13/1.

19. John Spencer, "James Beauttah: Kenya Patriot" (manuscript, 1972), KNA, MSS/35/1; "The Matter of Harry Thuku . . ." *Muigwithania* 1, no. 12 (May 1929): 3; Joseph Kang'ethe to Governor, 26 May 1926, KNA, PC/CP/8/5/2.

20. John Spencer, "Kikuyu Central Association," 68–70; John Spencer, "James Beauttah: Kenya Patriot."

21. E. A. Hutton to W. C. Bottomley, 26 November 1929, PRO, CO 533/384/9; Native Affairs Department, Annual Report, 1928, PRO, CO 544/25.

22. Jomo Kenyatta, while editing *Muigwithania*, corresponded with representatives of the West African Student Union, in London, and published news about the Industrial and Commercial Workers' Union in South Africa. Garveyite pamphlets were also discovered in the colony, although not to the extent uncovered in other regions. See "Black People and their Work," *Muigwithania* 1, no. 4 (August 1928): 9, and "Conditions in Other Countries," *Muigwithania* 1, no. 3 (July 1928): 8–9; Commissioner of Police to Colonial Secretary, Nairobi, 10 June 1936, KNA, AG 5/17.

23. Quoted in Presley, *Kikuyu Women*, 125–26.

24. Rotberg and Nottingham, *Myth*, 54.

25. Minutes of Meeting, Kahuhia, Fort Hall, 16 March 1928, KNA, PC/CP/8/5/3.

26. Edward Grigg to Lord Passfield, 12 October 1930, PRO, CO 533/392/1.

27. Spencer, "James Beauttah: Kenya Patriot"; DC, Kiambu, to Senior Commissioner, 24 December 1929, KNA, PC/CP/8/7/1; Rotberg and Nottingham, *Myth*, 123.

28. Hooper to Oldham, 1 August 1923, SOAS-IMC, Box 247, File A; E. A. Hutton to W. C. Bottomley, 26 November 1929, PRO, CO/533/384/9; Native Affairs Department, Annual Report, 1926, PRO, CO 544/21.

29. C.L.R. James, *The Black Jacobins: Toussaint L'Ouverture and the San Domingo Revolution*, Revised, 2nd ed. (New York: Random House, 1963), 397. Kenneth King writes that "it would be difficult to exaggerate the sort of effect [the *Negro World*] began to have from 1921 onwards." King, *Pan-Africanism*, 77.

30. While in exile, for example, Thuku received a smuggled copy of the first volume of *Philosophy and Opinions of Marcus Garvey*. Harry Thuku, *An Autobiography* (Nairobi: Oxford University Press, 1970), 38. See also Commissioner of Police to Colonial Secretary, Nairobi, 10 June 1936, KNA, AG 5/17. For Kenyatta, see Martin, *Race First: The Ideological and Organizational Struggles of Marcus Garvey and the Universal Negro Improvement Association* (Westport, CT: Greenwood Press, 1976), 45; Rev. Clarence W. Harding, Monrovia, to Honorable Thomas W. Harvey, Philadelphia, 30 October 1967, in UNIA, Box 11: Correspondence, 1965–1969.

31. Joseph Kang'ethe, "The Voice of the Leader," *Muigwithania* 1, no. 3 (1928): 12; George Ndegwa and Dishon C. Waihenya, "Riding in Motorcars," *Muigwithania* 1, no. 8 (1928): 6; Johnstone Kenyatta, "Let us agree among ourselves and exalt the Kikuyu," *Muigwithania* 1, no. 7 (1928): 1–4; Letter from George Ndegwa, *Muigwithania* 1, no. 4 (1928): 10; "Matters discussed by Elders at Kiambu," *Muigwithania* 1, no. 8 (1928): 8; "Enfeebling the Kikuyu," *Muigwithania* 1, no. 7 (1928): 10.

32. Johnstone Kenyatta, "The Editor and Land," and G.H.M. Kagika, "Unity in the Common Ancestor," *Muigwithania*, 1, no. 3 (1928): 1, 10; Henry M. Gichuiri, "Protection of the Land," Letter from George Ndegwa, Letter from Paulo K. Karanja, *Muigwithania* 1, no.4 (1928): 7, 10; S. Njuguna wa Karucha, "Kikuyu Time," *Muigwithania*, 1, no. 6 (1928): 10; Johnstone Kenyatta, "Have done with Trifling; let us go in for Self-Help," *Muigwithania* 1, no. 8 (1928): 1; Johnstone Kenyatta, "Muigwithania's Journey," *Muigwithania* 1, no. 12 (1929): 8–10.

33. Joseph Kang'ethe, "The Voice of the Leader," *Muigwithania* 1, no. 3 (1928): 12.

34. M. Reuben, "Work is accomplished by Self-Help," and Johnstone Kenyatta, "Set Yourself to Help," in *Muigwithania* 1, no. 6 (1928): 11, 1; "Conditions in Other Countries," *Muigwithania* 1, no. 3 (1928): 8–9; "Why do ask, Are you a Whiteman? Black People and their Work," *Muigwithania* 1, no. 4 (August 1928): 9; Johnstone Kenyatta, "Sending people to Europe," *Muigwithania* 1, no. 7 (1928): 10.

35. Bruce J. Berman and John M. Lonsdale, "The Labors of *Muigwithania*: Jomo Kenyatta as Author, 1928–1945," *Research in African Literatures* 29, no. 1 (1998): 16.

36. "In Memory of Chief Karuri wa Gakure," *Muigwithania* 1, no. 3 (1928): 9; S. Njuguna wa Karucha, "Kikuyu Time," *Muigwithania* 1, no. 6 (1928): 10; Johnstone Kenyatta, "Let us agree among ourselves and exalt the Kikuyu," *Muigwithania* 1, no. 7 (1928), 1–4; Letter from James Muigai, *Muigwithania* 1, no. 8 (1928/1929), 15; "The Matter of Harry Thuku . . ." *Muigwithania* 1, no. 12 (1929): 3.

37. John Lonsdale has brilliantly framed the work of the KCA as nation building in Berman and Lonsdale, *Unhappy Valley*, 371.

38. For a theoretical discussion of the gendering of space and place, see Doreen Massey, *Space, Place, and Gender* (Minneapolis: University of Minnesota Press, 1994), 9–11, 179–83.

39. Gideon M. Kaggka, "Hold Firmly to the Tribal Homes," and Johnstone Kenyatta, "Let us agree . . ." *Muigwithania* 1, no. 7 (1928): 1–4; George K. Ndegwa, "Riding in Motorcars," and Letter from K. Kirobi, *Muigwithania* 1, no. 8 (1928/1929): 6; Aanuiru wa Kinyau, "Wilfulness" [*sic*], *Muigwithania* 1, no. 12 (1929): 7–8; S. G. Kuria, "A Parable," *Muigwithania* 1, no. 10 (1929): 11.

40. Women supported the KCA by raising funds and by cooking food for the meetings, but they were not allowed to attend strategy meetings. In 1930, several women split from the KCA to form the Mumbi Central Association, returning to the KCA in 1933 after successfully negotiating positions of leadership within the organization—an act that marked a milestone in Kikuyu women's access to formal political power. See Presley, *Kikuyu Women*, 117–20.

41. In the twelve copies of *Muigwithania* preserved in the Kenya National Archives, two articles are written by women, both supportive of traditional gender norms. See Wanjiru wa Kinyau, "Wilfulness" [*sic*], *Muigwithania* 1, no. 12 (1929): 7–8; Tabitha Wangui wa Thomas Kamau, "A Woman's Voice," *Muigwithania* 2, no. 1 (1929): 10.

42. Members of the Committee of the Kikuyu Central Association to Sir Edward Grigg, 31 December 1925; Joseph Kang'ethe, et al. to Senior Commissioner, Nyeri, 10 July 1926; Minutes of a Meeting Held with Members of the KCA at Mwichuki's Camp, Fort Hall District, 30 August 1927. In KNA, PC/CP 8/5/2. Minutes of Meeting, Kahuhia, 16 March 1928, KNA, PC/CP 8/5/3; "Correspondence between the Kikuyu Central Association and the Colonial Office, 1929–1930," SOAS-IMC, Box 236, File F; David Anderson, *Histories of the Hanged: The Dirty War in Kenya and the End of Empire* (New York: W.W. Norton & Co., 2005), 21–22; Caroline Elkins, *Imperial Reckoning: The Untold Story of Britain's Gulag in Kenya* (Cambridge, MA: Harvard University Press, 2005), 14–18.

43. Native Affairs Department, Annual Report, 1926, PRO, CO 544/21; Kiambu District, Annual Report, 1932, KNA, DC/KBU/24a.

44. Church of Scotland Mission, Tumutumu, to DC, Nyeri, 17 November 1936, Johanna Kunyiha to Johanna Wanjau, 13 November 1926, PCEA, 1/AB/3; Edward Grigg to Lord Passfield, 12 October 1929, PRO, CO 533/392/1; Native Affairs Department, Annual Report, 1926, PRO, CO 544/21.

45. Chief Native Commissioner to PC, Kikuyu, Nyeri, 11 September 1929 and M.R.R. Vidal, DC, Kiambu, to Senior Commissioner, Nyeri, 21 September 1929, KNA, VQ 1/43; Edward Grigg to Lord Passfield, 12 October 1929, PRO, CO 533/392/1.

46. For examples of these petitions, see KNA, DC/KBU/4/4. See also Kiambu District, Annual Report, 1932, KNA, DC/KBU/24a.

47. Kiambu District Monthly Intelligence Report for November 1937, KNA, VQ/16/13.

48. John Spencer, "James Beauttah: Kenya Patriot" (manuscript, 1972), in KNA, MSS 35/1.

49. Johnstone Kenyatta, "Why do ask, Are you a Whiteman?" *Muigwithania* 1.4 (1928), 9; Kenyatta, "Sayings of 'Muigwithania,'" *Muigwithania* 1.7 (1928), 4.

50. Johnstone Kenyatta, "To All the Kikuyu who are Concerned for the Kikuyu Country," *Muigwithania* 1.9 (1929), 16; Letter from Koinange wa Mbiyu to President, KCA, Kiambu, *Muigwithania* 1, no. 10 (1929): 15; Johnstone Kenyatta, "Muigwithania's Journey," *Muigwithania* 1, no. 12 (1929): 8–10; Kunyiha is quoted in Spencer, "Kikuyu Central Association," 72.

51. Bruce Berman, "Ethnography as Politics, Politics as Ethnography: Kenyatta, Malinowski, and the Making of *Facing Mount Kenya,*" *Canadian Journal of African Studies* 30, no. 3 (1996): 318–30; Berman and Lonsdale, "Labours," 24–32.

52. Johnstone Kenyatta, "Kenya," in *Negro: An Anthology*, ed. Nancy Cunard (New York: Continuum, 1934): 452–56; Kenyatta quoted in Berman and Lonsdale, "Labours," 37.

53. Berman, "Ethnography," 340; Ras Makonnen, *Pan-Africanism from Within* (Nairobi: Oxford University Press, 1973), 162; C.L.R. James, "George Padmore: Black Marxist Revolutionary: A Memoir," in C.L.R. James, *At the Rendezvous of Victory: Selected Writings* (London: Allison & Busby, 1984), 257.

54. For example, in a work published the same year as *Facing Mount Kenya*, James described Garvey as a "reactionary," and his program "pitiable rubbish." C.L.R. James, *A History of Negro Revolt* (London: Fact International, 1938), 69–70.

55. Wilson, "Untold Story," 138; Police Report, 10 June 1930, PRO, CO 533/384/9; Makonnen, *Pan-Africanism*, 127–28.

56. Ladipo Solanke to the *Spokesman* 1, no. 7 (June 1925), in MGP, 10:303–4. See also Ladipo Solanke, *United West Africa (or Africa) at the Bar of the Family of Nations* (1927; London: African Publication Society, 1969); G. O. Olusanya, *The West African Students' Union and the Politics of Decolonisation, 1925–1958* (Ibadan: Daystar Press, 1982).

57. Amy Jacques Garvey, *Black Power in America* (Kingston: United Printers, Ltd., 1968), 33.

58. Kenyatta, *Facing Mount Kenya*, especially xvii–xviii, xix–xx, 1–6, 22–27, 115–28, 317–18.

59. Kenyatta, *Facing Mount Kenya*, 133–35.

60.   A. S. Adebola, "The London Connections: A Factor in the Survival of the Ki-kuyu Independent Schools' Movement, 1929–1939," *Journal of African Studies* 10, no. 1 (Spring 1983): 20–21; Derek R. Peterson, *Creative Writing: Translation, Bookkeeping, and the Work of Imagination in Colonial Kenya* (Portsmouth, NH: Heinemann, 2004), 153; Wilson, "Untold Story," 108–11, 219–20.

61.   According to Kenyatta's daughter, Koinange met with Garveyites after he arrived in New York in 1927. Wilson, "Untold Story," 138.

62.   Wilson, "Untold Story," 74–76; John Anderson, "Self Help," 12.

63.   Minutes of the District Commissioners' Meeting of the Kikuyu Province, 16 Feb 1931, KNA, PC/CP 8/4B/7; Annual Report, Kikuyu Province, 1937, KNA, PC/CP 4/3/1; J.Njoroge, et al., to Governor of Kenya, et al., Nairobi, 12 February 1952, KNA, MAC/KEN/35/3; Petition by S.R. Kimani, et al., to Governor, 23 February 1953, KNA, MAC/KEN/35/2; Report on Kikuyu Independent and Karinga Schools, PCEA, Box E-6, Folder EB/5, 1936–1938; Wilson, "Untold Story," 84–85.

64.   Wilson, "Untold Story," 28.

65.   For a sense of the political difficulties faced by the colonial government in its effort to support the hegemony of mission education in the aftermath of the cir-cumcision crisis, see H. S. Scott, Director of Education, Nairobi, to Chief Secretary, 10 January 1930, KNA, PC/CP 8/1/1. For the further complication created by sup-port for independent schools in both the Colonial Office and the House of Com-mons, see A.S. Adebola, "The London Connections," 14–21.

66.   Kunyiha quoted in John Spencer, "Kikuyu Central Association," 73; Wil-son, "Untold Story," 241–42, 251–55; James A. Wilson Jr., "Political Songs, Collec-tive Memories, and Kikuyu *Indi* Schools," *History in Africa* 33 (2006): 263–88; Derek Peterson, "Writing in Revolution: Independent Schooling & Mau Mau in Nyeri," in *Mau Mau & Nationhood: Arms, Authority & Narration*, eds. E. S. Atieno Odhiambo and John Lonsdale (Oxford: James Currey, 2003): 78–79.

67.   Richard Newman, "The Origins of the African Orthodox Church," in *Black Power and Black Religion: Essays and Reviews* (West Cornwall, CT: Locust Hill Press, 1987), 83–107; Theodore Natsoulas, "Patriarch McGuire and the Spread of the Afri-can Orthodox Church to Africa," *Journal of Religion in Africa* 12, no. 2 (1981): 81–104; Randall K. Burkett, *Black Redemption: Churchmen Speak for the Garvey Movement* (Philadelphia: Temple University Press, 1978), 157–65.

68.   George Alexander McGuire, "Ex Oriente Lux," *Negro Churchman* 1, no. 6 (1923): 1; Rev. F. A. Toote, "The Mission of the African Orthodox Church," *Negro Churchman* 2, no. 2 (1924): 3; McGuire, "Be Earnest," *Negro Churchman* 1 no. 1 (1923): 1; Archbishop Alexander (McGuire), "Timely Advice for 1926," *Negro Churchman* 4, no. 1 (1926): 1.

69.   *NW*, April 2, 1921, 5; *NW*, August 20, 1921, 3.

70.   Randall Burkett, *Garveyism as a Religious Movement: The Institutionalization of a Black Civil Religion* (Metuchen, NJ: Scarecrow Press, 1978), 66–67, 71.

71.   McGuire, "'Back To Africa'—The Other Side," *Negro Churchman* 1, no. 3 (1923): 1. See also McGuire, "Out of Tombs," *Negro Churchman* 1, no. 9/10 (1923): 11.

72.   "Report on the UNIA Convention Opening," MGP, 5:622–28. McGuire had developed this view of Garveyism at least a year and a half before the Convention. See "Back to Africa," *Negro Churchman* 1, no. 3 (1923): 1.

73. Daniel William Alexander, "The Harvest is Great: But the Labourers are Few—The Problem of Africa," n.d., in AOC, RG 005, Box 2, Folder 4. See also "Address of the Bishop-Elect of South Africa," *Negro Churchman* 5 no. 9 (October 1927): 4.

74. Richard Newman, "Archbishop Daniel William Alexander and the African Orthodox Church," *The International Journal of African Historical Studies* 16, no. 4 (1983): 615–20; Morris Johnson, *Archbishop Daniel William Alexander and the African Orthodox Church* (San Francisco: International Scholars Publications, 1999), 55–62.

75. Alexander calls the work "My higher education," but it seems clear that he is referring to Washington's *My Larger Education; Being Chapters from My Experience*, published in 1911. See Most Reverend D. W. Alexander, "Impression of my journey too [sic] and from America," *African Orthodox Churchman* 1, no. 5 (1929), in AOC, RG 005, Box 20, File 1.

76. "Address of the Bishop-Elect of South Africa," *Negro Churchman* 5, no. 9 (1927): 4; Minutes of the Preliminary Meeting held for the purpose of forming The African Orthodox Church, 6 October 1924, AOC, RG 005, Box 2, Folder 16.

77. "Is There Any Accursed Race?" *African Orthodox Churchman* 1, no. 3 (1929): 3; "The Spiritual Awakening of the African," *African Orthodox Church* 1, no. 4 (1929): 6–7; "The Primate's Charge," Fourth Provincial Synod, AOC, RG 005, Box 3, Folder 6; D. W. Alexander to Rev. Thomas Burns, 26 April 1929, AOC, RG 005, Box 10, Folder 9; "Carthage" and "The Price of Africa," *African Orthodox Churchman* 2, no. 2/3 (1930): 1; "Our Church in South Africa," *Negro Churchman* 3, no. 1 (1925): 4.

78. See Johnson, *Archbishop*, 74; Newman, "Archbishop," 619, 629–30; Michael O. West, "Ethiopianism and Colonialism: The African Orthodox Church in Zimbabwe, 1924–1934," in *Christian Missionaries & the State in the Third World*, ed. Holger Bernt Hansen and Michael Twaddle (Oxford: James Currey, 2002), 245.

79. Minutes of the 6th Provincial Synod, Beaconsfield, 5–7 September 1930, and Minutes of the 9th Provincial Synod, 15 December 1933, AOC, RG 005, Box 3, Folder 4; "The Primate's Charge," Sixth Synod of the AOC, 1930, AOC, RG 005, Box 3, Folder 7.

80. Johnson, *Archbishop*, 6–7; "The Sects," *African Orthodox Churchman* 1, no. 5 (1929): 1–4.

81. West, "Ethiopianism and Colonialism," 245; McGuire to Alexander, 24 October 1924, and McGuire to Alexander, 13 December 1924, in AOC, RG 005, Box 10, Folder 14. See also Statement of Rev. E. Urban Lewis to His Majesty's Consul General, New York, 24 September 1924 and E. Urban Lewis to Pro-Consul James, New York, 1 November 1924, in PRO, FO 115/2930.

82. Commissioner of South African Police to Superintendent, CID, British South African Police, Southern Rhodesia, 22 August 1929, and Gloster Armstrong to Secretary of State, Foreign Affairs, London, 5 October 1927, in MGP, 10:523–27.

83. "Travelogue of an African Missionary to Central Africa," AOC, RG 005, Box 1, Folder 15; Welbourn, *East African Rebels*, 79; Dick Dube to Editor, AO Churchman, 22 April 1929, AOC, RG 005, Box 10, Folder 9.

84. Letter from Daniel William Alexander, *NW*, February 7, 1925, 2; "Report of Primate," c. 1927, AOC, RG 005, Box 1, Folder 15; Minutes of the 8th Provincial Synod, 15 December 1932, AOC, RG 005, Box 3, Folder 4.

85. Welbourn, *East African Rebels*, 81; Alexander to PC, Buganda, Kampala, Uganda, 18 October 1931, and Alexander to McGuire, 22 September 1932, AOC, RG 005, Box 10, Folder 14; Alexander to James Poyah, 29 January 1930, AOC, RG 005, Box 10, Folder 5; "Our Church in South Africa," *Negro Churchman* 3, no. 1 (1925): 4.

86. Alexander, "Impressions of my journey . . ." *African Orthodox Churchman* 1, no. 5 (1929): 4. The story of the AOC's acquisition of the Apostolic Succession is a long and complicated one. See Welbourn, *East African Rebels*, 79–80; Richard Newman, "Origins," 92–95.

87. Rev. F. A. Toote, "The Mission of the African Orthodox Church," *Negro Churchman* 2, no. 2 (1924): 3; *African Orthodox Churchman* 1, no. 6 (1929): 6.

88. Diary of the Travel of the Most Rev. D. W. Alexander, AOC, RG 005, Box 1, Folder 14.

89. Alexander to McGuire, 22 September 1932, AOC, RG 005, Box 10, Folder 14; John Spencer, "James Beauttah: Kenya Patriot" (manuscript, 1972), in KNA, MSS 35/1; "Rules of the Kikuyu Independent Schools Association," 1935, AOC, RG 005, Box 20, Folder 23.

90. John Spencer, "James Beauttah: Kenya Patriot"; Newman, "Archbishop," 626; Johana Kunyiha, Nyeri, to D. W. Alexander, Beaconsfield, 1 July 1935, AOC, RG 005, Box 12, Folder 4.

91. D. W. Alexander to Rev. Canon William Miller, c. 1939, AOC, RG 005, Box 11, Folder 1; "Twenty-Fifth Anniversary of the Consecration of Archbishop Daniel William Alexander," 1952, AOC, RG 005, Box 2, Folder 3; Tomkinson, Acting PC, Central Province, to Chief Secretary, 19 February 1941, KNA, VQ/1/26.

92. District Officer, Fort Hall, to Acting PC, 6 January 1936; KISA, "Report and Constitution," 1938, KNA, MAC/KEN/35/4; John Spencer, "James Beauttah: Kenya Patriot."

AFTERWORD

1. Interview with T. R. Makonnen, in Kenneth King, "Early Pan-African Politicians in East Africa," *Mawazo* 2, no. 1 (June 1969): 9–10.

2. William Sherrill to Thomas Harvey, Ghana, 8 March 1957; Sherrill to Harvey, 15 March 1957; T.D.T. Banda to Sherrill, 16 April 1957. All in UNIA, Box 6: Correspondence, 1957.

3. Rev. Clarence W. Harding to Thomas W. Harvey, 25 September 1967, and Harding to Harvey, 30 October 1967, in UNIA, Box 11: Correspondence, 1965–1969.

4. Claudrena Harold, *The Rise and Fall of the Garvey Movement in the Urban South, 1918–1942* (New York: Routledge, 2007), 117–25; Mary G. Rolinson, *Grassroots Garveyism: The Universal Negro Improvement Association in the Rural South, 1920–1927* (Chapel Hill: University of North Carolina Press, 2007), 89, 100, 182–96; Charles M. Payne, *I've Got the Light of Freedom: The Organizing Tradition and the Mississippi Freedom Struggle* (Berkeley: University of California Press, 1995), 234; Malcolm X, as told to Alex Haley, *The Autobiography of Malcolm X* (1965; New York: Ballantine Books, 1992), 1–7; Barbara Bair, "True Women, Real Men," in *Gendered Domains: Rethinking Public and Private in Women's History*, eds. Dorothy O. Helly and Susan M. Reverby

(Ithaca, NY: Cornell University Press, 1992), 164; Regina Freer, "L.A. Race Woman: Charlotta Bass and the Complexities of Black Political Development in Los Angeles," *American Quarterly* 56, no. 3 (September 2004): 607–32; Jill Watts, *God, Harlem U.S.A.: The Father Divine Story* (Berkeley: University of California Press, 1992), 113–14; Ula Yvette Taylor, *The Veiled Garvey: The Life and Times of Amy Jacques Garvey* (Chapel Hill: University of North Carolina Press, 2002), 212–21.

5.   Adam Ewing, "Caribbean Labour Politics in the Age of Garvey, 1918–1938," *Race & Class* 55, no. 1 (2013): 35–38.

6.   Testimony of Tubal Uriah Butler and Testimony of Charles John, *Rex v. Butler*, PRO, CO 295/608/5.

7.   Rupert Lewis, "Marcus Garvey and the Early Rastafarians: Continuity and Discontinuity," in *Down Babylon: The Rastafari Reader*, ed. Nathaniel Samuel Murrell, et al. (Philadelphia: Temple University Press, 1998), 145–59.

8.   Robert A. Hill, "Redemption Works: From 'African Redemption' to 'Redemption Song,'" *Review: Literature and Arts of the Americas* 43, no. 2 (2010): 200–207.

9.   "Opening of UNIA Convention," MGP, 2:478; Harding to Harvey, 14 May 1966; Thomas W. Harvey, "UNIA Launches Five Point African Program," The Parent Body *Bulletin*, Month of October 1966; Harding to Hon. Andrew J. Crawford, 18 May 1967; Harding to Harvey, 19 June 1967; Harding to Harvey, 16 January 1968; Harding to Harvey, 17 August 1969. All in UNIA, Box 11: Correspondence, 1965–1969.

INDEX